DATE DUE

MY21 01			
JE 1 '01			
JA 8 '09			

DEMCO 38-296

FRANK SMITH

WRITING and the WRITER

SECOND EDITION

BOOKS BY FRANK SMITH

The Genesis of Language (edited, with George A. Miller)
Understanding Reading (five editions)
Psycholinguistics and Reading
Comprehension and Learning
Writing and the Writer (two editions)
Reading Without Nonsense ("Reading" in UK—two editions)
Essays Into Literacy
Awakening to Literacy (edited, with Hillel Goelman and Antoinette A.
    Oberg)
Insult to Intelligence
Joining the Literacy Club
to think
Whose Language? What Power?

R

FRANK SMITH

WRITING and the WRITER

SECOND EDITION

1994

LAWRENCE ERLBAUM ASSOCIATES, PUBLISHERS
Hillsdale, New Jersey   Hove, UK

Lawrence Erlbaum Associates, Inc., Publishers
365 Broadway
Hillsdale, New Jersey 07642

Library of Congress Cataloging-in-Publication Data

Smith, Frank, 1928-
    Writing and the writer / Frank Smith. -- 2nd ed.
        p.   cm.
    ISBN 0-8058-1421-3 (hardcover) -- ISBN 0-8058-1422-1 (pbk).
    1. Writing--Psychological aspects. 2. Creative writing.
    3. Creation (Literary, artistic, etc.)   I. Title.
    BF456.W8 1994
    808'.001'9--dc20   94-11555
                                                    CIP

Books published by Lawrence Erlbaum Associates are printed
on acid-free paper, and their bindings are chosen
for strength and durability.

Printed in the United States of America

10 9 8 7 6 5 4 3 2 1

Contents

Preface to the Second Edition

It is time, said my publisher, to bring *Writing and the Writer* up to date. But the first edition of *Writing and the Writer* was a journey, a reflexive exploration of writing a book as the book was being written. How can you bring up to date a journey made a dozen years ago? You cannot make a journey twice without obliterating the path you trod the first time, unless you follow a completely different route. And you cannot observe the landscape with the same eyes on a return visit. To reflect upon a book *after* it is written is not the same as contemplating the writing while it is being done. The vantage points are different.

But I saw my publisher's point of view. The world has changed since the first edition of this book was written, and so have I. While I cannot make the same journey twice, I can review and reflect upon the original journey from a distance, perhaps even from higher ground. In addition, as a friendly reviewer has pointed out, a second edition could add a new element to the writerly topics discussed in the first—the difficulties and opportunities confronting an author in returning to an earlier piece of writing.

Preparing a new edition is not the same as editing. Editing may be a form of revision, but it is revision made before the die is cast—before the letter mailed, the poem published, or the final draft surrendered to the printer. Revision, in the sense in which I must now use the term, is a second look, literally re-vision, an opportunity to recollect, observe and comment upon an enterprise once considered completed.

There are technical problems, of course. If I want to comment on the first edition of this book, the first edition must be present. And if I would like readers to follow my comments, they must have the first edition too. But I don't want to present the reader with two books—the original and a commentary upon it—nor even with a book and a half—the original and a package of emendations.

Furthermore, while I do not want to erase the steps I originally trod in composing this book, there are changes that I feel I should make—not changes to the journey itself, but to the landscape I ventured through, if I think I can now offer a clearer or more appropriate description (for example, from the point of view of more recent ideas and research).

My solution (to change the metaphor) has been to construct a sandwich in which the filling is the first edition and the outsides this brief "Preface to the Second Edition" at the beginning and "Second Thoughts" at the end. In this Preface I declare my intentions and manner in which I propose to proceed. In the filling I retain as much of the original edition as I can, with the background refreshed where I have thought (or been advised) that amendment is called for. And in "Second Thoughts" I discuss the changes I have made and the reasons I made them.

"Second Thoughts" consists of two parts that might be termed *technical* and *textual*. The technical part could be of general interest as it adds another dimension to aspects of writing already discussed, namely the insights, opportunities, and difficulties that can come with "second editions." The textual part, listing the changes made to "the filling," will probably be of interest to instructors and other specialists curious about how my views have developed or my approach changed.

ENDLESS CONTROVERSIES

In the introduction to the latest edition of *Understanding Reading*, the companion volume to this book, I comment on the fact that 20 years of recent research had failed to resolve a basic controversy concerning the nature of reading and how it should be taught. Scores of books and thousands of research studies are published every year reflecting one side of the issue or the other, taking their own position for granted if not violently denouncing the other side. Ostensibly the debate is over the question whether the "mechanics" of reading—relating the sounds of speech to the alphabetic characters of writing—should be a basis of instruction. But the issue will never be resolved by research because it is based on much deeper and intensely personal attitudes toward the nature of human beings—whether they can be trusted to learn through experience (with some specific help when the learner requires it) or whether the learner (and the teacher) must be told exactly what should be learned. Every generation seems destined to continue the campaigns of its predecessors, rediscovering their wisdom but also repeating many of their errors. And the only new aspect is the language in which it is all done.

The same applies to writing. In reviewing research that has been published since the first edition of *Writing and the Writer* in 1982, I am struck that there has been no resolution to the debate about whether writing should be approached through the "mechanics"—like spelling and punctuation—or through a kind of *total immersion* in writing, in which students are expected to learn through a series of successive approximations, always moving toward greater competence. While presenting these alternative points of view, my own position goes further, arguing that very little can be learned about writing either from explicit "direct instruction" or from extensive writing experience, unless there is considerable reading, which is the essential source of knowledge about writing.

Not only does research in writing seem to leave basic issues unresolved, it appears to have little effect on actual educational practice. Farnan, Lapp, and Flood (1992) note that over 18,000 articles on writing were added to the ERIC registry between 1980 and 1989, and over 160 writing projects were established in the United States during the decade, without any progress being documented in writing ability, or even in the amount of writing done in schools, which remained pitifully inadequate (less than three per cent of student writing stretching to a complete paragraph or longer).

I try not to engage in *debate* in the main section of this book, avoiding the digressions of argument with other people. In the main section I usually only cite people (or statements) that I agree with, leaving controversy and alternative points of view to the Notes. This is not because I want to hide deep and evident differences of opinion, but to keep the book as coherent as possible, a not uncommon practice among writers on educational topics, though not always acknowledged.

The first edition of *Writing and the Writer* was different from most other books on the topic of writing, and I have kept the second edition so. It is not a discussion of rhetorical techniques and styles, and it says nothing about *how* people should write, or what they should write about. Nor is it a scientific (or pseudo-scientific) tract, founded on models of hypothetical brain processes or computer simulations. Finally, it is not an instruction manual for teachers, with menus and recipes for their behavior. *Writing and the Writer* remains an exploration, something for teachers, learners and all students of the act and art of writing to think about, a description of a territory that must be personally experienced to be understood.

Preface to the First Edition

The common metaphors of childbirth for the genesis of books are apt. A book—like any piece of writing—is conceived, it gestates, and its delivery is frequently overdue, accompanied by severe labor pains and followed by postpartum depression. Close relatives often suffer sympathetically. More relevantly, a book is at all times during and after its prenatal development an entity separate from the individual who bears it. A book must be nourished if it is to develop, but it will develop according to its own characteristics quite independently of the expectations of the person who bears it, a person who will in turn be changed by the growth of this offspring. A book, like a baby, has an interdependent but separate existence from the moment of its conception. A book is never part of its author—except as a remote abstraction, the object of an intention—before it is written, while it is being written, and after it is completed. The book and its author can only interact, at every stage of their mutual development.

The purpose of the present book is to explore this relationship between the writer and what the writer happens to be writing. The general topic might be termed the psychology of the writing act, the manner in which individuals develop and perform the various skills that enable them to write, and the reciprocal consequences that learning to write and the act of writing have on those who write.

Thus the book is concerned with the physical activity of writing, the way the nervous system recruits the muscles to move the pen or manipulate the typewriter. It considers the necessary disciplines of writing, such as knowledge of the conventions of grammar, spelling, and punctuation. And primarily it examines the creative and productive aspects of writing, the genesis of what is written. In particular, there is a concern with how the skills underlying all these aspects of writing are learned and orchestrated. In none of these areas of inquiry, incidentally, could scientific understanding be said to be complete or even adequate. This book is an investigation, not an exposition.

The kind of writing with which this book is primarily concerned might be called mature writing, or *fluent writing* (my preferred term)—that is, writing that is being done by someone who knows how to write whatever is being written. I am not talking exclusively about professional writing of any kind, but neither am I excluding it. Professional writers do not do anything different from occasional or casual writers, though they may do it more efficiently and more effectively. They may know what the occasional writer strives to know. But an argument implicit throughout this book is that most of us could write more—and more effectively—than we do.

The concern is with the act of writing generally, with the writing of books and letters and memoranda, diaries and journals, public and professional reports; even, by extension at least, poetry and drama. Often I shall refer to the object of discussion as the *text*, which is anything that can be written. I look at writing the way one might look at the knowledge and skills underlying acts of cooking, from the boiling of an egg to the preparation of a banquet. "The writer" to whom I refer is the person who happens to be writing anything, at any time, just as the person who boils the egg can be called "the cook." My illustrations may tend to involve books rather than shorter texts, but that is because it is easier to dissect an elephant than a mosquito.

One reason for focusing attention on fluent writing is to try to determine what a child—or any other learner—must achieve in order to become a writer. Note that I said achieve rather than know or do. This book is not a primer on how to write, or on improving your own or anyone else's writing. It does not even attempt to differentiate good writing from bad, except in the most general ways. There are no exercises.

Nevertheless this book does have an educational orientation. Its ultimate concern is with learning. I hope therefore that it will prove relevant and useful to anyone who teaches about writing or endeavors to teach writing itself. In the first group would be instructors of college courses on educational or cognitive psychology whose main concern is with the higher cognitive functions of the brain, especially those functions involving language. In the second group would be teachers at all levels of education concerned with the development of writing fluency. To both I would like to offer at least a framework for thinking about the act of writing in both theoretical and practical ways.

More generally this book is intended for anyone interested in writing, and I make such a claim only because it reflects my own motivation. I have written this book because I have always been fascinated by its topic. My intention has been far less to teach others than to seize an opportunity to develop and share questions, ideas, and research about writing, which I still believe to be the most powerful means devised by the human race for exploring and expressing its own potential.

1 Introduction

My intention with this book was to explore the interaction between the writer and text by making use of it. I wanted to write about writing in order to understand better the act of writing and how it is learned. This is an enormous power of writing, as I see it. Not only can a piece of writing communicate thought from writer to reader (an assertion I shall examine rather critically in due course), but also the act of writing can tell the author things that were not known (or not known to be known) before the writing began. Thus we might build a boat to learn more about how boats are built, or climb a hill without knowing in advance the view that will be attained or even the route that we will be able to take. Writing can extend both our imagination and our understanding.[1] (Superscript numbers refer to the Notes, which begin on page 241.)

ON WRITING ON WRITING

Part of the original intention was to make this book the record of its own odyssey, to write of what I might discover about writing as the discovery was made. In principle this was a misconception—no more possible than to make a film about the making of that particular film. Always an additional camera is required to film the camera filming the camera that is filming. . . . Telescopes, microscopes, and eyes themselves are limited in the extent to which they can examine their own processes, even with the supplementary use of pictures or mirrors. Another instrument is always required to observe the instrument observing the image.[2]

But the idea was also misconceived in practice. Something I had to realize about writing is that it covers its own traces. The record is erased of the false starts, the dead ends, the deletions, and the rearrangements. The seams do not (I hope) show. An enormous advantage of writing over speech is that ideas can easily be reorganized in both time and space. They do not have to remain in the order in which they are produced. Conclusions can appear to follow inevitably from prior arguments or evidence, although the arguments and evidence may in fact be produced only after the conclusions are decided. Authors of mysteries and of scientific articles alike take advantage of this possibility of rearranging the temporal sequence of events in what they write. Certainly the present book as it was written would be both unpublishable and incomprehensible.

Thus the story of any writing enterprise can only be related retrospectively, in another piece of writing, and for anyone who is interested that is what I have done. Now, obviously manipulating time and space, I am explaining at the beginning of the final draft of this book something that I decided upon when I was well past this point as I wrote the first draft. I am discussing something yet to appear in the book although I have already written it. At the end of the text (page 233) is a kind of case study of how the book developed during its writing, beyond my original intentions and expectations, and of how the book changed me or, as we might more conventionally say, what I learned from writing it. There are also some second thoughts about how the original text looked to me when I had the opportunity to rewrite it.

OUTLINE OF THE BOOK

One of the paradoxes of writing is that a text will erase its own history but can look into its own future. In the following paragraphs I outline briefly the course and contents of the remainder of this book.

The following two chapters are brief but basic. Chapter 2 ("Why Write?") is concerned with both the motivation for writing and its consequences. I propose that writing is relevant to all human endeavors, and cannot be replaced by alternative technologies. Writing has many values, whether or not it is a requirement of our occupation or role in life to write. Chapter 3 ("Writing: Collaboration and Competition") draws a distinction between what is said in writing, the *composition*, and what has to be done to say it, the conventions of *transcription*, such as spelling, punctuation, grammar, and neatness. These are literally two sides of writing, sometimes confused and often in opposition.

Chapter 4 ("The Thought Behind Language") is the first of four relatively long chapters devoted to composition (to show where the emphasis in this book lies). The meaning of language ultimately lies beyond language, and this opening excursion ventures into those realms of thought that are quite literally speechless—and therefore frustratingly difficult to attempt to discern and describe. But to restrict the study of language to what can be seen or heard is to stay forever at the surface, in synonyms and paraphrases. The depths may be obscure, but they must be entered.

Chapter 5 ("Putting Meaning into Words") attempts the impossible task of constructing a one-sided bridge between the unobservable, preverbal processes of thought and the explicit, self-evident elements of language, whether spoken or written. Although the connection cannot be described, the gulf is crossed every time an individual produces or understands a meaningful utterance. How are the noises or marks of language made meaningful?

Chapter 6 ("Language: Spoken and Written") acknowledges that for all their similarities, spoken and written language are not the same, and considers possible reasons for the differences. There are some reflections on how and why differences in language come about, and on an issue very close to many writers on writing (though considered more peripheral by this one), the role of an audience.

Chapter 7 ("The Writer-Reader Contract") shows that the effort to be meaningful is not just a responsibility of the writer. If written language is to be intelligible in any way, writers and readers must implicitly agree on how it is to be interpreted. Communication involves getting into the other person's mind, and this can only be done if a number of conventions are observed and respected. The particular conventions may be arbitrary, but the fact of conventions is essential, for it is shared expectations that make communication and comprehensibility possible.

Chapter 8 ("The Act of Writing") attempts to draw the preceding chapters together, interrelating the demands of transcription and the problems of composition, both theoretically and in the mind of a writer actually trying to put ideas that make sense on paper.

Chapter 9 ("Starting and Stopping") recognizes that the act of writing is not so easily disposed of, either in this book or in practice. The previous chapter summed up writing as if it could be done without a hitch; what we are doing when we do it. This chapter, perhaps more realistically, considers problems of getting started, and of keeping going at times when one does not want to come to a standstill.

Chapter 10 ("The Tapestry of Transcription") examines in more detail some conventions of transcription. The concern is not with setting out the "rules" of such conventions as spelling or punctuation, certainly not with whether particular forms are right, wrong, or even desirable. Instead they are examined for their purpose and utility, including the extent to which any convention helps a writer or a reader and the price that each might pay in the compromise that is inevitably reached.

Chapter 11 ("The Tools of the Trade") begins with pens and pencils and ends with a substantial section on the differences that computers and word processors might make to writing, teaching, and written language. Cataloging the varied items of equipment and support that writers may call upon also helps to underline the frequently idiosyncratic individuality of those who write.

Chapter 12 ("Learning to be a Writer") looks at learning to write as an aspect of learning in general, and especially at the enormous (and usually unsuspected) amounts of learning all of us accomplish if we learn to use spoken and written language with any degree of fluency. The necessary conditions of learning are explored.

Chapter 13 ("Learning the Technicalities") takes the major aspects of composition and transcription and examines what is involved in their learning, both from reading and from writing. Beginners can and must be trusted to be able to learn to write.

Chapter 14 ("The Writing Teacher") contrasts what teachers reasonably might do, and almost certainly cannot do, to help students of any age learn to write. The way schools are organized might inhibit writing even by people who know very well how to do it, so that teaching to write is often much more complicated than it need be. The dilemma is examined.

An aim throughout the book is to avoid technicalities, unnecessary detail, and the frequent citation of related work, which for the writer is supposed to reflect scholarship but for the reader often constitutes little more than obstacles to comprehension. Notes for every chapter are presented together, in somewhat smaller type, beginning on page 241. In these Notes are references for particular topics discussed in the main text, some additional detail or elaborations into new areas that would constitute digressions in the main text, and occasional suggestions for further reading.

WRITING AND THE WRITER

My preview has perhaps already indicated that I have not found it possible to write a book about writing without going very far afield. There is a great deal in this book about language in general and about the thought that underlies language, much of it without specific reference to writing. But writing should not be isolated from other aspects of language and certainly cannot be separated from thought. Writing is a reflection of the mind, and to understand writing the mind in all its power and mystery has to be approached. For a similar reason the chapters on learning to write include discussions on learning in general, because we learn to write in the same ways that we learn anything else.

All this is to say that any inquiry into writing is by necessity fundamentally psychological; in particular, it must always be concerned with the perceptions and intentions of the writer, even when that writer is learning to write. I am not saying that it is necessary to inquire into the psychology of the writer in order to understand a book. Such an inquiry may help to *explain* the book, but as I have asserted, a book exists independently of its author and from many points of view must be dealt with on its own merits. Linguists, literary critics, and readers much of the time rightly ignore the history of how what they are reading was written, and even why it was written. But to understand the *act* of writing, the writer's perspective cannot be ignored, because it affects the act itself. Writing is always personal (even though what is written may not be personal). Writers' intentions cannot be explained away or ignored by the use of such vague expressions as "trying to communicate" or "getting thoughts on paper." A specific question must always be borne in mind: What was the purpose of the writing in the first place? And this will prove very complex. But I consider this question of "Why write?" so fundamental that it is the first to be explored in this book.

My final point enlarges upon one aspect of the personal nature of writing; it is that there is a tremendous range of differences among individuals. For some people writing often comes easily, although others find it a continual struggle (including many professional writers). Some find writing a strain, others a release. Some need absolute silence and freedom from distraction, while others are able to write in any circumstances. A few seem incapable of writing an ungrammatical sentence; others must concentrate on ideas first and attend to matters of grammar and style later. Some cannot bear to have their writing revised; others are reluctant to let it go without multiple revisions. Some flourish under deadlines, but many find it impossible to write to order. All this is apart from such obvious individual differences as ability to spell (certainly not a reliable indicator of the fluency or creativity of a writer), to punctuate, or to write grammatically or neatly.

In other words, there are many dimensions to writing, and individuals can be found at widely separated points on each dimension. One moral is that we should never assume that the way we ourselves write is the way everyone writes. Teachers must not assume that their own idiosyncrasies are the only or even the best way to write. And the author of a book on writing must take care not to make it autobiographical.

(Notes to Chapter 1 begin on page 241.)

2 Why Write?

To write about writing in all its aspects would be to write about every facet of our private and social lives, about the functions of the written word in religion, law, government, politics, industry, commerce, education, art, and entertainment, in all formal and informal relationships among people, all mechanisms for organizing, informing, instructing, persuading, exciting, amusing, tranquilizing, and otherwise controlling or influencing individuals. Writing touches every part of our lives, and not even the illiterate escape its consequences. Indeed, not being able to write is often regarded as an affront to literate society, a societal and an individual inadequacy. For decades, ability to read and to write has been a central issue in the politics of education and in educational research.

The question "Why write?" can be interpreted as an inquiry into the utility of written language to a culture or in our everyday interactions. It can also mean "What is the use of writing to an individual?" I attend to the more general cultural issue first because I do not intend to explore it in depth. I propose to take the general utility of writing to be axiomatic; it has earned its place in any culture in which it is found.

THE CULTURAL UTILITY OF WRITTEN LANGUAGE

Many cultures have developed writing systems of their own, or have adopted the writing systems of other cultures, but there is no record of any culture having given up writing or having allowed it to fall into disuse. Obviously, writing has been generally considered useful, and at least three broad reasons can be found for this.

The first reason for the persistence of writing is its evident utility as a tool for *communication*; it conveys information over time and space in a way not open to speech. You are probably reading these words many months after I wrote them and probably many miles from where I wrote them. It would be far less convenient for both of us if you had to listen to me talking about writing. The second general utility of writing is to provide a more or less permanent *record*, ranging from the accounts in a bookkeeper's ledger to histories and laws whose purpose is not so much to communicate as to institutionalize. All that some cultures have left of their existence is some written records and a few other artifacts. And the third cultural value of writing is as *art*, the product of creativity: novels, poems, plays. The fact that writing, wherever it has existed, seems to have participated in these three general roles demonstrates its broad utility to cultures.

I do not agree with the view that writing will become redundant in our own culture because other technologies are taking its place. I cannot imagine any technology making writing obsolete, in the sense of providing a complete alternative to writing. Technologies may sometimes offer acceptable substitutes—they may occasionally be more efficient than writing, occasionally less—but they are not the same; they do not do what writing does in the way writing does it. Therefore they cannot wholly take the place of writing, any more than photography can take the place of the painter's art (though photography introduces new possibilities for art). Consider the technological alternatives that are commonly proposed for writing, the telephone or radio and television, and their more permanent forms, recording and film.

Apart from the fact that the telephone (or radio) can overcome barriers of space, the telephone has the same disadvantages as spoken language; its utility is restricted to the moment it is uttered. A telephone call cannot take the place of a book or even a letter as a means of communication across time, as a record, or as a work of art. Recordings can only overcome constraints of time in a limited way, taking a spoken language event out of one particular moment of time, the moment it is produced, so that it can be heard and repeated at other times. But listeners to a recording do not have the power to manipulate time that readers have; they cannot skip, hurry ahead, or go back and review, at least not with the facility of a reader. You could not ask me to repeat a sentence I produced five minutes ago if you were listening to me talk, nor could you so easily find that sentence on a tape recording or even a computer disk. Certainly you could not ask me to tell you in advance the sentence I might produce five minutes from now, although you can easily look forward in a letter or a book. Nor could you attend to either of those sentences *at your own pace*, as slowly or as rapidly as you might wish, as you can with a written text. For such reasons (as well as other advantages of writing as a record), audio recordings of legal and political proceedings are usually transcribed into written form.

Even in ways that might seem trivial—though they are not—writing often has to be used to supplement recorded speech. It is difficult to edit recordings and impossible to mark them for emphasis or comment, to annotate, underline, or put exclamation marks in the margin. Once again I am not saying that recording might not have some advantages over writing, or even over the written transcription of speech. Some information is carried in the quality and intonation of speech that is lost when speech is transcribed into writing, although it can be put into written language in other ways. I am simply saying that the written form of language functions differently and cannot therefore be wholly replaced by direct or recorded speech.

It is essential to consider the different characteristics of various media in terms of the degree to which they can be manipulated to overcome constraints of time and space. Obviously, writing and other technologies are relatively independent of time and space *extrinsically*, text and recordings can be taken from one place to another and will persist far longer than the time taken to produce them. But there is also a matter of *intrinsic* control of time and space, both for the producer and recipients of the language form. A writer can (within limits) write fast or slowly, and can reorganize what is written so that the final product is not in the order in which it was produced. Readers can then impose their own rate and sequence of reading. Other media do not offer these possibilities so conveniently to everyone concerned.

Consider television and film. Immediacy may have a value—seeing a televised event as it occurs rather than reading about it—but it is not always convenient. A direct television broadcast, like the event itself, may occupy more time than I have available or may occur at a time when I cannot be watching. Film or videotape can be edited and seen at different times, but not with the ease of text editing, and—like tape recordings— they still offer less control over rate and sequence to the viewer than written language does to the reader.

Besides, film and language achieve their effects in different ways; they offer different perspectives. All this is perhaps most marked, although not exclusively, in the case of art. I would not be satisfied with a written description of the Mona Lisa or the Statue of Liberty, nor with the text of a film like *Modern Times* or *Battleship Potemkin*; so much of this art is visual. But on the other hand a picture of a storm at sea may not be as compelling as a written description, and I would certainly not want to have the films of many novels, no matter how well they are made, in place of the novels themselves. I would not be content with a picture of an art critic examining a painting. The various media can substitute in some ways for writing, but they cannot take its place. Films and recordings have introduced new art forms, but they have not made writing outdated. A picture can rarely take the place of a description, especially one that includes the intentions or morality of an act, any more than a description can provide the detail offered by a picture.[1]

Everything is relative. One might be tempted to argue that neither a written description nor a film could be better than actually participating in an event, but both book and film can be concerned with imaginary events, or events that we could not possibly attend or might not want to attend. A film or a book can convey to me in different ways something of what it is like to face a firing squad or to be in a plane crash, neither of which I would care to experience at first hand or even as an observer. But once again there are other experiences, like friendship, good meals, and sunny beaches, that can never be replaced by films or descriptions.

Computers do not threaten to make reading and writing obsolete, but they do promise to change reading and writing, or at least to introduce new forms of both, matters which I discuss in a later chapter on electronic and other tools of writing. Computers might also be perceived as threatening *paper* (or alternatively, as protecting some of the forests from which enormous quantities of paper are currently derived). But at the moment, paper is more than holding its own. Computers themselves are great devourers of paper, not only in the printouts involved in almost everything that computers do, including multiple drafts for writers. (I must confess that I use more paper to write a book or an article by computer than I used for composing similar texts by hand.) Computers and the software programs that run on them demand immense quantities of paper just to explain themselves. Manuals totaling many hundreds of pages are not unusual. The designers of these materials may expect and hope that this reliance on paper will diminish as people become more accustomed to computers—much of the text in manuals is also available on the monitor screen—but there is not much indication of this actually happening.

All the preceding considerations can be summed up by saying that the different technologies of communication, record, and art that we have available are options but not true alternatives. They do not work in the same way, nor can they always achieve the same ends. It is not possible to say that one is better than another, or even more convenient; it depends on the purposes of the producer and the recipient and on their situations.

And as a final complication it should be remembered that these various options are not even equally convenient or useful to the producer and to the recipient. It may be more convenient for me to telephone what you would rather have in a letter or an electronic bulletin board, or for me to write what you would prefer to see in a film. One characteristic of language that seems to apply to all its aspects is that the interests of the producer and recipient rarely coincide; language itself is frequently a compromise. It is easier for me to scribble, but you prefer clear print. I would rather not repeat myself, but you want to hear some things twice. One way of evaluating technologies is to consider the benefit they give to one participant in contrast to the cost to the other.

Certainly for our culture as a whole, other technologies do not seem to be taking the place of writing. Rather they might appear to generate more writing, from the scripts for films and programs for performances to the mass of documentation that underlies every new scientific and technical development and legislates its use. With every new step in science and art comes more print.

The amount of writing being done today might appear to be overwhelming many cultures. So much "information" has accumulated in the memories of computers and on various auxiliary electronic storage devices that it has already reached the saturation point that books had previously reached. So much exists that most of it will never be used and much of it can't be found— like the misplaced or uncataloged books in libraries. Governments and other bureaucracies are probably as much to blame as computers for this glut of written language. Apart from all the "archival" material that is produced, from presidential doodlings to the minutes and transcripts of the most mundane committees, laws and regulations are being produced at a faster rate than anyone could possibly read them. It is ironic that schools may be the only places where *less* writing is being done (Farnan, Lapp, & Flood, 1992).

However, in this book I am not concerned with the utility of writing to cultures but to individuals. It might be argued that all the aspects of writing that I have talked about—as communication, record, and art—could be a tool of an elite, of a special class of literates, certain lawyers, priests, scientists, artists, academics, and administrators. It might be argued that it is useful for most people to be able to read, but not a necessity that all should write. There is a profound political issue here. The implication is that individuals must read to be kept in order, but that writing is revolutionary and could be used to change the current order.

I could respond that in any case I am concerned with the *act* of writing, so I want to analyze what it is that certain lawyers, priests, scientists, artists, academics, and administrators do. But I want to go much further than that. I think writing has a utility to all individuals, that anyone who does not write loses both power and potential, comparable to losing a limb or sight or hearing. To look at the value of writing to cultures is basically to examine its effects on readers, the consequence of its existence. But writing also makes a difference because of what it does for writers. People gain by writing. And that leads to the more interesting interpretation of the "Why write?" question: What is its utility to the person who writes? What is the use of the act of writing?

THE PERSONAL UTILITY OF WRITING

I start with a broader question: not "What is the use of writing?" but "What is the use of language in general?" Writing is a form of language and not, as I shall argue, simply spoken language written down. In some important respects, writing is a far more powerful form of language than speech. First we must examine what language in general can do (for the individual), then see whether both spoken and written language can independently do these things, and then consider whether they can do them all equally well. We shall find, to get ahead of the discussion a little, that everything that language can do can be accomplished in other nonlanguage ways. There is nothing exclusive about language, except its versatility. Sometimes language works better, sometimes not; once again it depends on circumstances. But we also find that for each of the ends to which language can be put, sometimes spoken language and sometimes written language would appear to be more efficient. Writing may do nothing that is unique, but it can do some things enormously well.

There are no easy generalizations. Language is so much a part of our complicated lives that it is difficult if not impossible to say anything about it that is not complicated.

The Uses of Language[2]

First we consider the general question: What are the uses of language, both spoken and written? The issue is put in the plural, not "What is the use of language?" but "What are its uses?" because this is a case where undue simplification sidesteps all the interesting issues. Nothing is clarified, for example, by such assertions as "language is for communication" or "language is used to convey information." There are many instances when language is used for quite different reasons. Besides, such statements as the two I have just given beg the question; even if we were to agree with them we would still have to ask the supplementary questions "What is communication?" or "What is information?" Instead, it is better to ask directly, "What does language do? What are the uses to which it is put?" The answers will be complex enough.

Here is a short list of ways in which language can be used: (1) to get our material needs met, (2) to change the behavior or beliefs of others, (3) to establish or reflect personal relationships with others, (4) to express our perception of ourselves, (5) to seek new knowledge, (6) to exercise the imagination, (7) to describe and criticize situations or ideas, (8) for fun, (9) to establish agreement or expectations, (10) as a record of the past.

I do not want to claim that my catalog of language uses is complete; possibly you can think of other uses as well, or will argue that some of my categories are overlapping.[3] But for the moment I want to make only two brief points, and for these my list will serve.

The first point is that language, both spoken and written, has a wide variety of uses, so much so that I do not think it productive in the present context to summarize language uses under the traditional categories of "expressive," "communicative," and "descriptive" functions, which seem to me better considered as descriptions of the type of language that is produced on particular occasions rather than of the uses to which language is put. Indeed,

I avoid using the term *functions*, which might be considered far too limited where language is concerned. The uses to which tools are put are often far broader than their functions, which are usually narrowly prescribed with reference to the main reason for the tools' being fabricated in the first place. For example, I suppose the conventional function of knives is to cut, but they can be used for a variety of purposes ranging from digging holes in the ground to driving in screws. It is not a function of forks to comb the hair, but they might be used for that purpose.

Wood, steel, plastics, and electricity have so many uses that it would not even make sense to ask what their functions are. The actual uses depend on the intentions and initiative of people, rather than on any limitations of the material. I think the same applies to language; it can be employed in every kind of human enterprise. My list is a catalog not of what *might* be done as of what *is* done; the items are all things that people currently *do* with spoken and written language. Language in all its manifestations is around us, like a huge and endlessly renewable natural resource, waiting to be exploited by everyone.

My second point is that despite all of the multifarious uses to which language is put, none of them is unique. Language is always an alternative; there are always other ways of trying to achieve the same ends. I am not saying that these other means are necessarily more efficient; however, I am not saying that language is necessarily more efficient either, but simply that alternatives always exist. Language is not something apart from everything else we might do; it is a different means of achieving quite general ends. The argument will perhaps be clearer if I expand my list of language uses in the table on page 14, giving (on the left) a simple label for the particular kind of language use and also an example in words of how language might fulfill that use, and adding (on the right) examples of nonlanguage ways in which the same ends might be achieved.

The range of uses to which language may be put will be relevant at various points throughout this book, especially in approaching such complex issues as the relationships between thought and language, between written and spoken language, and between readers and writers, as well as when questions of how writing might best be learned and taught are raised. Neither spoken nor written language use should be segregated into a category apart from every other kind of human enterprise. Rather, language is an alternative or supplementary means, often particularly powerful, by which we can engage in any of the endeavors that occupy our lives. Language reflects and extends every kind of human intention and aspiration; there is no part of our lives in which it cannot be productive.

I do not want to argue that language is necessarily more efficient for all the various kinds of uses listed in Table 1; obviously this is not the case. Language is not conspicuously successful in expressing emotion or deep feeling (compared, for example, with dancing) and may be less adequate than a touch of the hand in conveying affection or sympathy. Language may fail to help us get material needs met or to change the behavior of others, in which event there appears to be a natural tendency to revert to alternative and more direct means of expressing determination, frustration, or outrage. On the other hand, one enormous advantage that language often has over certain alternative means of achieving the same ends is that it *can* be indirect; we can use language to suggest, to cajole, or to persuade. (Music, scents, and color can of

TABLE 1.
The Uses of Language[4]

LANGUAGE USE	NONLANGUAGE ALTERNATIVE
1. *Instrumental:* "I want." (Language as a means of getting things, satisfying material needs)	Pantomime, facial expressions, screaming, pointing, grabbing
2. *Regulatory:* "Do as I tell you." (Controlling the behavior, feelings, or attitudes of others)	Pushing and pulling people around; modeling behavior for others to copy; gestures, traffic lights
3. *Interactional:* "Me and you." (Getting along with others, establishing relative status; also "Me against you," establishing separateness)	Waving, smiling, linking arms, holding hands, shaking fist; sport; gifts; uniforms, shared activities
4. *Personal:* "Here I come." (Expressing individuality, awareness of self, pride, pleasure, anger, grief)	Art, music, dress, cosmetics, ornamentation
5. *Heuristic:* "Tell me why." (Seeking and testing knowledge)	Exploration, investigation, experimentation
6. *Imaginative:* "Let's pretend." (Creating new worlds, making up stories, poems)	Play, art, mime
7. *Representational:* "I've got something to tell you." (Communicating information, descriptions, expressing propositions)	Pointing, rituals, diagrams, dials, maps, mathematics
8. *Divertive:* "Enjoy this." (Puns, jokes, riddles)	Games, puzzles, magic
9. *Authoritative/contractual:* "How it must be." (Statutes, laws, regulations, agreements, contracts)	Roles, rituals, regalia, uniforms, architecture, money
10. *Perpetuating:* "How it was." (Records, histories, diaries, notes, scores)	Cave drawings, photographs, sculpture, monuments, memorials

course be employed for the same purpose, perhaps even more subtly or insinuatingly.) We can use language for *argument*, which not only permits us to construct and examine states of affairs that do not actually exist in the world around us, but can be a little more socially acceptable than beating someone who holds an opposing position about the head with a club.

In Table 1, I enumerated various uses of language in terms that are socially neutral, if not benign. But I should acknowledge that language can be employed in insidious ways too. Language can agitate, aggravate, betray, bewilder, confound, confuse, corrupt, deceive, defame, demoralize, disparage, and disrupt (and that is to confine myself to words beginning with the first four letters of the alphabet). I would certainly add antisocial practices as an additional—possibly the largest—category of uses in the Table, were they not a part of every category in the list. Language does not necessarily make us better people, and improving our language abilities can also improve our chances of accomplishing nefarious ends.

One rather specialized but still widespread use of language, which certainly did not exist before language, is to talk about language itself—that is, to describe and analyze linguistic phenomena. Such a use is called *metalinguistic*, or *metalanguage*. Many words in our language are metalinguistic, including the words *word*, *language*, and *metalinguistic*. This entire book is metalinguistic, and so is much instruction about reading and writing. The distinction is particularly important with respect to instruction, because it is often assumed that children need to understand metalinguistic terms like *noun*, *verb*, *sentence* (and *read* and *write*) in order to learn to read and write, when in fact the opposite applies. One can learn to read and write without knowing the meaning of such terms; in fact, one cannot completely understand the terms without having first learned to read and write.

To say that there is nothing language does that cannot be attempted by other means (and that sometimes the other means may be more effective than language) is not to undervalue language. Quite the contrary, language is perhaps the only universal all-purpose tool; none of the various alternatives available can be used for so many ends. (Only dance or mime can come even close to fulfilling most of the uses to which language can be put that are listed in Table 1.)

A final point about language in general, which will become particularly relevant as we move on to consider writing in particular, is that all of the uses of language that I have listed can be rehearsed and sometimes completed in the privacy of our own minds. Language is often thought about solely as a tool of communication, and I illustrated in Table 1 the various aspects of language use as if there were always a second participant, or at least a potential observer. But we can try things out mentally in language—we can generate, test, and if necessary reject all manner of ideas—without interference and without risk. The inner world as well as the world around us can be an arena for exploiting all the possibilities of language.

The Uses of Writing

I can now offer a simple answer to my original question about the utility of writing to the individual. Writing can do everything that language in general can do. All of the uses of language that are listed in Table 1 are uses to which writing can be put. And this should not be surprising, since writing is a form of language. Writing is not speech written down, any more than the word "language" should be regarded as synonymous with "speech." Speech and writing are alternative forms of language, and all of the uses to which language can be put apply to these alternative forms, to both writing and speech.[5]

Once again, I am not suggesting that the two alternatives are identical, that speech and writing can be substituted for each other with no difference in consequence. Sometimes speech might be considered more effective or appropriate—for example, in establishing interpersonal relations. Sometimes writing may be the preferred form, as it is for most contractual and recording purposes, or because, as I would argue, it separates our ideas from ourselves in a way that is easiest for us to examine, explore, and develop. Writing permits ideas and events to be created and manipulated in ways that would not exist if all language had to be as transient as thought or spoken words. You might find it an interesting exercise to go through the list of language uses in Table 1, considering whether each might be better performed in speech, in writing, or by one of the nonlanguage means. You will probably find that in each case the answer is "It all depends," which is the reason I shall not attempt at this point to discuss further the relative merits of speech, writing, or other forms of action or expression.

With one exception. I have already pointed out that although language is usually considered to be an interchange involving two or more people, it can be rehearsed or otherwise performed in the mind, where it not only can provide an opportunity to try out and even refine things we might want to say, but can give rise to new ideas we did not think we were capable of. Now one of the beautiful things about writing is that it does not have to be performed in the head to be a private or provisional undertaking. We can write for ourselves just as clearly and permanently as we can write for other people. This is an important difference between writing and speech; not only can writing separate the producer of language from its recipient in time and space, with the possibility of reflection and review, but writing can also separate the producer from him or herself, so that one's own ideas can be examined more objectively. Writers can look at the language they produce in a way that speakers cannot. Writing is a tangible construction.[6]

All this is not just a matter of getting thoughts onto paper and seeing what they look like. Things happen when we write. Ideas can be generated and developed in the interaction between writer and what is being written that would not be possible if the ideas were left to flower and perhaps fade in the transience of the mind. Writing can be used in the same way that a rough sketch is used by a painter or an architect, because no one can plan and work on an entire painting or building in all its interrelated detail in one's head. Even when we think we are writing solely for others, excepting perhaps the most trivial of communications, the writing is helping us to organize and develop the possibilities of our own minds. The advantages of writing may be accidental as well as incidental. All this is a major theme of this book—the mutually modifying interaction during the act of writing between the writer and what is being written.

Being able to write is generally regarded as a "good thing"—and I feel that way about it myself. But like language in general, writing is not an unalloyed good. It can be put to antisocial purposes, sometimes with great effect. And ability to write can itself be used as a means of discrimination, as an emblem of superiority. Just as speakers of particular dialects may be discriminated against simply because of the way they talk, so literate people often look down on and penalize those they call illiterate. And this despite the fact that the ability gap between those who consider themselves literate and their victims may not be as wide as the former claim. In schools, small differences in writing ability can lead to enormous consequences, when tests are so pervasive and when little allowance is made for individuals who might require slightly more time or consideration than others.

To sum up, writing can do everything that language in general can do, which means that it can contribute to every aspect of our lives. Writing can be an extension and reflection of all our efforts to develop and express ourselves in the world around us, to make sense of that world, and to impose order upon it. I make these points because I think some of the mystification should be taken out of writing. It is unproductive to regard writing as a special kind of activity that requires unusual talents or lengthy training and can only be used for a few specialized ends, which perhaps do not concern many people. It is wrong to regard writing ability as a particularly esoteric skill that only a few can achieve, and then usually only with a great deal of effort. The power of writing could be open to anyone who can use speech.

It is true that not many people write very much, and that those who do so often exhibit little skill or pleasure in the activity. There are two ways of looking at these facts. One can argue that writing is indeed a very difficult and specialized activity that few of us have the taste, talent, or training to perform well. Alternatively, one can hypothesize that writing is something that everyone ought to be able to do and enjoy, as naturally as singing, dancing, or play. Like singing, dancing, and play, writing may be one of those activities that all children enjoy—and enjoy learning to do better—until, all too often, they become discouraged or uninterested because something happens to inhibit their free and natural expression. And that something can often be associated with education or training; it results in a loss of spontaneity, a painful self-consciousness of "error," a reluctance to perform and learn because of a perceived inability to achieve certain extrinsic standards. Writing is full of inhibitions for most of us. Instead of asking why so few people learn to write well and to enjoy writing, we might ask why so many come not to enjoy it, and therefore lose the desire to engage in it. That people may deprive themselves of the pleasure and benefit of writing as a consequence of efforts that are made to teach them to write is an issue that will come up again.

(Notes to Chapter 2 begin on page 241.)

3 Writing: Collaboration and Competition

Like all of the common and most useful words of our language, the word *writing* has multiple meanings. The word even has more than one grammatical function, serving verbally when the reference is to an act of writing and as a noun when the reference is to the product of that act, a piece of writing. In the present chapter we examine writing as a verb.

TRANSCRIPTION AND COMPOSITION

Even when used as a verb, the word *writing* can have two quite different kinds of meaning. Two people might in fact claim to be writing the same words at the same time, although each is doing different things. An author dictating to a secretary or into a tape recorder could claim to be writing a book without actually putting a mark on paper. The secretary or person doing the transcribing could also claim to be writing the same words, by performing a conventional act with a pen, pencil, typewriter, or word processor.

To debate who was really doing the writing, author or secretary, could start one of those endless and pointless arguments based on a perfectly innocuous semantic ambiguity. It is sufficient to say that both are engaged in writing in different senses of the word, and if we want to clarify exactly what each is doing then we have to use different terms to distinguish the different ways in which the word is being used. Fortunately these alternative terms exist in English; we can say that the author is *composing* the words and that the secretary is *transcribing* them.

We can elaborate upon the distinction by listing some of the various responsibilities of the two parties:

COMPOSITION (author)	TRANSCRIPTION (secretary)
Getting ideas	Physical effort of writing
Selecting words	Spelling
Grammar	Capitalization
	Punctuation
	Paragraphs
	Legibility

The distinctions and division of responsibilities are not as clear-cut in the world as in the list. Authors may be concerned with some aspects of transcription; they may spell words as they are dictated, put in punctuation, and indicate which letters or words are to be capitalized and where new paragraphs begin. Secretaries may play an active role in composition, amending the author's grammar and choice of words and perhaps introducing new ideas. Furthermore, the author and secretary may not be limited to just one interaction with the same piece of writing; there may be *editing* when the author reviews the text to make changes to some of the secretary's concerns, to the spelling or punctuation, or to the actual composition. The secretary may make a "clean" copy that introduces further changes to the text. In very general terms, however, it is possible to distinguish the responsibilities of composer and transcriber as they collaborate to produce a single piece of writing in the noun sense.

THE TWO SIDES IN CONFLICT

I have been talking about composing and transcribing as if they were performed by two different people. This was for ease of exposition, to distinguish the two broad aspects of writing and to show that they need not have a great deal to do with each other, in the sense that the author need not be able to spell or punctuate and the secretary need not be able to put ideas together or write grammatically (provided, of course, that each can rely on the other to attend to those particular aspects of the task).

However, for most of us, most of the time, there is no such division of labor; we have to play both roles concurrently. As I sit at my keyboard writing these words in their original, unedited form, I am both composing and transcribing. I began with an illustration of two individuals in collaboration not only to show how the two aspects of writing can be distinguished, but also to make a further point. When two individuals undertake these complementary activities, they *facilitate* each other's contribution. Each one's tasks can be done better because the other takes exclusive responsibility for some of the work; the author does not have to worry about spelling or neatness, and the secretary does not have the bother of actually thinking of the words. When the two aspects are done by the same person at the same time, however, they can *interfere* with each other. What is collaboration between two people becomes competition when done by the same person.

The preceding point warrants spelling out, because it makes a particularly big difference when writing is difficult for any reason, when we are struggling for ideas or for the right words, when we are unsure of spelling or anxious about neatness, or when we are learning to write. *Composition and transcription can interfere with each other.* The more attention you give to one, the more the other is likely to suffer.

The problem is basically one of competition for attention. If we are struggling for ideas, or for particular words or constructions, or if our thoughts are coming too fast, then the quality of our handwriting or typing, our spelling or punctuation is likely to decline. If we concentrate on the transcription or appearance of what we write, on the other hand, then composition will be affected; we are more likely to produce impeccable nonsense.

There are several factors contributing to this conflict, to the writer's dilemma. The first is that writing is literally hard work; it requires more physical effort than any other aspect of language. We can talk a great deal before our jaws begin to ache, and provided that what we are attending to is of interest and comprehensible, we can listen and read for hours on end with little risk of fatiguing the ears or the eyes. Writing, however, can be physically tiring, to our fingers and arms and backs, especially if we are tense about the writing we are engaged in. Anything that can reduce the effort of writing is likely to improve its quality—hence the value of electric typewriters and word processors, together with skill in using them.

Perhaps more important than the physical demands of writing are the relative speeds of its two aspects. A major difficulty with the act of writing is that it is *slow* compared with every other aspect of language and with thought itself. It is not possible to make a direct measurement of the speed of thought because there are no units that can be used to express such a measure; it does not make sense to say that the human brain runs best at the rate of so many thoughts a minute, or so many ideas per hour. We can, however, very roughly get an indirect indication of the speed at which thought most comfortably progresses by looking at the rate at which the brain deals with language. Thought is not words, but the rate at which we can deal with words can be taken as a reflection of the rate at which thought itself proceeds. And that natural, comfortable rate of thought, it would seem to me, is in the range of between 200 and 300 words a minute.

Between 200 and 300 words a minute is a comfortable rate of *talking* (I am referring to the continuous parts of utterance, not including the breaks or hesitations when we are thinking about what we might say next). To talk faster than 300 words a minute is difficult and fatiguing; try it. It is not so much a matter of not being able to speak faster as of running out of things to say; the brain cannot keep up. But it is also difficult to speak much slower than 200 words a minute; the problem now is that memory is overburdened, and we forget what we intend to say while we wait to say it. Slow speech is not a sign that we are thinking more about what we are trying to say as much as an indication that we do not know what to say, or how to say it. Fluent speech, when tongue and thought function in synchrony (the brain always a little bit ahead of the tongue), occurs in the 200- to 300-word-a-minute range.

The same rate also seems to be the most comfortable and efficient for *listening*. If we understand and have an interest in what someone is saying, we can sit contentedly and listen at the rate of about 250 words a minute. At rates faster than that we have to struggle to keep up and to match our thoughts to what we hear; at slower rates the speaker becomes much more of a strain on our patience and on our memory, much harder to understand because now the words are not keeping up with our thoughts. Similarly with *reading*, there are many indications that the most comfortable and natural rate of reading is in the range of 200 to 300 words a minute. At faster rates we are looking for specific information, bypassing much of the detail that the author has provided (which may of course be the most efficient manner of reading on particular occasions); at slower rates memory becomes overburdened and we are likely to have forgotten the beginning of a sentence by the time we reach the end of it.

Contrasted with this average 250-word-a-minute rate for talking, listening, and reading, however, *writing* is painfully slow; often no less than ten times slower. An average rate of writing neatly by hand—try it—is not much more than 25 words a minute. The remarkable thing is that thought can ever slow down to produce itself in words at that rate at all. Certainly most of us would find it extremely difficult if we were constrained—to—talk—at—25—words—a—minute. It is not surprising that handwriting and neatness are likely to degenerate into a sloppy scrawl as we try to speed up writing to match the speed of thought.[1] But, on the other hand, the act of composition is hobbled if we try to slow it down to the rate of tidy handwriting or even, for many people, of errorless typing (or keyboarding). The most efficient typists and word processors rarely exceed 60 words a minute, still only a quarter of the average speed of speech. I can always tell on looking back at my notes when the ideas were coming fastest and most fluently; the evidence is everywhere in the scribble, the erratic spelling, and the incomplete sentences. It is in recognition of the discrepancy between the most comfortable speeds of thinking and of physically writing that many people believe that a recording machine is the solution. But as I have already indicated, speaking is not the same as writing, and not having a visible record of what you compose loses one of the greatest advantages of writing in the first place.

There is a limit to how much the human brain can be aware of, can consciously direct, at any one time.[2] The attention that is given to transcription aspects of writing—whether to neatness, spelling, or punctuation—is not available for composition. Neatness, spelling, and punctuation and other aspects of transcription can become habitual or automatic; we do not have to stop and think about spelling the words we have already learned how to spell. But the occasions when composition is most difficult—when we are struggling to produce ideas that are not fully worked out in our mind, especially if they are to be produced in a style of language with which we are not particularly familiar (and this, of course, is frequently the condition of anyone learning to write)—are unfortunately likely also to be the occasions when our resources of relevant habitual behaviors demanding a minimum of attention are least.[3]

Anxiety will always fuel the conflict. Anyone particularly apprehensive about the subsequent evaluation of what is being written will pay the most attention to those aspects of the writing that are most likely to be evaluated. If we expect that someone is likely to assess our ability on the basis of our spelling, punctuation, or neatness, then these are the aspects of our writing to which we will devote the most attention; and the more we are concerned about the evaluation, the more attention we are likely to commit. This of course is one reason why many people find themselves thinking and writing ineffectually at examinations; the very desire to be legible and to give the impression of a tidy and organized mind distracts even further a reserve of attention already dispersed by general anxiety about the situation.

RESOLVING THE CONFLICT

If the composition and transcription sides of writing are fundamentally incompatible, how then can the conflict be resolved so that what is written represents writing that is both worthwhile and conventionally acceptable in terms of its general appearance? There can be only one answer: The two aspects of writing have to be separated. Thus rewriting and editing can be as important as writing.

The matter of rewriting also involves two considerations. One consideration is the important interaction of the author with the current text in the process of composition, modifying what has already been done as a consequence of new insights and ideas that arise. Because this will usually result in an even messier transcription, with more scribbles and rearrangements, additions, and deletions, such rewriting will not be considered at this point. But the other consideration is the final production of a clean copy, the final *editing*, the stage when almost all the attention can be given to transcription because the composition has been satisfactorily completed.

The rule is simple: Composition and transcription must be separated, and transcription must come last. It is asking too much of anyone, and especially of students trying to improve all aspects of their writing ability, to expect that they can concern themselves with polished transcription at the same time that they are trying to compose. The effort to concentrate on spelling, handwriting, and punctuation at the same time that one is struggling with ideas and their expression not only interferes with composition but creates the least favorable situation in which to develop transcription skills as well.

It is ironic that although composition suffers to the extent that attention is devoted to transcription, the better one becomes at composition the less transcription skills are likely to be required. The successful writer can leave it to other people to look after spelling and punctuation. I am not saying that learning to spell and punctuate correctly and to write neatly are not important, and not only as good manners toward people you expect to read your work. The conventions of grammar and spelling and punctuation actually facilitate writing, provided you do not have to think about them. But facility in transcription skills is obviously achieved at too high a price if the cost is reluctance or inability to compose anything in the first place.

Both the composition and the transcription aspects of writing are important and, following my own precepts, I propose to deal with them separately. In accordance with what I have argued to be their relative priority when writing is actually taking place, I shall deal with transcription last. For all its complexity, transcription is a self-contained aspect of writing compared with the intricate links of composition to every facet of human understanding and motivation, a topic that will occupy the next six chapters.

Author–Author Collaboration

The collaboration I have been discussing is the rather unusual circumstance when one person takes care of composition while the other attends to the demands of transcription. Except in certain professional situations, becoming rarer, such collaboration is unusual and I discussed it only to make a contrast with the more usual "competitive" state of affairs when the same person is responsible for both composition and transcription.

Writers often collaborate with each other, however, and there is a growing interest in encouraging collaboration among students, or between students and their teacher, to improve their writing. Computers are facilitating such author–author partnerships.

Collaboration in writing—or "co-authorship"—usually involves cycles of composition or revision by one participant followed by criticism and suggestions by another. Such an arrangement requires tact as well as collegiality; a partner who does most of the composition *and* transcription but is also the recipient of most of the criticism and good advice may soon be wishing for solo authorship. Only the most tough-skinned professionals appreciate someone else making gratuitous comments all over their cherished manuscripts.

But it is also possible for two people to sit together—one at the keyboard and the other alongside (occasionally changing places, perhaps)—both contributing ideas, suggestions, words, phrases, or longer sections, or simply talking about what has been written or what might be written. Between two compatible people, this can be a productive and even pleasant process. It can be an ideal situation in some circumstances, because the two collaborators can help and even inspire each other in the composition task, while only one of them has to worry about transcription (and the other can perhaps act as a supplementary "short-term memory" if the transcribing partner forgets what is to be typed next). Such a collaboration may be particularly productive when a lot of incidental activity is involved that the non-typing partner can take care of, like looking up references, reading passages to be quoted, or making notes for future consideration. With networked computers, two people can engage in an "on-line" collaboration while in different rooms, even in different cities, avoiding the inconvenience of one partner constantly leaning over the shoulder of the other.

Wason (1980) briefly discusses some advantages of collaboration on texts among academic writers, and incidentally claims to have found some success in requiring children to write alternate sentences of stories in such a way that the final result looks as if it was written by just one person.

(Notes to Chapter 3 begin on page 243.)

4 The Thought Behind Language

Our starting point is at the threshold of a shadowy realm of enigma and paradox, the human brain. Any attempt to understand writing must begin with the relationship between language and thought, and this requires entering a world where language does not exist. There lies the first paradox, that the meaning of language is beyond words or direct inspection. The exploration of writing must begin before words or images are even formed. Consider the problem.

ENIGMAS OF THE BRAIN

The object of our concern, the human brain, rests securely lodged within the amphitheater of the skull, relatively protected from outside intervention but entirely deprived of any direct contact with the world around. Poetically the eyes might be considered the brain's windows on the world, just as one might imagine that the brain uses our ears for listening to its sounds. But in prosaic fact the brain leads a life of almost complete isolation in a world without sights or sounds, without even smells or tastes or any kind of tactile sensation. All of these *experiences* the brain conjures up for itself. The eyes do not send pictures to the brain; nerve impulses travel between eye and brain that do not contain color or texture or even shape in any simple way. The nerve fibers between the ears and the brain do not conduct sound, but are again merely channels along which neural impulses pass. The nerve impulses between ear and brain are no different in quality from those between eye and brain, or those from the nose, the tongue, the fingers, or the feet. There are no more differences among the nerve impulses that travel to and from the various parts of the body than there are differences in the electric currents that drive or control the washing machine, the television, the lights, or the refrigerator in the home.

But it is only through a constant barrage of indistinguishable neural impulses from the various receptor systems of the body (and how does the brain even know about its own body?) that the brain has any contact with the outside world. The brain sits like a technician in a sealed control room at the center of a vast communications network, receiving messages in code from every quarter of a complex organization outside—except that *the brain has never been outside*. The brain cannot know what the "code" is for. The brain has never "seen" the world at the other end of its incoming nerve fibers. Helen Keller might provide a better metaphor; deaf and blind, she had to make sense of a world of sight and sounds that she could not experience at first hand. But she did have access to that world through touch, taste, smell, and eventually language. The brain knows nothing at first hand. Everything it pictures as occurring in the world it depicts for itself, all the colors and textures and sounds and smells, presumably using the same palette that it employs for painting its dreams and fantasies.

Oddly enough, although the brain's only access to the outside world is through these neural networks, the incoming neural activity is not anything of which we can ever be directly aware. We can no more see (from the inside) the neural impulses reaching the visual areas of the brain than we can examine the chemical changes that light produces on the retina of the eye or hear the arrival of the neural impulses that travel to the brain along the auditory nerve fibers from the ears. The brain is aware only of its own products, the images and sensations that it constructs; and we seem destined to remain ignorant of the immediate evidence upon which the brain bases its perceptual decisions.

On the other hand, scientists using their microscopes and other instruments to explore what goes on in the brain can *only* see the neural activity to which the brain is apparently blind and deaf, or the equally uninformative (in this context) molecular structures of the chemistry of the brain. Scientists have no instruments to see in other brains the images and feelings that their own brains experience; these sensations do not exist in the physical structure of the brain. There is a gulf without any apparent way over or around it. From inside the brain we can see only mental images and from the outside we can detect only physical activity, and the two are so different in quality and complexity that it is, I think, impossible to imagine what kind of a bridge might be looked for.

Suppose that the eyes did send pictures to the brain, and that researchers discovered a screen in the brain on which scenes from the world outside were faithfully reproduced. That would solve nothing. What good is a picture in the brain? We would still need an eye in the brain to look at the picture in the brain, and a brain behind that eye to make sense of the picture the eye is seeing—and so on, eyes behind eyes behind eyes, with a brain between each pair. How could the chain ever be broken? Suppose that researchers could describe exactly what occurs in the neurochemistry of the brain when we have the experience of seeing blue or green, or smell burning, or sense sourness or warmth? How could the alchemy be explained? Why should we *see* anything just because certain cells of a particular neural subsystem become active in a particular part of the brain? Why should we *smell* freshly cut grass just because a certain chemical change takes place in a few brain cells somewhere else? How can any chemical formula or wiring diagram explain what goes on when we recognize a friend, hear a voice, and understand what that person is saying? This is nothing like explaining how a refrigerator works; the whole enterprise is beyond words—beyond conception.

At least, I think so. I must admit that many contemporary psychologists and brain researchers talk as if there were no mystery left about the brain. Any question that cannot be answered is regarded as a meaningless question. Even if science does not yet know all the answers, at least it is on the way to getting them. The only need is for more research, not for more questions. It is a rare scientist indeed who admits there might be some doubt about what the questions should be.[1]

I do not know why we are so reluctant to acknowledge mystery, especially since the world seems so full of it in so many fundamental ways. Children are rarely taught about mystery, although I am sure they understand and respect it. Instead we tend to encourage them to believe that only knowledge exists. The educated person knows everything that it is necessary to know, or at least knows where to look it up. Why do we associate ignorance with stupidity, and value dogma over doubt? Is it a political matter? Would our institutions crumble if we admitted that there were fundamental uncertainties in our lives?

So here is the frustrating dilemma. There is ultimately no way to examine how what goes on inside the brain is related to the words that suddenly appear outside, whether we write or speak. And we cannot expect brain research to answer such questions for us. Even if we imagine we hear words in our head before we say or write them, we cannot say where *those* words come from. Their beginnings are lost in the recesses of the mind, in the brain behind the voices in the brain.

Having belabored all this, I must quickly acknowledge that it does not mean there is nothing that can be said about the way in which words are generated by the brain. We can talk about the circumstances in which words occur and the circumstances in which they do not, and we can obviously talk about what the words are like when they come out. We can compare words produced on one occasion with those produced on another, and from these comparisons we can make inferences about underlying processes. We can even talk about instruction that might develop the underlying processes that we infer.

Fortunately, most of the time, most of us succeed in producing and comprehending language without being privy to any special knowledge of what is taking place in the brain, and there is no evidence that access to such knowledge would make our use of language any better (though it might make us more sensitive teachers). Most of us are perfectly capable of seeing (with our spectacles, if necessary) without awareness or understanding of the movement of the muscles of each eye to bring about the convergence of our gaze, or of the accommodation of the irises to light. We do not need this special information in order to see, and if we cannot see, there is no way in which this special information can restore our vision. A specialist might make use of this special information to make better spectacles for us, but once again, we do not need the special information before we can wear the spectacles. There is some knowledge that is irrelevant to ability.

So what I shall do for the remainder of this chapter is talk around the relationship of language and thought, trying to construct an impression of what goes on or of any inference that might be made about what goes on, retaining a respect for the fact that there is much that is just not known. A good beginning might be to consider the extent to which language itself contributes to confounding our understanding.

The Meanings of "Thought"

I have already avoided a precise definition of the word *writing*, and I now intend similar evasions with *language* and *thought*. To discuss the "meaning" of these words would be a lengthy semantic exercise, an involved discussion of the way the words are used, and would bring us no further toward understanding what goes on in the brain. And checking in a dictionary to discover how the words are defined by language experts will not bring us any closer to our goal. Dictionaries offer synonyms—similar meanings clothed in different words—or examples of the use of words; they do not tell us anything about their real or imagined referents.

In fact, the dictionary may seem to add to the confusion. For example, it tells us that the word *thought* (and its cognate, *thinking*) can be used in a multiplicity of ways, some of them quite opposite to others (such as *ponder* and *decide*, *anticipate* and *remember*). As just a short selection, the dictionary notes that thinking can mean: formulate in the mind, reason about; reflect, ponder, meditate; decide, judge, intend, plan; believe, suppose; expect, anticipate, hope; remember, call to mind; visualize, conceive, fancy; invent, speculate. . . .

Does all this flexibility and potential ambiguity mean that our language is a sloppy, inexact kind of instrument? Not at all. There is usually little doubt about a speaker's intention when words are used in a meaningful context. This flexibility is one of the most interesting and productive aspects of the way language works; instead of our being unable to use a word because it is restricted to a narrowly constrained definition, or because the concept it represents is difficult to define, we can usually embed the word in a context that is appropriate for the occasion and there will be no problem. If I say I am *thinking* of visiting some friends, that I *think* a certain team will win its next game, or that I *thought* a film was poorly directed, you will be most unlikely to ask me to define what I mean by the words I have italicized or to expect me to specify which of their many alternative senses I have in mind. Language in context usually makes sense.

The problem arises when we look for a specific referent for words taken out of context, especially the more ponderous "conceptual" ones. The fact that a word exists in our language, and that it can be used meaningfully, is no guarantee that it refers to something that actually exists outside of the mind. Thoughts are not like apples, teeth, or even like breaths; they cannot be pointed to or examined, and not even a surgeon can dissect them. They cannot be seen under a microscope or be weighed. So there is no guarantee that the way language seems to divide up the world reflects the way the world is constructed. Language merely reflects our way of trying to make sense of the world.

In face of the multiplicity of meanings that dictionaries often offer, an alternative sometimes resorted to is to limit the application of a word arbitrarily, to say "I shall use the word *thought* in this sense and this sense alone." But my object is to explore thought, and I am hardly likely to do so by narrowly restricting in advance what I shall be talking about.

So instead I want to go to the opposite extreme and embrace all the senses of thinking and thought that I find in the dictionary or in everyday usage. I want to employ the word without restriction. And it seems to me there is only one thing that all the different senses of the word have in common: They all refer to something the brain does that is not directly observable. Thought is exclusively the business of the brain.

Thus I regard thought as any activity of the brain. I do not propose to distinguish thought from reasoning, perception, comprehending, or problem solving, or any of the other categories of brain activity philosophers or psychologists might want to establish, nor do I intend to break thinking down into these categories. (The categories are all arbitrary in any case, and cannot be distinguished anatomically as separate and distinct processes of the brain.)

Such a blanket decision leaves me vulnerable. I could be caught out by anyone who wanted to ask "Ah, so you think that even the lowest forms of animal life think, provided they have a brain that has some function?" But this would not be a question about animals, but again about how words should be used. Anyone, for example, who believes by definition that only human beings think is bound to argue with my use of the term. I might also be asked whether thought underlies such reflex activities as walking, blinking, and even sneezing since they are also orchestrated by the brain. My only answer must be that it does not matter to my argument whether those activities are regarded as a consequence of thinking or not, even by my proposed use of the word, because they do not involve the kind of mental event I shall consider in any case. I am talking about everything that might normally be termed thought in statements employing the term, not in questions about its meaning.

The World of Thought

Thinking is the business of the brain—but how does the brain transact this business? What does the brain manipulate, in order that thinking can take place? What does the brain contain?

Conventional answers do not even begin to confront the issues. To say that the brain consists of thoughts, memories, ideas, concepts, associations, beliefs or knowledge, is too limited, too fragmentary. Whatever is inside the brain is all of a piece, not compartmentalized into sections, or functions, or aspects. Our understanding of the present cannot be separated from our experience of the past or from our expectations of the future; perceptions cannot be distinguished from intentions or understandings from feelings. To the extent that the world around us seems coherent and organized and systematic, so the content of the brain must be coherent and organized and systematic. In my view the brain must contain nothing less than a working model of the world, a theoretical model that every living brain has constructed for itself, with nothing more specific to work on than the cryptic neural bulletins it receives from whatever constitutes the world outside.

This model or theory of what the world is like is all the brain possesses to make sense of the world. It has no other resource. Nothing in the world is obvious. Every object that we can distinguish or identify, every relationship that we can perceive or intuit, everything that seems self-evident—all must reflect a part of our theory of the world. The moment we find ourselves in a situation where our theory of the world is inadequate, where something happens that our theory cannot account for, then we are bewildered or at the very least surprised. This theory of the world, which we carry around with us all the time in order to make sense of the world, and which we constantly test and modify (in a process we call learning) is more than just a representation of the world, however. It is the place where alternative worlds can be constructed, where we can explore ideas, generate fantasies, experience wishes, hopes, and fears, and plan all our activities.[2] How complex is this theory? It must be at least as complex as the world we perceive around us. To try to catalog the theory of any individual would be as enormous an undertaking as to attempt to catalog the world that the individual perceives. That is one reason it is impossible to describe the theory of the world in our head.

But there is another reason the theory cannot be described, another of the brain's frustrating paradoxes. This theory of the world, locked in a brain that is insulated from the world, is also concealed from its own direct inspection. We have no immediate access to the theory of the world in our own head. We cannot experience directly whatever it is that enables us to experience the world.

Obviously researchers have no access to anyone's theory of the world. It is not possible to look into an individual's brain, even with the most sophisticated of instruments, in order to discover whether its owner can write, or goes to church, or speaks French, or even whether the individual knows the difference between apples and oranges. But we cannot look into our own brains either. We cannot observe the operation of our own brains from the inside, to see how we know what we know or how we do what we can do.

One way of expressing this paradox is to say that the knowledge (or beliefs) in our theory of the world is "implicit." No one can catalog the complex and subtle differences that we look for to make everyday distinctions so rapidly, to distinguish on sight the letters of the alphabet, the written words of language, faces, places, and a multitude of objects like chairs, tables, cars, and trees—all the visible furniture of the world, not to mention how much of it can also be identified by taste, touch, smell, or sound. We must have our entire world in our head—but we cannot look inside and see, either from the inside or the outside.

What do we know about language? We can all talk, we can all understand speech. But we cannot say what it is we know that enables us to make sense of language. Linguists say we have "internalized" rules of language that enable us to understand and produce speech, but can only hypothesize what those rules might be. They are rules that have never been "externalized." Linguists, like everyone else, can usually say whether sentences in their language make sense and whether they are grammatical, but they cannot look inside their own brains to examine what enables them to make these judgments. They cannot inspect rules they themselves respect. The life's work of many linguists is to find out what they already know about language.

Many linguists and theoretical psychologists are busy these days trying to find a way of accounting for comprehension. What exactly takes place when we understand sentences? There is no way we can look into our own brain to find out, and no way we can look into anyone else's. Meaning defies language. What does "bachelor" mean? "Unmarried man." But what does "unmarried man" mean? The brain is not like a dictionary, producing synonyms to make sense of language; where would that get it? The English word *dog* means the same as the French word *chien*, but what is the meaning the two words have in common? The answer cannot be in words. Meaning always eludes us in the end. What would we look for in the brain to resolve the riddle?

We all have an enormously complex and efficient theory of the world in our head, so coherent and comprehensive that it enables us to write and understand sentences we have never heard or read before. And there is no way we can direct our gaze into our own mind to explore what this theory is, to examine how it works, to map its possibilities and limitations. Our theory of the world is where we think—but that thought is beyond language, beyond awareness, and even perhaps forever beyond our understanding.

Does all this mean that we can know nothing about the knowledge and skills embedded in our own brains? Not at all; there is one way we can become aware of the brain's secrets, but one way only. *We have to put our theory of the world to work.* We cannot observe ourselves thinking, but we can observe the products of thought. And one of the most powerful tools for doing so is *writing*.

The Products of Thought

We can observe the products of thought in the same way that researchers attempt to examine thought itself, by looking at what the brain can do, by looking at *action*. Do we know how to drive a car, to repair a bicycle, to speak French? We must see whether we can in practice drive a car, repair a bicycle, or speak French. Anything we can discriminate or do in the world around us must reflect part of the world in our head. But it must be noted that in doing any of these things we are not exactly demonstrating what the brain knew at the moment we began to do them. We learn in the course of action. The moment we begin to repair a bicycle, we may find out something about bicycles we did not know before. So that in observing action we are examining not what the brain *knows* so much as what the brain is capable of knowing. By observation we explore the brain's *potential*. It might in fact be better to regard the theory of the world as all potential, rather than a settled state or finished structure, a potential that may constantly expand as a consequence of its own activity.

A particularly instructive form of action to observe in order to explore the theory of the world is language itself, not as a linguistic exercise but as an observable manifestation of that theory. What does the brain know about bicycles or the French revolution or theories of education? Ask the individual, or ourselves, to talk or write about bicycles, the French revolution, or theories of education. This is one major aspect of writing that I constantly emphasize in this book: that by writing we find out what we know, what we think. Writing is an extremely efficient way of gaining access to that knowledge that we cannot explore directly. It is more efficient than speaking in many respects because of its relative permanence and because we can stand back and examine it as an independent entity.

But once again the action is not simply a direct reproduction of what the brain knows or can do at a particular moment; what I am writing now does not represent a time slice of something I could say I already had in my brain. My behavior of writing right now modifies and develops whatever was its source in my brain. By writing what I think I know, I develop what I potentially knew. Writing does more than reflect underlying thought, it liberates and develops it.

So far I have talked about exploring the content of our theory of the world in the way an outside observer might study it, by observing some overt form of action. But we have one other recourse to the products of thought that is not available to the external observer; we can examine the products of thought in *imagination*.

Do we know how to repair a bicycle? Could we ask someone the time of day in French? Do we have a coherent set of opinions about education? We can imagine repairing a bicycle, holding a conversation in French, or discussing education. We can put our theory of the world to work and examine its products in the theater of our own imagination. (And nobody can look over our shoulder and see us doing it.)

These exercises of the imagination should not themselves be regarded as the underlying processes of thought. We can no more say what the brain is doing in order to imagine distinguishing an apple from an orange than we can when we compare real apples or oranges. But imagination does give us access to what the brain can do (and once again we can expand what the brain can do in the process). The figures in the theater of our imagination are puppets that the unseen hands of thought again manipulate. Imagination, fantasy, daydreaming (and dreaming itself), subvocal speech, and implicit rehearsal all provide avenues for examining and developing the products of that elusive world where thought itself resides.

Action and imagination: These are the two avenues available to every individual to gain access to the implicit theory of the world concealed within the brain. And, through action and imagination, not only can we reveal some of these hidden potentials and make use of them, but we can develop them as well. Action and imagination are in fact both *interaction*, our means of operating on thought as well as observing it.

Of course, action and imagination are not the same. Each has its advantages and limitations. The great advantage of imagination is its privacy. We can put ourselves in situations that would not be logically or physically possible in the world outside, and we can also vicariously explore possibilities that for one reason or another we would rather try out in private before exposing ourselves to the world. No one can tell us we are doing wrong in our imagination (except that strong insistent voice of conscience, which is another matter altogether). No one can censure us for making a mental mistake. In the arena of the imagination we have a freedom to hypothesize, to test and to explore consequences that is rarely available to us in the world outside.

But on the other hand, there is a limit to how much we can handle in our imagination, especially where language is concerned. It is difficult to remember what we have just imagined saying; hard to hold a thought in words and then to evaluate that thought to see if it is really what we want to say in precisely the best way of saying it. Imagined speech is even more ephemeral than actual speech. If we try to hold a complete sentence in the imagination— unless it has already been sufficiently rehearsed to be memorized—we are unlikely to have enough attention left to remember exactly why we wanted to produce the sentence in the first place. (This is the explanation of the phenomenon I like to call "seminar speechlessness"; we may be so concerned with constructing the best wording in our own mind that we lose track of why we wanted to say it, or miss the moment when we should have said it, so that no one but ourselves ever gets to admire the verbal gem we have so carefully polished.)

Writing, however, allows us to transfer imagination to paper while still retaining the possibility of privacy. Because writing overcomes limitations of memory and attention, bringing imagination and action closer than speech can ever do, it is a superb instrument not only for exploring the potential of thought but for developing it as well.

For once, the paradox seems to work in our favor. Though we do not have direct access to the thought that underlies writing, writing provides us with a highly efficient way of interacting with the underlying thought. We do not think and then write, at least not without putting an unnecessary handicap on ourselves. We find out what we think when we write, and in the process put thinking to work—and increase its possibilities.

DYNAMICS OF THE WORLD IN THE HEAD

The world in the head may sound a rather dull and lifeless place, especially if the metaphor is interpreted too literally and the theory of the world is visualized as an empty stage where a variety of scenes can be set and dramas of life played out. But the theory of the world is far more than fixtures and fittings; it is more than the props required for real or imagined scenarios to be enacted. The theory of the world has currents pulsing through, forces that are not part of the world outside. These are the aspects of our theory that determine how we interact with the world, how precisely we behave and think. They are the truly personal aspects of every individual's theory of the world. And they are three in number: skills, feelings, and intentions.

Skills

The first dynamic aspect of the world in our head is our repertoire of *skills*, the means we have available for interacting with the world that we experience, for comprehending it, and for changing it. Skills, in other words, are the way we get things done. I shall not attempt to list all the different kinds of skill that can be available to us; I would have to cite just about every movement, every mental operation of which anyone is capable. There is one class of skills, however, which must be a constant concern, the skills of language. Two things that distinguish a skill (in my terms) from the knowledge or beliefs that constitute the relatively static part of our theory of the world are that skill is constructive, it changes the world around in some way, and it always involves time.

For every skill the order in which the elements of the act are performed makes a difference, whether it is the sequence of playing particular cards in a game of bridge, the operations involved in programming a computer, or the arrangement of one word after another in the construction of a meaningful sentence. But for many skills far more than a mere ordering of events is involved. There is a crucial requirement of precise timing, of tempo. Playing the piano is not just a matter of hitting the right notes in the right order, but of hitting them at just the right time. Tempo is critical in many skills of physical activity, such as dancing, skiing, or playing tennis, and also in the movement of the vocal apparatus in speech. Whenever tempo is a consideration, intensity is also a concern—how hard we strike the note, how firmly we move the leg, how loudly we utter the word. One of the pervasive problems of teaching any subject involving skill is that language can describe only those parts of a skill that involve order without timing (and intensity), such as the moves of chess or aspects of the grammar of language. Language is extremely limited when it comes to trying to describe relative tempo, which is the reason I would have little difficulty in telling you how to spell precisely the words in a phrase of a foreign language (with a familiar alphabet), but face an impossible task if I try to convey in writing how you should say the words like a native speaker.

Skills are a part of everyone's theory of the world; they are always rooted in the way we understand the world, the means by which we relate our knowledge to experience. Everything we know or believe or can imagine owes its existence to a skill, and cannot in fact be separated from that skill. Psychologists have demonstrated that the way in which we recall anything we have learned reflects the manner in which we learned it in the first place.[3]

Feelings

The second dynamic and personal aspect of our theory of the world is all our *feelings* and *attitudes*, our preferences and values, which jointly determine how we behave and how we perceive the world at any particular time. None of our behavior is independent of feeling. If we say we have no feelings or are doing something without feeling, we are in fact describing a feeling. We attribute a value to everything we do, even when we say there is no value. We never learn anything neutrally, without feeling; recollection of an event always includes a recollection of our feeling about that event. Sometimes the feeling is all we recollect; we know we dislike a certain room, or book, or person, but we cannot reason or remember why. Once again I shall not attempt to list every human feeling or value or motive, nor even try to elucidate how the referents for various terms of temperament and disposition differ, if indeed they do. Feelings are as complex as the rest of our theory of the world, from which they are inseparable.[4]

Intentions, Global and Focal

The third personal aspect of the theory of the world is, however, one with which I shall be most concerned, since it is the driving force within the theory of the world, the energizer that directs and controls it. I am referring to *intention*. Intention is fundamental to all behavior and learning, and therefore must be crucial to our consideration of writing. Indeed, everything we write has such an intimate relation to the purpose for which it is written that intention will be impossible to ignore.

I must begin with a shift from singular to plural. Not only is every individual capable of harboring a multiplicity of different intentions simultaneously, but we probably rarely function on the basis of just one intention at a time. And intentions are always liable to change; they are often too elusive to capture and pin down. A few basic intentions might appear to persist throughout our lives, to be instinctive, such as the intention to stay alive, to breathe, to have nourishment and shelter, to have companionship and mobility. But even these are susceptible to being overridden by other intentions at particular times. Intentions are always interlocked with each other; they cannot be neatly separated from other intentions operating concurrently or successively. Intentions are fluid, multiplex, interrelated, and contrapuntal.

Take, for example, what might be regarded as a relatively straightforward intention, such as visiting a library to borrow a book. Such a very general intention—I call it *global*—carries along with it and generates a number of smaller intentions—call them *focal*—that are essential to its execution. To enter the library we intend to cross the road, and while crossing the road we intend to avoid traffic. Each intention influences our behavior. Before we begin the journey we intend to travel by car, but perhaps we see that the weather is fine, so we change our intention and walk instead. At the same time we may have other intentions: to mail some letters, and to visit a friend on the way. Usually we try to combine global intentions, or at least to avoid conflicting ones, so that more focal intentions may serve several purposes. The terms global and focal are only relative, incidentally; they do not denote different kinds of intention but relations among intentions. Visiting the library is a global intention with respect to the manner in which we get there, but focal to some even more global intention that we might have, such as pursuing a particular course of study.

Intentions are always likely to be modified, the focal more often and more suddenly than the global. Our intention to cross the road at a particular point on the way to the library may be changed because an excavation is in progress. It may begin to rain, so we modify our intention about walking directly to the library and decide to spend some time in a department store until the rain passes. How closely we restrict our focal intentions to the more global end we have in view depends upon how determined and single-minded we happen to be, a matter that again will vary from intention to intention (and again depend on other aspects of our theory of the world).

Our more global intentions are less likely to change, but nothing is entirely immutable. Perhaps we wish to visit the library to borrow a book that is relevant to a paper we want to write as part of a particular course of study. But as a consequence of examining that book, or perhaps of not finding it on the shelf, we could conceivably change our intentions about the paper, about the course, even about the entire subject that we were studying. We might decide that studying is pointless in any case and give it all up in favor of building a yacht in our backyard with the new, overarching global intention of sailing alone around the world. Intentions cannot be exhaustively itemized; they encompass all our behavior. The variety of uses to which language can be put (Chapter 2) reflect the range of human intentions.

The Awareness of Intentions

Skills, feelings, and intentions—I have argued that all are part of our theory of the world, a part of the very fabric of our thought, interwoven with everything we know about the world. Indeed, I do not see how knowledge, skills, feelings, and intentions can be separated from each other, not from the brain's point of view. It is impossible to conceive of any one aspect that is not permeated by the others, any more than one can conceive of the ceiling of a room without considering walls and a floor.

But skills, feelings, and intentions have other characteristics in common with the rest of our theory of the world, with thought in general. One common basic characteristic is that they are not open to direct inspection or immediately accessible to awareness; all are part of the concealed, mysterious, inconceivable realm of the mind's internal processes. As I said before, if you want to test whether something is part of your theory of the world, you have to put the theory into action. It must produce something, in behavior or in language, either overt or imagined. If you want to test whether you have a particular skill, you must perform a relevant act or at least imagine performing the act, just as you would have to see another individual demonstrating a skill if you wanted to verify a claim that the individual has that skill. We might at least think that our own feelings are immediately accessible to us, but in fact if we want to discover how we feel about a particular person or activity or event we have to imagine the existence of that person, activity or event; we cannot inspect a catalog of our feelings the way we might inspect the card index of books in a library. And our intentions are hidden in the inner world underlying behavior. We can specify our intentions by analyzing our behavior, or our intended behavior, but we cannot examine the intentions directly. Indeed, it is impossible once again to conceive what an intention would be like if it had to be separated from an actual event, real or imagined, involving either participation on our part or a verbal description. Intention lies beyond words; we can sometimes put an intention into words, but the intention is not the words. Psychoanalysis can be seen as an effort to put our most global and pervasive intentions into highly metaphorical words. What we write can reveal many of our skills, our feelings, and our intentions.

Language, like other products of thought, can be an intermediary between all aspects of our thought and awareness, like the ripple on the surface that allows us to perceive a movement in an otherwise opaque body of water. Language is not thought, although it is produced and interpreted by thought. And thought is not language, although it is only through language or some other manifest product that its currents can be perceived.

Facts and Subvocal Speech

There are two aspects of thought, of our dynamic world in the head, that might appear to exist in the form of language, and that might even seem to depend on language. I am referring to all the remembered assertions and quotations and information that we call *facts*, and to the language we hear when we talk (silently) to ourselves.

The accumulation of language-embedded facts that we all carry around in our brains is enormous. I know my name, address, telephone number, and those of many other people; I can recite the days of the week, the months of the year; I can remember that two times two is four, that Paris is the capital of France, that *chien* is the French word for dog, and that *dog* is the English word for the same animal. I remember thousands of spellings. All of this, an immeasurable amount of knowledge of varying degrees of permanent or transient utility, is stored away in my brain in the form of language. But none of this is *thought*. Rather, all of these facts are a resource of thought; they are not part of any process of thought, but instead are raw material available for thought to operate upon. They are available in a convenient form, it is true, but no more an immediate part of our thought than they were when we first read them or heard someone else saying them, or wrote or said them ourselves. Facts, in other words, need to be *interpreted*, whether we hear them from someone else or have them in our own head to begin with. Facts are language, not meaning, remembered sequences of sounds like the sounds we remember of music. I remember that two times two is four the way I remember hickory dickory dock, as a sequence of sounds; the first is meaningful only because I can make it meaningful. I can remember (I have the fact in my brain) that H_2O is the composition of water, but that fact is less meaningful to me than the fact that Paris is the capital of France because there is a limit to what my thought can do with the image of two molecules of something and one molecule of something else. $E=mc^2$ is completely meaningless to me, although it is another fact that I have memorized (a fact that may be meaningful to someone else).

In other words, all that the memorization of facts does for us is save us the trouble of having to look them up when we need them, or of asking someone else. The meaning of facts does not lie in the facts themselves, in the language, but in their comprehension, in the underlying thought. The same applies to all the explicit "rules" that we have remembered, like the rules of spelling, for example, or of grammar. The rules are not themselves thought, but resources available to thought. Thought itself is beyond facts, beyond rules, beyond language.

Thought is not even the "subvocal speech" that we hear when we talk to ourselves. When we silently rehearse what we think we might say, or when we have a conversation with ourselves, the voice that we hear with our inner ear is still not the sound of thought itself, but only another product of thought. Thought underlies the words we produce to hear ourselves just as it underlies the words we produce for others to hear, and we have to comprehend the language we produce in our heads just as we have to comprehend the language of others. We can be aware of the inner language, but not of the thought that produces it. We may believe we hear ourselves thinking when we hear ourselves manipulating language problems silently—such as "Tom is taller than Dick, and Dick is taller than Harry. So is Tom taller than Harry?"—but each proposition has to be interpreted. Even if we visualize Tom, Dick, and Harry standing in line, the processes of thought by which we solve the problem lie far beyond our awareness. We surely would not want to say that no thought is involved if we actually observe that one person is taller than another. Why then should we think there is nothing left to be thought if we imagine the two individuals?

Visual imagery is in fact no more thought than subvocal speech, even the particularly vivid and complex visual reconstructions that are sometimes termed photographic memory. To be meaningful, to make sense, every mental image has to be interpreted. The scenes and events that we can conjure up in the mind still have to be dealt with by the elusive processes of thought, just as much as the actual scenes and events that we perceive in the world outside the head.

TIME, THOUGHT, AND AWARENESS

There is one further set of enigmas to be confronted before we can turn to the task of trying to relate language and nonverbal thought. These puzzles concern the nature of thought and language in relation to the passage of time. I have already noted that one advantage of written language is that it can overcome barriers of time and space, for example, by allowing the writer to change the order of words after they are written, to write faster or slower than the events that are described, and to write independently of the rate or order at which the text will subsequently be read. But this independence of writing from time is double-edged; writing (like speech) is extremely limited in the way in which it can deal with time, either time as it seems to unroll in the world around us or time as it is involved in the underlying activity of the brain. Language scarcely functions in one dimension of thought at all.

The beginning of the problem is that although most of our experiences of the world seem to involve events that occupy a particular location in time and space, it is impossible to find these events neatly demarcated in the actual situations in which we think they occur. We see someone open a door, but when exactly did that event begin and end? Did it begin when the person first grasped the door, when the handle began to move, or when the door began to move? Did the event end the moment the door began to move, while it was moving (when it was certainly no longer closed), or when it had come to a stop? What in any case was the precise instant when any of these "subevents" of the event of opening the door occurred? There is no distinct point in time at which the event can be separated from whatever the person was doing before or after opening the door. There are no small and empty intervals of time between successive incidents in the world; occurrences flow into each other. Events do not occur in the world at all; they are constructed by the brain, the products of thought.

There is another dimension to the mystery. Not only are events not separated from each other in the world in time, they are also not neatly separated from other events that might be perceived as taking place at the same time. Where exactly are the spatial limits to the event of the door being opened? Is the event restricted to the door itself, to the door and the handle, or should the hand that grasps the handle be included? Is the door frame part of the event of the door being opened? Is the person whose hand is opening the door? What about the wall that the door and its frame are in, or the floor on which the person stands? What are the *boundaries* to the event of the door being opened? How is this event to be separated from anything else that might occur at the same time? The rest of the world does not stop while a door is opened. Co-occurrences are no more separated from each other in space than successive events are separated from each other in time.

Put into a more technical nutshell, occurrences in the world are *undifferentiated* and *continuous*; they do not group themselves into discrete events in either time or space. Doors, handles, and persons who open doors are all categories of the mind, part of our theory of the world, and so also are the events in which we see them participating. Events are superimposed by the brain on a continuous flux of occurrences in the world, the brain's way of interpreting its interactions with the world. Although we live in a world of continuous change and undifferentiated occurrences, we perceive our experience in terms of discrete and distinguishable events.

But now a number of closely connected issues arise that will have to be dealt with successively (because language only works in a linear and fragmentary fashion), although to demonstrate their interrelatedness I introduce them jointly here: (1) Although events are not discrete parts of the world around us, they are also not part of our continual ongoing interaction with the world. Events are relatively rare occurrences in the mind, most of the time. (2) Awareness freezes time. We can only be aware of the events we perceive in the world by separating ourselves from our experience. Events exist only in reflection, in prospect or retrospect; they are manufactured cross sections of the continual flow of time. (3) Language also freezes time; it cannot describe or represent the flow of time, only states of affairs that we arbitrarily presume to exist at particular moments in time.

Experience—and Talking About Experience

The preceding considerations lead to a number of issues concerning both the comprehension and composition of language, since language whose elements are relatively differentiated and discontinuous must frequently be translated into (or from) experiences that are not. These fundamental questions of time and awareness have been very much a concern of some philosophers,[5] but they have received little attention from researchers, no doubt because it is difficult to contrive experiments to illuminate the mysteries.

(1) Events are Relatively Rare Occurrences in the Mind.

The world is in a continuous state of flux, and so is the brain as it interacts with the world. The thought that underlies all our transactions with the world must be as continuous and undifferentiated as the flow of occurrences in the world itself. We do not go through the day dividing up life into events or intentions; indeed, the moment we try to perceive our interaction with the world in terms of events or intentions, we must divert thought from the interaction and thus distract ourselves. We cannot simultaneously attend to something and attend to ourselves attending to it.

Thought does not proceed in fits and starts, it does not leap from one instant to the next. We do not at one moment think "I am driving a car," then "I am on Main Street," then "I must avoid that pedestrian"; rather, we drive our car on Main Street in such a way as to avoid pedestrians. If we pause to reflect "Where am I?" or "How can I avoid that pedestrian?" then our attention is withdrawn from the constantly changing situation of which we are a part to one historical or potential aspect of the situation, to an event. The same applies when we read a book. We do not tell ourselves "The car is driving down Main Street; it has crashed a red light; the police are in pursuit" (even though the author may have used those very words); our comprehension is holistic, continuous, unfragmented. We do not usually attend to the world or to language in the slices across time which the division of experience into events requires. Instead we are wholly involved in the constant change and development of a real or imagined world.

Of course, we may from time to time become aware of particular events as we drive down a street (or read about a car being driven down a street). But the price we pay for awareness is stopping the action, interrupting the thought. Events are static cross sections of time, and hence to contemplate events we must withdraw from the present, stop time, and view experience in retrospect. Events are the products of contemplation, not of action. When we are involved in action, in interaction, then we have no awareness.

All this may sound unlikely, implying as it does that we may not be aware of what we are doing most of the time. But how could we be aware that we are not aware? Part of the difficulty of conceptualizing this situation also lies once more in the ambiguity of language. The word *attention* (like the word *aware* in this context) sometimes implies conscious knowledge and sometimes not. In the latter (and most common) case, attention simply means a kind of orientation, concentration, or focus. If we successfully drive our car we have presumably "attended" to that action, we were focused upon it, but not in the sense that we were consciously aware of what we were doing. If we are engrossed in what we are doing, it is only afterwards that we can remove ourselves from the situation and say what we have done.[6]

Usually we become aware of events, or of our own behavior or thought, only when something goes wrong, when we find ourselves in an unexpected or confusing situation, or when we are confronted by a choice. We become aware when it is necessary to reflect, to remove ourselves from our ongoing involvement with the world, and to contemplate alternatives. Then thought (of which we are not aware) can generate and select among alternatives (of which we become aware) as if the alternatives were actual events or descriptions of possible events. But the cost of such conscious reflection is removal from ongoing involvement with the world.

The problem arises if we want to write or talk about our own experience and try to reflect upon events as they occur. We can label feelings or states of affairs in retrospect, but the moment we want to describe something that transpires over time we have to stop the action, to break it down into events. This is not such a great handicap when we try to write in retrospect, since our writing is a reconstruction in any case. But it is a distinct obstacle if we try to live the experience with the intention of recounting it afterward. To describe occurrences as they take place we must separate ourselves from the experience.

More than one writer has noted the dilemma of having to choose between interaction with the world and awareness of that interaction in the form of an event that can be remembered and written about. Yukio Mishima wrote "You cannot see and exist"; Sartre said "You cannot live and tell"; Robertson Davies wrote "Understanding and experience are not interchangeable"; and, to quote T. S. Eliot, "We had the experience but missed the meaning."

(2) Awareness Freezes Time.

The reason we cannot be aware of our interactions with the world while they are taking place is that thought develops through time, but awareness has to stop time, to slice it into the cross sections of events that can be inspected and described. Awareness is retrospective; it always involves reflection. Sometimes we can weave smoothly and continuously between attention to an activity (concentration) and attention to the product or progress of that activity (contemplation), just as an artist will alternately step up to the canvas to apply a stroke or two of paint, then stand back to contemplate the effect of that action. The paint is applied over a brief period of time without awareness of how the action is organized, fulfilling an intention that has been formulated during the previous moment of reflection.

Most of the time we are not aware of what we write or read (or say and hear)—certainly not while we are writing or reading it—although we can become aware of what we have written or read in retrospect. We can answer questions afterward, or move on to write or read the next thing in some kind of logical sequence, without being aware of writing or reading. But we can also weave in and out of awareness when we write or read; perhaps you are doing so right now, to test my assertion that you cannot attend to what you read and be aware of what you are reading simultaneously. But frequently this withdrawal for reflection can be disruptive, and when done involuntarily it is probably a sign that we are having difficulty in formulating something that we want to write or in comprehending what we are trying to read.

Sometimes we listen to ourselves talking very intently, if we are answering questions at an examination, for example, or trying to impress people with what we are saying at a meeting. But these are the times when we are most likely to become tongue-tied, victims of self-conscious "seminar speechlessness." I know of no data, but my feeling is that we spend relatively little time withdrawing ourselves from the activity in which we are involved in order to reflect upon what we are doing, certainly not in speech. No doubt there is a good deal of individual variation from person to person and time to time. Often there may be good reason for standing back, stopping the action, and taking stock of where we are and where we might be going. But at other times there is good reason for doing none of these things, and for permitting attention to concentrate on whatever we are doing or saying. We may not always say or write what we want if we just allow it to come out without reflection. But, on the other hand, nothing at all may come out if we reflect too much at the crucial moment.

(3) Language Freezes Time.

Now I am saying something different. I am not reiterating that in order to recount ongoing experience we must become aware of that experience, thereby interrupting the experience, stopping the action. Instead, I am saying that language in any case cannot directly represent time. Language cannot describe action the way it can describe color, size, or spatial relations; it only can describe static states of affairs and differences in successive states of affairs.

Language cannot describe everything that is part of a door being opened, the actual *occurrences* through time in the world, although it can label the *event* that the brain may superimpose on the occurrences in the world. It can say "The door was opened." Language can describe the state of the door before it was opened or after it was opened. It can label the manner in which the door was opened (quickly, slowly, smoothly, jerkily), but such words do not contain a description of every moment of that change. Language can do less to indicate how time actually passes, or how events occur in time, than a musical score, which itself can represent time precisely only if slaved to the beat of a metronome.

How could language represent time? There is a contradiction in the terms, like asking how color might represent weight. Words die in the air or lie dead on the page, flat and immutable. They do not map directly onto the occurrence they describe, they have a structure or sequence of their own. We say "The fielder caught the ball," putting the fielder first and the ball last, although catching the ball was all one event, a concurrence of occurrences. Sentences are laid out one word after another, with beginnings and ends in time and space, while occurrences are as diffuse and interwoven as the changing currents in a stream.

As users of language—speakers, listeners, writers, readers—we need not let these theoretical conundrums confound us. We can usually understand what is being talked about when we read of doors being opened and balls being caught. And we can usually produce sentences that will receive the appropriate interpretation. Certainly we have all learned to talk, to read and write, without the dubious benefit of involvement in these mysteries of time and awareness. But *how* we are able to do these things is the problem. The mysteries are relevant if our aim is to understand writing, to grasp how something as static as words on a page can be related to ideas and occurrences that are imbued with life and movement. To assume that speech is just thinking aloud, or that writing is a simple matter of putting thought (or speech) on paper, is to ignore the fundamental transmutation that must take place, a transmutation that I must now attempt to explicate.

(Notes to Chapter 4 begin on page 244.)

5 Putting Meaning into Words

How is our static and disjointed language produced from dynamic and continuous nonverbal thought? I tried in the previous chapter to show that thought is beyond language, that meaning lies beyond language, and that it is therefore impossible to distill the essence of words into words. But there is another problem. The study of language reveals that our spoken or written words have only a partial and indirect relation to meaning and thought in any case. Nevertheless, we talk and we write, and the words we produce are quite frequently understood by ourselves and by other people. The present chapter examines how the feat might be accomplished.

LANGUAGE—THE DEPTHS AND SURFACE

A general distinction may be made between two aspects of language, its surface structure and deep structure. The *surface structure* of language can be regarded as its physical properties—the sounds of speech, the written marks on the page for writing. *Deep structure*, on the other hand, is meaning. Most languages have more than one form of surface structure: not only speech and writing but also, for example, the gestures of sign language for the deaf and the tactile symbols of Braille. However, there is only one deep structure. No one would want to claim that the meaning of written language is in essence different from the meaning of speech.[1]

One way to look at the distinction is to regard surface structure as the part of language that exists in the world, however transiently, outside the minds of language users. We produce surface structure when we speak or write; we interpret surface structure when we listen or read.[2] Surface structure can be counted or measured, numbers can be put to the relative loudness of speech, to the size of print, or to the rate at which words are produced. Meaning, on the other hand, defies measurement. Meaning exists in our minds—in the nonverbal, inaccessible theory of the world in our head—underlying the language we produce and making sense of the language we understand.

Meaning is not directly represented in the surface structure of language; that is the central paradox of language. Surface structure and deep structure are not reflections of each other; in fact, there is a gulf between them. There is no "one-to-one" correspondence between the surface structure and deep structure of language; every meaning can be represented by more than one surface structure, and every surface structure can have more than one meaning. The grammatical structure of a statement is not the same as the meaning structure underlying it.

That the same literal meaning can be represented in more than one surface structure is demonstrated by sentences that are paraphrases of each other. *Everyone seeks truth, truth is sought by all,* and *humanity pursues verity* are three different ways of saying the same thing, roughly at least. Conversely, sentences like *the turkey was too old to eat* and *the policeman held up the motorcyclist* each represent more than one meaning. (It may take a moment to discover two meanings for the examples I have just given, because the brain resists interpreting the same surface structure in more than one way; thus puns are not always immediately seen or invariably appreciated.) The fact that all the common words of our language have multiple meanings under-lines the absence of a simple relationship between surface structure and meaning. If the word *bank* (or *time,* or *house,* or *table*—think of any common word) has more than one possible meaning, then any sentence containing that word must have more than one possible meaning. That some interpretations would not make sense is beside the point, which is that more than language is required to make sense of language. The additional factor is commonly regarded as "knowledge of the world"—a theory of the world—so that we can disentangle an anomaly like *the thieves drowned trying to reach the bank.* But the ability to make sense of language depends on more than just a theory of the world, it depends on an implicit understanding between speakers and listeners (or between writers and readers) about each other's expectations and intentions. The complex global structures of expectations and intentions are very different from the linear surface structures of sentences.

Oddly enough, although surface structure is the only aspect of language that is accessible to direct observation, the only part that can ever be counted or measured, it is usually an aspect of which we are completely unaware. We do not pay attention to individual words, and certainly not to the sounds or letters of which words are constructed, when we hear someone talk or when we read. Language is transparent; we look through the actual words to perceive the meaning beyond, in the way that we perceive a scene through a window without being aware of the window itself. We *can* become aware of words when we listen or read, but only if we make a conscious effort, in which case we are likely to miss the meaning (just as we can focus on the glass in the window at the cost of our perception of the scene beyond). Usually we only become aware of particular words if we cannot make sense of what we are reading or hearing, when the window is obscured in some way. Meaning commands our attention.

But how is this done? How do we succeed in perceiving meaning through the ambiguous surface structures that are presented to our ears or eyes? If we cannot embed meaning in the words we speak or write, how do we manage to make ourselves understood?

A common view is that the gulf is bridged through formal grammar— that surface structure plus grammar equals meaning. But we can all understand ungrammatical sentences, for example, when small children talk. And it is not possible to say what the grammar of many words and sentences is until we understand them. We cannot say whether *bank, time, take, walk,* and many other words are nouns or verbs unless we make sense of them in a sentence. The single-word utterance "Fire" can be a noun or a verb, depending on whether it is shouted at a conflagration or an execution. In *open the empty bottle, open* is a verb and *empty* an adjective; in *empty the open bottle* it is the other way around. *He was seated by the usher* is a passive sentence in one sense *(the usher seated him)* but not in another *(he sat next to the usher).* Certainly we do not produce sentences by first thinking of a grammatical structure, and then putting words of the appropriate parts of speech to that structure. Grammar is not a strong candidate to account for our ability to attribute meaning to the surface structure of language. It is not possible to get to the meaning of language from the surface down.

There is an alternative point of view that proposes what might at first glance seem an unlikely possibility, that language is understood by having meaning brought to it. We do not understand words by deriving meaning *from* them, but by bringing meaning *to* them. This perspective solves the problem of why we are not aware of the potential ambiguity of language when we speak or write. Since we normally only produce language when we have at least a general idea of what we want to say, it is not surprising that we tend to find in the language we produce the meaning we hope to express. Indeed, one of the hazards of writing is that we may know so well what we want to say that we find it difficult to examine what we have written with the less-informed eye of an independent reader. But how can we bring meaning to language when we are the listener or reader? Surely the whole point of attending to language is to discover meaning that the producer intended, not something we already know ourselves. Examination of this question will I hope throw more light on some of the operations of thought that underlie language in the first place.

During the next few pages I have a particular concern with comprehension—with the use the reader (or listener) makes of language—as well as with composition. I have not forgotten that this book is supposed to be about writing, but one way to an understanding of what the writer does is by trying to grasp what the reader must do. After all, writers generally aim to produce something that readers can comprehend. Besides, comprehension—as I shall argue later—is the way language and its uses are learned in the first place. Composition and comprehension are in many respects inseparable.

So having failed to relate language and thought by descending from the surface to the depths, I shall now take an opposite course and consider the nature of deep structure, to see if it is any easier to move from there to the surface.

THREE GRAMMARS OF LANGUAGE

It is not difficult to talk about the surface structure of language. We can look at the printed marks on a page of text or at transcriptions of speech and make all kinds of enumerations and analyses of words and their interrelations. All marks of grammar as it is conventionally understood reside in the surface structure of language, although there has to be some understanding of meaning before we can specify the grammatical function of particular words. We need to understand sentences to explain the purposes of their punctuation—for example, whether an apostrophe indicates a possessive or an omission. Deep structure also has a grammar, though it is different from the grammar of surface structure, and there is a grammar which links the grammars of the deep and surface structures. The surface grammar is usually the only one taught in schools. But it is the other two grammars that will be my concern for the next few pages.

Syntactic and Semantic Grammar

What does the deep structure of language look like? The question is meaningless if taken literally, because meaning is itself an abstraction; there is no way it can be laid out for inspection as if it were surface structure; it can only be represented symbolically. Deep structure can be conceptualized in terms of elements with different kinds of relationships with each other (which is the reason it is appropriate to use the term "grammar" for the organization of deep structure), just as the elements of surface structure—the sounds, letters, and words—have varied but distinctive relationships with each other. The grammar of surface structure is *syntactic*, its relationships are concerned with the ordering or arrangement of elements. But the grammar of deep structure is *semantic*; its relationships are concerned with meaning. For example, in the deep structure of the sentence *John is playing the guitar* there are three meaningful elements, namely whatever "John," "playing," and "guitar" mean to us, and a set of meaningful relationships among them.

The deep structure of language can be represented in a number of ways, centering usually on the notion that the meaning of any sentence can be expressed in the form of a network of *propositions*, or underlying assertions. The focus of such propositions is generally an action, an event, or a state of affairs, usually but not invariably corresponding to a word that is a verb in the surface structure. For example, the deep structure of the sentence *John is playing his guitar in the garden* consists of three propositions: that John is playing, that his guitar is being played, and that the garden is the place where the playing is occurring. All of these propositions can be represented diagrammatically as follows:

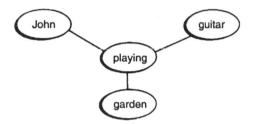

Of course, these relationships—or *"cases"* as they are known technically—are not the same. John does not have the same relationship to the playing as the guitar or the garden have. John might be called the subject of the playing, the guitar the instrument (no pun intended), and the garden the location. Linguists have identified nearly a score of common underlying relationships for English (and for all other languages, since we are now talking about the nature of *thought*, which is universal. Only surface structures differ from one language to another.)[3] Some of these relationships can be illustrated if I elaborate a little more on my exemplary sentence and deep structure: *John was enthusiastically playing Chopin mazurkas on his guitar in the garden in the rain on Tuesday to entertain his friends.*

Each of the relationships can be seen as the answer to a possible question about the playing: Who was doing it? (John) How was it done? (enthusiastically) Where was it done? (in the garden) On what? When? For what reason? and so forth.

The fact that the number of deep structure elements in the examples I have given might seem to be the same as the number of major elements ("content words") in the surface structure is purely coincidental. Deep structure can and usually does contain many more elements and relationships than surface structure makes explicit, the missing parts being what the writer and reader take for granted. For example, the surface structure *John was playing his guitar on Tuesday* would usually be regarded as a reasonably complete sentence, though it leaves out, it takes for granted, any reference to the music that John was playing, where he was playing, and how and why he was playing. The sentence *A guitar was played in the garden on Tuesday* does not even specify that someone was playing the guitar.

So now we have a second grammar, a meaningful or semantic rather than a syntactic one, representing the various ways in which elements of meaning can be organized and interrelated in the deep structure of language. The two grammars are obviously not the same, or even mirror images of each other. The grammar of surface structure is *linear*, it proceeds (in written English) from left to right and the order of elements (words) makes a difference, as does their form. The grammar of deep structure does not have a sequence; thoughts are holistic, global, and no one part is prior in time to another. The semantic network remains the same, no matter how its parts might be moved around on paper. How then does the writer move from the conceptual grammar of deep structure to the syntactic grammar of surface structure? How are thoughts transformed into words? The answer is by the third grammar, a *transformational* grammar, which gives form to the elements of deep structure that the writer wishes to represent and organizes them into linear sequences of words. Transformational grammar is in theory the only grammar a writer (or speaker) actually *uses*.

Transforming Thought into Words

Though it is not a grammar that is taught, transformational grammar is something that all speakers and writers must have, whether or not they produce language in conventionally grammatical surface structures. No one, not even an infant putting baby-talk words together in the first two-word sentences, puts words together randomly.[4] Even if some of our sentences ain't never grammatical by conventional standards, they tend to be consistently "wrong," they ain't never random arrangements of words. (I would not say "never ain't" as well as "ain't never" unless that were also a consistent practice, a rule of my personal transformational grammar.) Transformational grammar is the link between the two other grammars, between surface structure and meaning. The other two grammars are merely descriptive; they describe the actual arrangement of word elements in a surface structure or the presumed arrangement of thought elements in a deep structure. But the transformational grammar is productive; it *generates* surface structures from meaning. Drawing upon an inner dictionary or "lexicon" of its own, our personal transformational grammar selects lexical items which are appropriate to the deep structure elements which are to be expressed, and modifies and organizes these elements into what we can recognize as a surface structure of words in speech or writing.

Transformational grammars employ three principal devices to represent in surface structure some of the meaningful elements and interrelationships of deep structure. The first device is word order. In English, usually, the agent or subject of a sentence tends to be at the beginning. Thus, *John is playing the guitar* does not mean the same as *the guitar is playing John*. The order of words in a sentence is a crucial part of English, although it does not make a difference in other languages which rely more on the second transformational device for representing deep structure interrelationships, namely variation in the form of a word. The change in the form of a noun depending on its meaningful function in a sentence is the sense in which the word *case* is usually used in formal grammar, for example in referring to heavily inflected languages like Latin, Greek, or German. In such languages the form of a word like *John* or *guitar* would change depending on whether it was the subject or object of a sentence, while in English only pronouns change depending on the subject-object distinction (we say *he saw her* but *she was seen by him*). The third device for representing underlying case relationships is employed much more in English than in many other languages, namely the use of special words to express relationships. The special words in English (and many other European languages) are primarily prepositions such as *in*, *at*, *by*, *with*, *to*, and so forth, small ubiquitous words with a wide variety of uses, making them the hardest part of language to learn or to translate.

For some reason, which has never been adequately explained or even (I think) considered, there is a remarkable complexity among the prepositions that represent various case relationships. The same prepositions can be used to represent quite different kinds of relationship; I can say I hope to be *on* form *on* Friday when I shall be *on* the platform *on* time to talk *on* linguistics to a group *on* vacation from their courses *on* education—seven different uses of the preposition *on*. We also use different prepositions to express similar kinds of relationship. For example, we may say there was a party *at* someone's home, or *in* their house, or *on* their premises (*under* their auspices, *with* their approval, *by* their leave).

Because the same preposition can be used for quite different case relationships, the preposition alone cannot be taken as an indication of the underlying case relationship; this is a major cause of the ambiguity of the surface structure of English. For example, John may have been playing Chopin on his guitar on Tuesday, but the two instances of the word *on* represent different case relationships; they have different meanings, as we see if we try to join the phrases they are in with *and*. We cannot say John was playing Chopin on his guitar and Wednesday, any more than we can say he was playing in the rain and his best suit, or that we plan to send him an invitation by mail and Friday. But prepositional phrases with the same underlying meaning can be connected by *and*, so that we can say that John was in his blue shirt and white shoes, or entertaining on his flute and guitar. Sometimes the same surface structure word order will similarly represent quite different underlying meanings, as when we say that John was cooking at the barbecue and that hamburgers were cooking at the barbecue, but again the "and" test for similarity of underlying relationships applies and we find we cannot say that John and hamburgers were cooking at the barbecue (unless they were indeed both cooking in the same sense). The similarity of surface structures for different underlying meanings is a linguistic coincidence that writers can generally ignore.

Transforming Words into Thought

But what about comprehension? Will transformational grammar work in reverse for readers (or listeners), and why are they not usually aware of the potential ambiguity of the surface structures of language? The answer is that transformational grammar does not work in the reverse direction, and that readers must understand writing by employing their own transformational grammars in the same direction as the writer, proceeding from the deep structure to the surface.

At first sight it might seem absurd to suggest that readers are themselves responsible for bringing meaning to what we write, for imposing sense upon the printed marks on the page. But all that this assertion entails is that readers understand what the author is talking about, which does not I hope sound such an enormous or mystifying requirement. It is obvious that a reader who does not already know something about the language the author is using and the subject matter the author is dealing with will not make sense of what the author writes. By bringing to bear prior knowledge of the author's language and subject matter, the reader can anticipate possible surface structures on the page and thus find sense in them. The writer must anticipate what the reader will expect. I am not arguing that a reader should be able to forecast exactly what the author will say. If the reader has that much prior knowledge, there would be no point in reading in the first place. But the reader must always anticipate what the writer *might* say, in order to understand what the author *does* say.

It is not difficult to demonstrate that prediction is a constant part of the way we understand language (although it is again not a part of which we are usually aware); indeed, prediction is a constant part of the way we understand the world in general. The demonstration is that it is always possible to be surprised. I could write something that surprises you—by suddenly changing the subject matter to a discussion of scuba diving, or by switching the language from English to French, or by doing a variety of other idiosyncratic things. It is always possible that something will surprise you as you drive your car downtown—it is conceivable that you might see a giraffe or a deep sea diver in the main square, or you might meet your Uncle Fred who you thought had taken up permanent residence in Nepal. But events like these would surprise you for the very reason that you did not anticipate them. That is what a surprise is, something that is unexpected. The fact that we are so rarely surprised is not because we usually expect that anything might happen, but because our expectations are usually very accurate predictions of what indeed does happen (or rather, of what might happen).

I suspect that it is the reader's need to predict that explains and even justifies the importance frequently attributed to formal grammar, the rules of usage that are taught at schools and in the grammar books. Grammar is not essential for comprehension. If we can detect errors in the grammar of a sentence and put them right, then we do not need the grammar to tell us what the sentence intends in the first place. But writing that is ungrammatical confounds our expectations. Like unconventional spelling and punctuation, it makes writing more difficult to anticipate, although it is rarely the cause of its being incomprehensible.

What Transformational Grammar Lacks

Transformational grammar is a theory that endeavors to describe hypothetically the manner in which language and thought are related. The theory is entirely conjectural, of course; there is no means by which we can look inside the brain to see if such a grammar is really there. But the grammar is a useful metaphor, a way of thinking about what might otherwise be completely unthinkable and indescribable, the actual processes of the brain. It has its limitations, nonetheless.

The theory is simplistic, for a start. Transformational grammar as I have outlined it can only produce simple declarative sentences—nothing like the complicated compound constructions that the present sentence exemplifies, nor such alternative sentence structures as interrogatives or imperatives. But these objections can be dealt with handily. Additional transformational rules can be proposed for combining two or more simple sentences into one compound one, or for generating alternative sentence structures. More serious are objections that transformational grammar, no matter how well it might appear to relate the surface and deep structures of language, still is a very unrealistic model of the way in which language production and comprehension actually take place. As a working model, transformational grammar has a certain lack.

Consider writing. While logically transformational grammar might seem able to generate surface structures from meaning, the entire mechanism looks remarkably inert. What puts it to work? What determines that one transformational rule rather than another will be employed? Where exactly do deep structures come from, what do semantic networks represent, how does a writer move from one deep structure to another, and what decides exactly which deep structure elements will be represented in surface structure? Where is the dynamic element to put some force and direction into it all?

Consider reading. It is tempting to believe that an appropriate semantic network (like the guitar-playing example on page 53) is the meaning of the sentence, that a sentence has been understood if it has been reduced to deep structure elements and relationships. Many language researchers seem to assume that this is the case, and they write computer programs that are considered to simulate comprehension if they can reproduce underlying semantic structures or can answer questions about the surface structure. But comprehension is not paraphrase. We do not usually understand what we read or hear by translating it into other words, or even into some abstract or symbolic form. Something even deeper would then be required to interpret the deep structure. Where again is the direction, the reason behind the transformation?

Something is lacking in transformational grammar from both the writer's and the reader's point of view. And that lack has something to do with the dynamics underlying language, with purpose and direction. What is lacking is *intention.*

Because we intend to say something, one deep structure rather than another is selected. Deep structures are part of our theory of the world generated and shaped by intentions. Because we want to write or say a particular thing to a particular audience in particular circumstances, one way of saying it rather than another is selected. We do not blindly express everything that is in a deep structure, but only that which we believe our reader or listener needs to know in order to understand or respond appropriately to our intention. Once one thing is said, we become ready to say another, or to stop. We do not repeat unless we have a reason. Intentions provide continuity as well as purpose. Each new step along the way is determined with respect to the point we have just reached, where we might get to next and our more general, global intentions.

Intentions underlie comprehension as well. We never attend to language for no reason at all. When we read, we have a purpose. We read with certain expectations. Our purpose reflects global intentions and our expectations generate focal intentions (to look for particular things); there is nothing passive about reading or listening. We do not read a sentence in order to generate a deep structure; we read it *from* a deep structure, seeking to fill gaps, to answer questions, to confirm expectations, and to reduce uncertainty among alternatives. The deep structures of comprehension are no more static than those of writing. We move from one to another—or rather our deep structures merge one into another—as our thought moves through the text we are reading. It is true that our intentions as we read might seem to develop along lines determined by the text, by the author. But unless we have intentions to explore the text in a particular way (constrained by the text in just the same way that our intention to explore a river is constrained by the actual course of that river), then there can be no way for the author to capture our attention in the first place. The complex and intimate relationship between a writer's intentions and a reader's expectations—the manner in which each influences the other across time and space and through the barrier of a solid wall of text—will be the topic of Chapter 7.

THE CONVENTIONS OF LANGUAGE

The metaphorical manner in which I have talked of transformational grammar—as if it were a machine, a "device for producing sentences" or a set of procedures by which grammatical and meaningful sentences are generated—is not uncommon. These are all useful analogies, but they can be misleading. They are especially misleading if they are taken to suggest that there is some kind of logical necessity about the particular ways in which the surface structures of language are constructed, reinforcing perhaps an already widespread assumption that certain forms of language have an inherent "rightness" about them.

I have an alternative point of view—that every aspect of language is permeated by conventions which are in essence arbitrary and accidental. There is no inevitable logic about the particular forms of grammar, of spelling, of punctuation, or any other aspect of language apart from the fact that every convention serves a purpose; it is useful. Every convention of language could be changed and still function as effectively, provided the changed form became accepted as the convention. There is no inherent "rightness" about any aspect of language, only accepted or imposed custom. This is the reason I prefer to talk about grammar, spelling, and punctuation in terms of "conventional" and "unconventional" rather than "correct" or "incorrect." In language, as in every other form of human behavior, it is the conventional that tends to be regarded as correct, logical, and inevitable, especially by those who themselves observe the convention. The surface structures produced by our transformational grammars become grammatical and meaningful to the extent that they conform to convention, not because they contain some intrinsic appropriateness or relationship to meaning. Conventions work because they exist, and totally different conventions would work just as well—"yes" could mean "no" and "no" mean "yes"—provided we all agreed to use words in the new way.

The Utility of Conventions

By "convention" I mean simply an expected way of doing something that is accepted by all parties concerned, an implicit understanding that there is just one most appropriate way of doing something, not because that way is necessarily best or obvious or even particularly logical but because absence of a convention or disagreement about what it should be would cause inconvenience if not confusion. Conventions are so important and pervasive in human affairs that they often have the force of law behind them. But such is their importance and pervasiveness that generally they arise and persist without any need for legal enforcement at all.[5]

Take, as a general example, the fact that in every culture that has roads and traffic it is conventional for vehicles to drive on one side of the road rather than the other. It does not matter whether all vehicles drive on the right or on the left—different regions of the world have different conventions—provided that everyone in a particular region drives and expects everyone else to drive on the same conventional side. There is no logic behind the particular convention except consistency, established practice, or historical precedent—in other words, conformity with a convention that already exists. No committee ever sat down to debate whether there was any *essential* advantage to driving on the left (or right) rather than the other. The only possible consideration is conformity with other conventions. (The fact that vehicles might already have their steering mechanisms on one particular side is an existing convention.) You can predict that traffic everywhere in the world will be driven consistently on one side of the road rather than the other, but unless you have relevant historical information you will be unable to predict what that side will be. Reasoning will not help because there is no particular reason, only the historical accident of custom.

Here is another example, closer to language. Every literate culture that has an alphabet also has a conventional sequence in which the letters of that alphabet are arranged, an alphabetical order. I can find no logical reason for the particular order that exists for the English or any other alphabet except tradition and historical precedent. Alphabetical order is a convention, and is respected as such. There is certainly a logic in having an alphabetical order, without which dictionaries, directories, libraries, and all bureaucracies would be thrown into complete disarray. But there is no particular logic in the order itself. Any other order would work just as well provided the new order became the conventional one. Some logic could be introduced into the order; letters could be arranged in order of relative frequency as printers sometimes organize them, or all the vowels could come first, or thin letters could be at the beginning and fat letters at the end. Any logic would make the order more predictable. But there is nothing but historical knowledge of earlier conventions that would make our alphabetical order or any other predictable. Just as there is no intrinsic logic in alphabetical order in the first place, so there would be no particular logic in changing it. Alphabetical order is useful because it exists, and to try to change the convention would undermine its utility. Spelling reformers have always had limited success because they try to pit logic against convention and underestimate the utility of convention itself. It is convention, not habit, that is hard to change.

I am not saying that language itself is illogical or irrational. There is a good reason behind every convention in language. But that good reason never explains the particular convention, only the existence of convention. I am also not saying that there is not consistency in language. With various self-evident exceptions, English forms its plurals in consistent ways, just as there are consistent ways of forming the past tense. But plurals and tenses are formed in other ways in other languages, so there is no particular logical necessity about the English conventions, and knowledge of how the plural is formed in English (or any other language) will not help one predict how the different tenses will be formed. Consistency within a convention does not permit prediction beyond the convention; only a prior knowledge of the kinds of conventions to which a language adheres allows one to anticipate what a convention might be or what it might mean.

Why emphasize that the forms of language are conventional, established arbitrarily or by chance rather than on the basis of reason or intrinsic logic? For the important reason that language can never be produced or understood on the basis of its own intrinsic reason or logic; language does not explain itself. Writers and readers must share the conventions they employ and encounter; they cannot work out what a convention is likely to be. To express a conventional meaning a writer must embed it in a conventional form; there is no "logical" or "rational" form for any meaning to take beyond consistency with the conventions of the language itself. Readers must know the conventions too; they cannot work out (without clues from an understood context) the meaning that an unfamiliar convention is intended to express; they cannot *deduce* a meaning or intention from surface structure itself.

The arbitrary nature of language is also critical when considering how ability in writing or any other aspect of language is developed. Aspiring writers cannot predict or work out what particular forms of written language are likely to be; rather, they must discover what the conventions are. The conventions that are language must be experienced and *learned*.

The Pervasiveness of Conventions

Language consists of a truly staggering number of conventions. There is a convention for everything that language does. Writing has all its conventions for spelling, for punctuation, for paragraphing and capitalization, just as spoken language has its unique conventions for the sounds of words and for intonation. No two languages even share the same set of sounds from which their words can be constructed.[6] There are conventions for the words themselves, for their "names," and for their meanings. There is no logical reason (apart from conformity to an earlier convention) why a particular object should be called "table" in English or "mesa" in Spanish, or why these words have the particular range of different meanings that they do in each language. There are conventions for the ways in which words may be arranged grammatically and meaningfully into sentences and conventions about how sentences themselves are interrelated. In spoken language there are complicated yet extensively employed and understood conventions for taking turns in conversation and for other language interactions, for who can interrupt, and when and how to interrupt, and how to ignore an interruption. And all of these conventions vary in conventional ways depending on who is talking (or writing) to whom, their relative status, and other circumstances. How I ask someone to pass the salt depends on whether I am making the request at home or in a restaurant; whether I am asking a friend, a stranger, or a server; on our relative ages and the various relationships that we might have to each other; whether one or other of us has an arm in a sling or whether there is some other reason for my not being willing or able to reach for the salt myself. There are conventions for everything—easily demonstrated because there is always a multitude of wrong ways of saying anything, in speech or in writing.

Just as spoken language conventionally differs depending on the situation in which people are speaking, so different conventions of writing must be respected according to the circumstances that writers and readers are in, on the role of the text. These clusters of conventions are known as *genres*. Personal correspondence is one written language genre and business correspondence another—you do not write in the same way for both. Newspapers are a different genre (or rather, set of genres) from magazines, and articles must be written differently depending on the journal they are intended for. Stories constitute different genres from company reports, and both are different from poetry and plays. There are countless written language genres, which have arisen—like the conventions of which they are comprised—in countless arbitrary and accidental ways. Newspapers in Europe do not *look* like newspapers in North America, not because of any fundamental differences between European and North American writers or readers, but because of a myriad of unpredictable events in the evolution of newspapers on both sides of the Atlantic. There is no way of *figuring out* what the conventions of any particular genre might be, and very little chance of having it *explained*; the only way to gain a working acquaintance with the conventions of a language genre is to participate in that genre, which for the genres of writing means *reading*.

The term genre originally referred to broad different categories of writing, such as comedy, tragedy, epic. More recently the term has been used to refer to the structure and organization of different kinds of media—newspapers, periodicals, novels, "nonfiction"—all of which have their own conventions. Current emphasis is on complete settings—the language and the total situation in which it is embedded—and includes conversations, interrogations, and classroom procedures. The teaching of genre has been the center of a notable educational controversy in Australia, as I describe in Chapter 14.

There are even conventions for every nonverbal aspect of language.[7] There are conventions for how long you may look people in the eyes when you talk to them, how close you may stand to them, how much you may touch them, and where you may touch them, and again these conventions—the "appropriate behavior"—vary depending upon a complex range of factors including the number of people involved, their relative ages and status, the formality of the occasion, and their intentions and expectations.

It is entirely predictable that there will be conventions for all these aspects of language in every culture in the world. But it is entirely unpredictable what the particular conventions will be; there is no way for a visitor to an unfamiliar country or culture to anticipate the form of any convention. The mark of respect may be to gaze steadfastly at the other person or to avert one's eyes, to be higher than the other person or lower, to stand close to the other person or to keep distant. Every movement has a meaning, an implication; there is a convention for everything and every convention serves a purpose. Yet what makes the convention work is simply that it exists, not what it happens to be. Every aspect of language that we take for granted is a convention that we must have learned. Every language user's knowledge of language is enormous. Yet we acquire this knowledge—for the language to which we are accustomed—so easily and imperceptibly that we are rarely aware that the conventions exist, let alone that we have learned them.

There is no completely free choice in language; there is a convention for everything, and every convention makes a difference. I mean that there are never two entirely substitutable ways of saying the same thing. Words cannot be selected and organized idiosyncratically. Say something in one way and it has one set of implications; say it with even the slightest of changes and something different is said. The differences are often most obvious when the change is slightest, saying "Would you pass the salt" rather than "Could you pass the salt," for example. If alternatives exist, then they serve different purposes. While different surface structures may represent the same literal meaning (as I showed earlier in this chapter), they are never substitutable in practice. One form is always more appropriate or preferred than another in a particular context. The choice does not depend upon the intrinsic meaning of the sentence, on the proposition that it expresses, but on the purpose for which it is produced.[8]

Conventions and Creativity

The idea that language affords no freedom offends many people (as it unsettled me when I first considered it). I am not saying that we are not free to say anything we want to say—a different question altogether—but that given that we have something to say, there will be only one conventional way of saying it on any particular occasion. Where we feel we have a choice, it is always between saying two different things, however slight the difference, rather than between alternative ways of saying the same thing. There are no identical alternatives in language, no paraphrases, no synonyms. *The dog chases the ball* may represent the same literal meaning as *the ball is chased by the dog*, but in a meaningful context or setting the two phrases are not substitutable. The first phrase is a statement about the dog, the second a statement about the ball. The terms *bachelor* and *unmarried man* may appear to have the same meaning, but one term is always more appropriate in a given situation. If I tell you my brother is an unmarried man you will wonder if I think you do not know the meaning of "bachelor." If I say "petrol" rather than "gas," "biscuit" rather than "cookie," I reveal something about my own language background or about my perception of the language environment that I am in.

It may also be objected that if everything in language is conventional, if there is a convention for everything and no freedom of choice, then how can anything original ever be said? How can we find language to express something new? But paradoxically, it is because conventions exist that new things can be said. Without convention, how could one ever be unconventional? Creative writers deliberately contravene convention to make a point. James Joyce flouted conventional grammar and e. e. cummings disregarded conventional punctuation, just as Picasso rejected conventions of naturalistic painting. Artists and innovators of every kind use convention by selectively ignoring it. Their unconventionality expresses new meanings, different purposes. But they would be unable to make their statements if there were no conventions in the first place. Of course, the innovator runs risks. If unconventionality is attributed to ignorance or intransigence or if its purpose remains opaque, the creativity will fail. Unconventionality only works when its purpose is understood. And when a contravention of convention is particularly successful, when its utility becomes evident to a number of people, then it may well become conventional itself. Thus new conventions arise and old conventions die.

Conventions can always be broken; we are always free to express something unconventionally, though not if we wish to convey a conventional meaning. Conventions may always be broken for good reason, and there are basically two good reasons for conventions to be broken. The first reason is ignorance, and the second is to say something new. It is always permissible to break a convention through ignorance—provided we are prepared to be characterized as a person not familiar with the convention. Foreigners are expected to break convention—that is a condition of their foreignness. If they demonstrate knowledge of relevant conventions then they are not regarded as foreign—and unconventional behavior is regarded differently. Sometimes it is convenient to be "foreign," because different behavior may then be excused. But when convention is contravened and ignorance is not an explanation, it is always assumed that the contravention is for a purpose, that the contravener has something particular to say.

Metaphors are deliberate contraventions of the conventional use of words. It has often been argued that it is only through metaphor that we can get new ideas into the brain. The first automobiles were horseless carriages. Certainly children learn by using language metaphorically. A cow is a horse with horns and the moon a lamp in the sky. Metaphors lose their force when their meaning becomes conventional—like *dead ends* and *frozen metaphors*. Many of today's most common words and expressions began as metaphors; their utility has made them conventional.[9]

Why have conventions? Why not allow language to be creative all the time? I have argued that the existence of conventions permits new things to be said, and also alluded to the important consideration that different conventions permit us to claim status and show membership of particular social and cultural groups. But there are two more fundamental reasons why conventions develop in the first place. The first is simply the nature of the human brain. Fortuitously or not, the brain does not care for alternatives that do not have a distinct purpose. Variation is expected to be motivated. Perhaps the brain has enough difficulty trying to find one meaning, one explanation, for every phenomenon it experiences in the world, without the complication of differences that do not make a difference. The brain likes to predict what will happen in every circumstance. This leads to the second basic reason for convention: It makes communication possible.

Bridging the Language Gulf

I have tried to show that a gulf always exists between the surface structure and deep structure of language, that the basis of language comprehension is prediction. If listeners and readers are to understand language, then they must anticipate the surface structures that speakers and writers are likely to produce. And, conversely, speakers and writers must produce the kinds of surface structure that listeners and readers will anticipate. For all their complexity, the languages of the world are not fundamentally different from the kind of mutual mind reading that takes place when two entirely isolated prisoners try to communicate by tapping on the cell wall between them. Each has to imagine what the other would be most likely to want to say and how the other would be most likely to try to say it.[10]

Conventions permit static sequences of words to convey information and create images of a world in flux. Words can never directly represent either continuous changes of state that occur with the passage of time, or the simultaneity of all aspects of a simple event.[11] But if I say "The door was opened suddenly" in circumstances in which you would use the same words, then I can in fact describe the movement to you. If I put together the words "John was playing the guitar in the rain" in a conventional order then you can reconstruct an event that did not have a sequential order but was an indivisible whole. What matters is not the convention, but the implicit agreement behind the convention. Give anything a name and you can talk about it with anyone else who gives the same thing the same name. Agree on the significance of a descriptive label, and objects or events can be described in terms of that label. Every infant who learns language makes an implicit contract to use and interpret language in the terms in which the infant perceives people around using and interpreting language. It is all tapping on the cell walls but on an incredibly subtle and complex scale.

Language works to the extent that it is predictable. But for readers to predict they must anticipate the conventions that writers will observe (or contravene), and writers must respect (or carefully contravene) conventions that readers will expect. It may seem paradoxical that the conventions themselves should be quite unpredictable, that they need to be learned in advance, but it is due to its essential arbitrariness that language succeeds in conveying meaning, in making sense, and in constructing worlds in which different people may have similar experiences.

THE INTERACTION OF THOUGHT AND LANGUAGE

To recapitulate briefly from this and the previous chapter: Thought is essentially nonverbal. It proceeds in its complex and unobservable ways in and through the theory of the world that is contained within our brains. We cannot inspect thought directly any more than we can directly inspect what we know, but we can make our thought and knowledge manifest. We can observe the products of thought, through the conventions of language and through other kinds of behavior, either overt or imagined, just as we can observe the language of others and other kinds of occurrences in the world around us.

Our language is generated by our thought, but it is not itself thought, to which it is arbitrarily and conventionally related. Language is a product of thought, but not its image. Language is related to thought the way cooking is related to thought; both are products of the human brain and both reflect the way we think. Neither is an *image* of underlying brain processes. We should no more expect to find sentences in the brain than we should expect to find soups or casseroles there. But while language (like cooking) owes its existence to thought, it also *influences* our thought. Even when we keep our language to ourselves, either in our own minds or in writing which is not shown to anyone else, the language affects how we think. There is an interaction between language and thought.[12]

First, the language that our thought produces modifies our thought as it is produced, just as the image in a painter's mind develops as each brush stroke is applied to the canvas. The brush stroke is never in the painter's mind until it is produced or imagined; until that moment there is just a generalized intention, as intangible as the intention that sparks a word. Language permits thought to fold back on itself; the product of thought itself becomes an object that thought can operate upon, like the painter's brush mark, and thereby provides a basis for new or modified ideas. We can contemplate a statement we have ourselves made just as we contemplate the statements of others, and go forward to make further statements that would not have been possible if the original statement had not been contemplated. In the same way that a painter reflecting upon an unfinished picture can move ahead in new ways that would not have been possible—or conceivable—before the picture had progressed so far, so does language offer ways to create and explore new worlds.

Language is able to influence thought because it is able to—in fact, it has to—freeze time. Language slices a continuous progression into separate events, into instants of time. Thought is always ongoing and undifferentiated; it is not a sequence of separate states or acts. To examine itself thought must halt its progression through time in the same way that a still photograph stops action. Language can only be manifested in terms of concurrent and successive events, both in its own structure and in its descriptions. So what is a limitation when language is used to describe thought or the world—that it must arbitrarily categorize and partition continuities into events—becomes an advantage when thought tries to become reflective. Language gives thought something different to consider.

This constant possibility of interaction between thought and the surface structure of language—each remaining apart yet powerfully capable of influencing the other—is perhaps best represented in a diagram:

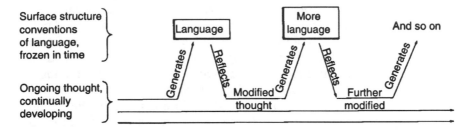

The diagram could be taken as a representation of the manner in which thought responds to language produced by others—the top part representing a speaker or writer, the lower part a listener or reader. But we can read what we ourselves have written, hear what we ourselves say, and respond to the language we produce as if it were something new because in fact our own language can be something new. What we say is created out of our minds but was never part of our minds. The conventions of language can create a new world—or at least a different world—for ourselves as well as for other people.

This potential of language to construct new worlds is one reason I regret the tendency, especially widespread in education, to regard language primarily as *communication*, as a vehicle for transmitting *information* from one person to another. How can one communicate anything new to oneself? How can you inform yourself of something you did not know already? The perspective completely ignores the possibility that language can be the means of creating worlds and of exploring ideas, our own as well as other people's, that language creates as well as communicates.

And for the exploration of our own ideas, writing has particular advantages over speech and over imagined language as well. It is to the differences between writing and speech that I now turn.

(Notes to Chapter 5 begin on page 245.)

6 Language: Spoken and Written

It is not difficult to see, or to hear, that written and spoken language are not the same. The written transcript of a spontaneous speech reads quite differently from a text written to be read, and we can always detect whether a speaker is talking extemporaneously or reading aloud from a text.

The exact differences between written and spoken language are many and complex. They are also subtle. It is not that written language has one vocabulary and grammar, and spoken language another, but that the vocabulary and grammar they share are used in different ways. They employ different conventions. And they differ, I argue, for good reasons.

WHY WRITTEN AND SPOKEN LANGUAGE SHOULD BE DIFFERENT

Take first the point of view of the language producer, the writer or the speaker. Why should language that flows from the fingers be different from that emerging from the mouth?

One obvious reason for a difference is that speakers are likely to get more direct and immediate reactions from their intended audience than writers. If I talk to you, I can see whether you understand, whether you are puzzled or bored, involved or impatient, behind me or ahead. You signal to me whether I should repeat a remark, add a detail, or hurry along and skip a point or two that I was intending to make. Less obviously, the mere fact of your attention provides an incentive for me to keep talking, and I am unlikely to grind to a halt in the middle of a statement doubting whether I am being heard at all.

Often a listener will contribute to what the speaker is trying to say, by starting or finishing sentences. In face-to-face situations both speaker and listener can also make use of nonverbal means to facilitate the speaker's task, through body language or facial gestures, by pointing to or otherwise indicating relevant aspects of the surrounding scene. All this possibility of interaction and even collaboration between speaker and listener tends not only to facilitate speech but also to fragment it. Speech of the face-to-face kind does not require a high degree of precision or organization; rather, it becomes elliptical, fragmentary, and discursive. With the help of a supportive listener, speech might seem to make little demand on the producer at all.

Some aspects of speech, however, demand more attention than writing. Paradoxically, speech may be more permanent than writing. Usually we have at least one chance to erase or modify a written word before anyone else can see it, but once a spoken word is uttered there may be no taking it back. We may argue that we did not mean what we said, or intend how we were interpreted, but the very transience of the spoken word protects it from eradication. It is not easy to *unsay*, so if we say something we did not quite intend, our only recourse is to elaborate or qualify—leading to repetition and digression. And qualification is often necessary because we cannot usually spend time thinking about what we are going to say before we say it. If we spend too long deciding we may lose the opportunity of saying anything. Often it is necessary to begin a statement before we know how we shall finish it, before we even know exactly what we want to say. Small wonder we sometimes become stranded in the middle of a sentence into which we have precipitately launched ourselves. As a consequence, speech tends to be highly sporadic, with lengthy hesitations as well as false starts. We pause to think of what to say next, or to reflect upon what we have already said, or for a sign from our listener about how we should continue—and all of these pauses tend to occur in the middle of sentences rather than at the end. Pause at the end of a sentence and your listener is likely to take over the talking.

Because writing can be more deliberate, because we can be more precise and organized about what we have to say, and also because we can have more time to be precise and organized, written language is generally far more structured than speech. Texts are usually more compact, more internally consistent, and more logical and coherent in the manner in which they proceed from start to finish, with a relative absence of digressions, repetitions, and false starts. Ideally, at least, every necessary word but no unnecessary one is included. Texts are more polished, so that speech sounds "formal" when it is read from a prepared text. Speech is less demanding and should reflect that fact; not only is more idiosyncrasy allowed, it is expected.

In one sense, the possibility of deliberation in writing makes it easier; we can revise, suppress false starts, and edit our errors; we can have second thoughts. But in another sense the remoteness of writing from an intended audience is a handicap; we can take much less for granted, and must do without the visible supports of understanding or encouragement. Indeed, one cause of the discouraging blocks that all writers experience from time to time is the uncertainty that anyone will attend to us. A blank page can be as disconcerting as a blank face.

Writers must consider a great many contingencies. They cannot afford to be misunderstood and therefore must include enough information to satisfy every prospective reader, at the same time trying to avoid the repetition or redundancy that will irritate or antagonize. It is perhaps not surprising that written language is often regarded as language in its purest form, as language at its best. The language itself must carry most of the burden of communication. Such self-sufficient language would be out of place in many spoken-language situations. We use spoken language inefficiently if we do not allow the setting to convey appropriate information; we do not say "Kindly pass the mottled brown crazed-glaze double-handled drinking mug over there" when our listener can see that the mottled brown crazed-glaze double-handled object is the only mug in the room.

There is the important matter of rate. The need for speech to be relatively fast may not leave the speaker much time to reflect, but the slowness with which most of us write throws a different kind of burden on the writer. The speaker beginning a sentence can often leave the end to take care of itself, and in any case the end of the sentence is usually reached soon enough. (When the end of a sentence is delayed, speakers characteristically begin to ramble.) But a writer frequently has to know where a sentence is going from the beginning. Trying to remember how a complex sentence will end while laboriously putting it on paper can be a considerable burden that leaves little memory capacity for anything else. We may find ourselves knowing that we wanted to write a particular sentence but forgetting why. We do not fully understand where to go from where the sentence has brought us. On the other hand, writing is much more helpful than speech in telling us where we have been, especially in the course of a long discussion. Professional speakers often have to rely on notes, not only to remind themselves of where to go but to keep track of where they have been.

Varying memory demands also help to explain major differences between written and spoken language as we move to the points of view of readers and listeners. The reader, like the writer, can use the text as a record of what has just been said, but listeners have no choice but to remember the immediately preceding language, sometimes in considerable detail if the topic is difficult, until they make sense of the whole. Because of this memory disadvantage it may be just as well that the listener can appeal so easily to a speaker for clarification. And in one respect the reader has an enormous advantage over the listener, a power over the text far greater than anyone can have over spoken language. I am referring to control over temporal aspects of comprehension, the power to manipulate time.

A listener is almost completely in the speaker's hands in terms of time. The listener occasionally may ask the speaker to repeat something that has been said, but with nothing like the facility with which a reader can go back to an earlier passage. Demand for repetition does not disrupt the writer in any way; the writer will never falter or object. A reader can reexamine an earlier passage any number of times, while a speaker is hardly likely to keep repeating. More strikingly, the reader can look forward to discover what the writer is about to say a few or even many sentences ahead. The order in which the author writes is not the order in which the reader must read, although again a listener has no choice. (If the listener does manage to divert the speaker, they are both then committed to the new direction, and cannot easily go back to where the speaker was and resume from there.)

In addition to the control over sequence, however, the reader can also determine the *rate* of comprehension, not being limited to the speed at which the author wrote the words. A reader may linger over a passage, read it several times, sometimes quickly, sometimes slowly. A reader can skip entire passages, removing from time something that took the author's time and that would necessarily fill the same time for the listener as the speaker, even if the listener chose to ignore what the speaker was saying. The consequence of all these considerations is not only that readers in general require more structure and organization than listeners (because readers have far less control over the language to which they are attending). Readers can also tolerate and even profit from much more structure and organization—it is easier to follow a complex argument—because of the control they have over time. Similarly, listeners can tolerate more digressions and ellipses because of the influence they have over what speakers say.

The differences between speaking and writing are not unlike the differences between accompanying a visitor on a tour of your city and having to provide all the sightseeing information in advance. In the first case, the "speaking" situation, you and your visitor can wander where your whims take you; your instructions can be a terse "turn here," "look over there," and "follow me"; and your descriptions can be related to immediate situations and to your visitor's particular needs and interests. But in the "writing" situation, if you have to organize in advance sightseeing that will be done in your absence, your best course is to offer a detailed map with many routes marked out, including a lot of information that your visitor might not, in fact, need.

One final point. My contrasts between the relative advantages and disadvantages of writing and speaking have concerned only those spoken-language situations where there is a face-to-face interaction between a speaker and one listener (or at the most only a few). I have tried to show that in some respects reading has advantages (there is always an audience of one for reading—no two people need read the same book at the same rate and in the same way); and that in some respects a solitary listener is better off. But the worst of both worlds is to be one of a large group of listeners, deprived both of the reader's temporal control over the author's words and of the solitary listener's influence over what the speaker says. Listeners in an audience have neither form of control, which would suggest that comprehensible public speaking may be the most difficult language skill of all.

A DIFFERENT DIFFERENCE IN LANGUAGE

The language we use cannot be divided categorically into written and spoken versions. Occasionally writing is very much like certain forms of speech, while at other times our spoken language is not dissimilar to the way we write. The circumstances in which language is used determine how the language shall be, as much as the relatively superficial matter of whether it is spoken or written.

Indeed, I think the rather obvious difference between speech and writing—that one is manifested in sound and the other visually—can be overemphasized; it does not constitute the most important distinction between different forms of language. There is a radical difference that cuts across the spoken-written distinction completely, so that there is in effect one form of speech and of written language with a good deal in common, quite different from another form of speech and of written language.

The first similar form of speech and written language I call *situation-dependent*. This is language that is intimately related to the physical environment in which it is produced. Much of the everyday spoken language we hear around the home could only be uttered in the very situation in which it occurs. If you ask me if I would like more coffee, then the setting in which you ask the question must include you, me, an empty coffee cup, and the possibility of a refill, together with an intention on your part to give me coffee should I desire it. If I suggest that we might close the window, or put the cat out, a number of reasonable assumptions could be made about the situation, including windows, cats, and the purpose behind my uttering the particular remark. The language and the situation are obviously closely related; on the basis of the language alone one could reconstruct a large part of the situation in which it was produced.

Alternatively, the situation in which the language is produced provides many clues to its meaning, a fact that we sometimes capitalize upon to make sense of foreign languages with which we are relatively unfamiliar. If someone says something we do not understand in a restaurant or at the airline terminal, a good strategy is to look around, to see what the person is doing, and thus to deduce the intention behind the unintelligible remark. A waiter waving a check is probably raising a question of payment; a clerk holding baggage labels is likely to be saying something related to baggage. The relationship of this kind of speech to the situation in which it occurs provides its meaningfulness. The language cannot be changed arbitrarily. One incidental consequence of this relationship is that very often the speech can be brief, fragmentary, and have very little grammar ("Coffee?" "Please!"). The situation carries most of the meaning.

There is a very common form of *written* language that functions in exactly the same way as the speech that I have been describing, because once again the language is almost entirely situation-dependent. Our vocabulary does not have one convenient term for situation-dependent writing (any more than it has for situation-dependent speech or for the contrasting forms of writing and speech that I shall go on to discuss), so I refer loosely to such situation-dependent writing as "print" or "signs." I am referring to the written language that appears on labels, packages, street signs, storefronts, and in department stores and supermarkets. Much of the world around us is an ocean of print that is entirely dependent on the situation in which it occurs. The package is labeled *detergent* because that is what it contains. The sign reads *exit* or *shoes* because it is located at the exit or the shoe department.

Once again this kind of language tends to be terse, incomplete even, and to have very little grammar. Once again this language cannot be changed arbitrarily; there can be nothing arbitrary about it. The word *toothpaste* cannot be printed on the shampoo tube, or the exit sign placed in the middle of a blank wall. The situation in which it occurs imposes necessity and meaningfulness upon situation-dependent written language. The situation in which it occurs can again help you to understand it. There really is not a great deal of difference between written and spoken situation-dependent language. What is important (from the reader's or listener's point of view) is that both have a similar kind of necessity that can be exploited in order to make sense of them. What is important (from the writer's or speaker's point of view) is that the relation between the situation and the language must be honored in similar ways; you can no more be arbitrary or idiosyncratic about such written words than you can about the speech. You must choose your words in the way your reader or listener would expect to find them in the particular situation in which they occur.

The kind of print I have been describing functions very differently from the written language of newspapers, magazines, letters, and books (a language which for convenience I refer to as *text*). Indeed, the difference is so great that many people do not believe children can read if they can only read signs (although this is something that many "nonreaders" are very good at). And being able to write the words of signs and labels is obviously very different from being able to write text. The written language of text has nothing to do with the situation in which it is produced or in which it is read. If you do not understand something I have written, it will not help you to look around the location in which you found the book or even to examine the situation in which it was written. If I am not sure what to write in a story or article, I cannot direct arrows off the page to events occurring in the room.

Nevertheless, there is a necessity about the written language of text, just as there is about situation-dependent spoken and written language. I can no more arbitrarily alter the words that I write in text than I can say "door" if I want the window closed or change the sign on the door from *men* to *women*. I cannot decide that because I have not written the word *rhinoceros* for a long time, I shall write it next, nor can I suddenly start writing French, or use the familiar language I would use in a letter to my Aunt Lucy. There are constraints upon the words I write in producing text just as there are constraints upon what I may say when asking for a second cup of coffee, except that now the constraints do not come from the situation in which the language is produced. The constraint upon the words I choose when I am writing depend upon two factors: the subject matter under discussion and the language I am using to discuss it. In short, it is the context of the text itself that determines what the language must be. This kind of written language may be called *context-dependent* (short for "language-context-dependent"), in contrast to situation-dependent speech and writing, where the context does not include language.

It is not difficult to demonstrate the context dependence of the written language of texts. It is possible————have one word in seven deleted———— passages of comprehensible text, and still————able to read with comprehension, even————find substitutes for many of the————words. The text as a whole determines what each individual word might be. Indeed, if a reader is not able to replace an occasional missing word from text (or to work out the meaning of an unfamiliar word in that text), then the reader is just not finding that text comprehensible. If the words or the order of words in text could be arbitrarily changed, if the sentences could be reordered and no one notice the difference, then the text must be meaningless. There has to be a necessity about the words we choose when we write text, just as there is a necessity about the words we speak or write in situation-dependent circumstances. But now the necessity is imposed by the language itself. We must put words together in such a way that they reflect this necessity; this is what I meant earlier by my references to the "structure" or "organization" of written language. This language cannot be terse, idiosyncratic, or elliptical; it is much more elaborated. The elaboration does not make it harder to understand, but easier. To be understood, the words we write must respect the context dependence that readers exploit in order to read text.

Among the special conventions of text in any language is a wide variety of devices whose purpose is *cohesion*.[1] These provide ways in which sentences may be knitted together. For example, the word *these* in the previous sentence referred back to the *wide variety of devices* mentioned in the sentence before, locking the two sentences together, making them cohere. Their order could not be reversed without rewriting them. Such cohesive devices are far less important in situation-dependent language.

The great differences between context-dependent written language and the situation-dependent speech with which many children may be most familiar before they come to school is one reason that learning to read and to write is sometimes difficult for them. Children not familiar with the way context-dependent language works—who do not know that you can look around the text for clues to meaning just as you can look around the room for clues to the sense of speech—will have difficulty learning to read. Just having "language," even a language rich enough to be understood in most everyday situations, will also not help anyone write clearly. A child does not become a comprehensible writer by putting words together the way they go together in situation-dependent speech. The prospective writer must also be familiar with context-dependent language.

Several times now I have used the term "context-dependent language" rather than "context-dependent writing," because it is not just the written language of books that is context-dependent, that can be contrasted with the situation-dependent language of everyday speech. There is context-dependent spoken language as well; speech that is not tied to the situation in which it occurs. It is easy to identify such speech; it is the spoken language that does not become easier to understand however much you gaze around the room or wherever the language happens to be uttered. This is the language of stories and of arguments, of everything that is not "here and now." The words still have a necessity, but only within the context of the language itself; the context of the language determines its own meaningfulness. Such context-dependent spoken language is under the same kinds of constraints as the written language of texts, and so not surprisingly is much more like the written language of texts.[2]

Indeed, some theorists have argued that it is only because we are literate that we can have conversations in context-dependent speech, or sit and listen to a lecturer discussing an abstract subject (such as the differences between spoken and written language).[3] I would not want to agree that writing is responsible for any of the basic ways in which we are able to think, but there can be no doubt that familiarity with written language facilitates our ability to follow a sustained argument in speech. On the other hand, familiarity with context-dependent spoken language facilitates reading texts; the two facets of language understanding are mutually supportive. As societies have moved into literacy, I suspect that the need for context-dependent language, literacy, and the ability to exploit literacy have tended to advance together.

I do not wish to imply that every instance of language can be neatly classified as either situation-dependent or context-dependent; often obviously there will be mixtures of both. A book—such as a guidebook—may at times be related to the situation in front of your eyes, and diagrams or illustrations may accompany a speech, so situation dependence is a possibility if not a necessity. And there can be grammar and context-dependent elaboration in speech about here-and-now situations. Nevertheless language must always reflect the particular dependencies that determine its necessity. Similarly, I do not want to imply that context-dependent writing and context-dependent speech are *identical*, because there are other considerations that I have already discussed concerning inevitable differences between the acts of listening and reading (or of speaking and writing).

It seems to be inherent in the nature of language—or in the brains of language users—that exquisite subtlety should be employed to differentiate one kind of situation from another, to respond to the demands of various kinds of need, and to establish conventions to differentiate and signpost these various forms. Even the four-way distinction between situation-dependent and context-dependent spoken and written language is a simplification. Language offers many more variations on its basic themes.[4]

THE REGISTERS OF LANGUAGE

Language takes a multitude of forms; there is no one "best way" of using language, no "correct form" that is appropriate for all occasions. We speak in one way to adults and in another way to children; we speak differently to adults singly and to adults in groups; to friends, strangers, and acquaintances; to colleagues at work and to colleagues over a drink; to professors and to policemen; to our own children, to friends' children, and to children in school; to anyone when we can reasonably request something from them and to anyone when we require a favor. All of these different ways of using language are given a special name by linguists, they are called *registers*.[5]

Some of the differences among registers are attributable to the subject being discussed; you would not talk to a colleague about a picnic the way you would about a death or a shortage in the pension fund. Some differences must be attributed to the relative age, status, and physical and emotional condition of the person you are talking to, together with your perception of what that person knows and would be interested in. You would not talk about an animal doctor to someone who knew very well the meaning of the word *veterinarian* or, in other circumstances, the word *vet*. Some differences are determined by the way you wish to be perceived as talking: seriously, humorously, persuasively, authoritatively. It even makes a difference whether you and the person to whom you are talking are standing or sitting, facing each other, or side by side, and how far apart you are.

Just as there are many different registers of language as it is spoken, so written language has different registers from speech. The difference should not now be regarded as surprising, nor should any particular written or spoken register be considered intrinsically "better" than the rest. All the different registers of language have become specialized for their particular uses, and written language has developed registers in its own right. As I noted in the previous chapter in the discussion of genres, every kind of text has its own rules. Letters are written in different registers from diaries, from company reports, and from business memoranda, newspaper articles, and novels. Letters to aunts are not the same as letters to bankers, even if they are both on the topic of borrowing money. And both are different again if the topic is playing golf. Lawyers do not write for lawyers the way scientists write for scientists, and both write differently (or should try to write differently) when they write for lay people. Novels for adults are written differently from stories for children, and stories for 12-year-olds are different from those for 8-year-olds.

Some of the differences in register must be attributed to the subject matter. Scientific themes demand different treatment from sports reports. Some differences are attributable to variations in the understanding and interest of the audience, and some are attributable to age (although it is surprising what young children can understand when they have the relevant background knowledge and interest). But most of the differences are conventional. The conventions of the different registers of writing are expected and have to be observed (unless there is good reason for disregarding them), but there is no point in looking for a particular reason or logic behind each one. Our inclusion of "Dear Aunt Lucy" and "Affectionately yours" might not seem to add much to the information in a letter, but she would be puzzled, surprised, or offended if the salutations were not there. There is a rigid formula for most scientific articles; they begin with an introduction and rationale, followed by the methodology, presentation of results, discussion of results, and conclusion. But the experiments discussed in such articles were probably not performed in the sequence in which they are written up, the articles were probably not written in that sequence, and very possibly they are not read in that sequence either. The conventional sequence is followed even though it does little to help either writer or reader except to provide a format that is predictable.

It is true that the individual voice may often come through. And it is true that written styles vary with fashion and fad. But to the extent that writers wander from the expected register they become less easy to read and less "acceptable" to their readers, at least until their idiosyncrasies have become familiar. A style is simply the particular conventions an author customarily chooses to employ.[6]

Once again it is difficult to specify exactly the differences among various registers of written language, although it is not hard to say who knows how to write them. Scientists know how to write in scientific registers; at least those do who are published in scientific journals. Lawyers know how to write legal language. Teachers tend to know school language best (though they may not recognize it as such, or understand that children may not be familiar with it). Newspaper and magazine writers probably write the best written language for popular consumption and professional novelists in general know the best language for novels. I am not trying to set up these various individuals as ultimate authorities, nor am I making a value judgment about the "standards" or "quality" (whatever those terms might mean) of their writing. I am simply expressing an empirical fact that the persons who best know the most appropriate register of written language for particular occasions are those who succeed in making themselves understood by the relevant audience on those occasions, no matter how much professors of English or literature might lament the way the trick is done. The person who knows best how to write for a particular audience is the author who succeeds in being consistently understood by that audience. If the conventions you observe when you write are the conventions your reading audience expects, then you are writing in the appropriate register for that audience.

THE SENSE OF AUDIENCE

The term "sense of audience" is widely used by a number of investigators who have studied writing for a long time and with great insight. The sense to which they refer is often considered to be a necessary and central characteristic of competent writing. It is not always clear what exactly the term is supposed to refer to; a sense of audience hardly functions like a sense of smell or touch; it is not (presumably) part of our innate biological equipment, nor does it function to enable us to construct within the brain perceptions of things impinging upon us from the world outside. It does not fully account for the ability of skilled writers to write in appropriate registers for intended audiences. Such writers are not skilled because they have this special sense; they may be said to have this sense because they are skilled writers. Effective writing is writing that meets the conventional demands of the text, demands that impose themselves on both writers and readers.

Awareness of a potential audience may of course play a considerable part in the original motivation for writing. We may write because we want someone else to read what we write; the audience provides the incentive. But there are occasions when we write for our own eyes only. And even when we write for other people we are still our own primary audience. Sometimes, in any case, the intention to write can long precede any decision about the audience that will be addressed. We may decide to write because we want to explore an idea or to express a feeling. Decisions about the intended audience may be postponed until quite late in the proceedings, and may not be made at all. (Publishers often surprise authors by asking to whom a particular book is addressed. Authors may not necessarily have thought of this question.)

The intended audience also often determines the manner of writing that is selected. We may decide to send a greeting card to Aunt Lucy, a letter to the bank manager, to write a book about the idea, and a poem about the feeling. But once again, the decision to begin a particular kind of writing may precede any decision about audience or even topic. We might feel like writing letters without any firm idea about whom to write to or what to write about. A journalist or author might decide to undertake a writing enterprise for reasons initially quite unrelated to a specific topic or audience—to earn some royalties, for example, or because writing anything might be preferable to writing nothing. Decisions about topic and audience follow, and may require a good deal of prior writing before the author can decide what exactly the topic is and whom the audience should be. Sense of audience can be more a matter of selection of audience.

But this still leaves to be considered the role of the audience during the actual writing. Certainly for any writing that is directed toward a particular reader, the reader's interests and prior understanding must be respected. But such a consideration influences the original intentions behind the writing and the intentions about what will be written, rather than the actual way the writing is done. We do not write to anyone in the way we would talk to them if they were physically present, or even if they were on the other end of a telephone connection. No one begins a conversation with "Dear Aunt Lucy." Stories for children are not written as if the children were gathered around the author's feet (though the author may imagine reading the story to the children), and articles in scientific journals do not (or should not) sound like a speech at a scientific conference.

There are conventions for letters that are written to aunts, for scientific papers, and for novels for adults and children. And these conventions are primarily related to the form of the genre, not to the nature of the audience. We do not write *to* Aunt Lucy, we write *a letter* for Aunt Lucy to read. Authors who write *for* children do not write *to* children, they write *stories* that children will read or have read to them. Always there are the conventions, the constraints, of the particular kind of text that is being produced. A public notice, a television commercial, and a personal letter will all be different, though they may be addressed to the same audience on the same topic. The text itself—the task at hand—is the primary concern in what exactly is written.

In other words, between the author and audience is always a specific task, the task of writing an appropriate text in an appropriate register. An author who is sensitive to a particular audience must of course select an appropriate register in which to write, but the ability of the author to write comprehensibly for that audience depends as much on knowledge of the appropriate register as on knowledge of the audience. Indeed, the register to some extent takes the place of a direct understanding of the audience. One expects an audience to understand an appropriate register, just as the audience expects the author to observe it.

Scientists who try to write on their subject for a general audience often fail miserably. So do lawyers, doctors, politicians, professors, and other professionals who are more used to writing for their colleagues than for a lay public. It is not that these individuals do not know or understand the general audience for whom they want to write, which might include members of their own family. But they do not know the conventions of "plain language." They have never learned (or they have forgotten) how to write in this kind of register. No matter how much they visualize their intended audience, they fail to write appropriately because they are unfamiliar with the task.

It is essential for writers who hope to reach any kind of audience to select an appropriate genre (and to read a few texts in that genre to learn and habituate themselves to its conventions). Flower (1979) says that writers who overlook the potential audience for what they write are likely to write in a manner that seems detached and even unskilled, as if they do not know the appropriate way to write. She refers to text that neglects the reader's perspective as "writer-based," as opposed to "reader-based" texts that respect the reader's concerns. Writer-based texts are likely to be less "context-dependent" than they should be, since the writer is able to read much more into the text than the reader.

Every form of text, every register of writing, has conventions that both writers and readers must respect; that is how communication takes place. In very general terms, writers need a sense of audience just as readers need a sense of writers, but what they both must share is something that is prior, a sense of the conventional written register.

THE NATURAL HISTORY OF LANGUAGE

The differences between written and spoken language, I have proposed, stem partly from the fact that there are some fundamental differences between the acts of writing and speaking, and between the acts of reading and listening, and also the fact that a number of conventions exist to distinguish different forms of language on different occasions. How do the differences between all the different forms of language come about, especially the more arbitrary conventions? My explanation might be called a natural selection theory of language evolution.

Languages are constantly changing because the people who use them are always likely to introduce spontaneous variations for one reason or another. These differences are rarely widespread or dramatic, certainly not in their beginnings—just a new or altered word here, an innovative or modified phrase there. The differences are rarely introduced with the intention of producing a lasting change in language; rather they are likely to be a consequence of individuals trying out a new word that they feel is needed (possibly because they cannot think of an existing word), seeking a new way of saying something (perhaps because they are tired or lazy), or desiring to be different from everyone else. The difference may simply be a mistake, a consequence of ignorance. Children are probably responsible for many of the changes that occur in spoken language, with adults copying them if the changes catch on (which may in turn provoke the children to change language again).

Language may change in many ways for many reasons, usually without premeditation. There are so many possibilities that I think language change should in general be regarded as accidental—a matter of random variation, of chance mutation. Nature is profligate in the evolution of alternative forms. But the fact that language is changed on a particular occasion is no guarantee that the difference will persist and survive to become part of the language in general. For a mutation to become part of the language, it must be adaptive, it must reproduce. The majority of changes that occur in the continual evolution of language probably appear only once, or on a few occasions over a limited area, and then die unreproduced and unregretted.

Changes in language are rarely legislated. Few innovations in the way people write or talk are introduced by linguists or by teachers (and change is rarely prevented by national academies). If a change is adaptive, if it can survive and be reproduced in its particular environment, then it will become part of the language; the language will have changed. The environment in which every mutation of language is tested is the human brain, and there is just one stark requirement that determines whether the mutation will survive or die. That requirement is that the language must be found meaningful by the audience to whom it is addressed. If a modification of language is understood, if it achieves its purpose, then there is a chance that it will be repeated and adopted by other language users. But a mutation that is not understood will fail to become a lasting part of the language, no matter how much it is repeated. The death knell tolls for innovations in the harsh struggle for language survival when the listener (or reader) objects "I don't understand" or the speaker (or writer) complains "I wasn't understood." The language that evolves is always the language that is easiest to understand among the people who use it in the particular situations in which they put it to use. Natural selection favors the most efficient forms of language, the survival of the fittest.

This has been one of my main points in this chapter—that written language has probably evolved to be different from spoken language for very good reasons, including the fact that written language is easier to read. Spoken language, with whatever its particular characteristics are, is more peculiarly adapted to being heard. The producer plays a role, of course. When we speak we tend to produce the language that we find easiest to utter, just as we tend to prefer the easy to the difficult when we write. But the recipient has the ultimate power. Innovations in spoken language that bewilder listeners will no more survive than changes in written language that confuse readers. Language always tends toward efficiency, toward functional adequacy in the situations in which it occurs.

The idea that the language we have must be a relatively efficient system for the demands to which it is put is perhaps not widespread, but it should not come as a surprise. It is not often that we hear someone complain that language is inadequate. There are complaints that language is not *used* properly, or that certain people have not sufficiently mastered it in one way or another, but it is rare that anyone criticizes language itself. Groups of activists do not go around demonstrating in favor of introducing a few new sounds into our spoken language, or for the suppression of the passive voice. There are criticisms of written language from time to time, generally from educators who would like to reform the spelling system or who think beginning reading books should be more like children's speech than adult writing. But such objections are based on the misconception that writing should be speech written down.

Groups of people tend to develop their language in ways that fulfill their own purposes best, or they modify their language in ways that will make it function better. The language that one particular group uses may not be the best language for other people to use, nor may it be the language that other people think best for the group to use. But the group will take from other languages to which they are exposed to the extent that they want and ignore aspects of other languages that they do not want to adopt. We get the language that serves us best. I am not suggesting that any language (or language use) represents the only solution to a particular language need; the existence of so many different languages, dialects, and conventions indicates that there is always more than one way to solve any language problem. But dysfunctional or outworn language just does not survive in natural environments, which is one reason it is so hard to perpetuate language through instruction or prescription alone.

Written language seems to change less rapidly than speech; it is more consistent across time and space. Probably, I suspect, this consistency is due to the need of readers for written language to be more predictable. Therefore writers have to be more cautious about introducing innovations. We tend to be more conservative about written language (which leads some people to think that written language must be a particularly "pure" form of language, so they are alarmed when speech fails to be the same as writing).

Sometimes it might appear that language evolves that is not easily understood, like the languages used by lawyers, doctors, and bureaucrats. But for some lawyers and doctors at least, one of the functions of their language may be that it should not be understood by lay people. Some languages become so specialized for use within subversive and secretive groups—such as long-term prisoners, political terrorists, and children—that they must be changed the moment they are understood outside the group. But they are never changed in a way that cannot be understood within the group.

Language is constantly changing, far more by accident than by design, but the changes tend to keep language alive, to keep it relevant and functional. If language seems no longer to fulfill certain purposes, it must be because those purposes no longer exist, not because language has failed. If individuals seem content to use language that is inadequate for comprehension, it must be because they are content not to be comprehended. If children seem incapable of learning a particular kind of language, it must be because they see no obvious utility in that language. Language can always change to meet the demands placed upon it, but if there is no demand placed upon it, if no one cares whether the language is understood or not, then the evolution of that language will stop—and a dead language will result.

On the other hand, to end on a more positive note, language is always susceptible to change, and changes that persist tend always to be in the direction of comprehensibility. As long as there is one person who cares about being understood, and another who cares to understand, then language will continue to evolve and perform effectively in the circumstances in which it is required, whether spoken or written.

THE ORIGINS OF WRITING

Many lengthy treatises have been written on the origins of writing, but they are all speculative, at least in attempting to locate and identify a single spark that actually ignited people to begin making language out of marks on solid surfaces. Where the *history* of writing systems is discussed—where there is an obvious record—the research is more scholarly, of course. Recent examples are Senner (1989) and Sampson (1985).

But no one knows how writing actually *started*. I think it most unlikely that it was in one place, at one time, for one particular reason, or in one particular way. Rather I see individuals all over the inhabited globe coming to realize that visible marks can be made in various ways for various useful and satisfying purposes. Written language has become what it is in contemporary cultures through what might be called "contingent dissemination"—the chance ways in which people using writing systems over the ages have happened to contact and influence each other. Cultures that did not develop writing systems of their own did not lack anything intellectually and socially; the particular ripples of writing that grew into the great tidal waves of today's systems simply washed by them. Writing, like all other aspects of language, was not invented or even discovered by individuals or cultures—it *enveloped* them.

I don't even think there is any strong evidence that writing originated in speech. The earliest existing representations of any written language are usually concerned more with mathematics, with *counting*, than with saying anything. Of course, counting is part of speech—but one could equally well say that speech itself developed from counting. Similarly it could be said that writing developed from drawing—many early scripts were "pictographic." And today, illustration is taking the place of writing in many public situations, as well as in instruction manuals and on computer screens, in the form of "logos" (for example for different services and facilities at airports) or "icons" (for different functions in computer programs). Writing is clearly independent of speech in many ways—for example, in punctuation (which as I note elsewhere does *not* reflect structures marked in speech; see p. 152), spelling (which does not reflect the sounds of spoken words; see p. 141), capitalization and quotation marks (see p. 154), together with other conventions of writing like paragraphing and heading systems. Of course, efforts to *relate* all these aspects of writing to speech are frequently made, especially in instructional situations, but the connections are tenuous, difficult to teach and difficult to understand. Writing is best understood when it is regarded as a system in its own right.[7]

There is a good deal of cultural hegemony involved in written language, and proponents of the alphabetic system have been particularly imperialistic. There is no evidence that alphabetic writing is more efficient for readers and writers than other writing systems (any more than one spoken language has ever been demonstrated to be superior to others). The spread of the English language across the world is not an indication of its superiority as a language, but simply a historical reflection of politics and power. Alphabetic writing has spread across the globe on the coattails of spoken English, abetted recently by demands of an international technology of keyboards. If the world had been politically and economically colonized by cultures that did not have an alphabetic writing system, the alphabet might not have risen independently to the position of dominance it has today.

A few theorists and researchers assert that written language is "parasitical on speech"—that written language is simply speech written down. We have seen that this is clearly not the case in any literal sense—it makes a difference whether language is spoken or written. Nevertheless it has been seriously argued (for example by Liberman and Liberman, 1992), that reading (and writing) are "unnatural" activities because they are not as universal as speech and do not appear as spontaneously. But by such a criterion, almost everything human beings do must be considered "unnatural," including wearing shoes, sitting on chairs, and using wheeled vehicles, and the value of making such a statement becomes limited. Speech itself should probably be put in the same "unnatural" category, because children will not develop it if they do not hear others talking and receive considerable help from them. Support for the view that writing but not speech is artifactual is taken from the *modular* theory that spoken language is an actual "hard-wired" neurological "module" in our brains, since it is universal, learned early and rapidly, and seemingly independent from other cognitive systems (Fodor, 1983; Mattingly and Studdert-Kennedy, 1991). But by the same token, we must all have modules for car driving and television watching, since few people have difficulty learning these when they have an opportunity. Besides, if we have a language module in our brains specialized only for speech, how can one account for the fluency with which deaf people can acquire a visual language at least as rich and elaborated as speech (Klima and Bellugi, 1979; Sacks, 1989). Modularity theory has a certain appeal to philosophers, but no physical basis for it has been found.

And talking is not learned all *that* quickly (it takes a number of years) nor is writing learned particularly slowly, once it is solidly under way (usually when learners start to see themselves as writers). Talking tends to *begin* before writing because children usually encounter speech earlier than writing, because situation-dependent language is initially easier to understand than context-dependent, and because writing demands a particular dexterity with tools.

(Notes to Chapter 6 begin on page 250.)

7 The Writer-Reader Contract

There are three parties to every transaction that written language makes possible: a writer, a reader, and a text. And of the three, the text is the pivot. Although texts may be (and often are) studied independently of the other two, neither writers nor readers can exist without a text. Writers must produce texts and readers must interpret them, and the text always stands between the two, a barrier as well as a bridge. Writers cannot reach through a text to the reader beyond, any more than a reader can penetrate the text to make direct contact with the writer. Like a river that permits communication between one shore and another, the text is also an obstacle that keeps the two sides apart.

In this book I have little to say about texts in themselves. Rather my concern is with the relation between writer and text, with how they interact with each other, just as the remarks I have had to make about reading are directed to the relation between reader and text. I have talked about writing almost as if the text were a mirror, reflecting back upon writers what writers themselves produce, as ideas develop in the act of writing. I have also talked about reading as if the text were a mirror reflecting in the other direction, generating meaning only to the extent that readers can themselves bring meaning to the text. Thus I have depicted text as a two-sided mirror rather than a window, with writers and readers unable to see through to each other but gazing upon reflections of their own minds.

Does this mean that writers and readers have nothing to do with each other? Obviously it should not. Writers cannot put what they like into a text, not if they wish the interpretation that a reader will bring to the text to bear some relevance to their own intentions. Readers have expectations that authors must respect if authors aspire to making their text meaningful. And readers are not free to infer anything they like from texts, not if they wish to stay in touch with the purposes of the author. Authors have expectations about readers that readers must respect. The text is where the two sides meet, where writers and readers exercise their influence upon each other.[1]

My aim in this chapter is to consider how writers and readers interact on the middle ground of the text. I want to consider text as the intersection of intentions and expectations, where the writer's art and the reader's skill converge. To do this I must look once more at how writers develop and express their particular intentions and how readers reciprocate with appropriate expectations.

THE INTENTIONS OF WRITERS

For convenience, the particular kind of text that I shall consider will be a book—in some cases the book you are at present reading. I need the substance and complexity of an extended text for the points I wish to make. But I propose that the general principles of my analysis apply to every kind of text, to short stories as well as novels, to plays and poems, magazine articles and newspaper reports, to business and personal letters and memoranda, to textbooks and term papers. Later I shall briefly indicate how the general principles might be relevant to various kinds of text.

In Chapter 4 I tried to illustrate the differences and interrelations among global and focal intentions generally with the example of a person going to a library to borrow a book. I shall now try to examine the intentions specifically involved in writing a book with an equally mundane analogy—driving a car. At the most *global* level, an author's intention to write a particular kind of book might be likened to a driver's intention to reach a particular destination, while chapter intentions to accomplish the author's overall aim might correspond to the driver's intentions about taking a particular route. At the opposite, more *focal* extreme, an author's intentions about the next word or phrase or sentence to be written correspond to important but transitory short-term intentions of the driver, to avoid an upcoming pothole or pedestrian or to reach the next traffic light before it changes to red. The more focal intentions of both author and driver depend to a large extent on the immediately pressing state of affairs; they are unpredictable more than a few moments in advance. But short-range focal intentions are also determined by the longer range overriding global considerations. The pothole is to be avoided, but preferably not by diverting to a different destination. I should end the present sentence in some manner that is coherent with its beginning, but not in a way that would distract me further from my more general intentions for this paragraph and for the entire book.

The interlayered, multifaceted intentions underlying the writing of a book are represented in a very schematic form in the following diagram, an attempt to depict how an author's intentions may arise and be disposed of at different points and with respect to different considerations. Each arch represents the conception of an intention (on the left), its extent or duration, and its accomplishment (on the right), when it ceases to be a consideration.

An author's most global intentions for a book as a whole arise before the book is even started and influence every step of its writing. In particular, these fundamental intentions about the entire book influence the general arrangement and context of chapters, although each successive chapter is also influenced by the chapters that have most recently gone before. Intentions relevant to each particular chapter influence in their turn every paragraph in that chapter, although successive paragraphs are also influenced by the paragraphs that have most immediately gone before. And so the intentions cascade down through sentences, phrases, and words. The author's intention at every point—about the next word, the next phrase, the next sentence—is influenced both by the immediately preceding words, phrases, and sentences and by the more general intentions for the paragraph, chapter, and book as a whole.

This word, this sentence that I am writing *now* was not a concern of mine when I began this book, or even the present chapter. My global intentions have brought me to the point where I am now, and my global intentions will, I hope, carry me to the end. But at each step of the way I have to attend to focal concerns—most specifically to the very next *word* I always have to write—if my more general intentions are to be realized. The driver's overriding aim is to reach a particular destination, but the driver had better concentrate on successfully negotiating every yard of road on the way if that destination is to be reached.

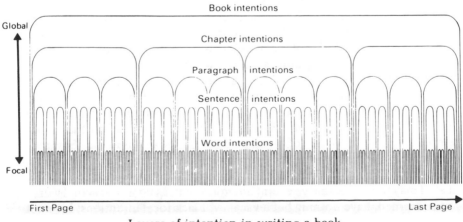

Layers of intention in writing a book.

Of course, writing and driving are not the same. The goal of a book is not necessarily its destination; I am not writing the present volume in order to say whatever I happen to say on the final page (though I shall be happy to reach the final page). For many books a better analogy might be a journey whose main purpose is the journey itself—for example, when the driver wants to explore or enjoy a certain stretch of countryside. For such a journey the destination marks the conclusion rather than the culmination of the enterprise. The purpose of the present book is in a sense realized in every sentence I write. I am not leading up to a grand finale.

And I am certainly not proposing that everything is ever laid out in an author's mind in the formal and organized manner my diagram might suggest. The diagram is like a terrain that reveals its features as it is explored but never exists in its entirety in the traveler's understanding, certainly not in all its detail. At any particular moment an author's attention might be concentrated upon a *particular* word, phrase, sentence, paragraph, and chapter—although there is always the possibility of distraction—but an author is never concerned with *every* word, phrase, sentence, paragraph, or chapter. Global intentions free the author's mind from concern about particular words and sentences that have gone or are yet to come. Indeed, for long periods the author need not think about words and sentences or even paragraphs and chapters at all. The mere fact that a book is being written, or intended to be written, sustains the author's purpose.

Nor does the diagram indicate *how* the book is written. I was careful to indicate that the progression from left to right across the bottom of the diagram represents the sequence of pages from first to last, not the passage of time from the beginning of writing to the end. Not only is an author likely to modify future intentions, even global ones, as the book progresses, but the record of past intentions, the words that have already been written, may be changed, sometimes radically, as a consequence of experience at wherever the author happens to be. Indeed, entire sentences, paragraphs, and even chapters may have their order changed after the author has written them, in the revision and editing that will be a major consideration of the next chapter. There is no way in which a static two-dimensional diagram could represent this dynamic, time-manipulating aspect of writing.

And finally, the diagram is an idealization. Certainly it does not accurately represent the specific concerns of an author at any given moment of writing. As I write these particular words I may have forgotten my more global intentions for the paragraph, chapter, or book as a whole, so that I am, temporarily at least, unsure of where I am going. The words as they flow may distract me completely from my overriding aims, so that I finish up with a completely irrelevant digression. On other occasions the words may not flow at all; I may be sure of fairly general intentions but, as far as the actual words are concerned, have nothing but a vacancy. I lack focal intentions; I cannot think of what to say. I have a block, and perhaps I shall have to modify some earlier intentions or push ahead and come back later for the fulfillment of the particular focal intentions that frustrate me now.

Although the diagram necessarily effaces all of the uncertainties, changes, and flaws that are part of the actual production of words in text, it constitutes a summary of how all the author's intentions, global and focal, are related to the words that are produced. My choice of words at this moment is determined—ideally—by my intentions concerning this particular sentence, this paragraph, this chapter, and the book as a whole, and I could, if I so desired, attempt to specify what in fact my intentions are for this particular sentence, paragraph, chapter, and the entire book.

It would be interesting to explore how many words would be required to specify these varying interrelated intentions. I suspect it would take me as long to determine and set out the intention behind a particular sentence, a particular word even, as it would for the paragraph, chapter, or book as a whole. Indeed, this may be a yardstick for the intellectual or cognitive "size" of an intention in writing. Whether global or focal, the intention has to be susceptible to being summed up in a sentence or two; it cannot be more than we can attend to in the forefront of our mind at any one time. The moment an intention becomes too complex to be contemplated in its entirety, an even more global intention has to be formulated to enable us to keep the parts of the whole together. This phenomenon is known in the psychology of perception and memory as "chunking," the organization of a number of parts into a more concise and independently manipulable whole.

So my diagram constitutes a static idealization of the constantly changing patchwork of an author's intentions as they become manifest, fixed, and immutable (eventually) in the text. And I am left with the question of how in fact authors transform their intentions into text. Intentions are intangible; they are abstractions, with no substance until they are expressed in action in some way. What do authors *do* in order to realize their intentions in written words? The answer I propose brings back the other term that I have used so much in recent chapters. Authors express or fulfill their intentions through *conventions*.

INTENTIONS AND CONVENTIONS

Conventions do not determine what an author writes. *Intentions* determine what an author wishes to say, and *conventions* permit it to be said. Conventions offer the means of expressing an intention.

At the most global level there are conventional ways of organizing any book, just as there are conventional means of producing books in the way that pages are bound inside covers and print is arranged on pages. A book is conventionally organized in one way if it is a textbook, in another if it is a novel, in another if it is a dictionary or telephone directory. Understanding of the appropriate *genre scheme*[2] is a fundamental requirement for the author of any kind of text. There are also conventions for organizing books into chapters and for organizing chapters into paragraphs, and there are conventions for the order and cohesive manner in which sentences may be arranged. An implicit knowledge of the appropriate *discourse structure*[3] by which sequences of sentences may be put together is another basic requirement for any writer. Sometimes the order of sentences, paragraphs, and chapters in a book might simply seem to be a matter of logic, or common sense. Events may be described in the temporal order in which they occur, a country in the sequence in which a traveler might travel though that country, and a structure—such as a building or an institution—in terms of the organization of the structure (buildings usually from the ground up, institutions from the top down). But use of these particular orders is itself a convention; one could say that it is a convention to be logical, except that the convention usually *seems* to be the most logical, whether it is or not. Even stories have their own rules, termed *story grammars*,[4] which successful tellers of stories (and understanders of stories) implicitly know and respect.

At the most focal level, the choice and organization of words into phrases and sentences is conventional. As I tried to show in Chapter 5, the internal grammar that enables us all to put thoughts into words is a purely conventional mechanism. There is no intrinsic logic about the root forms of words, about the rules that modify these roots for particular purposes, or about the rules by which words are organized into sentences.

Apart from exceptions, every word an author chooses follows conventions that reflect intentions at all levels. For every intention that can be expressed in text there is a convention, and conventions are interrelated globally and focally in the same manner as intentions. Thus my diagram on page 89 could be relabeled to represent the interlocking conventions of texts, simply by replacing the word *intention* on every occasion by *convention*. Organization into chapters is part of the conventional structure of books; paragraphs have a conventional place in chapters and sentences in paragraphs. The particular convention for a word, sentence, paragraph, or chapter depends in part on the convention observed in the immediately preceding words, sentences, paragraphs, or chapters, and in part on the overriding, more global conventions.

"Apart from exceptions..."—that was a key qualification at the beginning of the preceding paragraph. Obviously not everything that is written is conventional or expressed in a conventional way. Conventions are not laws, and authors are under no compulsion to respect them (although there are penalties if they are infringed capriciously). Authors may contravene conventions from time to time, and even find themselves in situations where no appropriate convention exists. The complex frameworks of convention in writing make the expression of intention possible in the first place and also permit writers to cultivate distinctive styles. Authors obviously have characteristic voices in their writing; no two authors would be likely to say the same thing in the same way. But then would two authors ever be likely to say the same thing? Differences in mode of expression reflect differences in what is said. To take extreme cases, are authors who write short sentences, like Hemingway, and those whose sentences are long, like Henry James, and those who sometimes ignore sentences altogether, like Joyce, really saying the same kind of thing in different ways, or did they try to express different things?

Language offers infinite possibilities for idiosyncrasy. But these possibilities exist not because the same thing can always be said in a variety of ways but because language permits so many subtle shades of meaning; it can reflect so many delicate tones of intention. Conventions do not force a person to say anything, but they offer many ways for things to be said.

Writers would have difficulty expressing any intentions if there were no conventions to be followed and occasionally contravened. The more appropriate conventions a writer knows, the easier it is to write. But conventions also help readers. The central point about conventions is that they are what people *expect*, and as I have already argued briefly, language is only understood because readers (and listeners) can form expectations about what is going to be said. Having tried to relate conventions to intentions, looking at their function from the writer's point of view, I can now turn to the role that conventions fulfill for readers.

EXPECTATIONS AND CONVENTIONS

I could also employ the analogy of a car journey to characterize the various kinds of expectation a reader might have about a text, the kinds of prediction the reader might make. Just as drivers might have certain *global* expectations about a journey as a whole—about the landmarks they should meet on the way—so readers usually have global expectations about a book, derived from their knowledge of the author, from the title of the book, and possibly from information from another source about the contents of the book. These global expectations would enable the reader to make certain predictions about the organization and content of the various chapters.[5]

Similarly the reader at any point in a book usually has *focal* expectations about immediately forthcoming words, sentences and paragraphs, just as a driver usually has expectations about what might happen in the next few yards and hundreds of yards of road. For the reader these focal expectations would be derived in part from more global expectations about the book and the specific chapter as a whole, and in part from the immediately preceding words, sentences, and paragraphs. All this can be put in the form of a diagram of cascading expectations identical with the diagram of cascading intentions on page 89 except that the word *expectations* replaces the word *intentions* on every occasion.

In Chapter 5 I discussed the importance of reader expectations if text is to be understood. By being able to anticipate what the author is likely to say in the present and immediately succeeding words and sentences, the reader can clear the ground of unlikely alternatives and become far better able to make sense of what actually the author is saying. In the same way it is far easier for a driver to "make sense of a journey" or to be less likely to become lost or have an accident when the driver is able to anticipate likely events along the route.

Once again, of course, the analogy is imperfect. Reading a book is not the same as driving a car, especially in terms of the constraints of time and space. A reader's journey does not have to proceed through a book from start to finish. The reader can miss entire segments, go forward or backward at will, and can generally choose how much time to spend at any point. Speed limits in reading are self-imposed, and there are no one-way streets.

The diagram is once more an idealized representation, this time of the relationship between a reader's expectations and the contents of the text. As you read this text you could, I hope, stop at any point and express in a few words certain expectations about the next one or two words, the next sentence, the next paragraph, and even the rest of the book. Try it when you reach the end of a right-hand page, before you turn the page over. I do not want to claim that you will predict *exactly* what the next word, sentence, paragraph and chapter might be; if you could do that there would be no need for you to read the book. But I hope you would have some expectations, otherwise a complete absence of comprehension would be indicated. It might

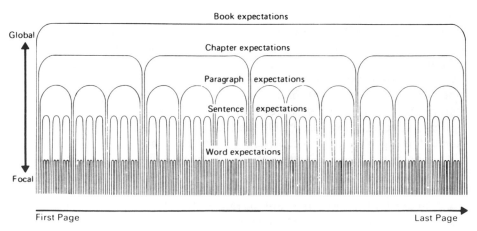

Layers of prediction in reading a book

indeed be interesting for you to examine your predictions to gauge the extent to which they are based on what you have just read and on your more global expectations about the paragraph, the chapter and the book. I would not expect you to be able to predict in the complex idealized manner represented in the diagram. Perhaps you will have fairly substantial expectations about the chapter and book but be in doubt at the more focal word and sentence levels because, for example, you are having difficulty in pursuing my particular argument at this time. On the other hand, you might be able to predict very well at the word and sentence level but be unable to relate this to more global expectations for the chapter or book.

Readers have expectations—but what exactly do they expect? How do readers translate anticipations of the text into actual predictions about the printed words that are in front of their eyes? They look for conventions. Readers anticipate not only what the author is likely to say—within a relatively narrow range of alternatives—they must anticipate the author's language as well. To the extent that a reader can anticipate the conventions an author is likely to observe at the book and chapter levels, that reader will be able to make relatively global predictions. To the extent that the reader can anticipate the conventions of language and expression that the author is likely to employ at the word and sentence levels, the reader will be able to make relatively focal predictions. The more unconventional the reader finds the text, the less the reader is likely to have any relevant expectations about it and the less understandable it is likely to be. But if the reader finds the text unconventional yet understandable, then the reader will have learned. The unconventional can be informative for a reader.

The conventions of the text reflect both the intentions that the writer expresses and the meanings that the reader anticipates. It is upon the conventions that the perspectives of writer and reader converge and intersect. The reader relies upon the writer to employ them and the writer relies upon the reader to expect them. Conventions are the contract on which writers and readers must agree if the text is to be comprehended in the manner the author desires. By understanding the conventions, writers and readers have less need to understand each other.

HOW WRITERS CONTROL READERS

I have used an identical diagram on pages 89 and 94, with just a single labeling change, to indicate the manner in which the intentions of writers and the expectations of readers are manifested in text. I do not see how there could ever be such a thing as a total or perfect comprehension of a text, certainly not from an author's point of view, but if there were I can now say what it would be. Perfect comprehension would occur when the writer's intentions and the reader's expectations coincided completely, when every intention of the author was correctly anticipated by the reader, and when every expectation of the reader was fulfilled.

Perfect comprehension in such terms could probably never occur because of two requirements which could never be fulfilled: an author who writes without possibility of ambiguity and a reader willing and able to read a text entirely from the author's point of view.

The philosopher Karl Popper gives one reason that the first requirement for perfect comprehension could never be met when he asserts that writers (and speakers) can never insure themselves against being misunderstood.[6] The meaning of any utterance depends upon the context in which it is understood, and this context will always change, if only as a consequence of the passage of time. A text is out of an author's hands the moment a reader sets eyes on it. In that independent existence the text can only talk for itself, and its interpretation is determined by the reader. Readers do not usually try to interpret the author's intentions—the second requirement; instead, they try to interpret the text, and the interpretation always depends upon the context in which they try to make their interpretation, on their current state of knowledge, and on what they themselves want and expect to find in the text.

Readers do not try to interpret a text from the author's point of view unless their aim is to understand the author rather than the book—for example, in the literary exploration of the sources of a book. Readers approach texts from their own point of view, with intentions of their own rather than those of the author. And readers comprehend when their own intentions are satisfied, when the questions they ask of the text are answered because their expectations are fulfilled.

Take, as a very simple example, the matter of looking up a number in a telephone directory. The reader does not have to understand the author's intentions in compiling the directory, except in the very global sense of providing an accessible list of telephone numbers in an area. The reader does not consult the text the way the author wrote it; quite the reverse. What the reader must understand and anticipate in order to find the directory comprehensible is the conventions the author followed in listing the numbers, primarily that of alphabetizing. If the reader succeeds in finding an answer to the question that led to the directory in the first place, if the desired number is located, then the reader has comprehended. But this comprehension will be achieved only if the reader's expectations about the focal intentions of the author (where specific telephone numbers should be located) are fulfilled.

But the important other side of the contract is that it is through such conventions as alphabetizing that the compiler of the directory manipulates the behavior of the reader. If a reader wants to know a particular telephone number (and it is not necessary for the author of course to know the specific number a particular reader might want to find) the conventions of alphabetizing enable the author to bring the distant reader's eye rapidly to the very page and line where the number will be found. This is a remarkable achievement (which we do not recognize because we take it for granted), made possible only because a convention exists that both author and reader of the directory understand and respect.

There is nothing *necessary* about the alphabetizing convention, of course; there could be others. Telephone numbers could be arranged (as they sometimes are) on a street location basis, by occupation (the yellow pages), even by the date of birth of telephone subscribers, provided both author and reader have the relevant information. As long as there is a convention that is shared, not only can readers generate expectations that will enable them to find answers to their own questions in text, but the writer can direct the reader's behavior—and the reader's focal expectations—and thereby influence the reader's comprehension.

In a textbook it seems to me to be the author's responsibility to bring a reader inexorably from beginning to end by contriving that the reader is never bereft of expectations and that expectations are always appropriate. This is again an ideal situation; it is most unlikely that an author would ever succeed completely. But, fortunately, readers are often flexible and forgiving about the frustration, uncertainty, and surprise they experience in trying to make sense of a textbook.

Readers usually come to a textbook with very little of the author's prior understanding of its content, so it would clearly be unrealistic to assume that a reader's expectations will match the author's intentions at all levels. It might be reasonable to assume that a prospective reader will have very global expectations about the subject matter (as given by the title of the book, for example), about the conventions usually employed in the organization of textbooks, and about the language intentions of the author (that the book is supposed to be in English, say, even though there might be a specialized vocabulary and terminology to be acquired on the way). But in general the reader will not start out with the possibility of generating many of the intermediate- and focal-level expectations required to understand the book and its subject matter; it is the author's responsibility to initiate the development of these expectations as the reader progresses through the book.

How can an author generate expectations in a distant reader? The diagram and discussion on page 94 indicate the general possibilities. A reader's expectations at any particular point in a text are determined by a combination of superordinate global expectations about book and chapter organization as a whole and of immediately preceding events at the word, sentence, and perhaps paragraph level. At the global level the conventions the author observes regarding the general organization of the book must be anticipated by the reader; these will be the reader's general guide throughout. At the focal level the author guides the reader's expectations by controlling where the reader has been.

Ideally (again), nothing should come as a surprise in a textbook. This does not mean that the reader should know everything in advance, but that everything should appear to unfold smoothly and inevitably, even if it leads to conclusions or raises possibilities contrary to what the reader believed at the beginning. Nothing should transpire contrary to focal expectations. Where a specialized terminology is required for understanding a book and its subject matter, the terminology itself has to be presented in a manner that conforms to the reader's expectations. The learning should in a sense be incidental (as I shall later argue, all of the important learning in our lives is incidental), a consequence of understanding. In one sense the reader should always be ahead of the author, but only because the author has indicated to the reader where the text is likely to go.

In the (nonexistent) perfect textbook, the path is determined by the author, proceeding usually from the first page to the last. But in reference books, encyclopedias, manuals, collections of recipes or prescriptions, dictionaries, television guides and various kinds of directories, authors must concede to readers the right to choose their own path and their own destinations. But the author must also facilitate the reader's choice; the reader should never be left wondering where to go next.

It may seem obvious that an author must guide a reader through a book, or enable a reader to reach an appropriate place depending upon the reader's particular need or interest. But I must stress that this obviously desirable state of affairs can be achieved only if there are conventions that are shared, if the reader can anticipate what the author is likely to do and the author can anticipate and control what the reader will expect. Signposts must be provided and utilized.

Protection from surprise and uncertainty is presumably the author's aim in plotting the course the reader will take from start to finish of a textbook or reference book. But the same considerations do not apply in other texts, such as novels. The *means* by which the author directs reader expectations remain the same, but the *manner* in which the manipulation is done can be entirely different.

The novelist must maintain a degree of uncertainty that would be intolerable in a textbook. Something has to be left that the reader cannot predict if there is to be any tension to sustain the reader's interest. How in fact tension is maintained—and the varying ways in which it is achieved in different novels and by different authors—is a complex question of textual analysis that I do not aspire to undertake here. I would speculate that usually authors strive to confound their readers' expectations at intermediate levels; they want readers to remain engaged in the book globally, to have some idea of what everything is about and where it might be leading, and they do not want to lose readers focally, to have readers bemused by the very words and sentences that are being used. But some authors seem deliberately to allow their readers little purchase at global levels. Sentences and even paragraphs seem to make sense, but it is quite unclear what the book as a whole is about. Others leave little doubt about general intentions but create considerable mystification at word and sentence levels. (And what a few do intentionally, by art, many others do accidentally, by incompetence.)

Novelists can play with readers' expectations. If the intention is a thriller, the unexpected must from time to time occur and there must be periods when the reader has no global expectations at all. Some signposts will be absent. If a mystery is the aim, red herrings will be set and readers' expectations led into blind alleys or false trails. Some signposts will be misleading. Authors transgress convention in some respects so that the reader cannot anticipate precisely where a book will lead. Globally, it is a convention that some conventions will be observed and others transgressed; all this is part of the contract between writer and reader that makes their interaction possible.

Interest

There are other ways in which authors control readers—and other ways of looking at my cascading diagrams on pages 89 and 94. For example, the diagrams could be relabeled from the point of view of *interest*. Some writers primarily hold their readers' attention globally—the general topic or theme is interesting but not necessarily all the detail that the author provides. Alternatively, novels and even abstruse technical works may be interesting on a focal sentence-by-sentence level, even though the broader concern is—by virtue of the subject matter or the organization of its exposition—boring or even incomprehensible. And of course, it would be unusual for a book (or a letter, or a term paper) to be equally interesting all the way through. Sometimes long sections hold the attention, sometimes nothing longer than a phrase, sometimes nothing at all. All this could perhaps be seen in terms of overlapping and intersecting waves—long swells that reach across the entire book (sometimes a roaring surf carrying writer and reader to a pounding conclusion), shorter waves that range over chapters, ripples of individual paragraphs or sentences, and occasional doldrums. Similar complex patterns can be found in many other facets of writing and reading—such as informativeness, comprehensibility, pleasure, frustration, anger, and even sympathy for the writer or for particular characters.

Interest in what they write may not necessarily help writers. We are all familiar with authors who get carried away by what ought to be brief digressions, allowing focal interests to lead them off course. I am not patronizing here. One of my constant frustrations as a writer is that I forget where I intended to go and become diverted down any sidestreet that attracts me. I say "forget"—but sometimes I think I willingly wander from where I am supposed to be going; I move down the meandering sidestreets much faster than I would forge along the long straight highway ahead. It is down these sidestreets that I often encounter ideas that are most interesting (to me at least).

A noteworthy research finding is that interest on the part of readers can actually interfere with their comprehension and memory of what they are reading. Hidi, Baird, and Hildyard (1982) report that "interesting" detail in a story may capture readers' attention to the detriment of their understanding and memory of the story as a whole. Readers, like writers, can be led down garden paths, and divert themselves willingly. Perhaps companion studies might be done examining how writers become disorganized and forgetful (in their writing if not in the rest of their lives) through infatuation with particular textual rambles. Experienced writers do not necessarily write in more detail on a topic than inexperienced writers—their skill is that they write *just enough*, for the topic, for their purpose, and for the purposes of anticipated readers.

Interest also increases the imagery that tends to occur spontaneously during reading (Long, Winograd, and Bridge, 1989), and imagery improves memory, thinking—and enjoyment. Kintsch and van Dijk (1978 and elsewhere, summarized in Kintsch, 1982) make similar observations. Anything that we are interested in tends to go into long-term memory, rather than remaining (transiently) in short-term memory. And what applies to readers must surely apply to writers, as they become immersed in what they are themselves writing.

THE CONVENTIONS OF TEXTS

A few pages ago I noted that every kind of text, every *genre*, has its particular conventions, the distinguishing characteristics by which the generic classification of individual texts can be asserted or disputed. The description, analysis, and classification of genres and their conventions is the vocation of professors of English and literary critics, more concerned with the text itself than with writers and readers, with the manner in which a text is produced and comprehended.

That every genre has its own conventions—that indeed it is by these conventions that a genre is identified—becomes evident when we reflect upon the recognizably different styles of writing to be found in newspapers, magazines, scientific publications, essays, letters, and so forth. That no one set of conventions is necessary, or even particularly logical (since other conventions could serve the same purpose) becomes evident when we consider the different forms a particular genre can take—for example, newspapers in different cultures. We can even see how the differing conventions persist in different cultures, with writers in a particular genre producing what readers of that genre expect such writers to produce, and with editors insisting that writers do so for no better reason than to honor the convention. Teachers do the same for students.

All conventions must conform to the basic requirement that they *work*, that they are capable of becoming a contract between particular writers and readers. Therefore they must be relatively easy to learn and produce (on the part of writers) and to learn and comprehend (on the part of readers). But provided the underlying necessity is fulfilled of providing a form that readers can expect and writers can expect readers to expect, any consistent practice might become a convention. No convention has ever been deliberately invented and imposed upon a genre by an author alone. Authors may devise changes and innovations, they may knowingly or accidentally contravene the conventions of a genre, but to establish a new convention they need the cooperation of readers who will anticipate it.

The conventions of some genres—such as those of newspapers, textbooks, and scientific publications—tend to be relatively consistent and stable over broad areas and long periods of time. The conventions of other genres are more loosely defined, and the category into which a particular text should be placed depends more on writer intentions and reader expectations than on the existence of a rigid set of conventions. What constitutes a poem, for example, the shadowy boundary between poetic prose and prosaic verse, has less to do with format than with author-reader agreement. Poems have rhyme and meter—unless they do not. Literary conventions have neither legal precision nor legal force; they are a matter of mutual consent.

Traditionally, the distinguishing characteristics of different genres of text have been considered in terms of such broad categories as expository, narrative, descriptive, and argumentative. These are classifications—or labels—that I have not found useful in trying to talk about writers (as opposed to talking about what writers write). I cannot see a difference between these various modes of writing in terms of what the writer does, only in terms of what the writer produces. One does not become a fluent expository or descriptive writer because one has particular powers of exposition or description, but because one knows the conventions and has something to say. These conventions are far more complex than a small set of descriptive labels.

In this chapter I have considered writer and reader as separate individuals, approaching texts from opposite though collaborative perspectives. But writers are always their own first readers, if only in the act of writing itself, and this is a major concern. I still want to discuss not only what goes on when writers write, but how writing affects the writer. These will be my topics in the next two chapters, as I try to consolidate and expand upon the writer, the text, and the dialectical processes that change them both.

(Notes to Chapter 7 begin on page 252.)

8 The Act of Writing

So far we have been concerned with many aspects of writing—except the act of writing itself. I have discussed some of the relationships between composition and transcription, language and thought, spoken and written language, and writing and reading, circling around but never focusing upon what the writer actually does. What exactly goes on in the mind, behind the scenes, when words flow from the hand? To what extent can we control, or even know, what transpires backstage in the brain during the act of writing?

Consider where we have been, from the writer's point of view. The two broad aspects of writing, composition and transcription, may compete for the writer's attention, demanding intricate memory and attention management. Composition, when it is taking place, wants to be relatively fast, but conventions of transcription such as spelling, punctuation, capitalization, and the onerous physical effort of making marks on paper can serve to slow down the formation of words. Thought must be transformed into words, a complex process since thought is global, diffuse, and independent of time and space, but the words have to go on paper sequentially and must stay there transfixed in time and space. Every kind of text and every aspect of text has its own conventions, so that composition is far more than getting words out; it requires finding appropriate words for every particular task. How is all this put together? How does a writer create a text, and in what manner is the writer changed in the process?

I shall avoid the strategy of a number of researchers (and myself in the first edition of this book) who rather arbitrarily separate actual episodes of *writing*, when words are put on the page, from a preceding *prewriting* period when the writer in one way or another prepares for what will be written, and a subsequent period of *rewriting* when the writer modifies and polishes what has been written.[1] Much of what is supposed to be done in "prewriting"—like making decisions about what will be written—is not done *before* writing, but rather during the act. And much "rewriting" is in fact revision—including substantial changes of mind—that are also typically done during writing as well as afterward. I employ the word *groundwork* in place of "prewriting," to try to get away from the notion that thinking about what is to be written ends when writing begins, and *review* in place of "rewriting" to try to escape the idea that revision does not begin until writing has ended. The present chapter is in any case concerned primarily with particularly intense episodes of writing, the climactic moments of composition and transcription, when words are flowing. The groundwork and reviewing aspects of writing are the topics of the following chapter, together with the matter of the "blocks" that so often inhibit us from writing anything at all.

THE FLOW OF WORDS

The actual flow of words at the moment of writing is something over which the writer has little control, beyond turning the faucet off. Words are independent. The writer does not "choose the words" that the pen will produce, but must accept or reject them as they occur. Before and after the act the writer has at least the possibility of conscious control. There can be contemplation before the event of writing and contemplation afterward. But the words that manifest themselves to express whatever thought lies behind them are neither premeditated nor predictable. The words just come (if they come at all). At least, that is the view I want to argue, which is why it seems most convenient for me to separate the intangible moment when words appear, the slim and elusive filling in the sandwich, from the more substantial and tractable periods available for reflection before and after.

But it is difficult to distinguish a "moment of writing" lying neatly between the groundwork and review. Rather the actual writing becomes lost in a fuzzy area of overlap between the two. One can talk about groundwork, as I do, when it is the thinking and reflecting and planning that can go on, consciously and unconsciously, before a word is even put on paper. And one can also discuss review, as again I do, when the draft of a text is reflected upon, modified, and ultimately polished editorially. But when we come to the actual production of words, groundwork, writing, and review frequently seem to be going on simultaneously.

The overlap becomes obvious if we consider a writer producing successive drafts of a chapter, a page, or even a paragraph or sentence or two. What is "review" of the draft just completed becomes "groundwork" of the draft to come. No writer ever produces words (or phrases or sentences) in a mental vacuum, first contemplating what should be written without reference to what has previously been written, and then revising it before beginning to contemplate what is to be written next. The consequence would be a sequence of unrelated words. Instead, every word (except the first) as it is written must be related to what has gone before, and also (unless it is the last) to what will come after. To think of a writing "moment" is misleading.

There is need for some research here, to examine the size and nature of a "writing episode," during which a writer's hand is on the move, when there is no manifest pause for reflection, and any groundwork or review that is being done occurs simultaneously with the act of writing itself. How many words are written, how far back do they seem to be related, and how far forward does the author appear to be looking? (What will probably be found is a considerable variation among individuals and for any one individual from one time to another.)

Other research is required (though it will doubtless show the same confounding range of variation) to illuminate the extent to which words are first written on the page or in the head. I said a few paragraphs ago that a writer has no control at all at the moment that written words are produced; they flow off the pen (or onto the keyboard), and we must look at them to see what we have written. In general, I believe, words do just flow from the end of the pen (if they flow at all); there is very little mental rehearsal of the words themselves before they are actually written.

But there are exceptions, of course. We can pause in the manual activity of writing and listen to ourselves rehearsing a few words, a sentence perhaps, before we write anything down, a muttering before the uttering. Sometimes we mull over a phrase or two and then reject them; they are not what we want to write. Sometimes we think of some words we want to write but cannot write them because we are walking or driving a car, or perhaps in the shower. So we hope to remember the words, and rehearse them from time to time in our head. On the other hand, sometimes the writing seems to come first, perhaps primed by a word or two that we have rehearsed. We have to look to see what we have written, and may even find it is not what we expected or wanted to write. Often the writing and the inner speech appear to be concurrent; it is not clear whether we are "reading" what we have written as we are writing or are writing to our own dictation. Perhaps any of the alternatives is possible and we switch from one to another—sometimes the hand leading the inner voice, sometimes the converse, and sometimes the two proceeding in tandem. And sometimes, for some people at least, the composition can be entirely focused on the hand alone, and there is no inner voice. Introspection is a poor guide in such matters. If we "listen" to hear if we are muttering words to ourselves as we write, then indeed we will discover that we are doing so, but that is because it is impossible to listen for that internal voice and not hear it.

Whether or whenever a writer mentally rehearses words immediately before they are written, however, does not essentially affect my argument (although it complicates the exposition). Whether the words are created as they are put onto paper (or onto a word processor) or whether they are first heard in the writer's mind does not change the basic fact that the writer has no control over their arrival, except for the ultimate control of not putting them on paper or of erasing them. We can make decisions about words when they are manifest, when they are accessible to conscious inspection in the imagination or on paper, but we cannot control what arrives in the first place.

Writing Episodes

Words flow, as the paper is marked by a pen (or the fingers strike a keyboard). What can be said about the circumstances of this act of writing? I do not think the following diagram is an appropriate representation:

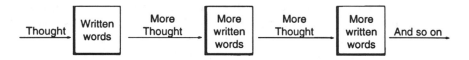

Instead, I visualize writing in the more complex manner outlined in the following diagram:

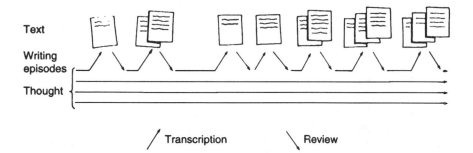

The continuous horizontal lines at the bottom of the diagram are intended to represent the continuity of thought through time, far below the level of awareness. Some or all of this ongoing mental activity may be relevant to the task at hand, part of the groundwork of writing, although it may all be distracted from time to time for greater or lesser periods. Every now and again some aspects of this thought are addressed to the act of making marks on paper—producing words—as indicated by the arrows leading up to the schematic pages of text across the top of the diagram. Each arrow arching up represents an *episode* of physically producing one or more words on paper, an extended act of transcription. (I make no important distinction between *acts* and *episodes*; an episode is the period of time during which an act takes place.)

The "pages" across the top of the diagram are intended to represent the progressive development of a piece of text. (For simplicity of exposition, once again, I am at the moment assuming that the text is part of a book.) The arrows returning from the pages of text to the continuous underlying thought are intended to represent the influence that each writing act has on the thought of the writer. Thus we have two parallel developments through time, the progressive construction of a piece of text and the continually changing flow of the writer's thought, each interacting with the other through the medium of the act of writing.

Writing episodes occur intermittently, although thought is continuous. Sometimes words literally flow, one act immediately following another (roughly indicated in the diagram by pages of text close together, although an episode is far more likely to be a few words or perhaps a sentence or two than an entire page). Usually there are pauses of varying length between episodes, because the writer's thought is reorganizing for forthcoming episodes or because of extraneous interruptions or distractions. But with every writing act—every upward arrow—there is a corresponding downward arrow to represent the influence of the particular episode on the writer's current thought. What is written (or revised) becomes in effect new information to the writer, a new basis for review and reflection, long before it is read by any other reader.

The diagram is, of course, a simplification, even in depicting the relatively more simple matter of the development of text over time. The huge advantage of writing over speech, and over pure all-in-the-mind thought, is that the writer can rearrange the past. This is one reason that writing can be such a learning experience. The diagram also implies that in each writing episode the writer adds a few more words to words already written. But the words can be written anywhere, on pages already completed, on fresh sheets, in margins, on scratch pads, in notebooks. At any time a line can be erased, a page thrown away. And at any time everything that has been written can be changed, added to, deleted from, and put into a completely different order.

My present concern, however, is with something far more complex and elusive than the changes that can be made to a developing piece of text, changes that at least one might observe as they take place. The question concerns what goes on in the mind in order that writing acts may occur. What happens to the writer? I am primarily concerned with composition, although later I shall have a few remarks to make regarding the conflict—or collaboration—between composition and transcription.

Controlling the Words

As I outlined in Chapter 5, every language-using individual must have a dynamic grammar in the brain that transforms underlying *deep structures* of meaning into conventional *surface structures* of words. These words must be further selected and organized in accordance with even more complex conventions concerned with such considerations as register, cohesion, discourse structure, and genre schemes.

What puts such a complicated device to work, generating words in such intricately conventional ways? Obviously, the system does not function of its own accord; we do not usually produce purposeless utterances, either spoken or written, no matter how impeccable their grammar might be. There are two rather obvious prior requirements, both founded in the preverbal depths of the mind. The first requirement is that there should be a reason for saying something, for any of the multiplicity of purposes for which language can be used. This "something to say" is part of the complex and continually changing fabric of global and focal intentions to which I so often refer. The second requirement is the desire to say or write what there is to be said, the act of will that sets the language-generating device to work, producing the desired flood (or disappointing trickle) of words. Without such an act of will we can and often do remain silent, for one reason or another, even though we could have words to say. The flow of words is deliberately constrained. But when the key of decision is turned, when we have both something to say and the will to say it, then the mechanism engages and the words come. We speak up (or write down).

None of this word-generating is conscious. Words come. They are shaped, as James Britton says, "at the point of utterance," on the tongue, the pen, the fingertips, or in the voice we hear in the mind if we rehearse them mentally.[2] But we cannot inspect the source of the words or the procedures by which they come; we let them come, and they arrive. This does not mean that we have no control over the words we produce, however.

One powerful long-range control that we can exercise is through learning. In general, the language we produce is the language we have learned to produce, and we can manipulate this learning so that we produce the language we want. But there are more immediate controls available to us. Although we can do nothing about the actual process by which words come, we can consciously change the circumstances of their coming, and we can decide whether or not we want to use the words we have generated after they arrive (in writing at least). We may not have control at the instant of word production, but we have control before and after.

Consider the latter first. We may not be able to manipulate the flow of words directly, but we can decide whether we want them. We can reject them if we wish, and this rejection can be a learning episode to modify the words that are likely to come in a similar context next time. Here again is an advantage that writing has over speech. If we want to review and possibly reject the words that we speak, then we have to rehearse them in our mind first of all—an inefficient procedure that tends to distract attention from other things that we and the people we are talking with are actually saying aloud.

And in any case, there are limits to how much we can rehearse in the mind at any one time. With writing it is easier to listen inwardly to the words the brain generates and to decide whether or not we want to keep them. There is usually not the immediate rush to make a decision and put words on paper that there is to produce words in speech. The reader does not make the "on-line" time demands of the listener. But with writing there is not in any case the necessity to keep words in the mind in order to review them; they can be put on paper, inspected and modified on paper, and, if necessary, rejected on paper. There can be even greater control of this kind on the word processor. Thus one form of control we have over the words we produce, the words that come, is the power of *selectivity*, of choosing whether or not we want to use the words in the form in which they happen to appear. It is a "take-it-or-leave-it" power that we always have in principle with language, although it is only with writing that we can exercise it fully. It is only in writing that we can be the first and only judge of what we have to say, because it is only in writing that we can inspect the product of our language-generating procedures and decide whether and how we want to modify what we have produced before we are irrevocably committed to producing it publicly.

There is also another control, another form of selectivity, that we can exercise before the words are actually produced, and that is control over our own underlying intentions for the words we produce. Our words, as I have said, reflect underlying purposes or intentions. These intentions are not themselves directly observable; we cannot be aware of our intentions unless we manifest them in some way. Nevertheless, we can control them to some extent and thereby indirectly control the words that they produce. Paradoxically, the way we can do this is by putting our intentions into words. By doing so, we can reflect upon which intentions should receive our attention; we can select the intentions that will determine the language we produce.[3]

To suggest that we should put intentions into words as a prerequisite to writing may not sound like much of an economy, as though I am proposing as a preliminary step what has to be the final product in any case. But the words in which we clothe our intentions in order to reflect upon them need not be as complex or elaborate as the words in which the intentions would finally be fulfilled. I can listen to myself reflecting on the next piece of writing that I should do—a letter to Aunt Lucy rather than to the bank manager, for example. I can put such global alternatives into words and decide among them without reciting to myself the entire letters to Aunt Lucy and the bank manager. The language in which the global intention is expressed and reflected upon is far more concise and condensed than the language that the intention would actually produce in the particular letter. While I am writing the letter to Aunt Lucy, I can reflect upon the more focal issue of whether to tell her next about my vacation plans or the recent weather. And again I can reflect upon these alternatives without actually reciting to myself the words that the particular intention I select to write about will generate. I can select an intention to focus upon, to direct my attention to, and that intention will be the one that determines the content of the words that are actually produced. Similarly I can make a prior decision about the *register* of the words I want to produce. I can decide I want to write to Aunt Lucy in a more formal way than I usually do, or to the bank manager in a rather more friendly tone than is perhaps conventional, and this will tune the convention procedures to the extent that they are more likely to produce the appropriate register.

Once again, writing itself can facilitate the prior reflection upon intentions. We can jot down in the form of notes the items we intend to discuss in the letter, the order in which we intend to discuss them, and the tone in which we wish to do so, and we can modify these notes in any way we wish before and during the actual writing of the letter. The notes help to focus attention on particular intentions, and the attention focused on particular intentions determines not just what particular meanings will be expressed as the words are formed "at point of utterance," but also the register in which they are expressed.

(As a final elaboration I should add that although the underlying intentions must be manifested in some way in order for us to have some prior conscious control over the words that are produced, the manifestation need not be in words. We might draw a picture, for example, or sketch a diagram or a map. Anything that we can inspect, reflect upon, and modify if we wish can be employed to control the direction our attention takes as the words are actually produced.)

Thus we have two possibilities of conscious control over the words that we produce at the time we produce them, even though we do not have access to the production procedures themselves. We can determine to some extent what we want to talk about—what we would like the words to be—and we can also determine whether to accept, reject, or modify the words that are actually produced. Usually this control is exercised in any case; we do not *need* to make a conscious decision to direct our attention along certain lines for coherent language to be produced nor need we decide consciously to review the language that is produced to see whether it conforms with our intentions. To the extent that we are practiced writers in the kind of writing that is involved, these procedures will be followed. But these are two ways in which we can in fact become aware of what we are doing and manipulate what we do. Words may come without our consciously plucking them like apples from a tree, but we can still do a great deal to ensure that the fruits that we get are the ones that are most appropriate for our purposes.

Both of these aspects of control warrant a clear examination. We shall look at the matter of selectivity again when we consider groundwork and review. The matter of intention is overdue for spelling out in more detail.

The Specification of Intentions

The intentions that determine our behavior are, of course, not restricted to writing; they are involved in all our interactions with the world (and with our occasional efforts to avoid interaction with the world). There is nothing special or unusual about having intricately organized intentions; indeed, you may recall that I illustrated the mundane yet complex nature of intentions by describing a visit to a library and a car journey. Sometimes there is an overlap of intentions among writing and nonwriting activities. The main intention of our car journey may be to discuss a mortgage with a bank manager, which is also the subject of a letter we intend to write.

But some intentions, the ones with which we are most concerned, are specifically related to writing (just as others may be specifically concerned with speech). As I have pointed out, they may range from the most global intentions involving the purpose or overall form of a text to quite focal intentions about the next word to be written. None of these intentions related to the text is part of the text itself; the text remains to be produced. The intentions are not a model of what the text will be like; many aspects of the text may be different from the original intentions, and intentions for what the text will be like may often be lacking until particular parts of the text are actually produced. In other words, the intentions are not the same as the text; they will probably never at any one time have the same form or detail as the text. Nevertheless, intentions are the basis upon which the text is formed.

I want to employ a special term for all of these intentions, which at one time or another are relevant to a potential or developing text; I shall refer to them as the *specification for the text*. It is with reference to this specification of intentions, this specification for a text, that we think about when we think about writing, when we write, and when we decide whether we have written what we wanted to write. And to the extent that we can put the specification into words at any time, so can we talk about what we would like to write.

The specification for a text is not unlike the specification given to an architect for drawing up the plans of a building. The specification is not the same thing as the building, or even as the plans for the building; if that were the case, there would be no need for the architect. The specification will however include some general guidelines concerning the building, that it should have certain overall dimensions, a particular style, a certain number of rooms, and perhaps be constructed primarily of certain materials. Some parts of the specification may be quite detailed and specific; for example, it may be specified that one particular room shall be of a certain size, with doors in particular places, or that one special kind of floor tile shall be employed. In general, however, there will be a good deal of scope for the architect. Many details, a number of them important and perhaps even substantial, (such as the number and location of staircases, or even the number of floors) may be left to the architect's discretion. And some aspects of the specification may be negotiable, depending on what the architect can produce, and such matters as cost. Indeed, the specification may well change as the plans are developed, because the specification was incomplete or impractical in the first place. Some aspects of the specification may even prove to be mutually contradictory; a desired kind of roof may not be possible with the specified number of supporting walls.

The specification does not insist entirely upon what the architect must do. It sets out in varying degrees of detail the expectations that the architect must fulfill and the constraints within which this fulfillment must be attained. In one sense, the specification presents the architect with a problem. And the architect solves the problem if the plans of the building conform to the specification. It should be noted that the plans are never the *only* possible solution to the problem. A different architect, or the same architect on another occasion, might draw up quite a different set of plans that still conform to the original specification. Nevertheless, the architect could claim to have designed the building that was specified if the plans in no way controvert the terms or *intentions* of the specification (perhaps as modified as the plans are being worked out). The plans may *look* as if they were exactly what the specification intended, but they were not uniquely determined by the specification.

So with writing. The specification does not set out in detail what the text will be like. The specification may be sketchy, but it will include some general expectations or intentions for the finished text, and possibly some guidelines about its form. Some parts of the specification may be quite detailed and specific—for example, that certain points will be covered in a certain order and even occasionally that certain words or phrases will be used. But, in general, many details—a number of them important and perhaps even substantial (such as how a particular state of affairs shall be explained, or even whether it should be explained), may be left to the actual moment of writing. And many aspects of the specification may be changed in some ways, not only for what has been written but for what is yet to be written. Some aspects of the specification may prove to be impossible to achieve; a particular kind of discussion may be beyond the competence of the writer or the tolerance of an intended reader.

The specification does not determine in advance what the final text will be like; rather, it includes in varying (and changing) degrees of detail expectations that the text should fulfill. In one sense the specification lays out the writer's problem, and the text is a solution to that problem if it conforms to the specification, if it meets the writer's intentions and expectations. But the text is not the *only* possible solution to the problem. No matter how perfect a poem might be considered on a particular theme, it would not be regarded as the only or even the best poem that could be composed on that theme. Nevertheless, we feel that something we have written is what we wanted to write if it does not controvert the terms or intentions of the specification (perhaps as modified in the course of writing). The text may read as if it was exactly what the specification intended, although it was not uniquely determined. Composition is not a simple matter of transforming intentions into words.

Take, for example, the current state of my own specification for this text, as I write it (the first draft) at this particular moment in *my* time. I have very general intentions about the title and contents of the book as a whole (although the working title has already changed three times and I am still not decided on a preferred alternative). I have a particular sequence of chapters in mind, which is not the sequence I set out with and probably will not be the sequence I finish with. I have intentions for this particular chapter, some of which I have already fulfilled, at least provisionally. I have intentions for this particular section of the chapter, although they have given me difficulty in working them out. (My original intentions were modified on several occasions, and until I did modify them, I had great difficulty in writing anything.) I have intentions for this particular paragraph but not in such detail that I could specify in advance the detail the paragraph would contain. (Indeed, the more detail I try to bring into the paragraph by prior intention, the more difficulty I have in writing the paragraph. At this point what I need is *flexibility*, so that I can make and develop my points in ways I could not have specified before I got into the paragraph.) Finally, I have intentions for particular sentences and words, but usually not until I am on the threshold of writing these particular sentences and words. I cannot predict now what I will write two sentences from now, although I can anticipate in general terms what the topic will be.

And when I am done—whether with a particular word, phrase, sentence, paragraph, section, chapter, or the book as a whole—I can say whether I have written what I wanted to write if what I have written conforms to the terms of the specification, if it reads like what I intended to write. My yardstick for deciding whether I have said what I wanted to say is not some model in my head of what I wanted to say; in that case there would be no composition, since the whole point of composition is to find the words to fit an intention. But I have not disregarded any intentions, I have not written anything that was irrelevant or contradictory to what I intended to write.

The specification is never complete and must always be flexible; at no point do I know everything about what I am likely to write. Sometimes I have a good general idea about what I want to put in a paragraph, but I cannot find the words or get the sentences ordered satisfactorily. Sometimes words seem to flow, but they take me in directions I do not intend; or I let the words come because I know they are relevant to my general concerns, although I am unsure of how to organize or constrain the particular paragraph.

Thus the specification for a text is not an "outline" of a proposed piece of writing, certainly not in the highly structured sense in which such outlines are often required in school (or in manuals on writing) as a preliminary to writing. An outline that sets out in detail—down to the level of individual paragraphs at least—the content and organization of a particular text is not so much a specification for that text as a text in itself, the working out of a specification. The specification for a text sets out the problems a writer has to solve in the process of writing; a complete and formal outline is a solution to these problems.

Indeed, the specification for a text may have many blanks. It may at times appear to be *all* blanks: a letter we know we should write but cannot think of what to say, a required paper on a subject we know little about. An intention to write does not mean that we have something to say, only that we want to say something. We can still determine afterwards whether we have written what we wanted to say, even if we began without knowing what this would be. Even though the intentions that constitute a specification may be far from complete, they nevertheless determine what we will write about and whether we will conclude ultimately that we have written what we intended to write.[4]

Composing is not a matter of developing a complete and acceptable specification, but of developing a complete and acceptable text. We begin to write with an incomplete specification and finish with an incomplete specification, different from the specification we began with. A while ago I was discussing my intentions concerning a particular paragraph and some sentences in that paragraph. I could not have said what those intentions were—except in global terms—before I reached that paragraph, and I could not now say what my intentions were at that time unless I look back at that paragraph. In other words, most of the detail in a specification exists only for as long as it is immediately relevant. The specification I shall have for this book when I have finished it will be different in some measure from the specification I had when I began it, but it will probably not be much more detailed, despite all the detail I am putting into the book. The detail does not concern me after I have written it, any more than it concerns me before I write it. Detail of the actual words and sentences concerns me only at the moment of composition, when I hope it comes with an act of will (if I am ready)—to be accepted, rejected, or modified. The book will be no more a part of me when I have written it than it was before I wrote it. It is a consequence of a constantly developing, constantly changing, and *constantly disappearing* specification of intentions. What I am left with is an ability to talk about the contents of a book more specifically than I could when I began, though probably not with any more detail or familiarity than I could talk about a book that I know reasonably well that has been written by someone else. Indeed, others may know more about what I have put into a particular piece of writing of my own than I do myself. Reviewers often develop their own specifications for texts other people have written.

Specifications need not exist in words. The words we write are the manifestation of intentions rather than alternative ways of putting intentions into words. We do not normally say to ourselves, or put down in a note, "I intend to write X"—where X represents a particular sequence of words. Instead we write that particular sequence of words. Nevertheless one thing that often characterizes the intentions we have that specify a text is that they can be put into words. I can say, "This book is about writing"; "This chapter is about composing"; "This paragraph is about putting intentions into words"; "This sentence gives examples of intentions put into words."

If we cannot put an intention into words, then our intentions are probably unclear or uncertain. I cannot say now what my intention is for my next paragraph because I do not yet have one (except the global intention that embraces all the paragraphs in this section as a whole). Although specifications—or particularly relevant aspects of them—can usually be put into words, I do not think they have to be. Intentions fundamentally are not in words; they lie beyond words, like every aspect of meaning in language and like all other thought. The intentions that specify what we will say or write do not have to be put into language before we can speak or write; they can be transformed directly into the speech or writing that we produce. The evidence for the preceding statement is the fact that the language we produce, spoken or written, normally conforms to what we would say our intentions are. We do not often have to say "I didn't intend to say that." We go (if we are able) directly from the intention to the utterance. But then it should not be surprising that we can go directly from an intention (or set of intentions) that is nonverbal to an utterance in speech or in writing, because if we want to put the intention into words before actually saying or writing something, we still have to produce *these* words directly from an intention that is essentially nonverbal. Whether our intentions are expressed directly in the written words of the text, or whether they are mediated through prior words of notes and outlines, speech, or the private rehearsal of language in the mind, they all have the same silent origin.

The Interaction Between Specification and Text

There is no one moment of composition. I do not see a neat progression between thinking about what one is going to write (the groundwork), writing it, and then revising or editing what is written (review). Composition is not simply a matter of translating a specification of intentions into words; the specification itself develops and changes. In some sense the development of the specification is analogous to the development of a text that begins in the form of a very rough draft, perhaps as disorganized notes, and becomes more and more ordered. But the analogy is not precise. The text may come to have much more detail, and much more formal organization, than the specification ever has. What the author knows about the book may always be much less than is contained in the book itself. Earlier in this chapter I tried to show nonverbal thought generating and reflecting upon pages of text with the following diagram:

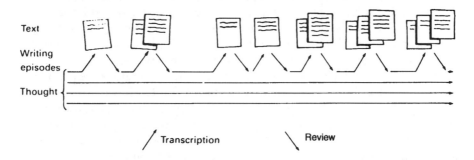

In more recent pages I have tried to elaborate upon the nature of the thought that is relevant to writing, referring to it as *intentions*, which constitute a specification of what the text will be like. At any particular moment of writing, that specification determines what will be written. The specification may then change, partly as a result of what has been written, and something else is perhaps written. As a consequence, as the text develops, the specification changes. All this I have tried to represent in the following elaboration of my diagram, showing the developing pages of text involved in an interaction with a constantly changing specification that is the part of thought specifically relevant to writing the text. (Unfortunately I cannot prevent the specification from looking like pages of text in the head. But it is not. As thought it is nonverbal, although it may be put into words for review and reflection. In any case the specification is not the words of the text; rather it is the considerations that shape the words of the text.)

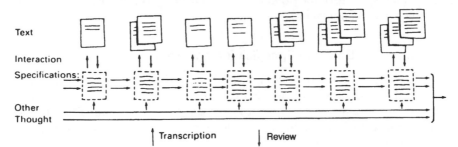

The text, as I have commented earlier, is not (and cannot be) represented accurately in a diagram like the one above. There is no *moment* of composition. Some of the "pages" of text depicted may be rough notes on various scraps of paper; some of the lines on the pages may be marginal notes of emendation; words, sentences, paragraphs and entire pages may be revised, reorganized, or dispensed with. The text part of my diagram might be more appropriately represented as I indicate below, with the time sequence of the text's development being completely rearranged.

The specification part of the diagram will similarly change over time, except that in the brain we cannot go back and rearrange the past. Each "page" of the specification represents relevant intentions at the time of a particular writing episode—the constraints upon the actual words that are written. And when that episode is done, the specification will change. *The specification continually rewrites itself.*

What causes the changes in specification? In the first place, the very fact of writing. The focal intention is to produce certain words, and when these words are produced, the focal intention is accomplished; it can be dispensed with; we can move on. The second factor is the consequence of writing, that what has been produced is no longer a relatively shifting ephemeral thought in the head but a tangible part of the outside world, a basis for further thought. This is the interaction between text and specification, when the writer can reflect upon and respond to ideas in text just as an artist can interact with brush marks on canvas. And third, the constantly changing specification can interact with other aspects of thought in general. Reflection can produce changes in what we want to write.

From a different point of view, the groundwork and review that I discuss in the next chapter are always done on the specification. *Groundwork* (often narrowly referred to as "prewriting") is essentially development and modification of the writer's specification at any stage of a writing enterprise—the growth and refinement of intentions in the writer's mind—though some traces may become manifest in a written outline or notes. And the *review* is also directed to the specification, although it may also result in revision of text already written. But a primary consequence of the review (ignored when the term "rewriting" is employed) is modification and further development of the specification. Thus both groundwork and review function in the same funda-

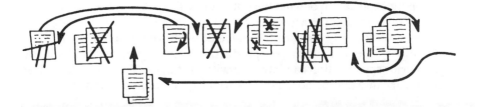

mental way—in development and modification of the specification, although review may also result in changes to text. But sometimes the only consequences of review may be the modification of the specification, with no changes to the text (another reason the term "rewriting" can be misleading). The compositional consequences of both groundwork and review may always be substantial, though they may not leave any conspicuous trace in the developing text.

How do specifications change? The discarding and replacing of focal intentions as they are accomplished has already been referred to. The less frequent modification of global intentions as a result of the development of the text has also been mentioned. But there can also be what might be called *blank-filling*, where incomplete specifications are filled out with new understandings. These may come from elsewhere; we reflect a little more, consult a reference book, or do some more reading. But blanks can also be filled during the interaction with the text. Ideas often do not seem the same when we get them on paper, and ideas that we did not think we had can appear on paper too.

Thus the interaction between specification and text is not smooth, and the development of one does not reflect the development of the other. To expect a detailed specification before beginning to write may prevent writing from beginning at all. A specification may be incomplete, inappropriate, confused, or contradictory, and it may only be in the development of the text that these problems can work themselves out. We may *never* create a clearly organized specification, yet nevertheless a text can be the result. The coherence may be in the text rather than the specification. But whatever transpires, neither is independent of the influence of the other.

To summarize, composition is not a matter of putting down one word after another, or of translating successive ideas into words, but rather of building a structure (the text) from materials (the conventions) according to an incomplete and constantly changing plan (the specification of intentions). Building comes easily as an appropriate metaphor, but so does any creative and constructive activity—painting a picture, composing music, sculpting, sewing, or cooking—where what we are still to do is both directed and stimulated by what we have already done. There is always some aspect of the conventional involved (the entire activity may sometimes be conventional), and there is always a specification, no matter how incomplete, a constantly developing expectation of what the outcome will be. And if we are lucky we finish by saying "That's exactly what I wanted to achieve," even though when we began we had only the sketchiest idea of what we wanted to achieve.

Creativity does not just shape a product, it shapes a producer. Indeed, too rigid a prior specification can interfere with creativity. We may reject ideas too soon because they do not conform to our expectations or intentions, or we may fail to reject them because they do conform. We inhibit the development of ourselves and of the text.

THE CONTRIBUTION OF CONVENTIONS

I have discussed earlier how all conventions, no matter how arbitrary some might seem, assist the reader if the reader is aware of them and anticipates them in reading. But it might now be easier to see how conventions can also help the writer. Every convention frees the writer from the necessity of making a decision; it is a ready-made solution to a problem.

Global conventions provide writers with a framework upon which the specification of a text can be constructed. If the author of a scientific article, or of a term paper, knows the established conventions of the genre, then a substantial part of the specification is already decided. Genre schemes are templates for a writer; they predetermine and economically represent how intentions might best be ordered. To know in advance that chapters, or paragraphs, or even sentences, should be arranged in a particular way is like having a map of otherwise unknown territory. Such conventions will not determine for the writer every step along the way, nor will they anticipate every obstacle that might be encountered, but they will delineate the most likely routes to follow.

And like maps, conventions of structure not only indicate the most probable path to follow, but also can indicate where one has been. Conventions make it easier to locate one's present position. This applies even to conventions of transcription.

Punctuation, for example, signposts not only where a writer must go but also the route by which this particular point has been reached. A period indicates where the last sentence ended, and a question mark or exclamation point indicates the nature of that sentence. Commas, quotation marks, dashes, and parentheses indicate when the writer is in the *middle* of something, again showing not only the direction to be followed but also the nature of the ground that has been covered. Although I do not know of any research on the subject, I would conjecture that writers who for one reason or another are not following a well-structured genre scheme not only will have less certainty about where they are going, but also will have a poorer recollection of where they have been. And, at a less global level, I would anticipate the same shortening of perspective in both directions in cases where an author is using minimal punctuation.

Familiarity with spellings also helps writers. This statement may seem to contradict what I said earlier in the book about composition and transcription being in competition when they are the responsibility of the same person, but the conflict occurs only when the two aspects of writing both demand attention. If one has to think about spelling (or punctuation, or handwriting), then attention is bound to be diverted from composition. This potential conflict is a constant problem for beginning writers who have little experience in the conventions of transcription or who are otherwise required to pay undue attention to them. On the other hand, a spelling that is known does not require attention, it facilitates composition. Even incorrect spelling facilitates composition, as long as it does not have to be thought about.

I shall consider the nature of spelling, punctuation, and other aspects of transcription in more detail in a later chapter. For the moment, a general statement may suffice. The demands of composition and transcription are in conflict when they compete for attention, either because certain conventions of transcription are not known or because attention is concentrated upon these conventions in any case. To the extent that the conventions are known and do not preempt attention, they facilitate composition.[5]

When composition and transcription compete for attention, the consequences of the conflict may still be minimized, provided the two aspects are attended to one at a time. If the demands of composition and transcription are separated, then neither will interfere with the other. I would like to think that the solution I have just mentioned was obvious, and that it is equally obvious that composition would have to come first. What is the point of impeccably spelled, well-punctuated, and beautifully laid-out rubbish? The way to circumvent the pressures of transcription is to ignore them until they can be given full attention—that is, in the course of editing, when the prior demands of composition have been met.

(Notes to Chapter 8 begin on page 254.)

9 Starting and Stopping

This chapter is not the collection of loose ends it might appear to be at first glance, concerned as it is with groundwork, review, and writing blocks. But groundwork and review are arbitrary distinctions, inseparable from any act of writing assumed to come between them. They are different aspects of a coherent process by which ideas may be clothed in the form of written words. And writing blocks are those occasions when ideas fail to take form and words resist the writer.[1] So all are part of the psychological setting into which the act of writing must be placed.

GROUNDWORK AND REVIEW

There is no neatly organized progression from prewriting to rewriting in the form in which I have often seen it displayed:

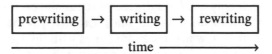

Instead, there is something impossible to represent in a two-dimensional diagram, the writing of one section of a text proceeding concurrently with the rewriting of the preceding section and the prewriting of the next. Ignoring the overlap, groundwork might be regarded as a particular case of manipulation of the specification of the text, reorganizing and developing intentions about what should be written prior to a major textual effort of "writing" (though the writing of notes, drafts, and outlines might be part of the groundwork). And review might be regarded as a particularly concentrated time of interaction with the text itself, when the writer responds to what has been written (although such a response can be part of the groundwork and main effort of writing as well).

I shall not recapitulate the various aspects of interaction between writer and text already discussed. Instead I shall take the opportunity to consider further aspects of composition that are not exclusive to groundwork and review, but perhaps become particularly relevant from these points of view. With groundwork, I shall discuss some of the more general creative and emotional aspects of writing, and with review I shall consider revision and editing, two circumstances in which the writer behaves more like a reader.

Groundwork: Getting the Ideas

It is impossible to make a precise demarcation between groundwork and writing; the brain is not necessarily doing anything different when words are simply being thought about rather than actually put on paper. The preparation, development, or "incubation" of ideas that may constitute the basis of a text can occur when we do not actually have a pen in hand minutes—or hours, even days or weeks—before we actually put words on paper. Or perhaps we might have a pen in hand but not be using it, or using it just to make notes, or outlines. We might even be writing something else or some other part of the particular text.

It is a mistake to regard the thinking that underlies writing as something special, as a unique kind of activity that calls for unusual efforts and abilities. The use of language in writing is basically no different from that in speech. The existence of special conventions does not constitute a major difference; spoken language itself involves wide ranges of different conventions. The "thinking" part of writing—the describing, exploring, explaining, arguing, and constructing in words—is also fundamentally no different from that of speech, indeed from the kind of thought the brain is engaged in all the time. Even writing at its most creative does not call for a special kind of activity from the brain (though it may call for a degree of focus and concentration that is not a common condition much of the time). Creativity is the business of the brain; it is the manner in which the brain copes with the world—and, as we shall see in a later chapter, the way it learns about the world. To understand the nature of creativity in writing ("where the ideas come from") it is necessary to consider a little further the more general activities of the brain.

Contrary to a general impression, the brain does not live in the here and now; it does not respond passively to the world around us. The brain is always anticipating future events (Chapter 4), whether the course of a conversation or journey during the next few moments or more global considerations over forthcoming hours, days, or longer periods. In other words, the brain is constantly *creating* possibilities for the future. Its normal mode of operation is to generate alternative worlds in order to anticipate the world which will actually come to be.

Of course, such anticipation is not necessarily highly imaginative. We predict that the world will be pretty much what the world will in fact be. For most of us, the only time we allow our brain free rein to imagine what the world could be like, as opposed to what it is likely to be like, or was like, is when we are engaged in wishful or rueful thinking. We plan how the world might be, with greater or lesser expectation of actually being able to experience that idealized world. Nevertheless, it is important to remember that hypothetical thought is the basis of our perception of the world and that it is not a special or unique type of activity. If the brain's function seems often to be mundane, it is because our intentions have become mundane, not because that is the nature of the brain.

Indeed, it is in children and young people (and in writers, artists, and inventors) that the propensity of the brain toward creativity is most apparent. I am not simply referring to the exercise of the imagination in play, but to the more general fact that the basis of all learning is imagination and anticipation. To find out the kind of world one is living in, possible worlds must be created. The person who lives in the narrowest world is the one who cannot conceive of richer possibilities. Imagination is the basis of reality, and the brain that cannot exercise creative thought is the one in which imagination has been constrained and shackled. It is as natural for the brain to invent as it is for muscles to move. As an organ, the brain is no more constructed to be passive than is the muscular system.

Once again, we are not normally *aware* of the creative nature of the brain; indeed, the very fact of its creativity usually has to be pointed out to us. We are certainly not usually aware of constructing hypothetical worlds as we go about the daily commerce of our existence. But it is partly because this creativity is so routine, and because we are so skilled at doing it, that its working does not rise into our consciousness. We may become aware of the need to create, to anticipate, when we are totally unable to do so or when our efforts meet with failure and consequent confusion. But usually there is no need for awareness; conscious attention to our interaction with the world could only interfere.

The actual process of imagination is, like all the brain's activities, not under our immediate conscious control. We can be aware of what we are imagining but not of the process by which we imagine. As with the generation of words in speech and writing, we can only be aware of our imaginings as they are manifested. The processes are the same, the brain generating inner scenarios and dialogues in forms of which we can become aware. The possibilities of control are also the same. First some behavior or state of affairs has to be imagined; then we can reflect upon what we have imagined. And we can direct attention into particular channels of thought through an effort of will.

Thus it is a normal everyday function of the brain to be imaginative, to construct worlds, to anticipate—and therefore imagine—possible states of affairs. And the groundwork for writing, when the brain's focus is upon something that might be written, does not require a particular kind of imagination; it is merely a general activity addressed to a particular end. Of course, experience is important. If we are not used to imagining dialogue, then dialogue will be difficult to imagine. And it is not easy to visualize any complex sequences of events unless one has had experience (actual or imagined) of doing that kind of thing before.

Prior reflection upon something to be composed, whether global or focal, is perhaps best regarded as the brain's endeavoring to solve problems or accomplish tasks. The problem may be concentrated upon a single word, it might involve a paragraph, or it might embrace the organization of an entire chapter, a paper, or a long and complex letter. Sometimes the task can be formally set up for the brain; we can sit down (or go for a walk) and *think* about the problem. Such resolution does not always help, even (or perhaps especially) if we have a pen expectantly in our hands. But often the task cannot be formally presented to the brain, certainly not at a particular time. We may consciously decide what the problem is, but we have to leave the brain to solve the problem in its own good time. Ideas, especially new ones, do not always come to order.

This period of "incubation" while a writer waits for the brain to solve problems is perhaps the most mysterious, variable, and frustrating aspect of writing.[2] Incubation is mysterious because it is difficult to specify what exactly the brain is doing except in such very general and nonexplanatory terms as exploring, hypothesizing, testing, and integrating. It is variable because the conditions of the fallow period differ so much from individual to individual, and from problem to problem. Perhaps more reading on the particular issue is required, perhaps less; perhaps the topic should be talked about, perhaps not; perhaps the mind should be deliberately focused on the problem, perhaps on some activity or concern that is quite different. And incubation is frustrating not only because it is almost impossible to control or organize progress, except in terms of setting up physical conditions or situations that the writer personally has previously found most conducive to productive thought, but also because it is generally impossible to *perceive* progress. We usually can tell when the brain has the solution to a problem, when a direction is clear for the way writing is to go, and it is similarly obvious if we have not yet found a solution. But it is impossible to detect whether we have moved toward a solution or even if the brain is productively working on the problem. The moment when an idea suddenly comes into consciousness after a period of incubation is something that almost all professional writers who have ever discussed composition have talked about with wonder. It is the moment when ideas are in control of the writer.

Groundwork can concern itself with any aspect of composition, any level of intention, and indeed may at times seem to concern itself unduly with intentions different from the ones we might consider to be most relevant. We may be struggling with relatively focal concerns like how to word the next sentence or two, while the unconscious mind prefers to concern itself with the next chapter, or with the letters we might be writing to other people. The length of time taken to work out ideas may bear little relation to their eventual size or apparent significance; we may spend weeks worrying about a few words while ideas for entire paragraphs shape themselves overnight.

The preparatory stage of composition can be more than just a time when ideas formulate themselves. It can be a time of tentative beginnings and of false starts. The products of incubation have to be manifested and evaluated; we should not expect our writing to come out right "the first time." Sometimes this manifestation can be entirely in the head; a large part of the testing of any idea consists of "talking to ourselves"—a phenomenon that I suspect is one of the most important aspects of language, yet one that has been largely ignored by linguists and by psychologists of language. The corollary of "talking to ourselves" should not be overlooked; "listening to ourselves" requires a certain quietness so that we can literally hear and reflect upon the ideas that come to us. Perhaps one of the most disabling aspects of having to write in rushed and noisy circumstances is the difficulty of hearing the words our mind produces. I am not implying that we need to rehearse everything to ourselves before we write it; indeed, when we are actually putting words on paper it can only be disruptive to try to hold and evaluate entire phrases and sentences in the mind rather than relieve the short-term memory burden and work with them on paper. But when global ideas rather than focal words are the matter of concern, listening to ourselves is perhaps the most direct route we have for getting in touch with the innermost activities of the brain—the most effective means to prime the pump of creativity.

Not that putting words on paper does not have a role. An equally important and productive part of groundwork is the making of notes, whether in carefully kept diaries and notebooks or in jottings on scraps of paper like old envelopes or on a word processor file. What I would call *disposable writing*, whose ultimate destiny is to be discarded with only the writer having seen it, serves as a tangible product of the mind's preliminary labors which can itself be operated upon. And some notes perhaps need never be looked at again, even by the writer. Their virtue is that an idea that leaves the mind and gets onto paper frees attention to move into quite different yet possibly far more profitable areas. The writing releases a block.

The time of incubation is often an emotional one. The intensity with which the internal attention is focused upon the unformulated issue can be reflected in the behavior of the individual, who may become distracted, preoccupied, or temperamental. If new ideas are bubbling, the individual may become restless and excitable, while lack of manifest progress may result in gloom and despondency. It is difficult to gauge whether these emotional concomitants of composition are *necessary*—whether they are an inevitable antecedent of writing, or whether they have become an habitual, difficult-to-erase, but nonetheless irrelevant side effect.

Do we have to go through days or weeks of indecision, unsettlement, even apparent inactivity before we can write a letter, a report, a paper, or a chapter of a book? I cannot argue that the fallow period is essential, because a few writers seem capable of doing without it. They can write—by their own report at least—a certain number of words in a certain period of every day, and forget about writing for the rest of the time. Perhaps indeed there is incubation for them at other times, but it is not something that seems to worry them or to affect their other behavior. But many other writers have written graphically of their need for silent periods, of heightened emotional states, and of sudden abrupt bursts of productivity. To a writer who has struggled for a month with a paragraph that the day before deadline springs fully formed onto paper it may be rather simplistic (and certainly discouraging) to suggest that the four weeks of searching and anxiety were unnecessary. On the other hand, deadlines and other forms of necessity often seem to bring laggardly incubation to a fruitful conclusion.

There is no reason to suspect that the brightest ideas take longer to come. Longer incubation time may give us alternative solutions but not necessarily better solutions to the same problem. And when the deadline falls and we have to commit ourselves to the best we can do at the moment, neither we nor anyone else will ever be able to tell whether we could have done better if we had waited longer. I know of no way of determining what is the right amount of incubation for any writer, let alone all writers. It may not even be true that writers know best for themselves, that a writer who writes successfully is necessarily writing in a manner that is personally optimal. But attempting to change a writer's habits may be more disruptive than the habits themselves. I shall return to this sensitive topic when I consider writing blocks.

Review: The Writer as a Reader

Just as there is no precise moment when groundwork ends and writing begins, so the activities that characterize review cannot be separated from composition. But there are aspects of review to which particular attention should be given because they reveal the writer from a special point of view; they reveal the writer as a reader. Review is the writer's own response to what has been written, and though it may occur at the end of every sentence, after individual words even, it is convenient to consider it when a draft of the text has been completed.

I propose to distinguish review from editing (although revision and editing are often lumped together as parts of "rewriting"). I am not arguing about how words should be used—I do not care whether editing "should be considered part of review/revision/rewriting" or not; that is purely a semantic matter. All we should do is make ourselves clear. Sometimes writers edit their work whenever they have an opportunity to review it, sometimes they do a thorough review whenever they edit, and sometimes they leave editing to the last (or even to someone else). Review is usually a constant activity.

For the sake of clarity, I shall use the words in the following way. When I refer to *editing*, I restrict myself to "cleaning up the text"—correcting or otherwise adjusting such technical matters as the spelling, punctuation, capitalization, paragraphing, and so forth, as well as points of grammar and even occasionally precision of expression. It may, in other words, involve revision or rewriting. To simplify, editing is the writer (or the editor) taking the reader's point of view, trying to make the text as clear and conventional as possible for a reader. Editing, as such, does nothing for the writer; it is purely a service for the reader.

Review, on the other hand, is purely for the writer; it is writers reading a text for their own purposes. They are not reading the text *for* readers, to make sure their exposition is conventional and clear, but reading it *as* readers, to see what they have said. As I have noted, review in this sense need not entail revision or rewriting; the text need not be touched. And if there is rewriting, it may be because the author has had a change of mind or a new idea, not to clean up the exposition. Review is when the author compares the text with the specification, modifying one or the other, or perhaps both, as the comparison is made. Review—in the sense that I have just described—may take place at the same time as editing, but the consequences are quite different. Editing changes the text; review changes the writer.

The aim of editing is to make the text optimally readable. It is not necessary for the writer to do the editing, in fact writers who publish typically are not responsible for the final copy editing, and it is always possible for any writer to employ someone else to take the responsibility for what is essentially a transcription skill. Often it is preferable for someone else to undertake the final editing, because it is difficult for writers to separate what they know and what they intended to write (or wished they had written) from the text that is actually produced. There is a constant risk that writers will see in a text only reflections of their own intentions.

Editing is a particularly conventional matter, making the text as easy as possible for the reader by presenting it in a manner that the reader is most likely to anticipate. Editing is a matter of communication rather than composition. Many writers are not good at it, and many dislike it. Why not? Editing one's own work can be boring, and probably should be boring. (If the writer is *interested* in the text while editing it, then the editing is likely to be poorly done; the writer is reading the text for its content rather than for its conventions.) A writer is unlikely to think differently after correcting the spelling and punctuation of a text. What is interesting about editing from the writer's point of view is how it is learned. And questions of learning are reserved for a later chapter.

In short, editing is a rather impersonal matter, not only because the editor must try to look at the text from the perspective of another person, the potential reader, but also because editing is probably better done, and almost certainly easier done, by a person who is not the writer. Review, on the other hand, is very personal, not only because it is best done by the writer, but also because of the effect it can have on the writer.

Review confronts writers with the text they have produced. It may be regarded as an occasion of dual reorganization: reorganization of the text as the writer responds to it as a reader, and reorganization of the specification of the text in the writer's mind. As I have said, ideas arise and develop in the original course of composition, both in the text and in the author's mind. When the author subsequently reviews the text there is the possibility of new developments among the ideas the author now finds in the text and those in the author's mind. The interaction resumes, but now with a new and substantial basis—the structure and content of the text itself.

Of course, the text being reviewed need not be a completed manuscript or draft; notes and fragments of a text can be the subject of revision. Review can be an important aspect of "groundwork"; indeed, the note form is particularly convenient for review since it facilitates the modification and reordering of parts of a text. Paragraphs, sentences, headings, comments, and what I like to call promissory notes—reminders to do something later on—can all be spread out, inspected, juxtaposed, and interrelated in two dimensions and even three, to take advantage of the fact that written language does not have to remain in the temporal or spatial sequence in which it is first produced. I am tempted to contrast groundwork and review in terms of emotional tone; groundwork can be a time of tension, of alternate impatience and excitement as possibilities conceal and reveal themselves, whereas review tends to be reflective, a contemplation of what an existing text or set of notes for a text is and might be. But just as there can be times of quiet reflection prior to composition, so review can produce moments of elation and despair as words take their effect on the writer.

"As words take their effect on the writer..." The text, I have argued, never exists in the author's head. The writer reviewing a text, therefore, may be confronted by ideas that could in effect be coming from a different writer. We can be surprised, confused, or delighted by the ideas we find in what we have written. Of course, we are quick to claim them as our own; after all, we were responsible for putting them on paper. But we can react to them the way artists can react to their paintings or sculptures, as something *accomplished*, separate from ourselves, stepping-stones to new creations.

The ideas that we create and represent on paper may not be ideas that we ever had before we began to write, but provided we can find in the text what we wanted to say (even at a very global level of intention) or what we are content to think we have said, then we will accept it for what we intended. And when we feel we can do no more with the text, or if we have neither the time nor the inclination to do any more with it, then the review ends, editing may or may not ensue, and we regard the text as done. We have finished with a text (ideally) when we decide that any further change would only detract from it.

BLOCKS

My argument throughout this book is that writing is a natural and frequently productive and satisfying activity. I may also seem to have implied that it usually proceeds easily and fluently. Yet often (with the few inevitable exceptions, of course) we find that writing is inhibited at the times when we most want or need to write. We are afflicted by writing blocks. In the present section of this chapter I first examine the relatively simple question of what the causes of writing blocks might be, and then consider the more difficult question of how such blocks might be removed and the flow of writing initiated or maintained.

Writing blocks may be put into two categories, *procedural* or *psychological*, depending on whether we cannot decide what to write next or we cannot bring ourselves to write anything next. There is I think a third general reason why writing might become difficult at times, and that might be called *physical*. Writing requires far more physical effort than reading, than talking or listening. It may occasionally be the case that we are too tired to write at all, but what is more likely, I think, is that fatigue is a supplementary but critical factor when we are experiencing writing difficulties with a psychological or procedural basis. We are too tired to solve our own problems, especially since overcoming writing blocks frequently requires effort and determination. To struggle for half an hour with an unyielding sentence that is not exactly what we want to say, while we do not know exactly what we want to say, can demand the concentration and stamina of an athlete.

Procedural Blocks

Quite literally, we can be in the position of not knowing what to write next. This need not mean that we have no idea why we are trying to write in the first place, nor that we are incapable of putting words together if we know what to say. The situation can perhaps best be expressed in terms of levels of intention. At a global level we know and can specify very well what we want to write about; and at a focal level we have no trouble putting one word after another—provided we can decide what we specifically want to say. But we are lost at an intermediate level—for example, in deciding the exact direction in which we want a paragraph to go. The situation is similar to the common one of knowing our way around a few streets in a neighborhood of a town we are visiting (a focal level) and understanding very well the relation of the town to the country as a whole (the global level) but having no idea about the relationship of the neighborhood to the town itself (an intermediate level).

This problem of lacking understanding at an intermediate level can occur at any point in a text. It may be particularly acute at the beginning (whether of a letter, a report, a chapter, or an entire book). Often the problem arises because a set of alternatives confronts us without obvious reason for the selection of any particular one; we have no text behind us to direct a decision and can see no particular reason ahead to prefer one alternative to another. This vacillation is intensified at the beginning of texts because the decision made at that time may commit us for the entire text. But a similar dilemma can arise at other places within the text, even occasionally at the end when we cannot find sufficiently persuasive reasons for selecting one conclusion rather than another.

There are several possible reasons for vacillation related to an unwieldy ramification of alternatives in writing. One reason is the packing of too much information into a sentence, into a paragraph even, leaving too many directions in which one might go and too many strands to be followed. There may be digressions into which we have been led by our own developing ideas, and we become entangled in the undergrowth of our own proliferating intentions. One incidental problem almost as disruptive as inability to start writing is inability to stop, even though the composition is taking us further and further from the path we intended to pursue. Writing difficulties are often not so much a matter of having nothing to say as the manipulation of dams and torrents, dams that must be carefully broached after words have built up behind them, and torrents that must be halted or channeled when the words burst through.[3]

Finally, there are uphill and downhill effects in writing that are both procedural and psychological (and therefore provide a convenient bridge to the next section). There are starting difficulties at the beginning of any piece or major section of text, where major decisions (and commitments) have to be made and the number of alternatives is perhaps greatest. After this relatively uphill struggle a freewheeling downhill period may ensue as an end comes in view, clarifying the route to get to that end. But this sudden fluency toward the end of a topic can prove discouraging if we expect it to continue across the boundary into a new section, with its new set of unresolved problems. The momentum is suddenly lost as the threads of focal concentration close themselves off and we are faced once again with decisions to be made at intermediate levels.

Psychological Blocks

The most difficult moment is often the moment when the first words should come. The preparations are complete; paper, pens, desk, and time are organized. We sit pen in hand, awaiting the words, with nothing else to do— and then we think of something else to do. We search for a distraction to release us from the tyranny of the words that might come but have not yet. We even write other words.

It is too easy to dismiss all this as a matter of discipline. Of course, writing requires discipline. Discipline brings the writer to the desk, to the paper, even to the point of writing, but it does not release the words. The cost of discipline may be a reduced probability that words will flow; composition is not enhanced by grim determination. Since there is no single cause of writing reluctance, there is no single cure. But it may help to understand some of the causes.

I am not now talking of the occasions when the writer has nothing to say, even though it may often be the case that the brain requires more time to sort out some ideas. Nor am I talking of procedural problems when the writer cannot decide a direction to take (although psychological factors may inhibit the writer from making the decision; we can take shelter behind our own self-induced problems). I am talking of the case when words should come, and could come, but we refuse to allow them to confront us. We cannot bring ourselves to let words appear on paper.

There are probably two main reasons for this reluctance. The first, which is relatively straightforward, is to do with the magnitude of the task. We may be committing ourselves to a considerable amount of effort, and even risk, and the first few words we put on a page may set a course from which we feel there will be no turning back or even opportunity for second thoughts. This degree of resistance to undertaking the enterprise will increase depending on the perceived magnitude, importance, and probability of succeeding in whatever our aims might be.

The second reason is complex. It is the apprehension that the product of our labors will fail to measure up to some standard. And the reluctance is intensified because this standard is often undefined. The standard need not be the approval of the reader to whom the text is addressed. And approval of an audience does not always generate confidence, whether for the writer of a personal letter or of a best-selling novel. Success on previous occasions may serve only to increase apprehension about failure to achieve success in the future. Nothing can be more inhibiting than success.

But the apprehension may be far more personal. The audience whom we are afraid of disappointing may exist only in our own mind. We are afraid that we will have nothing worthwhile to say—so we do not risk saying anything. This fear has an historical basis. Sitting on the shoulder of many writers is the wraith of a schoolteacher, waiting to jump on every fault of punctuation or spelling, on every infelicity of expression. Writing is so personal and so tangible that we are reluctant to risk displaying ourselves so openly on paper, where we can be questioned on every comma.

One other general psychological reason for writing blocks is simply expressed: habit. Just as we have our habitual and preferred writing materials, our preferred time of day and place for writing, so may we have our habitual and preferred strategies for avoiding it. Avoiding writing is usually much less of an immediate bother than doing it; it requires less effort and less inventiveness. Saying this does not make solving the problem any easier. Habits are not broken simply because we know we have them, or even because we want to break them.

Overcoming Writing Blocks

There is no shortage of ready advice on how to overcome writing blocks from people who ought to know, professional writers. And the advice is always the same: Make writing a daily habit, especially on those days when you least want to write. Banal advice, simple to give and difficult to follow; I can be disparaging about it because it is my advice too, and because it is advice that I have difficulty in following myself.

The "write at all costs, write anything, no matter how irrelevant" is most appropriate to the psychological aspects of writing-block problems, but not to the procedural aspects. Procedural problems arise when we do not know what to say, either because we *have* nothing to say or because we are confronted by too many possibilities. In the latter case the problem is organizational, and is best handled by capitalizing on the particular advantages of written language, its ability to overcome constraints of time and space. Instead of trying to puzzle over and remember alternative constructions in the head, we should put them on paper, where not only can they be inspected but also moved around to be evaluated in different order and different contexts. The difficulty of finding a beginning may be resolved by writing various alternatives, even the most mundane. You may find yourself writing something that takes off for you with a fluency you did not suspect. If you cannot think of anything else to write, write a summary statement of what in general you want to write about (a global intention). These possibilities also apply to blocks that occur at other places in the text—in the middle or at the end. But an alternative solution at these points may lie in not writing anything new at all, but in throwing away. The problem may not be that you do not know what to say next, but that you cannot get there from the last few sentences that you wrote. Inexperienced writers often fail to profit from this further advantage of written language: that anything we produce that is inappropriate or unproductive or simply not what we wished to say can initially, at least, be very easily disposed of. In writing, you can roll back the past.

On the other hand, the procedural problem may be that you do not have anything sufficiently worked out in your head; you are still waiting for inspiration, and no amount of doodling or looking at blank sheets of paper is going to help. There is much to be said for not beating one's head against the wall, and if what the brain requires is time and more incubation, then the brain should at least be given a chance. Take a walk, watch a movie, sleep on the problem; the brain does not always solve creative problems to order, under pressure, or as a consequence of deliberation. If we think the brain might in its own time come up with a spontaneous solution, we should not deny it the time and opportunity. We should learn to trust our own best way of writing.

Waiting for a better opportunity will not resolve the psychological problem, however. If we are reluctant to write because of the real or imagined consequences of writing, then the only solution is to write and be damned. And if the problem is that we have fallen into the habit of avoiding writing, the only solution is to establish the habit of writing, if not by writing a fixed amount at a fixed time every day, then at least by writing every time we sit down to write.

Many professionals recommend writing anything. If you cannot pick up from where you left off, begin by rewriting the last paragraph you wrote. (A useful idea for some people is always to stop at a point where you know you can continue, in the middle of a sentence even.) If you write one sentence and then come to a stop, rewrite the sentence. If you hesitate after a word, rewrite the word, to keep the pen moving while the brain collects itself. In any case, write. Keep a daily journal, keep notebooks. Write about how hard it is to write. Write anything.

But these suggestions may go too far. They may not apply to everyone, certainly not at all times. For me at least, writing can be a way to avoid writing. My problem often is not that I cannot write when I sit at my desk, but that I do not write what I should be writing. My book writing time is when I catch up with correspondence, with miscellaneous writing chores, and with making all kinds of notes and jottings. Sometimes, in order to write, I have to stop writing.

But if I want to devalue, however slightly, a traditional prescription for sufferers from writer's mental cramp, I would also offer two alternatives. The first is: *Do not expect the writing to come out right the first time.* Do not be afraid of the possibility that what you write will fail to live up to your expectations, or those of the schoolteacher on your shoulder. Anything you write can be changed. Anything you write can be thrown away. You have nothing to lose. But if you write nothing in the first place, you have nothing to gain, nothing to change. Most professional writers rewrite and rewrite. They would never publish their first drafts, and they would never publish at all if they did not write their first drafts. It is easier to work at writing on paper than in the mind.

My second suggestion will not help to remove writing blocks at all. It is: *Accept the block*. No one ever promised that writing would be easy. Most writers would testify that writing is work. It may be through the striving that the writing is forged and tempered. Even if a block is purely psychological, a needless apprehension, it may still be better to try to write despite the apprehension (which at least is part of you) than to try to change yourself in the fond hope that a fluent writer will suddenly materialize. All kinds of people write. What distinguishes the writers is not that they have hearts of stone and minds of steel. They probably run the range of anxieties and writing blocks as much as nonwriters. The main difference is that they write. They live with their uncertainties and difficulties, and they write.

Deadlines may help. Many writers agree that deadlines, especially hanging ones, concentrate the mind wonderfully. They can rarely be ignored (or only the rare individual can ignore them). They intensify. Either they magnify the immobilization, so that nothing is written until the pressure is off, or they focus the drive so that in desperation the writing is done. If one is simply indulging in the luxury of having time to spare, then the facilitating effect of a deadline is not difficult to explain. There is a Parkinson's law of procrastination: Unproductiveness expands to fill the time available for wasting. But deadlines have to be imposed and accepted judiciously. The best deadline is perhaps like the bar on the high jump, occasionally a little beyond anything we have ever reached before, never so low that there is shame in falling short but never so high that attainment is impossible.

Now I seek a conclusion. I have written my piece on writing blocks, and in doing so I overcame my own blocks. (Ironically, this section was one of the hardest for me to write, my blocks perhaps defying me to explode them.) What have I learned from my own analysis? I can only repeat the obvious.

Blocks are resolved only by writing, although occasionally the writing may be postponed. Writing may be facilitated if we lower our expectations for what we are likely to produce, initially at least. It is easier to polish and improve something that is already written. Blocks may be necessary—and even if they are not necessary, they may be unavoidable. But they seldom persist indefinitely, and no one as far as I know has ever died of one. Learning to live with writing blocks may be like learning to live with our families or colleagues—easier than trying to change them.

WRITERS AND WRITING

A British "media theorist," Daniel Chandler (1992), has extensively studied the work habits and preferences of many writers. He places them on a continuum ranging from *planners*—who tend to think of communicating ideas which they already have clear in their minds—to *discoverers*—who tend to experience writing primarily as a way of finding out what they want to say. Chandler proposes that extreme planners are relatively indifferent to the medium they employ for writing, while extreme discoverers may be virtually dependent on a particular medium. Chandler has also made a close analysis of the consequences of writing with different kinds of instrument—pens, pencils, typewriters, and word-processors—some of which I refer to in Chapter 11.

Chandler is engagingly adventurous with metaphors, elsewhere characterizing planners as doers, or Mozartians, and discoverers as thinkers, or Beethovians. In a different study, using different metaphors derived from Hayes and Flower (1980), Chandler (1993) asked academic writers which of four descriptions most characterized them. These were: *architects*, who do a lot of planning before writing and revising afterward; *water-colorists*, who usually produce single drafts with minimal revision; *oil painters*, who write down thoughts as they occur to them, organizing and revising later; and *bricklayers*, who usually try to perfect each sentence before moving on to the next. Of the 107 writers in Chandler's sample, 15 reported using none of these strategies and one reported using all four. Most (80 of them) reported just one or two of the strategies—57 were architects, 20 water-colorists, 33 oil painters, and 38 bricklayers. Most of the bricklayers were also architects. Chandler found that all four strategies "worked"—or at least, he found successful professional writers who said they wrote in those ways. By implication—though Chandler is not specific on this point—many of the writers who fitted themselves into one or two categories did *not* belong in the other categories. Bricklayers would probably find it difficult to be water-colorists, and vice versa. All of these matters are of importance in educational contexts, though generally ignored. Writing is not the same for everyone, and expectations that everyone should write in the same way, whether in classroom exercises or under examination conditions, may be unrealistic and inequitable.

(Notes to Chapter 9 begin on page 255.)

10 The Tapestry of Transcription

Apart from the mental activity involved in composing the words we write, the physical act of transcription is complex and demanding. The brain must orchestrate an intricate symphony of muscle movements to ensure that we operate our pencil, pen, or keyboard in a coordinated way, at the same time ensuring that the delicate tapestry that these movements produce contains appropriate patterns of spelling, capitalization, punctuation, and organization on the page.

This is the order in which I shall treat the transcription aspect of writing, considering first the coordination of the physical processes involved and then the kind of knowledge we must have in order to be able to spell. A few concluding remarks on such themes as punctuation, capitalization, and neatness will move me into the more general topics of how all these various aspects of writing are learned.

ORCHESTRATING THE WRITING ACT

Words leave our lips or fingers one at a time, but the brain does not produce them in that way. The brain does not choose one word, then the next, and then the next, deciding what is to come on the basis of what has just been done. Words that will arrive later in the sentence are as important in determining what a particular word will be as words that have gone before.

Each word is an integral part of the entire sentence in which it is embedded, just as (in writing) each sentence has to find its logical place among other sentences in a paragraph and each paragraph must be appropriately positioned between its neighbors on both sides in longer sequences of text. Indeed, the meaning of words in a sentence is inseparable from the meaning of the sentence as a whole; it is no more possible to produce or understand sentences one word at a time, from left to right, than it would be to do so from right to left.

A more technical way of saying all this is that language is *hierarchically organized*; decisions at any level are dependent upon more general decisions at higher (or deeper) levels. Word decisions are embedded in phrase decisions, which are embedded in sentence decisions, which are related to very general meanings and purposes. The brain must activate whole clusters of words (or of potential words) at a time, organize them into groups that are appropriate, and then line them up so that they come out one at a time and in the conventional order.

The same applies to the physical production of each word that we speak or write. When we speak, individual sounds require the precise coordination of delicate movements by widely separated groups of muscles controlling the tongue, lips, jaw, throat, and vocal cords. As the brain dispatches barrages of neural impulses to initiate and terminate these different movements, it must also ensure that the movements proceed smoothly from the configuration the various muscles were approaching at the conclusion of the previous sound and into a configuration that will be appropriate for the initiation of the following sound. To make these smooth transitions, the brain must have information about the position of each muscle group at all times during their operation. As a simple example, the movements of facial muscles to half-open the mouth for a particular sound will be in opposite directions depending on whether the mouth is closed or fully open in the first place. Thus there must be constant *feedback* for the brain in the form of neural information traveling back from the muscles themselves.

To complicate even further, none of these neural impulses either to or from the brain travel at the same rate; they pass along their own particular nerve fibers at different speeds and have different distances to travel. If tongue and lips are to begin a coordinated movement at the same time, the bursts of neural activity controlling them must leave the brain at different times, while the feedback about the position of the tongue and lips at any given time will return to the brain after different intervals. The complexity of putting all this together is doubtless one reason that infants spend a large part of the first months of their lives babbling, getting the feel of making the sounds that they will eventually manipulate to produce the words of their language.

All of these complex problems of coordination and control in what is termed the "serial order of behavior"[1] apply just as much to writing, although different groups of muscles are involved, of course. Now the brain has to coordinate the movements of fingers, wrists, arms, and even shoulders— sending and receiving neural messages over much longer distances. Movements must be integrated in space as well as time (we do not want the pen to go shooting off the page), and also in intensity (we do not want our touch to be so light that the pen leaves no mark or so heavy that it goes right through the paper).

And there is yet a further complication, relevant to both speech and writing. Although muscle movements must be made quickly and precisely, the downstream and upstream neural impulses that coordinate them travel relatively slowly, so the brain does not have time to wait for one set of movements to be completed before the next set is begun.[2] Fingers can be busy writing one letter before the brain learns that the previous letter was finished. The problem is now not so much one of timing as of time; the brain must always plan ahead of what the hands (or vocal apparatus) are doing. It must commit itself to movements, trusting that the muscles will be in the appropriate position. It is not possible to write, type, or speak words one letter or sound at a time without slowing the language we produce to an impossible crawl.

It is easy to see that we do not normally write one letter after another, whether we are using a pen, pencil, or keyboard. As people learn to type (or in the miserable contemporary jargon, acquire keyboarding skills), they make relatively slow progress at first while they strive to locate individual keys. Then there is a sudden spurt of progress as letters are typed not one at a time but in familiar pairs or triplets—*th* together, for example, or *ing*.[3] The brain is not now dealing with the letters one at a time, but in familiar groups. With further practice the typist improves even more as words and short phrases are typed as individual units, with the brain committing itself to the entire sequence before it has begun. There are two common illustrations that experienced typists write in units of a word or more rather than a letter at a time. It is extremely difficult for a skilled typist to type deliberate errors, to type *hte* for *the*, for example. The typist will have to slow down considerably and even then will frequently make the "mistake" of typing *the* correctly. On the other hand, an experienced typist will also occasionally have the frustrating knowledge that a mistake is on the way, that the fingers are going to hit some wrong keys, and yet not have the time to stop them.

These phenomena are not of course unique to writing; musicians will also be familiar with them. Many arpeggios are played so fast that it would be impossible for the brain to execute the individual notes one at a time. Instead the brain organizes rapid sequences of notes in the same way that the musician reads them in the score, as chords extended over time, treating entire phrases as a single unit. Like the typist, the experienced pianist will have difficulty striking unfamiliar sequences of keys and occasionally be helplessly aware that false notes are on the way. Sometimes the order will get mixed up, and keys are prematurely struck for letters or notes that should be two or three ahead. To become proficient at typing or playing a musical instrument it is necessary to develop a repertoire of *integrated movement patterns*, each combining a sequence of individual actions into a longer, smoothly coordinated whole.

Integrated movement patterns are the basis of fluent writing with pen or pencil. Handwriting would not be possible—not if we were trying to compose the words at the same time—if we had to labor along one letter after another. Too much time and too much attention would have to be given to remembering where we were at every moment and to ensuring that each letter occurred in its proper position at the proper time. Instead we write words as wholes, even if we are one of those individuals whose normal handwriting consists of separate letters rather than letters joined together. (An easy way to demonstrate that even the separate letters are being written in practiced groups rather than one at a time is to see how difficult it is to copy words that are written backwards—sdrawkcab nettirw—so that the letters are not in a familiar order.)

Interestingly, integrated movement patterns in writing are not entirely based upon sequences of *muscle* movements that have become habitual, because we can perform the movements with muscles that have never been called on for that purpose before. We can write a reasonable replica of our signature in letters several inches high with a pen clenched between our toes or in our teeth. Try writing a word or two on a card which you are holding against your forehead and you will probably find that you have been writing backwards, in mirror image, as though to be read by an eye peering through your skull and through the card. You are using muscle groups to produce writing in a way you may never have done before. The integrated movement patterns that we have acquired, in other words, are patterns for the *direction* of movements rather than for specific muscular activity. They are *plans* for movements.[4]

All this is very complicated, and possible only because the rapid and precise combinations of plans for movements have been what psychologists call "overlearned" or "automated," which means that they are so highly practiced that they demand little or no conscious attention. We are not aware of the enormous effort that is saved because the brain has done most of the work of planning the complex movements of writing in advance; the effort is largely unconscious.[5] To get an indication of the skill that has been achieved and the gains that can be made we must see how much attention is required, and how much disruption is caused, when appropriate movement patterns are not available. When we see a child (or an adult learning to write an unfamiliar script) laboring over the fundamental problem of forming letter shapes, then perhaps we can appreciate how little attention would be left over for consideration of what is being said.

How is the skill achieved of writing reasonably legible patterns of letters and words without incapacitating slowness? There can be only one answer: through practice. As with all the other coordinated movement patterns we acquire during our lives, like walking, standing, sitting, riding a bicycle, brushing our hair, and cleaning our teeth, very little can be learned by watching other people or listening to lectures. We learn to write—in the sense of making marks on paper—by writing, and primarily by writing when we do not have to worry about spelling, punctuation, or any other aspect of composition or transcription. All these other concerns will distract attention required for the purpose of establishing movement patterns that will become automatic.

There is one other advantage to establishing a repertoire of integrated movement patterns; it helps us to spell. Like writing legibly, spelling correctly is a skill that varies enormously in its achievement from one person to another. Like writing legibly, spelling is a skill that is not highly correlated with other facets of writing ability; the most prolific authors can be almost illegible scribblers and idiosyncratic spellers. Spelling, which can be the second great obstacle to fluent writing, is the subject to which we now turn.

THE WEB OF SPELLING

"Spelling" is another of the ambiguous words of our language. It can refer to what a person does, as when we say "I can't spell many words," but it can also refer to what is done, for example when we say "I don't know the spelling of many words." I begin by considering spelling in the noun sense, particularly the reason letters of an alphabet might be employed to represent written words in English and a number of other languages, and then go on to talk about spelling in the verb sense, the skill of using letters in conventional ways to produce written words.

The Alphabet and Reading[6]

The purpose of spelling is frequently confused, or at least oversimplified, by the notion that written language is speech written down. The idea that writing is speech made visible underlies the belief that reading is a matter of "decoding" spelling into sound, that we read by transforming letters into sounds in the head which we then try to recognize and understand by listening to them, and also the belief that writing is a matter of "coding" speech into spelling. Neither is the case. Speech and writing are alternative and concrete manifestations of the abstraction we call language, and it is no more necessary to translate writing into speech to comprehend what we read than it is adequate to translate speech into writing to write comprehensibly.

To begin with, spellings are themselves not necessary. Consistency is necessary, and spelling facilitates consistency, but many written languages function perfectly consistently and well without an alphabet at all. Chinese and Japanese, for example, employ logographic systems for their written languages. A *logograph* is a symbol that represents an entire word without indicating the meaning of that word pictorially or its sound alphabetically.

Here is an example of Chinese logographic writing, reading from left to right, *(The) man buys (a) big house:*

And here is an example of logographic writing that may be rather more familiar:

$$2 + 3 = 5$$

Logographic writing systems are not defective. Anything that can be expressed in alphabetic writing can be expressed in logographic form also. Indeed, logographic systems have some advantages over alphabetic writing. Because they are not tied to the sounds of a particular spoken language, logographs can be understood by speakers of different languages who would not understand each other's speech. Speakers of only Cantonese or Mandarin could both read the Chinese writing in the previous paragraph, but might not understand each other reading the sentence aloud. It is not even necessary to speak any form of Chinese to read the written language; a group of Harlem youths who had reading problems with written English (possibly because they had become confused by instruction about the way our alphabetic system works) very quickly learned to read Chinese sentences of the kind I have given above, giving their meanings in English of course and learning not a word of spoken Chinese in the process.[7] In the same way speakers of many languages can understand 2 + 3 = 5, even though it might be written by a French person who would not be understood saying "deux et trois font cinq."

Unlike the symbols of mathematics, the characters of logographic writing are not always precise in their meaning. It is sometimes not possible to argue that a particular written symbol represents a specific word in any spoken language. Again, this indeterminacy can be advantageous. The Korean written language has become largely alphabetic, but several thousand logographs have been retained for abstract terms such as "justice," in recognition that their meaning is not well-defined and perhaps needs thinking about. The fact that we can give a name to an idea sometimes gives a spurious suggestion that something specific exists that is being named.

There is no evidence that logographic writing is harder to read. Chinese and Japanese readers can read their texts just as fast as others read similar material in alphabetic script. And there is also no evidence that it is more difficult to learn to read logographic writing. Certainly it is not harder on the memory.

It is not difficult to show that readers of English do not concern themselves with the sounds of letters when they read; words are recognized as wholes, just as we recognize faces or particular makes of automobiles. We do not have the time to pay attention to letters. Reading at the relatively modest rate of 200 words a minute would entail recognizing more than three individual words a second, an average of 15 letters or more a second, with the added complication of trying to discover the appropriate sound for every letter and to blend these sounds together to try to make a recognizable word. The human brain works fast, but not as fast as that. It is much easier for the brain to recognize whole words, and this is what it quickly becomes skilled in doing, recognizing individual words as rapidly and as accurately as it can recognize individual letters.

And this precisely is what the Chinese reader does: recognize whole words at a time. It is not an enormous memory burden to hold in the brain the possibility of recognizing perhaps 50,000 written words on sight. We are able to recognize thousands upon thousands of other shapes, objects, properties, and relationships in our world without any evident strain; we have little difficulty in being able to recognize 50,000 or more spoken words. Readers of English and Chinese recognize the words of their superficially different written languages in exactly the same way, which is the same as the way they recognize cars and trees and faces; as wholes, as distinctive compound shapes.

I am not saying that the letters of the alphabet are not related to the sounds of speech, or even that knowledge of these correspondences is not helpful in reading. But this knowledge, even if a beginning reader could painfully acquire it all, will rarely permit the sounding out of visually unfamiliar words with sufficient precision to make them recognizable as known words in English speech. For a start, there are too many possibilities. There is not a single letter in English writing that does not correspond to more than one sound (or to silence) in speech. In a relatively small sample of 20,000 common words there are over 300 of these correspondences; over 300 different ways in which our 26 individual letters of the alphabet are collectively related to the sounds of English speech. It is scarcely possible to exaggerate how difficult it is for a child to identify an unfamiliar word in written English without any other kind of clue. The common initial letter combination *ho* is involved in no fewer than 11 different pronunciations: hop, hope, hoop, hook, horse, hoist, house, honey, honest, hour, horizon. Letter-to-sound correspondences only look obvious and simple when we know what a word is in the first place. Some other clue is needed, and that clue for the beginning readers of English is the same as for the beginning Chinese reader—the clue of context, which eliminates alternatives in advance. If the beginning reader can get the idea that an unfamiliar word is "horse," "cow," or "donkey," then even a little knowledge of spelling-to-sound correspondences will help; "cow" and "donkey" could not begin with *ho*———. But now, you will notice, there is no question of "sounding out" the entire word.

Thus the beginning reader of English is in the same position as the learner of Chinese; complete initial reliance on someone who can read to identify unfamiliar words, with the need for outside help decreasing rapidly the more the beginner can use context to provide clues to the identification of unfamiliar words. Spelling can provide only supporting evidence for what a tentatively identified word might possibly be.

Why then have an alphabet? If English spelling is as unreliable a guide to pronunciation as I have outlined, and if English readers have to rely on the total visual configuration of written words both for their identification and recognition, why should the English writing system be different from the Chinese? To understand the utility of alphabetic writing systems, we have to consider the matter from other points of view.

The Alphabet and Writing

Writing and reading are not in any literal sense mirror images of each other; they are not opposite sides of the same coin. Rather they are in conflict, since anything that tends to make writing easier usually tends to make reading more difficult, and vice versa. A writer might like to dash off words as they come to mind, but the reader prefers a good deal more organization. The less attention the writer gives to what is written, the more attention the reader must apply in order to read it. Similarly with legibility, the writer must slow down and work harder to make handwriting neater and clearer, while the reader must slow down and work harder when the writing is a scribble. Thus writers and readers do not have the same interests at heart; they are in competition with each other, and the characteristics of our written language might be seen as a compromise between the two. Since so much about writing is more difficult than reading, and since readers do not use or need the alphabet very much, we should consider whether the alphabet serves primarily to help the writer.

Certainly we need all the help we can get when we write. Not only is writing slower and physically more demanding than reading, but the writer has much more work to do than the reader, putting far more detail into every letter, word, and sentence than the reader will ever attend to. Readers can skim and skip; they can ignore the equivalent of every other letter in the text and identify whole series of words at a glance; they may be affronted by an occasional misspelling or punctuation error, but they usually have little difficulty in comprehending what the writer intended despite the faulty spelling or punctuation. And because it is the reader, not the writer, who decides what can be ignored, the writer has to strive for exactitude and comprehensiveness.

Furthermore, writing places a much heavier burden on memory than reading; it takes much more experience and skill to write words than to read them. This is partly because it is far easier to *recognize* something than to *reproduce* it. We can all recognize faces and objects that we could not possibly draw, just as we can enjoy and understand pictures we could never paint. Reproduction requires skill of a quite different order from recognition.

As I have said, the reader of English or of Chinese may identify an unfamiliar written word not simply by asking someone else what it is, but by the use of cues from context. But context will not help a writer wondering how to put the next word on paper. Either the writer knows (rightly or wrongly) how to produce the word, or the writer must ask someone else; no amount of thinking about the context surrounding the word will help. That, at least, is the situation confronting the Chinese writer. At first glance it might seem that our alphabetic system would be of help to the writer of English who need only write down the letters corresponding to the sounds of the particular word. But as I have shown, the sound of an English word is not a particularly good guide to the consistent spelling that readers expect. The worst spellers are the wuns hoo spel fonetikly. The learning problem for the English speller is really not much different from that for the Chinese; either some authority must be consulted— another person who knows how the word is spelled, or possibly a dictionary—or the writer must build up a knowledge of written forms prior to the need for their use.

Clearly, the only solution for the Chinese writer is to remember a stock of logographic forms; for the literate Chinese, many thousands of them. For the writer of English once again, the alphabetic nature of the language might appear to be of some help, but in practice it is not. For the English writer as for the Chinese, the ability to produce the correct form of a word when required is primarily a matter of memorization. If we can spell well, it is because we remember spellings. To understand why this is the case, it will be necessary to examine further the limitations of the alphabet as a system of correspondences between the sounds of speech and the letters of the written language.

There is no way that 26 letters of our alphabet could represent the sounds of speech on any one-to-one basis because there are 40 or more different sounds in any individual speech (the exact total varies with the speaker and the dialect). But even having an alphabet of 40 letters would not make the problem of representing speech any easier because there is always the question: whose speech? Should English spelling represent the speech of people from the North of England or the South; from the southern United

States, the West Coast, or from New England? Should it represent the way they speak now or their pronunciation 50 years ago? Should spelling change as pronunciation changes? At the moment the spelling of English represents no particular dialect, but it can be read by speakers of every dialect. No one really talks the way words are spelled; to do so would be conspicuously ostentatious, and to attempt to make English spelling a closer reflection of one particular dialect would make it harder for everyone else. Not only can written English be read by speakers of a wide variety of dialects around the globe (who certainly could not read so easily if it were written in a variety of dialects) but it can be *written* by speakers of a wide variety of dialects who would certainly have more trouble if they had to spell in different dialects for different readers rather than in one widely accepted conventional way. So one advantage of written English as it is spelled today is that it does not in fact represent the sounds of anyone's spoken language.[8]

A third party has become involved in the matter of spelling, apart from readers and writers. This third party is the printer and the printer's associates, the proofreader and the maker of keyboards for mechanical writing devices. Readers had to tolerate large amounts of variation in spelling for centuries, until the inventions of moveable type and the printing press made possible the mass production of books and papers. When manuscripts were copied by hand, books were sufficiently rare and idiosyncratic that there was little basis or possibility for standardization. But the printing press brought with it the need for "correctors of the press," for proofreaders, whose vocation it was to ensure that words were spelled consistently. Therefore there had to be some standard of correctness, and the printers and proofreaders turned to the makers of dictionaries. In Britain, Samuel Johnson endeavored to establish a conservative tradition by fiat, sometimes leaning on etymology (occasionally false), sometimes on customary "educated" usage, leavening it all with his own idiosyncrasies. Noah Webster later attempted a modest American revolution with only limited success and consistency, like the elimination of *u* from some *-our* words (*favor*, *flavor*) and the abolition of a few double letters (*waggon* to *wagon*).

The trend to consistency in spelling brought with it rules about spelling that had nothing to do with sound. There are *orthographic* rules solely concerned with the internal structure of the orthography, the spelling system, itself. Certain letter combinations are not allowed to occur in words, so that for example, *ie* in *lie* and *die* is changed to *y* in front of *ing* to make *lying* and *dying*, avoiding *iei* combinations. This rule obviously has nothing to do with how words are pronounced, any more than the converse change of *y* to *ie* when an *s* is added, as in *party* and *parties*, because *ys* is not a conventional ending for English words. That, incidentally, is the reason *have*, *love*, and *move* have a nonfunctional *e* on the end; because English words just do not end with a *v*.

(And like *money* and *women*, *love* and *move* have an *o* as their main vowels because early printers decided that *i* or *u* among all those thickets of up and down strokes would be visually confusing.)

But the main reason that English spelling so poorly represents the sounds of English is because representing the sounds of speech is a relatively low priority for spelling in any case; there are two overriding considerations, consistency and meaning. Despite the many apparent anomalies of English spelling for one historical reason or another, a basic principle that always has priority is that words and parts of words with similar meanings should be spelled alike. This is one facet of spelling that makes life easier for both reader and writer, although the extent to which either can capitalize upon it depends upon the number of words already known that can provide a basis for comparison. For the reader, words that look alike tend to have a similar meaning; for the writer, words that have similar meanings tend to be spelled alike. If you are in doubt about the spelling of a particular word, think of the sound or spelling of cognate words. Does *muscle* have a *c* in it? Think of *muscular*, where the *c* is pronounced. Does *bomb* end with a silent *b* and *damn* with a silent *n*? Think of *bombard* and *damnation*. *Critic* and *critical* answer the question whether there is a *c* or an *s* in the middle of *criticize*. The spelling (and sound) of *migrant* and *courageous* suggest the otherwise indeterminate vowel in the middle of *immigrant* and at the end of *courage*, while *horizontal* and *civilian* indicate the unstressed vowel at the end of *horizon* and *civil*.

Meaning would be much less clear if we allowed spelling to follow the idiosyncrasies of speech. Plurals spelled with an *s* (or *es* for orthographic reasons) may represent the sounds /s/ (as in *cats*), /z/ (as in *dogs*), or /iz/ (*judges*). In writing, the past tense is indicated by *ed*, but the related sound may be /t/ (*walked*), /d/ (*hugged*), or /id/ (*handed*). Would it be easier to read or write these important parts of written words if they were consistent with the sounds of speech rather than meaning?

Meaning is the basis upon which many common words are judged to be correctly or incorrectly spelled. There is nothing wrong with the spellings, *eye*, *eight, sum, meet, four, Ann, our*—unless we intend *I ate some meat for an hour*. It would be useless appealing that the first seven spellings represented the appropriate sound in spoken English; spellings are expected to represent appropriate meanings.

I am not trying to argue that written English bears no relation to the sounds of speech. The relationship of spelling to meaning in any case provides an indirect link with pronunciation. But for a number of reasons—including the wide variability of speech sounds, historical accident, and the priority given to meaning—correspondences between letters and sounds are so tenuous that they are at best an inadequate and unreliable guide for both readers and writers. So why have the alphabet? It must have some utility, and since readers seem able to do very well without it, we should look to see the advantages the alphabet might offer for the writer, and for anyone else who might have an interest in writing, notably the printer and the teacher.

Advantages of the Alphabet

A major advantage that I have already cited for the alphabet is that it facilitates consistency. If there is one thing readers (and especially teachers) can tolerate less than misspelling it is erratic spelling, two or three different spellings in the same sentence. As I have said, all aspects of language are conventional, and it is far more important that a convention exists than what a particular convention is. It would not matter if *H* were written like *O*, and vice versa, provided everyone understood and respected the new convention. Any other mutually agreed shapes would do just as well. Spellings are conventions as well. It makes writing much easier to know there is an agreed spelling for every word than to try to think of a spelling that a reader might be able to understand.

The second great advantage that I see for the alphabet might appear paradoxical; that is, it makes words easier to talk about. This also aids consistency because it makes written words easier to teach, learn, write, and remember. It is impossible to give a comprehensive description of most physical objects to anyone unfamiliar with their shapes; imagine trying to describe a horse to a person who has never seen one. It would be hard enough to provide a description sufficient for the person to recognize a horse (as opposed to say a cow or a deer), let alone to enable the person to draw one recognizably. But it is easy to describe the written word *horse* so precisely that not only can it be recognized among thousands of alternatives, it can be reproduced. That description is of course the letters *h-o-r-s-e*. What we call spelling, in other words, can be regarded as a very simple but extremely efficient system for describing how written words look, facilitating both their identification and reproduction. Here then is a major advantage of the alphabet over, for example, the logographic system of Chinese. With a simple repertoire of only 26 named shapes, the structure of every possible written word in the language can be uniquely described.

The possibility of breaking down scores of thousands of written words into 26 basic components greatly facilitates writing (just as the reduction of complex dance patterns to a relatively few basic steps and positions that have names facilitates both dance instruction and choreography). Writers of English do not have to learn how to reproduce the shapes of thousands of written words. They have to remember thousands of *spellings*—which is a matter we shall come to in a moment—but as for physically reproducing these spellings on paper, all that is required is an ability to draw the 26 letters.

This reduction of thousands of different visual patterns to a mere couple of dozen elements is where interests of the printer are again relevant. The matrices for one particular typeface of the alphabet take up very little space in a printer's composing room and from that one typeface the printer might put together an entire dictionary. Consider the space required if every word had to be separately stored. A similar problem arises wherever mechanical (or electric) machines are employed for reproducing writing. Typewriters, typesetting machines, and computer terminals all have keyboards on which the elements of a written language must be represented. No one had too much trouble with the logographic nature of Chinese writing when it was in the hands of scribes. But with the introduction of typewriters it was found impractical to include many of the characters on a conveniently sized keyboard, even with simplified ways of representing parts of characters. Thus the technological demands of printing have played a major part in moves to convert Chinese writing into an alphabetic system (or systems, since written Chinese will then no longer be mutually comprehensible to readers with different spoken languages).

The reduction of the complex patterns of whole words to a relatively small number of component shapes, each of which has a name (A, B, C, etc.), has also greatly simplified the writer's problem of *remembering* how the thousands of words are constructed (apart from the problem of actually writing them). Instead of striving to remember thousands of different shapes, the writer remembers thousands of different spellings.

Spelling and Memory

The difference may not seem significant, but remembering spellings is very much easier than remembering how to draw a similar number of complex visual patterns. Remembering a spelling is not very much different from remembering the name of a person or object—it is a matter of storing away a sequence of sounds. It is hardly less complicated to remember that a particular animal is called a "horse" than to remember that the spelling of "horse" is *h-o-r-s-e*. And that is the basic way in which we remember the spelling of words that we can spell. At the risk of sounding banal, I have to point out that the way we demonstrate our knowledge of the spelling of a particular word is by saying what that spelling is. We do not pause to think how the word sounds (unless we do not know how to spell it), nor do we hesitate over the possible application of particular spelling "rules" (unless again we do not know how to spell the word). But if we *know* how to spell a word (or think we know), out the spelling comes. How do you spell "horse"? *H-o-r-s-e*. How do you spell "cart"? *C-a-r-t*. And that is the way it is, for all of the thousands of words that we can spell (or think we can spell). If we can spell a word, it is because we have remembered the spelling.

The memory problem, as I have said, is not extraordinary. The human brain is perfectly capable of retaining thousands of spellings, just as it retains the sounds of thousands of words that constitute our spoken-language vocabulary. And it is just as well that the brain has this tremendous capacity, for we have no choice. As I have tried to show, the "rules" of spelling, especially when narrowly interpreted to mean the correspondences between the sounds of speech and letters, are a very poor guide indeed. Most of us do remember spelling rules; how could we avoid it when their importance is so often drummed into us at school? And we try to use those rules when we do not have a memory of how a word is spelled. But these rules are highly fallible. They will lead to incorrect spelling more than 50 percent of the time,[9] and they are particularly unreliable for the words we most want to spell, the common words of our language. The "regular" words that conform most to the rules tend to be infrequent words for which we rarely have a need.[10]

Ironically, when adults spell incorrectly the problem is often not so much failure of memory as inability to forget. Usually when we cannot decide how to spell a word, it is not because we cannot think of a spelling but because we think of two or more likely alternatives. We cannot decide whether a particular word ends with *ent* or *ant*; whether it is spelled with a *g* or a *j*. It is not that we have never been corrected on the spelling, or that we have never looked the spelling up in a dictionary; the problem is that the incorrect spelling keeps cropping up alongside the correct one and we cannot distinguish between the two. Spelling the word would be easy if only we could remember which of the alternatives is correct, or forget the alternative that is wrong.

Retaining thousands upon thousands of spellings (right or wrong) is not a problem for the brain, but *learning* them can be. The problem is too complicated to be dealt with adequately at this point, but the underlying issue can be simply stated. Put most concisely, deliberate learning is extremely difficult and unproductive, but incidental learning is so easy and effortless that we are rarely aware that it is going on at all. Children learn thousands of spoken words in their first few years of life, while they are going about their daily business of making sense of the world in general. They do not learn these words by doing exercises or by sitting down and committing them to memory one at a time.

We may learn to spell a few words intentionally, by consultation with dictionaries or by diligently performing classroom exercises, but most people who read and write know *thousands* of spellings, probably tens of thousands, (and the vast majority of these are *correct*). Where does all this knowledge come from? As I demonstrate in Chapter 12, there can be only one answer—from reading. Just as we learn how words are pronounced by hearing them spoken in meaningful ways by people around us, so we learn spellings by encountering them in meaningful contexts when we read. (I must be very clear here—I am not saying that reading guarantees spelling ability, but that spelling ability depends on reading.)

The practice of writing also gives us a completely different possibility for remembering the spelling of words, one that does not involve sounds at all. As I said in the section of this chapter on the physical process of writing, the only way the brain can orchestrate the complex movements involved in using a pencil, pen, or typewriter is to have them planned in advance. The brain does not decide to write one letter at a time, but rather whole groups of letters, often entire words, which it produces as integrated movement sequences. It is these integrated movement sequences—muscle memories, so to speak—that provide a completely independent alternative resource for remembering how to write words correctly.

If you are unsure about how to spell a word, if one certain sequence of letters does not pop out of your mind as you think about how the word might be spelled, write it. Provided the movement sequence is itself not habituated to an incorrect spelling, then your doubts may be resolved. We do not usually pause to think about spelling as we write. Your muscles may remember only one alternative, hopefully the correct one, while your brain, laboring with possible spellings, remembers two.

And writing a word we are unsure of permits one other contribution from our knowledge as readers; we know how words are supposed to *look*, and can often tell at a glance whether a spelling we have attempted is right or wrong.

On Neurotic Attitudes Toward Spelling

Spelling is one of the great phobias of our time. Not only is there constant national concern over declining "standards" of spelling, but many people, including many teachers, are needlessly convinced that they are poor spellers themselves—and feel ashamed of the fact. Spelling ability, for reasons unknown except perhaps the possibility that it is so immediately evident whenever anyone is called upon to write, has been widely adopted as an infallible sign of writing ability, educational attainment, intellectual potential, and social worth.

But there is no evidence that spelling ability has been falling over the years. There have been complaints about the decline in young people's competence in spelling and other aspects of literacy for over a hundred years. The actual success of schools in teaching literate behaviors has probably increased, but because so many more people have been staying longer in school, and entering college, test score averages have been kept down by the inclusion of individuals who in the past would have been outside the school system and not included in the count. There is also no evidence that spelling ability is correlated with other aspects of educational achievement, with intelligence, or social value. Certainly it is not related to any particular method of teaching. In fact the only thing that spelling *is* correlated with is reading (Krashen, 1989; Nagy, Herman, and Anderson, 1985). People who read a lot tend to be better spellers than people who read rarely. People who read a lot also tend to be better readers, writers, and academic achievers in general, an important point to which I shall return when learning is the topic.

In fact, as Krashen (1991) has pointed out, most people who condemn themselves for being poor spellers are in fact good spellers—the problem is that they are not *great* spellers. The "demons" that plague most of us, that we seem quite incapable of learning correctly, are few but conspicuous, a persecuted visible minority. I have noticed when talking with groups of teachers that not only did many of them claim they could not spell well—but they could tell me, almost defiantly, the words they could not spell. They remembered the words they spelt incorrectly, a miserable few among the thousands of words which I knew from their writing that they could spell correctly. Foolishly, I used to ask these teachers why they did not learn to spell the words they knew they could not spell, so that they could be "great" spellers. I say foolishly because the problem was not that the teachers had not tried to learn the correct spelling of their demons. Like most of us, they had constantly checked the dictionary to ascertain a correct spelling, and even practiced by writing out correct spelling twenty times or more. Yet the next time they needed to spell the word, they had to go to the dictionary again—because they could not stop remembering incorrect spellings. It took some time for us to work out that the teachers did not have a learning problem—they had learned too much. They *had* learned correct spellings, but they had learned incorrect spellings as well, and every time they wanted to write a demon word they remembered the correct and the incorrect spellings together. They had a *forgetting* problem—which is another kind of problem altogether. The human brain is very good at learning (even at learning incorrect spellings) and very poor at forgetting (especially things that would be best forgotten—like the "fact" that we are poor spellers).

PUNCTUATION AND OTHER CONVENTIONS

Punctuation and spelling have much in common—in addition to the difficulty they present to many learners and teachers. Both are highly arbitrary and conventional, have less to do with the sound of spoken language than is frequently supposed, and may be more of an aid to writers than is generally thought.

The importance of punctuation is greatly overrated. Early Greeks managed to write and read the first Western alphabetic language without periods, spaces between words, or capital letters (or rather without lowercase letters), all introduced by the Romans as they roughly adapted for their own Latin the writing system they had captured from the Greeks. Other punctuation marks with which we are familiar did not appear for centuries, and many other written languages today function without question marks, commas, apostrophes, capitals, or paragraphs. The first recorded occurrence of the word "punctuation" (in its grammatical sense) in English was in 1661. There is no record of a written language ever causing confusion by lack of punctuation. Indeed, where punctuation has been introduced in recent years, for example in Arabic and Chinese, it is as a consequence of contact with European conventions, perhaps because Europeans were disturbed by the absence of punctuation.

Punctuation and Speech

Like alphabetic spelling, the punctuation of English was originally related to the way the spoken language sounds, at least according to widespread belief. But like spelling, punctuation does a rather poor job of representing how speech actually sounds, and it is hard to see how it could be expected to do much better than it does.

The notion, for example, that periods represent relatively long pauses in speech and commas represent relatively shorter ones, just does not hold up. Speakers often pause longer within sentences than between them, either for emphasis or because they are not sure what to say next. Medieval grammarians introduced the period and comma into their texts to indicate breathing pauses, but this was for writing intended to be chanted and was more in the nature of musical notation than a guide to expression. The longest pauses in conversational speech usually occur where we would never place punctuation in writing, between an article or an adjective and the immediately following noun as we struggle to decide upon the next um-er-er-word. It is doubtful indeed whether our written language would be easier to read if we placed periods, colons, semicolons, and commas in the same positions where pauses of various duration occur in speech. And it would be circular to object that the incidental hesitations of speech are irrelevant because pauses should reflect punctuation when speech is "properly produced." Such an argument refers the whole matter back to writing again, to the not uncommon argument that when speech and writing do not closely correspond in some way, writing represents the ideal of what speech should be.

Just as the marks of punctuation do very little to indicate where pauses occur in speech, they give relatively few clues to intonation. The period marking the end of a sentence does not even indicate whether the voice should be rising or falling in pitch, a decision that depends on what one is trying to say and on the sentence that follows. Almost all of the nuances of intonation within sentences occur between commas or in sentences without commas; the commas themselves do not indicate how words should be read aloud. The correct placement of stress in the sentence *John ran to the bank* depends on whether it is asserted that *John* (rather than anyone else) ran, whether he *ran* (rather than walked), whether he ran *to* (rather than from), whether to *the* bank (rather than to any bank) and whether to the *bank* rather than to the butcher's. Emphasis could be placed on any of the five words in the sentence, representing at least five marked differences in meaning, yet none of this is indicated by the punctuation. On the other hand, the placement of stress can be clearly indicated without resort to punctuation (and without resort to underlining or any other artificial aids to emphasis), simply by providing a relevant context. Thus in *Peter called the police and John ran to the bank* the word *John* receives stress, while in *Peter strolled but John ran to the bank* the word *ran* is stressed. The reader's interpretation of the writer's intention determines how the sentence will be read, not the punctuation. Indeed, readers do not need punctuation to represent intonation; they can get that information from the context and from their prior knowledge of the sound patterns of English.

Punctuation does not directly indicate how texts should be read aloud, either with respect to pauses or to intonation. What then does punctuation represent, and does it have any utility to the reader?

Punctuation and Meaning

An alternative explanation is that punctuation is related to the *grammar* of written language. This is true, but only to the extent that grammar is related to meaning. As with spelling, the consistency of punctuation is determined mainly by the *meaning* of what is being expressed rather than by the sounds of speech.

The capital letter and period (or question mark or exclamation mark) that begin and end every sentence in written English might appear to have a purely grammatical function, except that sentences themselves can only be defined with respect to meaning. Generally a sentence is defined as a sequence of words that make complete sense or express a complete thought, definitions that require a good deal of qualification but are evidently concerned with the meaning of what is being expressed rather than grammatical structure. The alternative definition of a sentence, that it begins with a capital letter and ends with a period, question mark, or exclamation mark, is again circular, and also not always correct. The sequence *Mr.* in the sentence *I saw Mr. Jones* begins with a capital letter and ends with a period, but it is not in itself a sentence. (My example may appear to be rather contrived and of limited applicability, but so then are most examples used to argue the logical necessity of punctuation.)

Everything seems to support the advice commonly given to students that in order to punctuate a passage it is necessary first to understand it; punctuation is primarily related to meaning. The use of question marks, exclamation marks, and quotation marks is determined by the intention behind the words in the sentence, and so is the capitalization of proper names. In only a few cases, such as the apostrophe in possessive forms like *John's*, does punctuation seem to perform a purely grammatical function, a function that in this instance is not required (and not missed) in speech.

Punctuation largely reflects the *structure* of meaning in written language, providing a visible spatial framework for the sense of what is being said. It marks out the connected and embedded meanings in text, tracing how an argument or narrative is progressing—indicating where a particular train of thought comes to an end, where there has been a digression, and where an incomplete thread is picked up again.

Not all punctuation represents meaning, but that which does not reflect meaning also has nothing to do with speech either but is a matter of convention within the writing system itself—a convention observed more for the sake of consistency than for any other reason. I am referring to such aspects of punctuation as the capital letters at the beginning of lines of poetry, the commas that occur when there are two, three, or more adjectives in a sequence (as in this phrase), and the apostrophe to indicate where letters have been omitted in contractions, as in *don't* and *I've*.

Punctuation in fact is rarely a necessity for reading; it does little to tell readers anything they are unlikely to know already. In some contexts punctuation is even regarded as a *source* of ambiguity; legal documents generally try to avoid it. Punctuation is so redundant in English that readers can almost always detect when it is wrong and replace it when it is omitted. I am not referring to such esoteric questions as whether a colon or semicolon belongs at a particular point, or whether dashes are more appropriate than parentheses on certain occasions. Where there is room for dispute on such matters it usually does not make a difference to meaning which of the alternatives is chosen; the argument is about a convention rather than an interpretation. I am referring to the fact that even if the punctuation is radically—wrong for example in the present, sentence the reader can usually tell where the punctuation ought to be. If the reader can put the punctuation in its proper place, then the reader does not *need* the punctuation. Punctuation merely confirms what the reader already knows; the reader may be disconcerted when punctuation ? occurs in; places where it should not be, but the reader would have very little difficulty if there were no punctuation at all certainly not once the reader became accustomed to the punctuation not being there.

Sheer unfamiliarity has a great deal to do with the minor difficulty sometimes experienced when punctuation is absent or incorrect. Readers *expect* punctuation to occur in appropriate places. But they do not often need the punctuation. in the same way it can only be unfamiliarity i think that makes readers hesitate a little over the absence of capital letters in expected places; despite e. e. cummings and modern display graphics we expect to see ROME or Rome but not rome. But we obviously do not need the distinction between capital and small letters because we can EASILY READ WORDS WHEN THEY ARE ALL IN CAPITAL LETTERS. It is just a matter of what we have become used to.

Readers do not need quotation marks to indicate when they are reading reported speech, nor do they need the commas whose necessity is so often thought to be demonstrated by the following illustrations:

(1) The thief said the policeman was lying

(2) The thief, said the policeman, was lying

(3) "The thief," said the policeman, "was lying."

(4) The thief said, "The policeman was lying."

It is true that there is a possible difference in meaning between sentences (1) and (2) and an obvious one between (3) and (4) which only the punctuation indicates, but that is because the sentences occur out of context and in contrast. If the unpunctuated sentence (1) were produced for any meaningful reason (apart from the present illustrative purpose of examining language itself) either the context would dispel any ambiguity or it could be removed by a simple rearrangement of words. Ambiguities can always occur and be removed in language quite independently of punctuation. The fact that we can usually see where quotation marks belong again indicates that they are not really necessary. Even a written language as close to English in its punctuation as French manages without our intricate mechanisms of quotation marks. In French, example (3) would be written

(5) <<The thief, said the policeman, was lying.>>

indicating that some direct speech is present but that not every word between the marks is actually being quoted. The reader is expected to be able to decide which words are being quoted and which are commentary. But then, every speaker of English can do that with spoken language. If sentences (3) and (4) were read aloud, we would not expect the reader to tell us where the quotation marks occur.

Punctuation, in other words, is a matter of convention rather than necessity. Readers do not really need it, but they expect it to be there. As I argued for spelling, the *consistency* of the convention is probably more important—and logical—than its particular nature. Readers can use punctuation to confirm their interpretation of what they are reading; they need not worry as much as they might otherwise do that they might be making a mistake. This possibility is consistent with the more general view that reading always involves anticipating what the writer is likely to do. If readers find what they expect in text, then they are content that they understand. But if readers are surprised by what they find, if they encounter words or punctuation that they really did not expect, then they will suspect that they do not fully understand what they are reading.

The possibility that punctuation serves primarily to confirm for readers that an interpretation is probably correct may explain the frequently noted phenomenon that a good deal of English punctuation occurs *late*. The question mark cannot tell a reader that a question is coming because it does not appear until the end of the sentence (just as commas come at the end of phrases). Such punctuation gives little indication about where a reader is going but shows clearly where the reader has been. Punctuation, in other words, is more a matter of landmarks than of signposts.

Punctuation and the Writer

There remains the question of the possible value of punctuation to writers. Is punctuation just an unavoidable nuisance, a courtesy that writers have to provide for readers, or does it have a utility for writers as well? If my conjecture about the landmark nature of punctuation is correct, if it serves for looking back rather than for looking forward, then punctuation may indeed be of use to writers; it can enable them to keep track of what they have already written while engaged in the relatively laborious task of writing more. Punctuation, in other words, may be the writer's way of keeping in view, or easily accessible to the eyes, the structure of the text that is being constructed.

I am not suggesting that anyone should deliberately make punctuation a primary concern while striving to develop ideas on paper. Punctuation, like spelling, neatness, and other aspects of transcription, can usually be cleaned up in editing when the delicate work of composition has been largely completed. But some rough punctuation may occur in the free flow of composition in any case, left behind as unthinkingly but self-evidently as footprints in sand. The physical effort put into punctuation, especially when writing with a pencil or pen, might provide some indication of what punctuation actually means to a writer. A period may be quite deliberately bored into the paper during reflection upon the completion of a sentence (and possibly the reorganization of thought for the next). Alternatively, a period may be thumped into the paper with a satisfying flourish, indicating relief at having reached at least a temporary remission in the effort of composition. Commas, on the other hand, seem often to require a lighter touch, suggesting just a passing interruption of the flow of words. And the exclamation point may be nothing more than a writer's own breathlessness at what has been written down!! I do not usually find that exclamation marks help me when I read and

I avoid them in my own writing, but I often put them in the margin as I read as my own mark of pleasure or surprise at something someone else has written.

It should not be too difficult to get some idea of the extent to which punctuation is helpful to writers, but so far the role of punctuation seems to have been taken pretty much for granted, and not, I think, for very good reason. One problem discouraging the researcher may be that to some extent punctuation can appear idiosyncratic. No one has complete freedom; we are not permitted to scatter periods or quotation marks across the page at random. But there is a wide range of variation from one writer to another in the relative numbers of commas, colons, and semicolons used. Some writers—like the present author—scatter dashes all over the page, while others are more inclined (from time to time) to parentheses, or manage without these marks of digression at all. To some extent these evident differences among writers reflect stylistic preferences; not so much for the punctuation itself as for the kinds of sentence structure that demand particular marks of punctuation. Some writers just do not produce long sentences that require breaking up with subsidiary punctuation. Getting used to punctuation patterns may be one part of the sometimes difficult period of "settling down" to a new book that readers often experience.

Punctuation can be a problem both for learning and for teaching, perhaps further indication that punctuation has little intrinsic logic or necessity. The "rules" tend to be complex in their application, and it is not clear how easily they can be learned or appropriately applied simply by rote memorization. It may be the case that most experienced writers punctuate relatively well (with the possibility of exceptions acknowledged), but whether this is because knowledge of punctuation makes for good writing or because experience in writing leads to a tacit learning of the use of punctuation is an open question.

The Meanings of Neatness

There are several subtle reasons for the usual expectation that writing should be neat and that it should respect other conventions concerning margins, indentation, and the spacing and straightness of lines—apart from the most apparent one of legibility. Legibility is the bottom line of a complex structure of conventions concerning the appearance of text; writing can often be perfectly readable yet unacceptably untidy. What is acceptable depends on whom we are writing to and what we want to convey.

To a friend, alterations and occasional errors are acceptable; indeed, too much polish can be regarded as pretension or coolness. In a business letter, crossing out would be regarded as impolite, no matter how clear the meaning. But in a job application, neglect of conventions may be interpreted either as ignorance or, worse, a radical rejection of authority. And to someone who claims a higher status than ours, even a casual untidiness might be taken as a direct challenge. It may be interesting to reflect upon why teachers so often insist on neat work.

Neatness, in other words, is a matter of register. It tells readers something about how a writer perceives them, and it also says something about how writers perceive themselves. Neatness may not be the most important convention of writing—and word processors may be making it less of a concern for writers, at the cost perhaps of a certain blandness. But like all conventions, the *appearance* of what we write plays an inescapable part, whether we choose to respect it or ignore it.

(Notes to Chapter 10 begin on page 256.)

11 The Tools of the Trade

Many kinds of writing equipment will be considered in this chapter, beginning with the venerable instruments that we can hold in our hands, like medieval scribes, to make marks directly on paper—the pencil and pen. But the writing, printing, and publishing landscape is dominated today by the computer—a device hardly mentioned in the first edition of this book. Thus the bulk of this chapter will be concerned with electronic "word processing." After a general review of writing instruments and accessories, I examine three aspects of word processors—their utility in helping writers to write, their relevance in teaching writing, and their potential to bring about new kinds of writing and reading.

THE EQUIPMENT AT HAND

On most of the occasions when I have referred to the act of writing in this book, I have talked in terms of the pen. But the reference has been largely figurative—a metaphor that is rapidly becoming as dated as that of the quill. While some writers can compose with only pencils or pen, others need typewriters, a few like to dictate, and a growing number rely on the electronic services of a computer—the word processor. Every tool has its advantages and its disadvantages. Some differences are profound, others trivial, but all are important because writing is such an individual matter. Taste in writing equipment can be as varied and as personally significant as taste in clothes.

For some writers, a pencil might be the preferred instrument because it is small, light, transportable, and usually accessible; its marks are easily erased, there are no smudges, and nothing has to dry. A pen or typewriter, on the other hand, might be considered more desirable because of their relative permanence; there is a certain finality about the marks they make. And many writers prefer substantial pens because of the *feel* of them, and perhaps even for their aura and the rituals that accompany them. Not for such writers the utilitarian mug full of throwaway ballpoints; they crave the elegant solidity of a fountain pen, with its constant need for care and for cautious refilling from that traditional reservoir of words, the ink bottle.

One problem with trying to write fast with pencil or pen is that the letters and words quickly become illegible; one has to slow down. When typing at the limit of one's ability, the spelling and punctuation may suffer, but at least the letters are clear. Typing can be faster than handwriting, a little closer to the speed of speech. Faster still is dictating, a difficult technique for many people to learn, perhaps because it lacks immediate feedback. It is much easier to look back through sheets of paper than for a stenographer to recover a particular passage of dictation or for material to be found and played back on a tape recorder. And it is difficult to reorganize or edit material on tape or in a shorthand notebook. Nevertheless, a few writers dictate prolifically—or compose so prolifically that they have to dictate, writing without ever making a mark on paper.[1]

While the typewriter has the relative advantage of speed and neatness, it suffers from orientation problems. The typewriter forces writers to compose in the directions in which it is designed to operate, from left to right and one page at a time. It is not easy to erase or insert text while the paper is in the machine, or to put lines down the side of the page or a circle around a part of the text, with arrows indicating a transposition of that part to somewhere else.

Word processors combine many of the advantages of the typewriter and the pen or pencil—the speedy and legible production of characters, an easily accessible visual display of selected segments of text, and the possibility of easily inserting comments, and erasing, adding, or transposing anything from individual letters to entire paragraphs or more, followed by effortless storage, retrieval, and printing. The worst errors of computers, short of power or "memory" breakdowns, result from human negligence. Computers are still not very forgiving of user inattention or failure to follow their electronic conventions.

The research of Chandler (1992, 1993) confirms that for anyone who has been willing to switch from pen and pencil to typewriter, the word processor is likely to be found even more congenial. Typewriters today seem a transitional breed of instrument, terminally twitching to assert life by becoming more like computers with display windows, easy erasure, and memory. But simpler and more traditional devices like pencils and pens are surviving, as paper survives, in their own right and as necessary adjuncts to electronic text processing. The attraction for many may be largely nostalgic, but just as the almost omnipresent influence of television does not appear to be making reading obsolete, so even the most dedicated computer hacker may still be found with a pocket full of pens.

Because erasure and insertion are such important aspects of writing for many people, I must include in a list of the tools of writing not just marking instruments and paper but also erasers, correcting fluids and tapes, scissors, paper clips, staplers, paste, clear adhesive tape, and blocks of stick-on tabs. Other important accessories include all the different scraps of paper, index cards, and notebooks that can be used to address reminders to oneself concerning things to be written or already written. Different colors of paper and ink can be used to indicate separate parts or different stages of development of a text, and different colored folders to contain it all. Dictionaries and other reference works are often also required, together with supplies of coffee and other aids to composition. Two indispensable tools for many writers are a large work space on which all these impedimenta can be spread (including often a supplementary desk or table surface and a swivel chair), and perhaps most importantly, a large wastebasket, if not a floor, for the disposal of pieces of paper that are no longer required. I mention all of these items that might otherwise appear obvious or trivial because so often they are lacking from classrooms (and homes) where students are expected to compose fluently.

In listing alternative means of making marks on paper I have avoided saying which is "best." Almost all writers have idiosyncratic preferences, many to an extreme degree. Most favor a particular kind of writing instrument—pen, pencil, typewriter, tape recorder, word processor, or amanuensis. Some will type (or dictate) a rough draft but write the finished manuscript in longhand; for others it is the reverse. Among pencil users, some prefer pristine instruments with every centimeter of their original length, others are happier with the short and stubby. Tastes range between sharp pointed and blunt, soft lead or hard, with eraser or without, chewed or unchewed, yellow or blue, or any combination of the above. Some writers prefer particular kinds of paper, particular books as desk companions, facing a window or back toward it. Some work best alone, others in company; some in the morning, others in the evening or through the night; deadlines help some and dismay others. Some need a special place for writing, an ivory tower; others can write anywhere, on beaches and in the bath, in kitchens and laundries, on aircraft, buses, and subway trains.

The idiosyncratic habituation of writers to preferred tools and surroundings continues with computers. People settle in to the software that they use, to the particular word processing or spreadsheet program that they are accustomed to, and find it difficult to adapt to any other, even to "upgrade." They may prefer to learn two entirely different programs for different purposes than a slightly different alternative for the same purpose. This is not to be explained (or explained away) by a simple reference to "habit"; there is no compelling logical or physiological reason why we should not develop alternative ways of doing the same thing. In fact, having a "backup" system might seem to have considerable evolutionary advantage. The human difficulty of adjusting to the idea that there might be more than one way, even more than one best way, to accomplish something, seems to be more of a *reluctance* than a disability, another illustration of the significance of conventions in writing and in everything else. We expect there to be one particular way to do everything we do, and may have great difficulty in acknowledging any other.

In the study cited in the previous chapter, Chandler (1992) found that only four of the 107 academic writers that he interviewed used typewriters (and they were all in the Arts Faculty); 82 reported writing directly on word processors on some occasions if not all (and they were predominantly members of the Science Faculty). Only nine never used word processors, and only four wrote by dictating. Of the frequent word processor writers, 31 were also frequent users of pens and pencils, although another 39 said they rarely used pens and pencils. There were 33 who used pen or pencil frequently but were not frequent word processor users. The "water-colorist" writers (who did little revising) favored handwriting most, and the "oil painters" (who revised most) favored it least. The main objection to word processors, from people who used them and people who did not, was a "sense of restiveness" from having the text on a monitor.

It is impossible to say what will be best for any individual at any particular time. I have seen no evidence, in published research or in my own classroom observations, to suggest that children or older students *should* begin their writing careers with pencils or other hand-held writing instruments. But I have also seen no evidence that beginning to write on a word processor is the only way to go, although most children take computers in their stride, and the earlier they are introduced to electronic life, the more naturally it seems to come to them.

Writing is often a highly personal and emotionally charged activity, and consequently elicits deeply rooted habits and even superstitions. We all work best in circumstances that seem to have worked best for us before. It is perhaps easy to argue that many writerly idiosyncrasies are indulgences and should be unnecessary; that if there is something to be written and a person can write, then that person should not need a special kind of space, paper, pen, coffee mug, or heightened emotional tension. But for the individual the idiosyncrasies may be crucial supports for writing. Writing is a demanding business; writers challenge and expose themselves, making a commitment to what may be a long period of effort and frustration with no guarantee that the final product will live up to their own or other people's expectations, or whether indeed it will ever be finished, and if so whether it will reach the audience for whom it is intended. We should be slow to discourage anything that makes venturing out on the risky seas of writing more supportable.

WORLDS OF WORD PROCESSING

Though the term "word processing" is both ugly and inexact, it is perhaps appropriate that we have a new expression for the centuries-old practice of writing. The neologism may encourage us to adopt fresh perspectives in looking at developments more profound than anything else that has happened to written language since the invention of moveable type for the printing press, and to be ready for further rapid but unpredictable innovations. Word processors and their associated technologies constitute great possibilities, and possibly a few threats, to writers, teachers of writing, and to written language itself. I consider each of these in turn—the electronic writer, the electronic classroom, and the electronic text.

The Electronic Writer

The most apparent yet least celebrated benefit of word processors is their combination of speed and neatness. Touch a key with a fingertip, and a perfectly formed character appears on the screen, right where we want it to be, ready to be transformed into an equally immaculate figure printed on a sheet of paper. Press the same key again and there is an identical character lined up next to the first. Keep a finger on the key, and there is a regimented row of these characters, more alike than peas in a pod. Press alternative keys, and these characters will adopt any size we want in any position that we choose. Spaces can be inserted, along with numerals, and a variety of other symbols from ampersands to asterisks. With the appropriate equipment, it is easy to change type from upright to italic, from regular to bold, from small to large, from plain to fancy. With a little prior arrangement, a smorgasbord of type fonts and international orthographies becomes available.

This is *vast* power, an enormous saving in concentration and effort and an immeasurable increase in precision and utility. Never has it been so easy for people to express themselves and to communicate in writing (or, for that matter, in the visual and auditory arts and in mathematics); it is the current end of the road that began with the laborious incision of depressions in rocks with hammers and chisels. What we take for granted is a milestone. If we watch children, we can see how they respond to the power of producing letters and language at the touch of a finger, as magical as producing notes from a musical keyboard. One of the hardest parts of writing is—or was—the production of individual letters of a conventional size, shape, and consistency. The task of learning and perfecting handwriting still remains, but it can at last be separated from the exigencies of composition.

And equally as important as the power to produce written characters, singly or in massed array, is the ability to erase them, without a trace. No longer need a page be ruined by a slip of the finger. Exacting readers (or writers) need no longer confront rashes of rubbings out and crossings through. And even erasures can be erased. If on reflection we decide that we prefer to retain something that we have removed, we can get it back again. (There are limits, of course, but these are set by constraints of particular software programs and of human attention. There is no reason why everything we erase should not be retained for as long as we want—we just open an "erasures" file.)

There are at least three other major classes of delights for acclimatized word processor users. The first is the ability to *search* at high speed backward and forward through the text, to find a particular point or to check whether something has already been said. The second is the ability to *move* text around, individual letters or extended series of paragraphs, so that writers can change—or contemplate changing—the order in which things are said. The third is to *store* material away; to clear the decks for current concerns, yet to be able to retrieve whatever you need whenever you need it—all with almost lightning rapidity.

Most professional writers—and doubtless many students—appreciate the fact that word processing programs include an "on-line" spelling checker that can supply individual spellings on demand and rapidly scan entire documents for errors, and also a thesaurus that will almost instantly suggest synonyms and antonyms for whatever word the writer has in mind—and often provide a lively spur to the imagination for further ideas and their expression. Grammar checkers are constantly being refined, and though they may never guarantee that every document will be free of grammatical infelicities, they can alert writers to aspects of composition that might deserve attention. The marriage of compact disc technology with computers means that the contents of entire encyclopedias are open to immediate inquiry by writers, with full-color illustrations and sound capabilities, as are a host of other reference works from atlases and directories to specialized dictionaries and the latest fluctuations of the stock exchange.

There are other word-processing attributes that I could expound upon at length, but this section is not intended to be an encomium to the electronic age. So I merely note for the record the facilities offered by "desktop publishing," "graphic" capabilities for pictures and other kinds of illustration, alternative and preset text layouts, and printing options for all the colors of the rainbow, all of a quality that would have amazed professional printers and designers a generation ago.

It might be objected that anything that makes the transcription side of writing faster and easier can also make the composition side of it sloppy and graceless. There are people who argue that the braking constraints of writing by hand lead to more considered expression (e.g., Emig, 1978). But except for peculiar kinds of mechanical error that sometimes slip through in the final product, I don't think anyone has ever claimed or will be able to claim the ability to *detect* whether a particular text has been composed by hand or on a word processor.

If I had to express in a few words just one great boon that computers offer writers, even more than easing the physical demands of writing, I would say it is *the ease with which writers can change their mind.* This open invitation to second thoughts on word processors not only means increased opportunity and encouragement to think while writing, but facilitation of the ultimate demands of writing: revision and editing.

The word processor can do much to mitigate the internal conflict referred to in Chapter 3, where the competition for attention between the demands of composition and transcription was discussed. My suggestion at that time was the obvious one that writers attend to the demands of composition first, leaving such transcription concerns as spelling, punctuation, grammar, and neatness till later. The word processor can automatically take care of much of these concerns, facilitating composition and allowing easy return to the text to take care of spelling, punctuation, and the final organization and revision.

Computers, which once seemed the most isolated of work environments, have now contributed to opening up the world perhaps as much as jet aircraft and television. Through *local area networks*, writers in different rooms or even in different towns can work collaboratively with each other, each seeing on a personal monitor a document that is shared, and each contributing to the text. On a more extended basis, through electronic mail (E-mail) and electronic "bulletin boards," people across the globe can write to each other, leave messages, exchange ideas, participate in dialogues, overhear debates (with the participants' permission), and generally become part of communities of individuals with similar interests.

I should not neglect to note the almost mesmerizing delight that a word processor can exercise for those who fall within its spell. For anyone who has a substantial amount of correspondence, there can be simple but profound pleasure in putting a long and complex address into an "address book," knowing that it will never have to be typed again, on a letter or on an envelope, but that it is always on call, waiting to be beckoned like the Genie of the Lamp, and able to reproduce itself an infinite number of times, like the brooms of the Sorcerer's Apprentice. None of this guarantees *better* writing, of course; in fact the sheer *facility* of producing text on computers can doubtless lead to sloppy and unimaginative work, but so can writing with a pencil. Possibly anything a writer might want to do the word processor can help to do, more or less efficiently depending on the attitudes and discipline of the writer. And no doubt other possibilities remain to be discovered that writers and computer systems designers have not yet imagined.

Of course, I have been talking about the value of word processors to people who know how to use them. All of this virtuosity has to be learned, and getting started can be time consuming and onerous, particularly for anyone apprehensive about the mysteries of the microchip world. Procedures are not always simple and rarely intuitive. Instruction manuals tend to be voluminous, replete with jargon, and otherwise difficult to understand. Other people, particularly experienced users, may find it difficult to explain what beginners need to know, and will overload them with bewildering advice and information. It is a bit like swimming; the best way to learn is usually a little bit at a time, with progressively deeper immersion as confidence is gained, never getting out of one's depth, either in the element to be mastered or in the instruction to be understood.

Despite my obvious enthusiasm, I have to declare that, in general, research has failed to show any improvement in the quality of writing that is done on a word processor. And there are disadvantages. There are well-known problems of eye strain and back strain, and possible stresses of other nerve and muscle groups. People probably walk around less, and look around less, working with word processors than with pencils or pens. Keyboards and other pieces of equipment are excessively intolerant of dust, spills, crumbs, and other debris. Power failures and human slips of attention can lead to catastrophic results, with the loss of hours of work. It takes longer to proofread text on screen than to proofread "hard copy" on paper (Gould and Grischkowsky, 1984). Electronic composition is not always easy, particularly if computer technology has to be united with earlier means of writing, for example in the revision of a text that has already been produced by other means. Short of transferring an entire printed or handwritten text into a word processor, there is (currently) no convenient way to merge computer additions or deletions into previously printed text. My own experience in this regard with the present book is briefly mentioned near the beginning of the Notes.

The Electronic Classroom

There are three general ways in which computers are currently used in writing classrooms—to facilitate student writing, to "teach writing," and to assist in classroom management. Research and my own experience lead me to feel enthusiastic about the first, dubious about the second, and decidedly suspicious about the third.

Anything that helps writers to write will help students learn to write. Indeed, electronic technology tends to facilitate the things that learners find most difficult, like speed, legibility, organization, and spelling. Inexperienced writers have the greatest need to be able to change their minds. Word processors take much of the physical labor out of writing, and assist the mental labor as well. Young children can easily take their first steps in learning to write on a word processor, and the device can certainly be of use to high-school or college students struggling to improve written language fluency and expression. This is not to say that students should ever be *forced* to employ word processors, or even be distracted by the protracted business of learning to use them, if they are happier with more traditional ways of getting their thoughts and words onto paper. Word processors—and guidance on how to use them—should be optional classroom *aids* to writing, as available as but no more obligatory than dictionaries and pencil sharpeners.

And I should also emphasize that I am certainly not advocating that computers take the place of *books*, in classrooms or in schools. It is a tragedy when electronic equipment is purchased at the expense of libraries. Books (and other genres of reading matter) remain essential sources of experience, and—as I shall discuss in the chapters to come—are the primary foundation of learning about writing.

Word processors can help learners in every way that they help more experienced writers. I don't want to reiterate everything I have already written in this chapter, replacing the word "writer" with "learner," "child," or "student" (although the reader might briefly undertake that enterprise). But I should mention a few specifics, observed in a number of classrooms, from the most junior grades up.

Word processors can make it easier for students to write collaboratively with each other, or with a teacher or outside resource, in the manner I discussed in Chapter 3. A number of specialized "educational" computer programs are becoming available to facilitate composing collaborations. But such collaborations can be done with all nonspecialist word processing programs, on-line if the computers are networked or sequentially if students can share or exchange developing texts on printouts, on diskettes, or through modems.

Through what might be called community computing, using networked computer systems, students can join a variety of writing and other communities, observing how other people write, and getting the opportunity to participate in writing exchanges themselves. They can introduce themselves to other people, as well as to other ideas and alternative sources of information, all over the world. Writing becomes more authentic, more meaningful and purposeful, when students know that they have a good chance of finding a nonevaluative readership genuinely interested in what they have to say. Students will not learn about all genres of writing in such networks, but they can gain experience—and admission to the club of writers—that will support them in other enterprises.

During recent elections in Canada, students could of course read about the campaign and its issues in newspapers and journals. If they were so inspired they could write letters to editors, with a modest hope of seeing their thoughts in print. But major candidates were also making statements on the "bulletin boards" of networking computers, and anyone on the network was able to respond. Other people read and commented on the responses (even if the candidates did not). Even more people were able to read the debate—and observe how a political discussion was conducted. All this was a form of participatory democracy that every student could be involved in, provided there was a networking computer in the classroom. Students could *write* their own contributions, *see* what they had written displayed in a public forum, and possibly *read* the reaction to what they had written. This is not tomorrow's technology; it is today's (yesterday's, in fact, but there is always a lag while schools catch up). I am not saying that computers should or will take the place of face-to-face discussions, the press, or public debates. But all the alternatives have *their* limitations—debates and discussions are sometimes difficult to organize, often require many people to be in the same place at the same time, and many must simply sit and watch. Computers offer the choice of immediate participation, at times convenient to participants, and are universal invitations to practice writing and reading.

Computers offer broad opportunities for experience with real people in actual situations, providing students with more to write about and more reasons for writing. But computers also offer possibilities of highly realistic experience in situations which for various reasons are not possible or even desirable in actuality. I am referring to computer *simulations*. It is highly unlikely that I will ever get the opportunity to pilot a commercial airliner, with or without the help of a computer. But a computer can easily simulate what it would be like for me to pilot an airliner, and even simulate the crash that would be the probable outcome, which is something I would certainly not want to experience in reality. In order to pilot the simulated airliner, I would have to read all kinds of instructions and regulations (and possibly the biographies of other pilots and their flights) and write all kinds of notes, logs, and reports, (and possibly my own flying biography).

Computer simulations can turn classrooms into newsrooms or courtrooms, boardrooms or factory floors, cabinet offices or operating theaters, ocean liners or intergalactic spaceships. Imaginations can run free, and opportunities abound for authentic writing, reading, and thinking.

It is sometimes feared that word processing technology will discourage students from learning to spell and punctuate, and even from writing by hand. I do not understand the belief that students will most easily learn things that are made difficult for them. Spelling and punctuation are not particularly easy to learn, especially to order, as I explain in the following chapter. Requiring students to worry about spelling and punctuation at the same time that they are worrying about more creative aspects of composition is unlikely to make them more interested or proficient in any aspect of writing. I have seen no evidence that computers make people inferior spellers. I know it is sometimes claimed that hand and desk calculators have resulted in people losing simple arithmetical skills, but again, there is no hard evidence. It would certainly be false to suggest that everyone was arithmetically competent before calculators, or better spellers before word processors. And if electronic equipment contributes in any way to more reliable results, it must have advantages.

There are also fears that students given access to computers will only want to play arcade games, but if this is the case, teachers should ensure that students have the opportunity to discover that things other than playing arcade games can be done on computers. (And teachers themselves should not use arcade games as *rewards* for students whom they want to cajole into doing less interesting things on computers.) The task for teachers is to demonstrate that there is more to life than arcade games, to help students join the communities of people who find more interesting things to become involved in than arcade games.

It is sometimes thought that students using computers require closer supervision than those with pencils and paper. Sometimes teachers worry that students will not be able to use computers unless they have "appropriate keyboarding skills," and deny access to machines until the students can type with all 10 fingers (although many experienced computer users do not type conventionally, and learning to type fast and accurately, conventionally or otherwise, is a byproduct of using computers). I have seen children required to "practice keyboarding skills" on colored diagrams spread out on their computerless desks. This is like expecting them to learn handwriting with pencils without leads in them. I have similarly observed cases where students are categorized as "not ready" to use computers because they are unable to define technical terms ("What does central processing unit mean?") or describe technical functions ("What does the Alt key do?"). Anything anyone *needs* to learn in order to use a computer is best learned while using a computer, at the moment when the learning is necessary and meaningful.

I shall not attempt to prescribe which word processing programs and simulations teachers should use and how they should use them. The options are enormous, their number growing daily. But in any case I, like any outside "expert," lack vital information that is only in the possession of teachers. I am referring to knowledge of the interests and abilities of the students who will be affected. I would no more try to recommend a particular course of study or set of experiences for particular students, much less for a *group* of students, than I would try to prescribe an interesting and nourishing diet for them. In both cases I would need to know the individuals. What will be interesting and comprehensible to one student will not be productive and worthwhile for the next. Only a teacher can make these decisions, despite the frequent attempts by outsiders to say they know better, even though they never even *see* the students. This doesn't absolve teachers from the responsibility of finding out what is available, and how it is most appropriately used, but this is best done by critically reading and observing how other teachers use electronic equipment in their classrooms and how computers are used in real life. They must join the community of teachers who use electronic equipment discriminatingly, not those who unreflectingly swallow advertising hyperbole.

The mention of advertising brings me to the final use of computers in classrooms, which unfortunately is often the most prominent—their role in "teaching" and in classroom administration. I shall say little on these topics because I have little to say that is encouraging. Rather than making a totally negative statement about computers, let me express my opinion in positive form about teachers. The only way in which anyone learns anything useful about writing—in terms of spelling, punctuation, style, clarity, and every other aspect of writing, is by personal contact with *people*, either as individuals or as the authors of books. It is not necessary or desirable that computers should be used to set, correct, and mark drills and exercises that students must complete at the keyboard. Unfortunately, such mindless programs are among the easiest forms of software to produce—and the easiest to market and sell. And unfortunately for students, many administrators and teachers like them.

Computer-based exercises in writing are good for only one thing—for generating "marks" and "scores" that can be recorded for administrative purposes. And computers are also outstanding in their ability to help teachers and administrators record these scores, store them, retrieve them, compare them, and use them to inform and placate other people, usually to the detriment of the students from whom the scores were originally extracted. None of this helps anyone to learn to write, and as facilitators of such misguided manipulation, computers constitute an enormous threat to students, teachers, and education. All this is spelled out in more polemical detail in my book *Insult to Intelligence* (Smith, 1986).

I do not see computers driving teachers from the classroom—at least, I hope they don't. There is no research to show that computers can substitute for teachers, and it is difficult to see how aspiring writers might *identify* with electronic devices. Hawisher (1989) found that students given the opportunity to use word processors tended to develop positive attitudes to the machines and to writing, and wrote longer texts with fewer errors, but it was not clear whether their writing actually improved.

I should note that educational software companies, covering all bases, are becoming very involved in the "home schooling market." But in doing so they often transfer the most unimaginative parts of computer instructional technology from the classroom to the living room. If electronic educational technology is to develop further along the "drill and test" route, then not only might school-based and home-based education become more and more similar, but eventually the question will be asked whether schools are necessary. Could students do all their "learning" at home the way we are encouraged these days to do our "shopping" and banking at home, through computer-controlled choices and centralized administration?

To summarize, there are three positive reasons why computers should and no doubt will become a prominent but optional part of every classroom. The first is that word processors can help writers—and learner-writers—to write. The second is that they can help people in educational institutions, staff and students, to join extensive communities of writers. And the third is that it will give everyone in educational institutions the opportunity to keep abreast of the radical changes in writing and in social organization that computer technology is in the process of bringing about, some of which I shall discuss next.[2]

The Electronic Text

Word processing is not simply a matter of putting words on a monitor screen instead of on paper. Word processing is a new medium of writing in itself, and is generating a broad range of new genres. New problems are arising that will affect all writers, concerning privacy, copyright, and even the very notion of "authorship."

Networking and electronic mail are rapidly bringing about new ways of using language that may have profound consequences for all societies, bringing people closer together in many ways, but changing the language that they speak and write. I would have included word processing in my Table of Language Uses in Chapter 2, except that it is not (at the moment) so much a new use of language as a vast expansion of existing uses, establishing communities of scholars, researchers, and practitioners in virtually every profession, art, craft, and interest group. Just as the development of the telephone expanded the possibility of people all over the world to talk with each other, so electronic mail adds a written language advantage by providing permanency to world-spanning conversations and discussions. Individuals can address questions, answers, suggestions, and propositions to each other, even reaching out to people they haven't yet met. Yet by the use of codewords and scramblers, privacy can also be preserved. The web of spoken and written language in which we all live today might well become a web of computer-embedded spoken and written language in the future.

Spoken and written language constantly change, and the changes will accelerate. In the past, speech has changed faster than written language, but with word processing networks, the tail may soon wag the dog. The effluent of word processing jargon has already seeped into many people's language, starting with word processing itself (in place of writing), text processing (editing), keyboarding (typing), retrieving (remembering), accessing, impacting, inputting, outputting, programming, online, backup, default, virtual reality. . . . Language is always subject to change and is always metaphorical. But the impact of new terms and new images, which means new ways of thought, is increasing inexorably. Some examples, crucial to the way many people think about education, are provided in my discussion of "cognitive science" beginning on page 264.

Participants in computer networks are developing and adopting new styles and conventions of writing, from terse sequences of disconnected phrases and even single words to great convoluted streams of discourse that flow across the screen like streams of water finding their way across a plain. This is not the way individuals normally talk, or even the way they normally write—it is the way they discover a new voice with the combination of keyboard, monitor, and an audience.

The computer, like the typewriter before it, has had a great influence in standardizing writing systems (into Western alphabetic forms) and possibly in reducing the influence of non-alphabetic written languages. But on the other hand, fax technology (which has been facilitated by computers) may be instigating a revival of interest in handwriting, especially in Japan where there have been difficulties in converting keyboards to a 6000-character writing system. Faxes can be written by hand, and appearances again become important.

Spoken language has been affected internationally, especially among the young, by American movies and television programs that propagate particular dialects and idioms. Now computers may be doing the same for written language. "British spelling" (*centre, honour, waggon*) and "American spelling" (*center, honor, wagon*) have retained their distinctive differences primarily because of the deep historical roots of British and American national publishing houses and educational systems. Canada and Australia have been more schizophrenic, with publishers and school systems unsure of which way to go, because many of their books, magazines, and educational materials come from *both* Britain and the United States. But now Britain itself is beginning to tolerate and even to use American spelling because of the influence of computer software and manuals, most of which employ American spelling.

New kinds of text are being developed. Though *hypertexts* are still a relatively new, untried, and not widely accepted concept (at the time that I write this; nothing remains relatively new for long with computers), more and more writers and researchers are becoming interested in this new type of text that can only be produced on computers. At first glance, hypertexts are everything teachers of writing would abhor, since they consist primarily of disconnected paragraphs. Such texts are organized and stored on the basis of separate but interlocking units (of ideas, themes, or feelings) rather than as coherent indivisible wholes. Bolter (1991) explains: "Electronic text falls naturally into discrete units—paragraphs or sections that stand in multiple relation to one another. An electronic text is a network rather than the straight line suggested by the pages of a printed book. . . . Texts written explicitly for this new medium will probably favor short, concentrated expression, because each unit may be approached from a different perspective on each reading" (p. ix).

Obviously, writers of hypertexts need not and often cannot have specific readers in mind, nor any idea of the path a particular reader might take. Readers of hypertexts need not follow a path specifically set out for them by the author (although this is a freedom readers already possess, of course, with conventional texts).

Hypertexts could be seen as attempts to facilitate the constant modifications of specifications that I referred to in Chapter 8. Hypertext designers might even claim that the networks of interlocking notes their programs make possible *are* specifications, though I would be inclined to argue that specifications are required for the hypertexts themselves.

A hypertext, according to Bolter, is a *network* of subtexts. It is not an *outline*, but a *text* that branches out in many directions. If the beginning of this paragraph were part of an electronic text, it would be possible to "activate" any italicized words (network, outline, text), perhaps just by touching them on the screen, and another text would appear with a discussion of the selected topic, with its own keywords in italics or boldface so that readers might go off in all directions, including back to the point they had just left. Hypertexts do not have a table of contents but a "menu" of topics. There are no page numbers. Hypertexts (in a primitive and often irritating form) are already familiar to many users of word processors as the way in which "help" functions and other putatively explanatory sections of text are organized.

In such a text, there are no beginnings or endings; the selected topics are not digressions (unless the reader wishes to make them so) but different paths. Moving through such a text would be like exploring a city with high-rise buildings interconnected by multiple bridges and subways, with a choice of traveling in several directions, including up and down, at every corner. It would no longer make sense to debate the "meaning" of a text. Hypertexts may destroy the notion of "great books" as cultures construct a single "great book" that will be different for every reader. Will *authors* come back into their own as guides that take readers through hypertexts, "discovering" books rather than writing them?

Bolter sees electronic writing space as a new metaphor for the human mind and for the "collective mentality" of cultures. Whether all this is "progress," or even a convenience, is debatable, of course. The notion of what constitutes a writer and a reader may be changing rapidly, just as other traditional roles are being subjected to violent change as technology and society develop. Should literary productions have "beginnings," "middles," and "ends"?

Many contemporary books and plays don't follow this formula, television serials don't, *life* doesn't. We plunge into newspapers and magazines for our daily or weekly episode of one great interlocking set of stories, for none of which we can ever know the true beginnings or the eventual end. *Thought* is not linear. All of this might also be a model for education—not hypertexts, but *hyperexperience.*

Bolter's book is full of provocative and sometimes disturbing ideas about "the computer as a new writing space." In addition to extolling the virtues of texts that do not follow a linear sequence, he perhaps illustrates one of the dangers when he admits in his Preface to difficulty in organizing his text "in an appropriate manner" to the printed page rather than "intertextually" or "hypertextually." Finding ways to link everything together is of course a problem for most writers; Bolter is one of the first to think that the problem can be avoided altogether. His book is encyclopedic, difficult to read from beginning to end as the author suddenly sidetracks into new topics. The book is easier to read, perhaps, if the reader takes control of the sequence and continually moves forward and back to whatever is most interesting and relevant, much as one might browse through an encyclopedia from topic to topic—the basic idea behind hypertext. Appropriately, Bolter's book is also available on disk in a true hypertextual version, giving the reader alternative paths to follow, in written language and sound, including several voices (some of which are sceptical about electronic writing).

Inevitably, as individual voices, written and spoken, multiply and inter-mingle in electronic writing, so the individual voice of specific authors will be lost. No doubt by the time the words that I am writing now are being read, at some time in my future (and my reader's present), there will be many more hypertexts. Perhaps *Writing and the Writer*, with millions of others books and documents, will eventually become part of one vast continent of hypertext, never read in its entirety by anyone, occasionally "accessed" with a dozen other fragments as part of a specialist review. The world of writing is changing inexorably, and electronic devices are leading the way. They cannot be ignored.

(Notes to Chapter 11 begin on page 258.)

12 Learning to be a Writer

The more I think about writing the more impressed I become that anyone should ever learn to do it. This is not because I think writing requires a great deal of intelligence or a special kind of aptitude; there is no evidence to support any such view. Rather, it might seem that the ability to read and write makes us very much brighter than we otherwise would be. But writing encompasses familiarity with so many conventions in so many areas—in spelling, punctuation, vocabulary, grammar, cohesion, discourse structure, and register—that one wonders how anyone could find the time and the instruction to acquire it all. Even if we write only rarely, and reluctantly, there must still be an enormous lode of competence at our disposal so that we can, when we must, draft a halfway adequate letter, memorandum, or diary entry. It is perhaps especially difficult to explain the ability of people to write who do so only infrequently.

Not that I want to imply that learning to write must be intrinsically difficult. Learning to write obviously presents problems for many people, but that need not be because writing itself is a particularly arcane accomplishment. Learning to write might become difficult—it might be made difficult, even— for reasons quite unconnected with the intrinsic demands of the task. It is difficult to discover anything that accomplished writers have studied or exercises they have practiced in order to develop their ability.

No writer has ever claimed to have learned as a result of the grammar lessons given at school. Very little of what writers know in order to write can be explicitly taught; their ability is a matter of selecting conventions rather than of applying rules. You do not need to be *told* very much about writing in order to learn to write, which is just as well because there is very little understanding of what the conventions of the various aspects of writing are, even among specialists who spend a lifetime studying small aspects of the subject.

What is the difference between people who can write and those who cannot? How did we learn all the conventions of composition and transcription that we know, the incorrect as well as the correct? A facile answer comes to mind; we learn to write by writing. I have been tempted to make this argument myself, especially since I have long held the view that we learn to read by reading. But we just do not do enough writing, certainly most students do not, to account for the extensive facility that even mediocre and unenthusiastic writers are able to demonstrate. I am not saying that the act of writing is not important for developing fluency; obviously we can and often must learn by attempting to write something and having the errors we have made corrected. But correction when it comes is usually delayed and may be very sketchy; a few misspellings or grammatical errors are pointed out. And there is little evidence that students pay much attention to a teacher's annotations of work they hope they have finished with.

The writing we do cannot account for the writing we learn to do. Rather we must learn from *exposure* to writing, in other words from *reading*, and from acquaintanceship with writers. It is this vicarious learning accomplishment that is so impressive. And if we learn to write by reading it must be by reading done in a particular way, because many people who can read do not write very well, certainly not with the fluency of the writers they read. What we read does not inevitably rub off onto us as writers.

So explanations are required not only for how so much about writing is learned almost incidentally while we read, but also for why some aspects of learning so often prove elusive. The explanations of both must be sought in the nature of the brain as a learning instrument.

LEARNING—SENSE AND NONSENSE

The brain's capacity for learning at all ages is widely underrated. There is a disproportionate emphasis on those occasions when learning is difficult, with a tendency to lay the blame on the brain (or on the owner of the brain) rather than on the situations in which the learning is expected to take place. Many researchers in education and psychology might seem to regard the brain as a normally inactive organ whose usual state is to be doing nothing, and which only occasionally learns, and then only if particularly prodded into doing so. I take an opposing point of view. It is the business of the brain to learn— basically, the brain does nothing else—and it is no more "normal" for the brain not to be learning than it is for musculature to be limp. What needs to be explained is not how learning takes place on the occasions when it does but what is lacking on those occasions when it does not.

The brain is capable of enormous amounts of learning. Think of the complexity of the world in which we live, the thousands upon thousands of different objects, attributes, and events that we can discriminate (and talk about) and their multiple interrelationships. Think of our ability not only to make sense of events in the present and past but to anticipate their occurrence in the future. The occasional circumstance may find us surprised or leave us bewildered, but surprise and bewilderment are not common conditions of our lives. Most of the occurrences of our lives are so obvious that they have become boring; we take the world and the way it is organized for granted. Yet nothing in the world is self-evident; nothing announces itself. Everything we know about the world we must have learned, from the way doors are opened to the intricacy of language itself. All of the detail, complexity, and order we perceive in the world around us must reflect a detail, complexity, and order in our own brain.

The magnitude of the enterprise by which infants learn to use and understand spoken language is by now well documented. Obviously no one tells an infant how language works, or even what it can be used for. The complexity of a vocabulary and grammar and the subtlety of all the underlying conventions elude description, let alone formal instruction. What kind of a brain enables children to cope so effortlessly with the enormous task of making sense of the world around them, including its language, at least until adults feel they should orchestrate their learning for them?

The brain is perpetually learning. No one can tolerate boredom, and boredom is the inevitable consequence of having nothing to learn. Boredom is as aversive as suffocation and learning as natural and continual as breathing. The brain must learn; it requires a constant diet of new things to understand. Even when we pass our time in apparently trivial occupations, watching a mundane television program or reading a pulp novel, it is still the possibility of something new, some residual uncertainty, that holds our attention. If there is one thing more unbearable than watching an entirely predictable television program the first time, it would be watching the same program twice.

Because learning is such a natural and constant activity, we are not normally aware that it is taking place. We fail to credit the brain for the learning it achieves because the learning is usually so effortless, accomplished without strain. See someone sweating over learning, frowning over a book or grimacing with the burden of committing something to memory, and you know that learning is probably not taking place. We learn without knowing when and how, and if we become aware of the effort to learn, it is because there are impediments in the way; we are confused, or anxious, or simply going about learning in an inappropriate manner.

Obviously, when I characterize the brain as continually learning, I cannot mean that it will learn anything, at any time, in any circumstance, at anyone's beck. The brain is highly selective in the timing, content, and manner of its preferred and natural occupation. The brain insists upon being in control.[1]

Learning to write is less an intellectual achievement than a social one, depending on attitude rather than on application. Learning to write begins—whatever the learner's age—with *seeing oneself* as a writer, doing the things writers do, and thinking the way writers think. This is a matter of *identity*, not of instruction or of effort, even of desire to learn. Teachers have a crucial role to play here, not in teaching the technicalities of writing, but in engendering appropriate attitudes to writing. This matter is so important that I have divided the topic of learning to write into two parts. The present chapter is concerned with how individuals come to see themselves as writers, so that they become sensitized to learning everything that fluent writers have learned, and the next chapter is on "learning the technicalities"—the profusion of conventions of writing.

Inventing Worlds

Some researchers, impressed by the rich and idiosyncratic manner in which infants penetrate the mysteries of language, describe the achievement in a striking way. They say infants *invent* language in order to learn it. Children do not passively absorb the language they hear around them (which, until they understand it, can consist only of meaningless sounds) nor do they aimlessly imitate the noises that adults make when they speak. Instead infants strive to create language that will achieve ends for themselves, trying out a sound here, borrowing some noises there, staying with a possibility whenever it works for them, and discovering by trial and error when their notion of what language might be corresponds to the actuality of the language around them. The first language of babies may bear little resemblance to the language they hear adults producing, but it soon becomes more and more conventional. The child's language becomes that of the world around.

The language we develop as children is our set of solutions to problems of how the language works that we hear around us.[2] But solutions require inventiveness. Solutions do not exist in the world out there, one for every problem, conveniently waiting for us to stumble over them. To resolve a problem you may have to try out many solutions, more than one of which may have equal merit although only one happens to be appropriate at a particular time and place for purely accidental or historical reasons. All of the 3,000 or more natural languages in the world, for example, are alternative solutions to the particular problems that those languages have evolved to solve. There is no reason to believe other languages would not be equally possible. Infants must potentially have the capacity for inventing the forms and conventions of English, French, Chinese, and every other natural language, *and of possible languages that do not exist*, if they are to master the particular language that happens to be spoken around them. (Small children who spend a great deal of time exclusively together, especially twins, occasionally invent miniature languages of their own, which no one else uses or understands.) To find out what the world is "really like" in all respects, we must be capable of generating possibilities far beyond actuality. The brain creates many possible worlds, only one of which happens to correspond to the world we actually inhabit.

Invention plays an important role as individuals become writers. Spellings, punctuation, grammar, and many other conventions of writing are all invented, by children and by older learners, in the course of acquiring the tools of the writer's trade—and even experienced professional writers continue to invent from time to time, when they don't want transcription detail to interfere with the flow of composition. I discuss many aspects of such invention in the following chapter, but for the moment I want to concentrate on what may be the most crucial invention of all: *the invention of ourselves as writers*.

Becoming a writer is like becoming any other kind of person, a matter of finding and assuming a new identity, an extension of one's personality and self-image. Becoming a writer is not a matter of acquiring a kit of skills, but of enlarging the role of the character we play as we strive to compose the stories of our lives.

The Stories of Writers

A number of prominent psychological and educational theorists emphasize the importance of story-making and story-telling in people's lives. Rosen (1988) describes his research into memory for stories in a chapter entitled "Stories of stories: Footnotes on sly gossipy practices." He does not look the way many teachers do at how stories are remembered—to see how accurately readers can recall detail or structure—but at how creatively readers *change* stories in the retelling (like Bartlett, 1932). Rosen refers to this topic as "memory as art." Bruner (1986) also writes of the creative narrative nature of the human mind—a side which he says cognitive science has neglected in its emphasis on logical and problem solving mental activities. Wells (1986) has done extensive research into how children make sense of their experience through the construction of stories, in home and at school, in spoken and in written language. In what he terms "the guided reinvention of knowledge," Wells says that children always strive to "make meaning." Adults should give them evidence, guidance, and encouragement, aiming to help without overwhelming, willingly giving up control and being prepared to listen.

I suspect that story-telling is so central to the human mind that writing must be one of the most *natural* things for anyone to want to do—to tell stories about what they and the world are like, or about what they and the world *might be like*, or could be like, or ought to be like—with all of the permanence and plasticity that writing offers compared with speech.

Right from birth, we have all been composing and amending the story of who we are. This is the basis of all learning. In an article and book entitled *Joining the Literacy Club* (Smith, 1988) I have characterized the way infants learn to talk by saying they join a "spoken language club," where people around them show infants what can be done with speech, and help infants to do those things themselves. In effect, the grownups and other children help the infants to say what they want to say and to understand what they are trying to understand. I then extend the analogy to show that reading begins when learners (of any age) "join the reading club," where other people help them to read what they would like to read, and—most importantly—help them to see themselves as readers. Very soon the people who help learners consolidate themselves in the club of readers are not people who read to and with the learner, but the authors that the learners read. Similarly, learners (of any age) become writers when other people help them to see themselves as writers—when they help them "join the writing club."

Later in this chapter I go into detail about learning generally, and "identity learning" in particular; in the rest of the book, I discuss learning the technicalities of writing. But first I want to spend a little more time discussing how children are first helped to "join the spoken language club," partly because of its intrinsic interest, but also because of lessons that can be drawn for learning to write.[3]

Baby-Talk and Beyond

Scribbling and other aspects of children's early efforts to write are occasionally compared with "baby-talk" (professionally abbreviated to BT). At its most direct level, the comparison is evidently wrong. Scribbling is *not* like BT for the simple reason that children do not speak BT—adults do. By speaking BT to infants, grownups help them to learn to use spoken language, by simplifying, collaborating, and easing their task in understanding, all with a close eye on what the child is trying to do.

Two of the major authorities in the field of BT have edited an important volume (Snow and Ferguson, 1977) in which researchers describe how adults "fine-tune" BT to help infants understand and learn. In the volume, Snow (1977) describes how mothers modify their language (into "motherese") to help children understand—but the child makes as important a contribution as the mother, and mothers can't speak BT unless the child is there to cue them to do so. Snow notes that book reading elicits more complex speech by both mother and child. But the adult language has to be precisely produced to match the child's ability to comprehend on every individual occasion. Cross (1977), in the same volume, observes that mothers make critical adjustments as they attempt to converse with their infants so that they can be understood beyond the point that the children's language abilities have actually reached. In the terms of Vygotsky (1978), the parents are operating within the children's "zone of proximal development," where learners can do with help what they cannot do alone (although what they can do with help today they will be able to do alone tomorrow). Bruner (1983) makes similar points, employing the metaphor of "scaffolding" as the means by which parents support children's language development.

As a model for how more experienced adults can help children learn to write, BT exchanges could not be bettered. One wonders if the parents (and others) who do so much to help children and older learners to become readers and writers through collaboration and facilitation are not following some intuitive practices that both mentor and learner are sensitive to. Unfortunately, adult instincts sometimes seem to be overwritten by "teacher" caricatures that require them to become drill instructors and error-detectors, so that what should be a pleasant interaction becomes a frustrating one for all parties.

Calkins (1983) is one of a number of researchers who relate early writing to play. Becoming a young author can be seen as a "play-full" activity. Not only can learners emulate and even practice a range of writing activities, from producing real or pretend poems and stories to composing cafeteria menus and traffic citations, but they can joyfully adopt the role of being a person who writes. In a study of children's play, Schwartzman (1978) notes that children are "continually constructing and transforming the contexts in which they exist in their efforts to make sense, and sometimes nonsense, of the worlds in which they find themselves." (See also Gelman, 1979, Sutton-Smith, 1975, and Herron and Sutton-Smith, 1982.) Such ideas are scarcely new. A century ago, Francis Parker (1890) observed that "creation is the moving, central power and delight of the child. The baby creates out of its meagre store of ideas a new world, its own world, in which it lives and moves and has its being" (p. 7).

The effort to see ourselves as writers is not a trivial accomplishment, nor a passing phase. It is part of a continual struggle for most writers. The moment we suspect that we may have misjudged our vocation, or have lost our skills, we are in deep trouble as writers.

Composition, the creative aspect of writing, is simply a reflection of the brain's natural activity. Of course, the "quality" that we and the rest of the world might seek in composition depends on something more than turning the story-telling faucet. Quality implies standards and criteria, both in themselves conventions that focus upon the writer's use of conventions in general. And conventions have to be learned, by interaction with the world outside.

But now we are approaching the heart of the other question, how writers learn from their own efforts and from the efforts of others, not simply to improve the quality of composition, however that might be defined, but also to master all of the transcription conventions of written language. How does a theory of the world come to include everything that is expected of anyone who aspires to write?

THE DYNAMICS OF LEARNING

Memory is not the problem. The brain's capacity for storing knowledge of the world seems boundless, for both how much it can hold and how long it will persist. We remember prodigious numbers of things: all the people and objects we can recognize (by sight, sound, smell, taste, or touch), thousands of which have names and thousands of which do not, all of their manifold interrelationships, everything that is familiar or predictable about the world, all of the contents of our theory of the world. Memory does not seem to become overcrowded. And the persistence of memory can take us by surprise. A glimpse of a face not seen for years, a tune not heard since childhood, a fragrance redolent of a distant vacation, and we can be engulfed in a flood of recollection. Putting the bulk of all this knowledge into memory does not seem to have been a difficulty. Indeed, that is our question, how all the multiplicity and subtlety of everything we have ever learned, about writing, and everything else, became established so effortlessly. And getting things out of memory is usually no trouble either; everything we take for granted in our daily experience is something recollected instantly.

Memory itself we take for granted. We become aware of its operations only through its occasional shortcomings and lapses, so that we may regard our memory as far less efficient than it actually is. Because of course things can go wrong. We can labor mightily to commit names, spellings, definitions, or formulas to memory with a painful lack of success. And we can pick and probe to pry things out of memory and still frustratingly fail. Frustratingly, because in some sense the memory seems still to be there; we cannot think of the word, but it is on the tip of the tongue and if someone else suggests it, or offers a clue, we can say "Ah yes, that's it" or "No, it is not."

It is not difficult to account in general terms for the remarkable efficiency of memory most of the time and for the occasional and irritating failures. Memory is *organized*—indeed, memory *is* organization—and everything we know seems to be related to everything else we know in some way. It is difficult to imagine what a memory would be like, or what its utility would be, with no connection at all to anything else in our mind. Memorizing anything is effortless if it can become a coherent and relevant part of our understanding of the world. The basis of much of our memory is possibilities that we ourselves have generated, a matter not so much of struggling to insert alien information into the mind as of confirming something that tentatively existed there in the first place. Similarly, unless we are afflicted by one of those aggravating memory lapses that must reflect distraction, inhibition, or some temporary disorganization of the brain, recall of something immediately relevant does not require effort. Usually we have difficulty only in gaining access to something that is not part of our current theory of the world, when it is not something that we have anticipated. Our childhood memories are not lost to us because they have been erased from the brain, but because they have become remote from our present concerns. What we usually must recall right now we do not need to plunge and search for; it is already there at the surface of our mind because it is part of the world we inhabit right now. Neither aspect of memory—putting knowledge in and getting it out—is a problem if it is relevant to us at the moment, if it makes sense. From the brain's point of view, memory is part of the continual coherent process of creating, comprehending, and learning in which the brain is constantly engaged.

Ironically, almost all psychological and educational research into memory has overlooked this fundamental, natural, effortless process. Research has tended to look at learning and memory at their most difficult and unnatural. Learning is easy when it is meaningful, but the experimental focus is on learning that is meaningless.

The reasons for this regrettable distortion in the study of learning and memory are easy to identify. Scientific inquiry (according to the rules of science) has to be rigorous, controlled, and replicable. A phenomenon investigated today must be repeatable tomorrow; science must find *laws* that are generalizable across people. And the problem with meaningful learning, with the memorization of something that makes sense to a particular individual, is that it is not predictable, it cannot be neatly condensed into a curve on a graph or a mathematical formula. Whether a person will find something to be learned meaningful depends upon the individual's prior knowledge, motivation, and expectation; there are too many "uncontrolled variables." But everyone starts from the same place when learning is meaningless.

Learning has to be unnatural and difficult if it is to be broken down into discrete segments that can be dealt with at a controlled rate in a predetermined order under the direction of someone other than the learner, whose success or failure is then amenable to measurement, comparison, and prediction. I have been describing the dilemma of the experimental researcher, but it is not coincidental that I might also have been talking about "systematic instruction" in schools.

Research has had little to say about effortless learning and the circumstances in which such learning occurs. One handicap is that what can be said may appear obvious to the point of banality—that individuals learn better when they are interested, when they expect to learn, can make sense of what they want to learn, are not unduly apprehensive about the possibility or cost of making mistakes, and other people help them. Who would expect learning to be easier for anyone who is unmotivated, uninterested, disillusioned, confused, anxious, hostile, or unaided?

In the analysis I am about to make I want to examine learning when it is undirected (except by the learner), and uninhibited by lack of interest, anxiety, or confusion. I am not concerned now with the slow and transient way in which a dozen items might be learned on a spelling or vocabulary list, but with the ease with which many thousands of conventions of language are acquired without strain. I shall not focus on the "learning process," whatever that might be, but on the dynamics of the circumstances in which learning is manifested. As I have said, I do not think that learning itself requires explanation; it is the normal way the brain goes about its business. Indeed, I am not sure how a useful answer could be formulated to the pseudo-profundity "What *really* is learning?" (A particular kind of chemical change in the brain? A pattern of bioelectric activity?) It is the circumstances I propose to explore. I see three dynamically interrelated conditions involved, which I term *demonstration*, *engagement*, and *sensitivity*.

THE CONDITIONS OF LEARNING

Demonstration

The linguist M. A. K. Halliday has pointed out that children learn language and its uses simultaneously.[4] Children do not learn language as an abstraction, as a "tool" that they then apply to various uses; language and its uses are inseparable.

I would go a step further and argue not just that language and its uses are learned simultaneously, but that it is through its uses that language is learned. We learn the conventions of writing when we have a use for its conventions ourselves or when we understand the use that others make of them. It is necessary to see (or hear) something being done, and to understand why it is being done. There must be a *demonstration* which, in effect, says "This is how something is done."

And the world is full of demonstrations. Everything anyone does is a demonstration of something being done, in a right or in a wrong way, enthusiastically or otherwise. The clothes we wear demonstrate how clothes are worn and the clothes that people like us wear. The food we eat demonstrates how, what, and when we eat; the letters we write demonstrate how letters are written. Every act demonstrates not only what can be done and how it can be done, but what the person doing it feels about the act. If we are bored when we have to write, that is what is demonstrated to anyone observing us.

Just as people provide demonstrations, so do products. A table demonstrates what a table is like, how it can be made, and how it can be used. A book demonstrates how every word in that book is spelled, a use for each of these words, how words go together to make sentences, and every other convention that the book employs.[5] Every utterance, spoken or written, demonstrates some conventions of language and their relationships to the intentions of the people who use language.

We can even provide demonstrations for ourselves, intentionally or accidentally. Babies cry, parents pick them up, and there is a demonstration of what babies must do to be picked up. An infant says "Dadda go walk," demonstrating a hypothesis of how a particular observation might be put into words, and the mother says "Yes, dear, Daddy has gone for a walk," demonstrating how adults say the same thing. A teenager attempts to write a job application, a more experienced person lends a hand, and there is a demonstration of how job applications are written. Everything we write is a demonstration from which we can learn, from other people's reactions but also from our own. There is a demonstration of how something should be done, or perhaps how it should not be done, whenever something is done with a purpose or has been done with a purpose, in every human act and artifact.

We can even have demonstrations within the privacy of our own minds. We can imagine an act or an event, and we can examine its imagined consequences. And writing can provide us with demonstrations that are public only to ourselves.

Demonstrations are relative, of course. What to me may be a very clear demonstration of how a mainsail is reefed may be only a potential demonstration to you, or no demonstration at all, if you do not understand the function of reefing in the first place. We might dismantle an automobile engine to provide you with a demonstration of the relationships of tappets to valve stems, while I gain nothing more than grease on my shirt because I do not understand automobile engines in the first place. An object or event is a demonstration to a particular person only if that person understands the purpose behind that object or event. Every act or artifact involving language demonstrates how intentions and the conventions of language are related— to the extent that the purpose behind the convention is understood. Remember that it is not necessary to know something already in order to understand it. If we understand a convention of which we were previously not aware because we understand the intention that the convention reflects, then there is a demonstration from which learning can ensue.

Yet learning still may not take place. A demonstration shows us how something is done, but we will not learn without a complementary involvement on our part to be able to do or understand the same thing ourselves. For learning to take place there has to be *engagement* with a demonstration, as direct and immediate as the manner in which gears engage in a mechanical device.

Engagement

I use the term *engagement* to characterize the way a learner and a demonstration come together on those occasions when learning takes place. I am not saying that learning takes place as a *consequence* of a demonstration but that it occurs on the *occasion* of the demonstration, concurrently—if there is engagement. Before considering how engagement might occur I give two brief illustrations of engagement with which you may be familiar.

Have you had the experience of casually reading a book or newspaper when suddenly your attention is seized by the way a word is spelled, perhaps a name you have heard mentioned on radio or television but never seen written before? You may have read beyond the word in the text but you go back because you know there was something that reached for your attention. What you find is a word that you did not know how to spell, that you are interested in knowing how to spell (or about whose spelling you are at least mildly curious) but which you certainly did not expect to find or to learn when you began reading. Indeed, your reason for reading had nothing to do with spelling. Such, I think, is one of the rare occasions when we might be briefly aware of an engagement taking place, the brain capitalizing on a demonstration.

Here is a second illustration. You are again reading a novel or a magazine article, and once more you are quite unexpectedly halted because your attention has been seized, not this time by a spelling but by the way an idea has been expressed. You find the phrase or passage that stopped you, read it again, and think momentarily how well the words express a particular idea. You have become engaged with a demonstration of the way a particular expression in words has been made.

In each of my two illustrations it was as if you had little "learning hooks" unknowingly extended as you read, waiting to engage in an appropriate demonstration should one occur, in the first example for spellings and in the second for apt ways of saying things. You were possibly in a condition of "flow" (Csikzentmihalyi, 1990), immersed in an activity, unaware that the particular hooks were out or that the appropriate demonstrations would occur. But when the demonstrations and hooks coincided, engagement took place. On such occasions, I believe, you experienced a moment of learning. Usually, however, we learn without awareness; our engagements are unsuspected.

The learning hooks have to be out constantly, especially for the young, and engagement must be such a common experience it rarely intrudes upon awareness. How else could the brain accomplish the enormous amounts of learning it achieves? The brains of children especially must be ready to grasp at every relevant demonstration the world offers, to engage in learning at every opportunity. I see no other way to account for the great repertoire of skills and fund of knowledge possessed by every child who can talk, understand the speech of parents, friends, and television, and make sense of a complex world even before coming to school. But adults also learn without being aware that the learning is taking place.

Engagement occurs quite mundanely, as you can easily demonstrate to yourself. Take a few minutes to reflect upon the *last* newspaper you read, even if it was several days ago. I am sure you can still recollect the main news stories, the pictures on the front page, and the content of any particular section you read—the sports, entertainment, or review pages, for example. (You might also reflect briefly upon the last movie or television program that you saw, the last novel you read, the last time you went out to dinner, or any other recent event in your life. With a little patience you will be able to reconstruct far more of these occasions than you might have thought possible.)

My point in asking you to experience the kind of demonstration I have just described is not simply to impress you with the amount of learning that you must have accomplished but to show how such learning will take place without conscious effort.[6] I am sure you did not sit down with the newspaper and say that you were going to remember all the details you now remember. (If you had deliberately tried to learn, you would probably have remembered far less.) The learning took place concurrently with the understanding; it was part of the comprehension.

Here I suspect is the clue to how engagement takes place, the nature of the "hooks." Comprehension, as I argued in Chapter 4, is not a passive activity. To understand anything it is necessary to anticipate, to predict some alternative possibilities for what might occur. The very act of understanding entails the testing of hypotheses, a learning situation. The hooks that go out when engagement occurs are the hooks that are necessary for any understanding, for "grasping" a situation or a story.

Experimental psychologists have shown that our memory of an event cannot be separated from the way we made sense of that event.[7] To me this finding confirms that the way we make sense of a demonstration, relating it to the organization of what we already know, constitutes what we may learn from the demonstration. Such learning is frequently *vicarious*; we learn from what someone else is doing or has done as if we were doing it ourselves. Another person's demonstration becomes our own learning experience. But such learning is vicarious in the subtlest of ways; it does not even require an overt intention on our part, only the normal effort of involvement and understanding.

To master physical skills, of course, some deliberate practice is usually required. We will not become very good singers, typists, or skiers if we do not attempt these things ourselves. But by observation we may discover possibilities to attempt or to avoid ourselves. Whenever we participate with understanding in a situation, even one as ostensibly passive as reading a newspaper or watching a movie, engagement is likely to occur. The engagement is in the involvement.

Yet obviously there are many exceptions. Often we see new spellings and we do not learn them. We all have difficulty learning many things some of the time and some things all of the time. We do not all extend the same hooks. My own learning hooks seem reasonably efficient for spellings, but I have a terrible time with the names of trees and flowers. If learning is so natural and effortless, why does engagement so often fail to occur? Why in particular should some people have such difficulty learning to spell, punctuate, or write meaningfully and grammatically, although they may read as much as others who succeed? It is to account for this difference that I now want to explore what I term sensitivity, the third critical condition of learning.

Sensitivity

It might be thought that the reason we learn in some situations but not in others must be related to motivation; engagement takes place when we want to learn and does not occur when motivation is lacking. But such an explanation is most inadequate.

For a start, motivation is certainly no guarantee of learning. We would all like to learn things that will forever be beyond us. I could not be more motivated to learn to distinguish at least some common trees and flowers; constant failure to do so is embarrassing and discouraging. I make frequent attempts to remedy this deficiency, but without success. If anything, excess of motivation can be disruptive, we fail to learn because we try too hard, *confronting* what we would like to learn rather than embracing it. And then, the greater part of all the learning we do seems to take place without motivation, certainly not of the overt kind. To say that a baby is motivated to learn to talk or that a casual reader is motivated to learn what is in the evening newspaper both seem to me to make nonsense of the term, to confuse deliberate intention and effort with a very general interest in something that is going on. At best, motivation puts us in situations where relevant demonstrations are likely to occur, but then "motivation" in this context is practically synonymous with "interest."

Of course, motivation *not* to learn, a deliberate intention that learning shall not take place, will generally prove effective, but learning itself as I have tried to show usually takes us unawares. Motivation, I have decided, is largely an educational red herring, a convenient way of allocating fault. Some other factor must be involved, something that is particularly relevant to formal learning situations (both in school and outside) because it is in such situations that even greatly desired learning seems so often not to occur.

And that other factor has be *expectation*. It is when we expect learning to occur, when we take the learning for granted and do not give it a thought, that engagement takes place. Expect learning not to occur, and the hooks just do not go out; there is no possibility of engagement. Because we so often take learning for granted—when it occurs—I have to define sensitivity in negative terms. Sensitivity is the absence of expectation that learning will not take place.

The consideration is basically economic, a matter of profit and loss. Deliberate learning has a price as well as a value, a cost in terms of effort, of alternatives given up, of failure and error. We are unlikely to expose ourselves to an opportunity for learning if we think the possibility of success is remote or fear the consequence of error. Engagement requires a reaching toward the learning opportunity, not in the sense of strain or effort but in the sense of an openness, often characterized simply as "interest." Just as a demonstration can be conceived of in terms of "This is how something is done," so sensitivity reflects "I do not anticipate any difficulty in learning to do (or understand) this thing myself," a commitment with confidence to learning.

Such an expectation of learning is generally so pervasive, so much a part of our everyday commerce with the world, that it is taken for granted. Usually we are no more aware of our intention to learn or of our expectation of learning than we are of learning itself; all are reflections of the brain's continual interaction with what (to the brain) are relevant aspects of the world. Motivation and the expectation of learning are, like comprehension and learning, most evident in their absence, or when obstacles arise. We do not usually bother to remark that an infant is motivated to learn to walk or talk because the motivation for both, and the expectation of success, are like success itself taken for granted.

It is perhaps curious how expectations of failure on the part of young people seem so often to emanate from adults, and how prophetic such expectations often are; club membership is almost automatically denied. Everyone expects infants to learn to understand speech, and with very few exceptions every infant does, although as I have already argued the feat demands a considerable intellectual effort. Learning to read should be considerably less demanding, given the experience the child has already had with language learning, yet expectations of failure abound and failures duly occur. Everyone expects infants to learn to walk, and learn to walk they do. Swimming might be regarded as almost as natural and instinctive as walking—certainly many children take to it like ducks—yet prognostications of difficulty arise and difficulty ensues. Age is not the issue; no one expects teenagers to have difficulty learning to drive cars, and difficulties rarely occur.

Where does sensitivity come from? We must be born with it. Infants believe they can learn anything, until experience teaches them otherwise. The brain's propensity to learn can work against its own interests because it can learn that it is unlikely to learn certain things, a critically maladaptive idea that can be as difficult to dislodge from our unconscious mind as an incorrect spelling. Sensitivity does not have to be taught; it must be nurtured and protected. It is not easily restored. Neither I nor anyone else is likely to persuade me that I could become an automobile mechanic at this late stage, no matter how much I am told "it should be easy." I have been persuaded that I am not a member of the club.

Everyone is born sensitive to style and register, certainly in spoken language. Children can detect when someone is speaking to them in an unfamiliar or inappropriate tone for any reason. They can mimic the way parents and teachers talk. If they have had stories read to them, they will begin telling their own with "Once upon a time" and similar written language conventions. Such sensitivity can persist. I know that reading influences my own writing. If my current relaxation happens to be a humorist, I am tempted to crack jokes. Scientific articles tend to make me more analytical, while a mystery inclines me to devise a detective story from the pursuit of understanding. I recognize this sensitivity and occasionally try to exploit it, reading certain authors before I write not so much for what they say as how they say it, for the lucidity of X, the wisdom of Y, the wit of Z. Is it superstition that keeps these books close at hand as I write, a belief in sympathetic magic? Are they a convenient distraction, or do they indeed influence my own composition? A simple test would be for me to name my models, the sources of my preferred demonstrations. But such a confession would invite comparisons I do not feel I can afford.

Sensitivity is not something apart from learning; rather, it delineates what the brain will learn. It represents what the brain is interested in, what it expects to learn whenever there is an opportunity. We do not learn at random, nor does experience arbitrarily determine what we learn. We learn what we expect to learn, as a consequence of the way we perceive ourselves and our interactions with the world. Not learning is not the brain getting old, or shutting down: it is the brain rejecting learning opportunities because it has decided that learning is too much trouble, or that it knows enough, or that learning is unlikely to take place in any case.

(Notes to Chapter 12 begin on page 258.)

13 Learning the Technicalities

Becoming a writer begins with seeing oneself as a writer. But self-image is not enough; the technicalities must be learned. In essence, learners do this by apprenticing themselves to established writers, joining the club, keeping the company of more experienced authors, and vicariously doing themselves the things done by the writers they read.

LEARNING FROM READING AND FROM WRITING

There appears to be an asymmetrical if not parasitical relationship between writing and reading. Writing needs reading, but reading can do without writing, even though writing may provide shortcuts to understanding aspects of reading. In the same way we can recognize faces without first having to learn to draw them, although experience in drawing faces may enrich the way we see them.

It is important to distinguish how much can be learned about writing from reading and how much from writing. Reading is the essential source of knowledge about writing, from the conventions of transcription to the subtle nuances of register and discourse structures in various genres. No one writes enough to get all this information from the editing or correction, and very little of it can be imparted by direct instruction. Nevertheless, the act of writing is critical for several reasons, which I now enumerate.

Practice is required to shape and consolidate any skilled act. Writing is not a simple matter of transcribing on paper the letters of words whose spellings we already know or can work out (or even of typing those individual letters on a keyboard). To write with the fluency that composition requires, it is necessary to write (or type) words rather than letters, fast enough and with so little conscious effort that attention can be concentrated on composition. The physical burden of having to draw each unfamiliar individual letter is one of the greatest obstacles in the way of children striving to achieve fluency in writing.

Spelling is perhaps the only aspect of writing that might be learned entirely from reading. The spelling of each word in a text is a *fact*; it is there in front of our eyes. To spell this particular word, we write these particular letters. No other aspect of writing is presented so unambiguously. A text may show how some piece of punctuation has been done, but not how to do it. The same applies to capitalization, paragraphing, and all the other conventions of transcription; examples are demonstrated, not principles. So the second reason that writing is necessary for learning to write is that most of the demonstrations in a text do not show how to do something but only how something has been done. To learn to do these things ourselves, we must try them for ourselves, to work out possibilities in practice.

This leads to the third necessity. Unless you write, you cannot find out whether you have learned anything about writing. The act of writing does more than polish skills; it offers an opportunity, often the only opportunity, for testing conjectures, for confirming or rejecting hypotheses. Write something, and you have the possibility of learning from someone else whether you have punctuated appropriately, whether your intended meaning is clear, or whether you have indeed produced the correct spellings. Some things you can check, provisionally at least, simply by reading what you yourself have written. Just as a child does not need a teacher to explain that a fall from a bicycle is a consequence of doing something wrong, we become aware of shortcomings in our own writing ability without the involvement of a second party.

Moreover, writing can be a shortcut to encountering just the demonstrations that will be most relevant at a particular time. You may not be sure how best to phrase a particular remark, to achieve a certain effect, and you could have a long wait for the relevant demonstration to come your way by chance. If you make an attempt yourself, the response of an instructor or other interested reader may provide precisely the demonstration that you need. This evocation of relevant demonstrations is an important part of the way infants learn to talk. They do not wait for an adult to demonstrate something they want to say; they make their own best effort and allow the second party, politely or otherwise, to show them how more experienced exponents of the language think it should be done. Our own efforts are in themselves demonstrations of how something might be done and can effectively evoke an appropriate demonstration of how it should be done.

Finally, and perhaps most importantly, writing provides the incentive, the purpose for learning about writing from reading. Unless one wants to write, and sees oneself as a writer, there is no reason to be responsive to the facets of writing demonstrated in text. The key to learning about writing from reading is *to read like a writer*.

Learning about Writing from Reading

Having stressed the importance of engaging in writing as a groundwork for learning, I can now elaborate on the point that knowledge of all the conventions of writing can only come from reading.

Think of the knowledge that becomes available from a simple act of reading. Every book demonstrates how every word in that book is spelled—and it demonstrates the spelling in a meaningful context, which means that the spelling is easier to learn. Most of the time that is the way we all—children and "poor spellers" as well—learn how words are spelled (provided we read with the engagement of writers, as members of the club). The book also demonstrates the meaning of each of these words—in fact once anyone becomes a reader, it is the principal way that new words are learned (Nagy, Herman, and Anderson, 1985).

Every book also demonstrates how every word in the book is employed—its role in titles, headings, captions, idioms, slang, phrases, and sentences. In other words—books (and other kinds of text) demonstrate grammar, not in an abstract sense but in actual use, the way learners encounter spoken language. They also demonstrate how paragraphs are organized and many other aspects of style. Paragraphing itself is a matter of style, not of rules. Different authors organize their paragraphs—like their sentences—in different ways, depending on the tone and texture they wish to achieve, ranging from the telegraphic short sentences and paragraphs of Hemingway to the complex meandering constructions of Henry James. Every sentence in a published text also demonstrates how that kind of sentence is punctuated, and the roles of capital letters, dashes, parentheses, quotation marks, and various signs of emphasis. Story books demonstrate how stories are told; newspaper reports demonstrate how newspaper articles are written; poems demonstrate poetry. They also demonstrate how texts of their kind are presented typographically.

In other words, every text demonstrates all the conventions of that particular kind of text; the conventions of the genre, as well as the appropriate registers that are employed on particular occasions. For further details of everything that can be learned from "free voluntary reading," including a useful compendium of the research behind all the claims that are made, see Krashen (1993).[1]

Reading like a writer is *collaborative learning*, even though it might appear that the reader is alone. But reading like a writer means reading *with the author*, as if one were writing the text oneself. In effect, it is the author who shows the learner how every word is spelled, every sentence punctuated, and so forth—always at a time and in a way that is most meaningful to the reader. Authors—even dead ones—have this tremendous advantage over live teachers; they always proceed at the pace of the individual learner, and are able to repeat their lessons as often as the learner wants, without any coercion, embarrassment or punitive threat. (Teachers have other important responsibilities, like encouraging learners to see themselves as writers, demonstrating how members of the writers' club engage in club activities, and putting apprentice writers in the company of authors.)

Most of these things could never be learned from direct instruction, which would mean difficulty and frustration for teachers and learners alike. To understand this better, it is necessary to look more closely at all the technicalities of writing, and is a major reason for the detailed sections that follow.

THE ROLE OF INVENTION

There is a thread I shall follow through the remainder of this chapter, that the basis of learning to write is *inventiveness*, manifested through sensitivity in reading and experimentation in writing.[2] I look in more detail at how learners of any age begin to acquire expertise in various aspects of transcription and composition. Whether we examine handwriting, spelling, punctuation, or composition, we find both a necessity and evidence that inventiveness exists, right from the start, informed, wherever possible, by knowledge gained from reading.

I begin with aspects of transcription—with spelling, punctuation, and grammar—before proceeding to composition, revision, and editing. But this is an arbitrary choice, for convenience in exposition. In fact I leave handwriting to the end of the chapter, partly because it is a relatively long section, but also because I do not think it warrants *primary* attention. Handwriting has interesting aspects (one reason the section is long), and some people make a fetish of it, but unlike other aspects of transcription and composition, becoming a writer does not (or certainly should not) depend on quality of handwriting. And for learners who use word processors, handwriting need not be any kind of issue before they become fluent writers.

I do not want to imply that fluency in transcription skills has to precede development in composition, nor would I wish to suggest that transcription should come last or be learned independently from composition. Skill in transcription facilitates composition, but endeavor in composition provides the basis for learning about transcription. Learning to write advances most effectively on a broad front, in all areas concurrently, mutually supportive. It is only because the act of writing requires dealing with one topic at a time that I have segregated composition and transcription at any point in this book.

As I examine how particular conventions are learned, it may be useful occasionally to refer back to earlier sections of the book where the conventions were themselves discussed. Indicated in parentheses beside the next few side headings are the numbers of the pages where relevant prior discussion may be found.

Spelling (pages 141–152)

Spelling is another aspect of early writing where the inventiveness of children is particularly visible—perhaps too visible, some teachers might say. I am referring to such apparently tortuous efforts at "phonetic" spelling as *lovvabull* (lovable), *muther, kari* (carry), *nysli* (nicely), *hows, wos, plesman* (policeman), *lukt* (looked), *klimd* (climbed), *jres* (dress), and *chree* (tree), not to mention *alot* (a lot) and *wus a pone a tim*. But then I have also seen literate adults (schoolteachers no less) write *alot, frinstance* (for instance) and *nexstore* (next door).

The frequent violence done to conventional English orthography by children and older students, especially by the more enthusiastic young writers, should not be immediately attributed to laziness, perversity, or inadequate learning. Rather it can reflect eagerness to capitalize upon an overrated principle of our written language—that spelling represents the sounds of speech—and determination to get on with the essential business of writing, the construction of meaningful texts. (A more restrictive tactic subsequently adopted by astute students who become persuaded that creativity in spelling is not widely commended is to avoid writing words that they think they are likely to spell incorrectly.)

Invented spelling is not unique to the young. Experienced writers will also invent if a required spelling does not come immediately to mind, rather than have the disruption of consulting a dictionary. (Looking up a word can be particularly time-consuming when you have no idea of its spelling; dictionaries are not well organized for poor spellers.) Indeed, most of the words that individual adults spell incorrectly must be inventions; it is surely rare that we see words spelled incorrectly, and rarer still that we fail to recognize them as misspellings, unless we have produced the incorrect spelling ourselves.

Invented spellings are more conspicuous in beginners' writing because beginners have fewer correct spellings at their command. Learning to spell takes time; it begins with misspellings. Learners who write only the words they know how to spell end up writing (and knowing how to spell) very few words indeed. Besides, there are two powerful factors working against children's early efforts to spell phonetically, one being the nature of the spelling system itself and the other the way in which they hear.

I have already discussed the main problem with the spelling system, that an exact or even approximate representation of the sounds of speech is not spelling's overriding concern. Not only are there hundreds of "rules" relating spelling and sound, none of which is without exception, but spelling is in any case expected primarily to represent meaning. Different meanings can be spelled in quite different ways despite similarity in sound (*there* and *their; bear* and *bare*) for a variety of historical or accidental reasons, and other variations are determined by purely grammatical (walk*ed*, hugg*ed*, and hand*ed*) or visual (*tie, tying*) considerations. The spelling of individual words is more a matter of convention than rule, and to make matters even more complicated, the conventions of spelling, even when they are related to the sounds of speech, in fact represent *conventions* of what the sounds of speech are thought to be, rather than what the sounds actually are.

A literal representation of all shades of sound that are employed in speech requires an alphabet of well over a hundred characters; this is the minimum that linguists employ to make phonetic transcriptions capturing all of the nuances of speech. Adults with untrained ears usually find it difficult to detect such shades of difference in the sounds of spoken words for a rather peculiar reason. When we know something about spelling, we begin to persuade ourselves that we can *hear* the spelling in spoken words. For example, we may claim to hear a nonexistent /t/ sound in the middle of the usual pronunciation of the word *writer*. We may even distort the normal pronunciation of such words in order to demonstrate that spelling reflects sound, arguing that spoken language should reflect spelling.

Children do not share the adult inability to perceive the actual sounds of speech; this is their second problem, concerning the way they hear. Children hear too well from a spelling point of view. Since they are not familiar with spelling in the first place, they are not biased toward hearing spelling in spoken words and instead will attempt to reproduce the sounds of speech as they actually are, like a professional phonetician. And phonetic transcription does not result in conventional spelling.

Thus a critical step for anyone learning to spell is not so much to learn a principle that spelling reflects sound as to recognize its limitations. The lifelong difficulties of some poor spellers may have their roots in their early frustrations of trying to spell words—being urged to do so, in fact—in a way that could only be guaranteed to fail.

Why should anyone invent spellings? Obviously, because they do not know required spellings already. There are two parts to the task of learning to spell any word; the first is to discover the correct (the conventional) spelling, and the second is to remember it. Perhaps I might recapitulate what I have already said on this matter in a way that could seem self-evident if not absurd. Remembering spellings is no problem when it is not a problem and a considerable problem when it is. I mean that remembering depends on the elusive factor that I have called *sensitivity*. If spellings are the kinds of thing our brain remembers, then countless spellings will be remembered indefinitely, effortlessly. But if we do not remember spellings in this way, then learning spelling is likely to be a most difficult, sporadic, and frustrating business indeed.

But whether we remember spellings easily or not, there is still the fundamental matter of discovering correct spellings in the first place. Invention will not tell us; even if the invention is correct, we still have to check to find out. The only dependable ways to discover correct spellings are to look them up in a dictionary, to consult (or be told by) someone else who knows, or to come across them more or less by chance while reading or in spelling exercises. None of these circumstances is likely to happen with great frequency or especial relevance at the beginning of a writing and reading career. Beginners will have few learned spellings already in the bank, their reading may be limited in amount and content, and the major effort in their formal spelling instruction may be expended on rote memorization, which affords them little relevance or satisfaction. So anyone who wants to write or is interested in writing has little choice but to invent spellings.

The fact that invented spellings are almost certain to be wrong is not the crux of the matter. The purpose of invented spelling is not to enable the writer to spell correctly but to separate the specific problem of learning to spell from the other, more satisfying matter perhaps, of getting on with writing. Formal exercises in spelling and the effort to memorize spelling lists may provide an opportunity to discover some correct spellings at the beginning, but they are most likely to be useful and successful with students who would learn to spell from reading in any case. For others they may offer only discouragement and interfere with the essential sensitivity.[3]

Beginners do not learn to spell by writing, and they (and their teachers) may have to tolerate considerable misspelling if they are to get on with the practice of writing while waiting for a repertoire of correct spellings to accumulate from reading. Writing is *relevant* to spelling, but primarily in providing the reason and occasionally the direction for learning to spell. There is not much point in learning to spell if you have little intention of writing, but if you want to write with reasonably conventional spelling then there can be no substitute for reading.

Punctuation (pages 152–158)

Conventions of punctuation are demonstrated in every text we read, but while illustrating how particular conventions are employed, they do not tell us how to employ the conventions ourselves. There is not much point in remembering that a certain sentence ended with a period or employed quotation marks at a particular place. What we need to know is how to apply these particular conventions to sentences we ourselves produce.

Punctuation therefore requires more than memorization; an implicit understanding must be brought to it. It is not enough to observe punctuation, or even to be told the "rules"; its purposes must be deduced. This kind of learning need not be difficult; it is the way we learn speech. But like speech, punctuation can be learned only through comprehension of its uses.

However, punctuation does not seem to be quite the spontaneous kind of activity that speech or even spelling are. Children do not often invent punctuation. But then it has not such an evident utility. As I said in Chapter 10, many written languages exist without punctuation, and it is not clear what *essential* functions punctuation might perform. My conjecture was that the various manifestations of punctuation are fairly arbitrary conventions employed to consolidate the implicit contract between writers and readers, not something for which beginning writers would necessarily see an immediate need. The conventions of punctuation may also have come to serve as retrospective markers indicating to writers the path that has been covered, not again a matter of great concern for beginning writers producing relatively short texts.

But if children are not spontaneously inventive in producing punctuation, their use of punctuation as they become familiar with it is certainly creative. They invent applications for punctuation. As children perceive uses for punctuation they may employ it almost indiscriminately, scattering commas or capitals or exclamation marks across their texts rather in the way they frequently use new spoken words they have learned in contexts which might to an adult seem completely inappropriate. By exploring its uses so they learn the limitations of a convention.

Punctuation for children often begins with emphasis, the use of underlining, capital letters, or exclamation marks for effects that cannot yet be achieved though composition. Particular forms often spread through classrooms like a contagion. A teacher may give instruction for weeks on how exclamation marks should be employed, but not until children actually see them being used with a purpose—perhaps in the writing of just one child in the class—does the idea catch. And then the marks may spread rapidly from child to child, cropping up all over their texts like measles. In fact, children will produce texts especially to use the new punctuation. Where the intention is simply to accommodate the teacher, placement of punctuation may be almost random, but where the child has a purpose, then both the use of the punctuation and the composition of the text that justifies it become deliberate. Children have little interest in punctuation as a nicety, as a convention that other people might expect, but they can become fascinated by its use.[4]

Far more than spelling, punctuation requires the practice of writing and the confirmation of feedback, for learners of all ages. Writing is important initially not so much for punctuation to be *practiced*, to become automatic, as to provide opportunities for discovering whether it is right or wrong. Reading may be a source of hypotheses about punctuation, but the hypotheses still have to be tested by attempting to use punctuation and then having someone say whether it has been employed conventionally or not. Spelling can be checked in a dictionary, but it is rarely possible to consult a book to discover whether punctuation was appropriate. It is probably not until learners have begun to experiment with punctuation in their own writing that they can become sensitive to it in the writing of others. Once they can begin to *anticipate* certain kinds of punctuation, they can become sensitive to whether it is used elsewhere in the manner in which they would use it themselves.

I have stressed that punctuation is not self-evident but have not said anything very positive about instruction, about learning by being told something about rules of punctuation or by looking them up in a reference book. Punctuation can rarely be reduced to simple rules, especially rules that attempt to relate its conventions to the patterns of speech. As with spelling, people familiar with its conventions generally feel they can *hear* punctuation in speech; there seems to be a definite place for periods, commas, and quotation marks. Of course, if you know where punctuation should go, it is not difficult to hear where the punctuation belongs, where it is "required." But this impression is a consequence of being able to punctuate, not a basis for its necessity.

Instruction also tends to illustrate usage rather than explain principles. We are told, for example, that periods should be placed at the ends of sentences or after abbreviations, or that lists should be preceded by a colon, but these "rules" are no more than assertions of custom, like saying that brown shoes should not be worn with black socks. They are not a rationale. The major problem with formal statements about punctuation is that they require an understanding of what they are supposed to explain in the first place. They may also require an understanding of grammatical terminology, which itself is explained with respect to punctuation—complete circularity.

Not even the use of quotation marks around direct speech is self-evident; many contemporary written languages dispense with or employ them quite differently. The distinction between direct and indirect speech is particularly difficult for anyone to grasp before becoming a writer, if only because one does not listen to "the actual words" in speech, but rather to meaning. Not being able to understand the use of quotation marks does not mean an inability to understand spoken language, but only confusion over a complex written-language convention.

The use of the question mark demands a similar ability to make formal statements about language. Everyone knows in practice the difference between a question and answer; even children know how and when to ask questions and they recognize when an answer is given. They also know how to answer questions (if they know the answer). But they do not know how to talk about these abilities that they have. To understand what a teacher means by the word "question" confuses many 7- and 8-year-olds who have been asking questions for years. It does not help them to be told that a question is a request for information, because the paraphrase is perhaps even more difficult to understand than the original expression. And it is not necessarily helpful to be told that questions begin with *who*, *what*, *where*, *why*, *when*, or *how*, because many questions do not begin with any of these words, and many sentences that are not questions do.

How then does anyone ever learn to recognize a question, a clause, a sentence, or paragraph in order to make sense of instruction, or otherwise to place question marks, commas, periods, indentations, and so forth in conventional locations? The answer is in the same way that they once came to recognize dogs, cats, chairs, tables, and just about everything else in the world. Adults do not often try to define what constitutes a cat, dog, chair, or table. They do not attempt to teach rules of catness, dogness, or whatever. They simply point out instances of each category and leave children to work out the rules themselves, implicitly. Perhaps they best help beginners to understand punctuation by helping them to understand passages in their reading, which include various types of punctuation and to employ it appropriately in what they are actually writing.

Grammar (pages 49–59)

The creative manner in which children begin to write is also exemplified in their grammar, although perhaps less obviously than in their early spelling and punctuation because many of the grammatical structures with which they experiment can also be expressed and explored through speech. Children and older students' writing often differs from their speech simply because they cannot write fast enough to produce complex sentences they have no difficulty in saying. Their writing begins as a kind of truncated version of their spoken language, a compression that is in itself inventive because it does not reflect anything they could have heard or read elsewhere. Until they become aware of conventional differences between spoken and written language, their way of writing naturally reflects the conventions they respect in their speech—to the extent that they can get these conventions down on paper.

There are some important differences in the opportunities available to beginners for becoming aware of specifically grammatical conventions of written language. Insights about spelling and punctuation are primarily available through reading because neither is represented in speech; no understanding can be gained of either punctuation or spelling from the way people talk, or even from their reading aloud. However, the grammar of written language can be *heard*—for example, when someone reads aloud or talks in registers close to those of written language. Children who are read to can therefore become familiar with some of the grammatical structures of written language without having to write or read for themselves, and so can older students who read, or who "hear written language spoken," for example, in formal lecture or public speaking situations. Thus one might expect familiarity with specific grammatical structures of writing before a great grasp of either spelling or punctuation is achieved.

And indeed, there is evidence that many children are sensitive to constructions of written language before they can write or even read for themselves. Prereaders will usually relate an account of something that happened to them in a spoken language register, but if asked specifically to "tell a story" they are quite likely to employ other stylistic devices more characteristic of texts than of informal speech. Older students learning to write, especially if highly motivated, may demonstrate too much sensitivity to particular aspects of written language. They may strive deliberately to produce complicated sentences, recondite synonyms, and florid phraseology simply because they believe this is what written language is like. Such a disproportionate respect for relatively superficial aspects of written language, often at the expense of clarity, can be quite persistent, spreading like a weed, for example, over the written assignments of college students and in inexperienced attempts at formal letters, poetry, and various forms of technical writing. Such "poor writing" does not so much reveal ignorance as an undue sensitivity to conventions of written language without the leavening effect of relevant feedback. To write grammatically and appropriately, one needs more than demonstrations and engagement; one needs editing.

I should perhaps reiterate how I am using the terms "grammar" and "grammatical." I am not talking about the "rules" set out in formal grammar books, which are descriptions of sentences that are considered grammatical, descriptions of products rather than procedures by which grammatical sentences might be produced. Despite the frequent efforts to teach these rules, they are not the means by which children become writers. Noun-verb agreement, for example, is a convention of English that is learned in the process of tidying up language already produced; the rule makes no sense unless you are already producing nouns and verbs. It is not a tool that you can use for producing language; it does not help you say things. Indeed, we all know there is a difference between being able to produce language grammatically and being able to talk about its grammar. Most of us can speak or write conventionally without being able to specify the rules. Even the ability to write grammatically does not guarantee that we will understand what a grammarian is talking about.

By "grammar" I mean the implicit rules that mediate the production of sentences, the connections between the deep structures and surface structures of language (pages 52–54). And by "grammatical" I mean conformity with the conventions of other users of the same language, the conventions of a particular language use. The "rules" are implicit, describable only by analogy or metaphor, since one end of them is rooted in meaning, in the mental arena that lies beyond words. This implicit grammar cannot be taught or even be directly discussed. Beginners do not learn by collecting rules that they then apply to the business of being a writer. But in the process of trying to write they can become sensitive to conventions. Many authors have given credit to their teachers for encouraging them to write and helping them to avoid their own errors, but no authors to my knowledge have ever said that lessons in grammar—either the old grammar of the traditional grammarians or the new grammars of the transformational linguists—made them into writers.

I do not in fact want to make a distinction between the grammar of sentences and other aspects of word selection and organization in writing, such as the conventions of cohesion, discourse structures, and relevant genre schemes (pages 91–93). Although they can not all be learned at once, of course, they can be learned concurrently. The distinctions are arbitrary, drawn for our theoretical or instructional purposes but not separate parts of what a child has to learn. The structures required to express complex thought and the complex thought that employs those structures develop together. Beginners can learn all the conventions of letter writing in reading and attempting to write letters, and all the conventions of stories in telling, reading, and listening to stories. Intention, sensitivity, and skill develop together.

It may seem surprising, a dereliction of duty almost, that I have no more to say on a topic that fills so many fat books and occupies so much concern in school and out. But I do not see grammar as a learning topic in its own right, except for the language specialist. Exercises in the finer points of grammar will only make sense to students already writing. They will not make a beginner a writer. I am not saying that "good grammar" does not matter, but that there is no point in learning it instead of writing. Every convention of writing is tied to an intention that lies behind writing; conventions without intention are of only academic interest and extremely difficult to learn. Until inhibited, children who want to say things, to create worlds in writing, use any grammar that is available to them. They experiment with grammar, and become sensitive to relevant demonstrations either through instruction or through reading. For writers, grammar is inseparable from composition, which is the topic to which I now turn.

Composition (pages 104–119)

To learn to compose, beginners need not learn to be creative, which is the natural function of everyone's brain. But they do need to learn the conventions by which creativity can become manifest in composition; they need to discover what can be done with written language.

Everyone has a natural interest in stories. We all create imaginative worlds in the light of the realities of the world around us, constructing a theory of the world that works. We also create imaginative worlds just for the sake of living in them. In using their brains sometimes to establish fact, sometimes to explore fantasy, children (and not infrequently adults) often fail to distinguish between the two. They are as content to tell, hear, and reflect upon stories of possible worlds as they are to experience the "real" one.

But storytelling requires a knowledge of conventions with which anyone who is not a practicing reader will not be particularly familiar. One problem is that stories, just like individual sentences, have to be unraveled over time in order to be expressed. Language demands a beginning, a middle, and an end. But a story is a whole; its end is closure, completion, not a termination. Even the simplest narrative technique of unfolding a story in the order in which events occurred in time is only a convention, perhaps the easiest convention for anyone to understand and learn, but nonetheless arbitrary rather than "natural." Indeed, chronological exactitude in storytelling is a convention often broken. The "logical" place to begin is just as likely to be the concluding as the initial state of affairs. All stories are to some extent flashbacks.

The difficulty young children have in telling stories may have nothing to do with lack of something to say, with absence of content. Kindergarten children were asked to retell a favorite story they knew well, on which they had been especially coached. The children were reluctant to tell the story and argued that they did not know how to do so, an assertion they then demonstrated to be true. Questioning by the investigators (Dowley and Sulzby, undated), however, revealed that the children were in command of all the facts of the story. They could relate relevant incidents when specifically prompted. But they could not take the initiative in telling the story until halfway through and did not become enthusiastic about the task until near the end. The children had the entire story, at a global level, in their heads, but they could not unwind it in time. They were unsure where to begin and how episodes should be linked. In particular, it would seem, children lack familiarity with conventions at the intermediate levels involving the ordering and connecting of sentences and paragraphs. Globally they know what stories are about; they can understand and invent situations on broad canvases. And focally they can put words together in simple sentences. But they have difficulty in moving between these two extremes. This is a problem not unknown to adults.

It must be extremely difficult to practice conventions of composition while the underlying demands of transcription are so disproportionately great, when the physical act of writing is still slow and laborious. You do not learn to dance wearing heavy boots. Beginners have a tendency to stop writing after a few sentences, often after only one. Typically they stop when there is more that they could say. Partly I think this must be due to the physical effort of writing, but partly also to uncertainty about what should follow next. Many teachers have learned that students can be prompted to write more simply by being *asked* to write more—by being shown that continuation is both expected and possible. When additional sentences are elicited in this way, the composition as a whole tends to be disjointed and unstructured. But the disjointedness may be the reason the student came to a halt in the first place. If you do not know how to stop, you might as well stop now as later.

Another problem confronting beginners concerns what and how much detail should be put into what they write. Descriptions are determined not so much by the object being described as by the alternatives from which the object is to be distinguished. If I asked you to bring me the brown coffee cup with a chipped handle that I left in the kitchen, I would be indicating that there were probably other coffee cups in the kitchen (otherwise I would simply have asked you to bring *the* coffee cup) and that at least one of those other cups would be brown (otherwise I would not have mentioned the chipped handle) but that mine was the only brown cup with a chipped handle (otherwise I would have given some other detail). Adults are extremely good at both giving and comprehending this kind of implicit information, but then we have had years of practice at it; we take it for granted. Children are not so skilled; they leave out detail that we might consider critical and put in detail that to us is completely irrelevant. But this is a facility that requires *experience*; it is not something that anyone can acquire rapidly (and certainly not a "skill" that can be taught all at once). It is acquired progressively, in meaningful settings, when descriptions are required for a purpose.

Expository writing is notoriously difficult for beginners, far harder than narrative. Again, there are probably several explanations. One is unfamiliarity with the task itself. Most students have had some opportunities to produce narrative in spoken language, holding the floor for a minute or two to relate a true or imaginary story. They may even be accustomed to receiving helpful prompts. But describing objects and situations in exposition is not something that younger people are often called upon to do in their world out of school. And there is no natural or logical place to start upon and expand a description of a museum, a picnic, or a summer's day.

Problems of limited experience and familiarity are magnified in composition involving explanation and argument, which is even more difficult than description. Explanation—the why something happened as opposed to the what and how of it—inevitably requires more knowledge. The lack is not necessarily of a particularly abstract or esoteric kind of knowledge, but of more general knowledge. I need to know more to explain why my car will not start than I do merely to state that it does not start: there is more to know, more to say, and a need again for conventions that will organize how it is all to be said. There are many special conventions of formal or persuasive argument with which adults are often unfamiliar. Children and young adults are obviously capable of disputing, but they are usually actively discouraged from "arguing." The conventional ways in which arguments are developed in text have to be understood before they can be learned. What slows beginning writers here is not lack of formal instruction in rhetoric but exposure to forms of exposition and argument whose purposes they can understand.

Composition is often discussed as if it consisted of two separate and independent parts, the generation of something to be said (variously called ideas, thoughts, meaning, or content) and its expression in appropriate sequences of words. But these two aspects cannot be separated. Meaning is made manifest in its expression. We may not know an appropriate way of saying something we want to express, but until we find a way of saying it then what is to be said remains a chimera, at best a more diffuse form of image. As a manifest reflection or consequence of anything in the mind, idea and words must come into existence together.

Thoughts and the conventions by which they may be expressed cannot be separated in learning. Students cannot be taught or even encouraged to produce and manipulate ideas without the words and structures in which they can be manipulated (or some other manifest and conventional medium, such as acting or painting). It is impossible to run ahead with thought or meanings while waiting for techniques to catch up, whatever the medium. On the other hand, mastery of a medium will not develop unless there is something that is expressed or understood.

Conventions cannot precede ideas, nor can ideas precede conventions; the two must develop together. Therefore the development of composition in writing cannot reside in writing alone, but requires reading and being read to. Only from the written language of others can beginning writers observe and understand convention and idea together. When children begin to write, they must overcome the twin handicaps of the physical demands of the task and their own inexperience in clothing ideas in words. As Murray (1978) has argued, a child and a helping adult should write together, the blank page must be just as much of a challenge to the teacher as to the child. A child's first clumsy effort at composition may be a source of delight and satisfaction to both child and interested adults, but if the child is to learn through writing, the child must have opportunities to see not just how something is best written, but what might be written. Children and older learners must go beyond what they themselves can write.

Composition is learned through reading and writing; it can also be fostered by conversation and discussion. Talking with other people is in one sense just like writing in that it provides opportunity for the examination of ideas one already holds and for the generation of new ones. It is important to understand all the advantages of discussion. One can test one's own ideas on others; one can hear, borrow, and steal the ideas of others; but beyond that, new ideas can be generated that did not exist in any of the participants' heads before. This is a communal equivalent of the writer-text interaction I tried to represent in the diagram on page 106. Writing has the advantages of relative permanence and plasticity, but both writing and conversation must be seen as alternative and supplementary means by which ideas may be generated and "composed" in the first place.

Revision and Editing (pages 121–129)

The barrier through which young writers must burst is the enveloping cocoon of transcription. The butterfly of writing remains locked in a mental chrysalis unless the learner can speedily produce words on paper in place of words in the head. The solution for the beginner must be the same as the solution for the experienced writer: to get the words out as fast as possible and to clean them up later. Words on paper can be revised and edited; the spelling, punctuation, capitalization, grammar, cohesion, detail, and general neatness can be attended to at leisure, provided the words are on paper. And in the course of editing, with the help of a more experienced writer, the conventions of spelling and every other aspect of transcription can be observed, tested, and at least partially learned.

Unfortunately, none of these possibilities seems to be immediately self-evident to beginning writers. Perhaps because they are unused to a medium where they can have such immense control, perhaps because they are so impressed by what they can achieve the first time, learners of all ages do not seem particularly inventive in the matter of revision and editing. They tend to think a piece of writing is done at the first attempt. They need demonstrations of the potentialities of rewriting and editing.

Even more unfortunately, beginners rarely have the opportunity to observe that writing need not be considered finished when it is produced for the first time. They rarely see their teachers writing, let alone revising, editing, or throwing drafts away. Usually when they see a text it is a finished product, whether it is a letter, a newspaper or magazine article, or a printed story. They do not see its manner of production.[5]

One of the best kept secrets in school, to which even many teachers seem not to be privy, is that most professional writers produce draft after draft; that they *attack* what they write, erasing, adding, altering, and moving words around; that they rarely write on just one piece of paper at a time; and that they do more planning as they write than before they write.

Students whose mastery of writing is growing are generally not slow to capitalize upon the advantages of revising and editing once these are made apparent to them. They do not find it difficult or confusing to make notes on small pieces of paper, to move these pieces around in space, to dissect texts with scissors and to reorganize them with transparent tape, to insert words in sentences, and to draw loops and arrows that move entire groups of sentences from one place to another. They have little trouble in perceiving writing as a plastic art. Indeed, the power of these manipulative techniques sometimes so impresses children that they will deliberately misplace words or sentences in a draft just for the opportunity to move chunks of text around. Children also do not find it difficult to reread what they have written, provided that they retain an interest in the text they have produced, and there is a purpose for the rereading.

A substantial difference between good and poor writers of all ages and degrees of experience is that the good ones frequently look back and reread, during the writing as well as at the end, and that poor writers rarely read their work at all. Poor writers are much more likely to be satisfied with what they have written, without really knowing what they have written. Good writers, on the other hand, are frequently dissatisfied with what they have done, even after many revisions. Their problem often is deciding to stop, since every rewrite seems to offer the possibility of improvement.

There are differences in rereading too. Poor writers reread, perhaps rewrite a bit (or simply edit a bit), and then write on. Good writers reread, rework, reflect, and *reread again* before writing on. The second (or final) rereading may be less for the sake of revising what has already been written than for gaining momentum and continuity in what is to be written next. Such writing is not one thing after another but one thing flowing out of and into another, with seamless bonds among words, sentences, and paragraphs. Everything that is written or rewritten is groundwork for development of what has already been done and what is still to be done.

How does a beginner learn devices and procedures for facilitating composition, for relieving the pressure of transcription? Again, not by being instructed and exercised upon all the possibilities in advance, when the learner has nothing to say. At such a time all the aspects of revision and editing can only appear as a catalog of purposeless activities. To learn, the student must understand what can be achieved, which is unlikely unless the student is involved in the developing achievement. A student might possibly learn by seeing a teacher revise and edit something that the teacher is personally in the process of writing, but only if the learner understands the intention. Nothing can be learned from a text whose meaning is opaque before, during, and after the editing. Students can learn a great deal from seeing other students revising and editing, especially if the revision can be seen to be productive; then the techniques can become more of the useful contagions that spread rapidly from one student to another in classrooms. But the prime source of information about the means and utility of revision and editing must come when a beginner and a more experienced writer work together on something the beginner is interested in producing, when the advantages are immediately apparent. This is again the ideal learning situation with the more experienced member of the writing club helping the beginner, providing on-the-spot demonstrations that have the maximum relevance because the apprentice member in effect determines what demonstrations shall be given.

The evidence suggests that the mutual writing need not be done often, provided it is done when the learner most wants to write and is most receptive to help. If conventions and techniques are presented at the wrong time, when they are irrelevant or confusing, then any effort to teach and to learn is completely wasted. But if the beginner is involved in doing something—if there is demonstration, engagement, and sensitivity—then the learning takes care of itself.

Handwriting (pages 137–141)

Does writing begin with infant scribbling? It depends on what is meant by scribbling. Children as young as two years of age have been introduced to writing through typewriters[6] or computers, where there can be no question of scribbling in the sense of producing ill-formed or unrecognizable letters. It might be argued that children playing with a keyboard, exploring the potentialities of a machine, are engaging in a kind of scribble. What is important is not to become trapped into a debate about what should be called scribbling, a term also used to label the careless handwriting or composition of adults who know perfectly well how the letters of our alphabet are conventionally formed, but to examine what children might be attempting when they make marks on paper or a screen before they are able to produce conventional letters and words.

Indeed, the first scribbles that small children typically make when given the instruments of writing should be regarded as nothing more than marks on paper, meaningless and perhaps even pointless from the perspective of a literate adult. But these clumsy dots and dashes and tangles of spaghetti are of profound significance to the infant making them, not as an inadequate attempt to produce writing, about which the child may know nothing, but as the creation of something which did not exist in the visual world before. (And this, of course, could occur with a typewriter or computer.) This is not a matter of trying to copy or manipulate aspects of an existing world, but of creating a new world, a possibility which fascinates infants. Their first efforts are not to *represent* anything, but to *construct*, to explore the power of hand and tool.

Such scribbles are more than a precursor of writing; they are equally a preliminary to drawing and painting, to any activity where new aspects of the visual world can be intentionally constructed. The marks are initially of interest for what they constitute, not for what they might be developed to become. Children will begin to scribble before they know anything about writing.

A child's first significant insights about writing may become apparent when scribble is deliberately produced to run roughly horizontally across the page or underneath a picture. The line of the scribble may be broken in places, obviously with the intention of representing the spaces that occur between words. Now the intention behind the marks on paper reflects new knowledge, or at least new hypotheses that can only come from seeing and being sensitive to some conventions of print. The scribble is now intended to *represent* language, a remarkably sophisticated achievement, similar to the blocking out of lines by a graphic designer to indicate the place of printed words in the layout of an advertisement or a page of text. Obviously such scribble is not a poor attempt to copy print in any literal sense. The child may have no conception of letters or even of separate words. The insight is not so much into how writing looks as what it is for, what it can do.

Some investigators call such motivated scribbles "mock writing,"[7] but it should not be seen as a pretense or inadequate effort by the child to imitate something that adults can do better. To the child the scribble is *writing*, an invention that might very well work. The child will often tell an adult what the scribble says, or even ask the adult to read it aloud so that the child can find out what it says. The child has a clear idea of what marks on paper might do, and discovering the precise forms of the marks that are the conventions of the written language is a relatively minor undertaking compared with this first great insight about the potential uses of print.

It can be misleading to view these early demonstrations by children in terms of what we know as literate adults. A child scribbling across a page is not making a feeble effort to produce letters, the very notion of a letter may have no significance at that time. Children do not ape what adults do, except in games. They try, if they wish, to achieve the results that adults achieve. Adults see letters and spellings as obvious solutions that children must learn in order to solve the problems of becoming writers. But the *fact* of the alphabet and spelling and all the other conventions of language is something each child must discover personally, as possible but not unique solutions to the problems of making readable marks on paper. Obviously, the solutions achieved by Chinese children in their culture are different from those of English-writing children. An infant's scribble contains the seeds of English, Chinese, and every other script in the world.

Inventiveness and exploration are further displayed as children (on their way to becoming writers of English script) develop the insights that text can be broken down into words and letters. Children do not passively copy adult letters. Once they get an idea of what letters are like, of how they work, they begin to invent their own. Sometimes called "mock letters," these letterlike shapes are not playful; they are serious endeavor. The child is not producing forms that *look like* letters but forms that *could be* letters and just happen not to be. Of course, there is a copying aspect. When a child knows what letters can do, when they are recognizable for their relevance, then a deliberate effort to learn them can begin. Children will also try to copy letters if asked to do so, especially if the task seems important to an adult, but copying is a meaningless activity for children who see no purpose for what they copy. It may make little sense to a child to learn to draw a *Tee* or an *Oh* or an *Emm*—

meaningless names for such strange-looking configurations as *T* and *O* and *M*—but it can make a lot of sense to be able to write *TOM*, especially if that happens to be your name.

As I said earlier, an enormous advantage of the alphabet is that it enables us to talk about parts of written words. But parts of words have no meaning until there is an understanding of written words themselves. Learning to write does not proceed from scribble to letters to words and sentences, but from an understanding first of sentences, then of words, and finally of letters, with scribble being used to represent any of these. Copying letters is useful and perhaps essential in developing the fine muscular coordination required to produce them, but to expect children to master letters as a preliminary to writing is like expecting them to understand houses by first studying the shape of bricks. That children will sometimes learn to produce some or all of the letters of the alphabet before they understand their utility in written words does not disprove the preceding argument. It does demonstrate the astonishing tolerance of children for the foibles of adults and the trouble they will take to please them.

In learning to write letters, children almost invariably produce some of them backward, or inconsistently. This does not mean that any child might see some letters backward. Seeing anything backward is a physiological impossibility. The problem is that most of the letters of the alphabet are complicated and unusual shapes to remember and draw. Writing the alphabet may seem easy and obvious to adults, but they have been doing it for years. A child who writes *k* or *h* backward (or upside down for that matter) does not have a visual defect or an ignorance of what the letters look like. The reversal simply demonstrates that the child is not a very experienced artist. Children know very well what faces and cars look like, but they still do not find it easy to draw them. (Nor do most adults. For most of us numerals and the letters of the alphabet are by far the most complex figures we are ever able to draw.) Until the writing of letters becomes established as a matter of muscular habit, as integrated movement patterns, the only way to produce letters like *k* and *h* properly is to remember on which side of the upright stroke the rest of the letter is attached. The importance of this directionality is a most unusual idea for children to grasp; letters of the alphabet are among the few objects in this world that can only face in one direction. A dog does not become a cat when it turns from east to west, the way a *d* becomes a *b*. The initial difficulty for children is not in seeing (physically) that such letters are different but in seeing (intellectually) that the difference makes a difference. And the only way to remember the direction such letters should face is with respect to left and right; not an easy thing for children to do, even after they have learned to distinguish their left hand from their right.

The problem remains the same even if a model of the correct letter is in front of the child, if "all the child has to do" is copy an example printed alongside on the page. The concentrated attention required to reproduce the required shape one bit at a time—the loop not too big, the line not too crooked, and all the joins and starts and finishes in exactly the right place — so focuses the gaze that it is impossible for children to see an entire letter at one time, whether the model or their own effort, let alone the two of them together for comparison. The difficulties and their amateurish consequences are not unique to children; adults can make exactly the same kinds of directional error when they try to copy unfamiliar and complicated figures, like a map of a length of coastline or a line of Chinese characters, and would make even more if verbal props like "left" and "right" (and "top" and "bottom") were not available to them.

All the arbitrary directions in which we expect things to be produced in written language, the lines and words as well as letters, initially pose most unusual problems for children to solve. The correct solution is rarely obvious. We assume that a child asked to copy or trace over a word printed on a page will do so from left to right, as we would. But why should the child? What is there in a printed word, or even in seeing an adult write the word, to indicate that the child must begin on the left, rather than on the right or in the middle? To draw a car it is not necessary to begin with the front wheels; you could start if you wished with a door handle. Terms like left and right or top and bottom are extremely difficult for children to grasp until they have a familiarity with reading. The top and bottom of the page are not the same as the top and bottom of the table on which the page is placed. A child who takes instructions literally might object "Of course I'm starting at the top of the page, I couldn't very well start underneath it." We do not begin writing at the top of the page; the top of the page is where the writing begins.

There is nothing *natural* or necessary about our particular conventions of left to right and top to bottom; other written languages have scripts that proceed in other directions, and most children will cheerfully and spontaneously try all the alternatives. They invent before they learn. It is not even obvious that direction should be consistent, and in some respects it is perhaps not logical. Occasionally a child will alternate written lines from left to right and right to left, an economical behavior as far as the effort of hand movement is concerned, and one which was in fact a conventional style of writing in Greece—the *boustrophedon*—2,000 years ago. Sometimes when children first grasp that the idea is to start at the top left of the page and to finish at bottom right they take the most direct route, a single diagonal line through the center of the page. What is wrong with the reasoning?

With so many things to discover and learn about just the physical aspects of writing, it should not be surprising that children do not find it easy to keep the results up to adult standards of neatness. Neatness is perhaps something that children do not spontaneously invent, and in writing it always exacts a price. Speed and neatness are always in conflict, but especially so at the beginning. Conventionally, handwriting is relatively small, though not as small as it might be if the reader's convenience were the only concern. It is (I hope) not difficult to read type of the size in which this book is printed, but most of us would be hard pressed to write as small.

The advantage of the size of writing at which most of us conventionally write is that it is produced about as fast as we can go and still keep relatively neat. Larger script—say, letters a centimeter high or more—is slower to write, even with practice, especially if neatness is to be maintained. But paradoxically, larger letters are easier to write for a child learning how letters should be written in the first place. Thus children for a while face a dilemma; it is easier for them to write in large letters than small, but in the long run small letters can be written faster and neater than large. The solution obviously should be to make letters as large as required in order to learn and then as small as possible in order to develop speed. Neither effort is likely initially to contribute to neatness, but a straitjacket of conventional tidiness at the same time that fluency and speed are being developed can only make every other aspect of learning to write more difficult.

The basic problem is that learners have so much to think about. The solution, however, is not a simple matter of learning one thing before another. Of course it will be easier to compose, to give attention to spelling and to punctuation, when handwriting is not a focal concern. And in principle it is easier to learn to make letters when composition is not competing for attention. But this does not mean that a child should not attempt anything more ambitious than copying before an acceptable or complete repertoire of handwriting skills is achieved; a child unable to see the point of developing a neat and efficient hand is unlikely to practice sufficiently to acquire one. Perhaps the best policy for beginners is the rule that applies to fluent writers too. When there might be a conflict between neatness and getting ideas on paper, make at least two drafts, the first for the ideas and the last for tidying the transcription. To attempt to begin with the courtesies is as pointless as gift wrapping the package before the contents have been put inside.[8]

HIGH SCHOOL AND COLLEGE WRITERS

Except for a few specific references to "children" in this chapter, when the primary concern is with the introduction to writing at the primary grades, or before, I have usually referred to "beginners" or "learners."

My point is that the requirements of learning to write do not change as one grows older. Adolescents should not be treated as children, of course, but nevertheless what beginning writers need to learn and how they need to learn it are the same for people of all ages. The material in this book can be read by primary school teachers with primary school children in mind and by high school or college teachers with high school or college students in mind. Of course, students of different ages must be treated differently, not because they need to learn different things about writing, but because their experience and their interests will be different. The same conventions must be learned, they are learned primarily through collaboration and demonstration, and through reading, and they are learned in the same conditions, basically by the learner approaching the task *as a writer*. Membership in the club is critical for learners of any age. But interests and experience will differ among students of the same age as well. There can be no *formula* for teaching anyone to write. As I said earlier, the most important knowledge for teachers to have, which outside experts can never provide for them, is knowledge of the students they are teaching.

Augst (1992) observes that learning to write (in the sense of becoming a proficient writer) takes a long time, and lags behind speech. He compared students aged 13, 16, 19, and 23, all writing on a similar assignment (concerning whether homework should be abolished) and found a steady improvement in such writerly aspects as including a formulated introduction and conclusion, making a complete argument, being able to adopt the reader's point of view, and coping with "rewriting."

Emig (1983) remarks that there is no direct route that anyone can follow from beginning writer to experienced writer; that mastery over many kinds of technical, genre, and social considerations must be developed, and that what is learned depends on interests and consequences as well as content. She emphasizes that writing is learned rather than taught, and that learning to write is a recursive process rather than a linear one.

There are a few particular considerations to be taken into account in working with students of different ages, more to do with their experience than with what they must learn. The first is that young children are usually less inhibited in their learning and inventiveness than older students. One might think that the additional worldly and academic experience of older students would provide a greater basis for invention and imagination. But unfortunately while *ability* to invent might become richer as we get older, *willingness* to do so may decrease. For a variety of reasons, older students are less ready to take chances, to acknowledge ignorance, or to accept help. Sometimes they are not encouraged to do these things. None of these conditions can be addressed by the *content* of writing instruction; they must all be part of the personal relationship between teacher and student.

The broader experience of older students is not always to their advantage. They may have learned the wrong things. They may have learned to attach undue or untimely importance to spelling or neatness, or that it is a wise strategy not to write more than a minimum, or at the limit of one's competence. They may have learned to *avoid risk*. Even more disastrously, older students may have learned that they *can't* write, that writing is difficult and unpleasant, and that it is not for them. They may have learned failure, that they are not and are never likely to be members of the club. And getting bruised or distracted adolescents to see themselves as members of the club of writers can be far more difficult than getting a group of naive but enthusiastic five-year-olds to do the same. For older students, writing instruction often becomes remedial education, with the learner's self-image a more important consideration than the learner's competence.

I have discussed these differences—and lack of differences—under the heading of learning, but they are also of course central to the topic of teaching. Teaching is less a matter of presenting information than of establishing relationships, and with the final chapter I can now move deeper into this crucial consideration.

(Notes to Chapter 13 begin on page 260.)

14   The Writing Teacher

The main conclusion that must be drawn from the analyses of writing and learning in previous chapters is that the role of teachers is central in the development of writers. But the part teachers must play is subtle and different from the way it is widely perceived. There is very little that beginners can be taught directly, through the memorization of rules and imposition of exercises, that will transform nonwriters into writers. There are few "facts" of writing that students might usefully be required to memorize, in the way that they might be taught the nomenclature of geography or geology, nor do there appear to be relevant exercises that learners might be required to practice, in the way that they might rehearse mathematical skills (although the value of drills in learning mathematics has also been questioned).[1]

Instead, writing is learned by writing, by reading, and by perceiving oneself as a writer. In each of these requirements, a teacher can play a crucial part. The practice of writing develops interest, but needs the help of a more able collaborator to provide opportunity for discovering conventions relevant to what is being written. The practice of reading may also engender interest in writing and provide opportunity for encountering relevant conventions, but often calls for guidance and encouragement. And the perception of oneself as a writer—as the kind of person who is sensitive to the conventions of written language—demands membership in the club of writers, to which all teachers of writing should belong. Teachers are influential, as models as well as guides, as students explore the worlds of writing—or decide that writing is something they will never voluntarily undertake inside school or out.[2]

I have been tempted to make the present chapter particularly succinct by recommending that interested teachers reread the preceding chapters on how writing is learned and then consider how to promote the appropriate conditions themselves. Writing is fostered rather than taught, and what teachers require is not helpful advice about "methods" of writing instruction, nor an outline of appropriate "programs," but an understanding of the task a student faces in learning to write.

My reluctance to recommend or even discuss particular methods of teaching writing is partly because teacher understanding is more important than any system, because no method or program can be guaranteed to teach students to write, and also because even the best of ideas can be misused in the hands of a misguided or insensitive teacher. Like baseball bats, many instructional techniques can have a benign and even useful role in school until students are beaten over the head with them. For example, I have seen researchers recommending reading and writing games with newspapers, activities that I thought most students could enjoy and learn from. But some of the teachers and parents who were presented with these ideas wanted to know the level of performance that might be expected from particular groups of students. One visualizes those students who least liked or learned from the tasks being urged in effect: "Most people of your age can do this," or "Keep at it; this is fun," until they hated newspapers.

Some useful ideas and enjoyable activities should perhaps be kept out of school, if there is a risk that as school-type tasks they become confusing or meaningless chores. I have seen primary school children taught the techniques of revision and editing, showing how writing can flower on the page to produce texts that fill the young authors with pleasure and pride. But I have also seen teachers translate these techniques into exercises, so that revision is changed from a tool that facilitates writing to a "skill" on which children can be drilled and given so many marks out of ten. Then children do not see revision as a way of building upon a draft but as a process of "getting it right," reflecting a common school attitude that the only way to respond to a child's language is to classify it as correct or incorrect, good or bad.[3]

In the following pages I summarize very specifically some illustrative ways in which teachers may help students learn to write or to improve their writing. My aim is not to make decisions for teachers (which is a responsibility I do not think they should leave to anyone else) but to indicate those things that teachers involved with writing should particularly think about. But teachers by no means have total command over what goes on in their classrooms. Many things teachers might want to do to facilitate reading and writing may be difficult to introduce; moreover, teachers sometimes are unable to exclude activities and considerations that can serve only to sidetrack or inhibit learning to read and write. So I shall add a section on some handicaps that teachers of writing must overcome.

THE TEACHER'S ROLES

The main requirements are easily stated. The teacher must provide an environment in which students will want to write and in which they can learn about writing.

The environment in which students will want to write is an environment of demonstrations, not just of "this is the way we do things" but also "these are things that can be done." Books, magazines, newspapers, letters, announcements, advertisements, programs, catalogs—all these are demonstrations of how writing is done and essential sources of conventions of written language to which prospective writers of any age must have access. These are the artifacts that embody the clues to their own construction. But for demonstrations of *what* can be done students must see someone doing something. How much writing do most students see being done in school or at home, and what kind of writing is it?

One way to see writing being done is to see someone else doing it. But an even more potent experience is to be involved in the doing oneself. The most direct and relevant way for a teacher to demonstrate the power of writing is to write with the student, not by requiring the student to engage in writing that the teacher determines must be done, but by helping to bring out of the student writing that the student would like to do.

Joining in the discovery and development of a theme may provide an excellent stimulus and organizing basis for writing; nothing is as unhelpful as a blank sheet of paper when words refuse to come. But assisting with a theme is not the same as imposing a topic to write upon. Writing will not emerge without an underlying intention. In some circumstances there may be an adequate reason for requiring students to write to a given theme, to explore an issue in a particular subject area, for example. On other occasions a few suggested topics may be helpful. But if the aim is to help a student learn to write, and if the consequence of a selected theme is to make writing less probable, then its imposition will not help the student become a writer. Besides, students required to write something they are not interested in will also not be interested in any feedback, in any correction, that ensues. They will not learn.

The different aspects of a productive writing environment cannot be separated from each other and delivered to students one bit at a time. Reading, writing, talking about writing, and talking in order to write must be continual possibilities; they overlap and interlock. In theory, reading begins with the teacher reading *to* children, then *with* them, and finally with children reading for themselves. In practice, however, children able to read some texts for themselves will still learn more from other texts that are read to them. Reading alone and being read to can each be a welcome relief from the other.

Similarly with writing. It is not the case that the teacher should first write for the student, then with the student, and then leave the student alone. Rather the matter is one of *accessibility*; teachers have to develop a sense of when to offer help, when to intervene, and when to stand back.

It is impossible to overestimate the importance of teachers writing themselves, not only to understand writing better, and to reflect on their own teaching practices (Newman, 1991). They should write *with* their students, in order to provide demonstrations. I am not talking about teachers displaying to students the final drafts of their own hard-worked efforts, with all the effort being expended off-stage, but of actually writing at the same time as the students, at the same tasks as the students, as *publicly* as the students (the way a carpentry instructor might build a piece of furniture alongside the students). To readers who object that they would not want students to see them struggling to write something, I would reply that *that* is the point. Students need to see that writing can be a struggle; that there is nothing wrong with them if they do not find writing easy, or if their efforts are often less than perfect. By the same token, it is also important for students to see writing that is flawed, or still in progress; it is almost impossible to learn from perfect models. Learners in any subject need to be familiar with the pitfalls that they will encounter on the way.

There is no special time in a student's life when the various aspects of a productive writing environment become particularly appropriate, just as there is no particular sequence in which the writing, reading, or talking about writing will be most useful. It is no more necessary for teachers to conceal some aspects of reading and writing from students than it is for storekeepers to hide items that particular customers are unlikely to buy. Beginners can easily ignore what they do not understand, especially if more interesting or relevant alternatives are available to them. Teachers should not be dismayed if they cannot provide an optimum reading and writing environment all the time, provided they understand what helps and what hinders children. Even the youngest students do not expect a perfect world, and they can be remarkably tolerant when told to wait for help or to struggle through by themselves. Anyone who will wait in line an hour for a movie and survive a week or more in anticipation of a special treat will not be discouraged if assistance in writing is delayed, provided they can perceive the limitations under which a teacher works and also the teacher's good intentions.

In discussing the teacher's critical roles and responsibilities as motivator, model, guide, helper, audience, and editor for learners, I should emphasize that the burden can often be shared. Responsibilities can be delegated to other adults—to parents, aides, volunteer correspondents—and to other students. There are great advantages in students helping each other. They are less likely to be didactic, evaluative, impatient, and otherwise preoccupied, and more likely to be collaborative. It is a pity that teachers often overlook communal aspects of writing, where students work together to write a letter, poem, or story, to produce a play or a newspaper, sharing abilities as well as difficulties, increasing interest and involvement. Teachers may be most effective when they are most in the background.[4]

I do not propose to review the many kinds of organized, structured, teacher-directed activities that are available and frequently promoted for the writing class, even though they are often seen as a teacher's main concern, such as providing worksheet exercises for various skills of transcription. My general orientation toward their place in learning to write must be apparent from earlier discussions. Research rarely shows that a particular exercise or activity fails in its specific objectives; students usually succeed in doing better whatever it is the activity drills them to do. But research also rarely shows what such activity has to do with writing as a whole, whether it results in more writing, a keener interest in writing, or even better writing in any general sense. Students who can write beyond the level of such activities naturally cope with such activities best; they make the drills look good. In principle, every kind of writing activity might contribute something to ability to write, but in principle also it might bore or confuse. We are all capable of learning when we expect to learn, but it is impossible to predict what individuals will learn as the result of a particular activity.

As always, the teacher's best guides are the learners themselves—their interest, creativity, and the amount of writing they willingly or voluntarily do. Teachers themselves must develop the insight and exercise the judgment about whether a particular activity will help or handicap a particular student. The profit-and-loss equation applies: How exactly is this activity supposed to help, and what is its likely cost in effort and possible failure? Writing is not learned in steps; there is no ladder of separate and incremental skills to be ascended. Writing develops as an individual develops, in many directions, continually, usually inconspicuously, but occasionally in dramatic and unforeseeable spurts. And, like individual human development, writing requires nourishment and encouragement rather than a restrictive regimen.

Some General Observations

The only conclusion that can be drawn from masses of fragmented research is that there is no guaranteed *method* of turning students into writers, but that anything that encourages interest, effort, thinking, and pride is likely to do good, while anything that produces anxiety, resentment, despair, or a negative self-image can only do harm. Unfortunately a teaching approach that is on the positive side of the ledger for some learners will be on the negative side for others. The cardinal rule is to watch for the effect on the learner, and on the learner's writing.

The "writing problem" for many students, from children to adults, is often perceived as a matter of having nothing to say. It is true that on particular topics anyone may lack specific knowledge that would facilitate writing (especially when an instructor will determine whether what is written is "right" or "wrong"). But research has never demonstrated that anyone has nothing to say. Quite the contrary. Inexperienced writers usually stop writing because they are tired, lose interest, or become uncertain of what in particular to say next—or simply because they think they have written enough. It is the easiest thing in the world to persuade a learner to write another sentence, and another, and another. Teachers can always ask another leading question, and learners can be trained to ask themselves questions to elicit yet another sentence. In theory I suppose the process might be continued until the entire content of a person's head is unraveled. But what the process achieves is what puts a brake on the beginning writer, a disconnected sequence of sentences, each of which constitutes as good a place to stop as any other.

Part of the problem, I think, is the potency of what is already written. Beginners encouraged to keep writing find it difficult not to repeat what they have just said in slightly different words. What they have just said may also lead them further and further along a digression; their brains are much better at "furthermore . . ." than at "on the other hand, . . ." But one of the hardest things for adult writers to learn is that the best way to go forward may be to change or even delete the sentence that has gone before. In writing, the old rural joke often applies: It may not be possible to get where you want to go from where you are at present.[5]

More generally, the beginner's problem seems to be doubt about the most appropriate thing to say next, to bridge what has already been said with what might be still to come. There are two complementary ways to overcome this difficulty. The first is to become familiar with conventions of extended discourse that provide a route from the beginning to the end of a piece of text. Teachers may not be aware of all the relevant conventions, not in an explicit sense, but if they can write themselves they can still guide a learner's writing by helping the learner to write. They can also foster sensitivity in reading, demonstrating how stories are told, explanations developed, and arguments presented. The second part of the solution is for beginners not to worry unduly about the order in which sentences are first produced because they can always be rearranged later. Writers can cut up and otherwise reshuffle anything they have written on a single sheet of paper, and they can write on more than one piece of paper at a time. Word processors can make this experimentation even easier. Beginners can even, if they wish, include in their revision additional sentences that an obliging helper has provided for them. (And in revision they can develop insights that will perhaps produce sentences in a more appropriate order in the first draft next time.) The burden of the sequential, left-to-right demands of writing may be reduced by taking advantage of the fact that writing does not have to remain in the sequential, left-to-right order in which it is originally produced.

A point that might be mentioned here is that learning to write—like writing—requires space. If words are to be shuffled around on paper and inserted between lines and along margins, then students need access to sheets of paper as large as they feel comfortable with. And if students are also to write on many pieces of paper, on index cards, and notepads as well as on manuscript paper, then they also need ample room on the desk and on the floor. (They may also need a few demonstrations of support activities such as keeping index cards together with rubber bands and the use of paper clips and files, though not if these activities are made ends in themselves, with learners evaluated on the quality of their rough work and the contents of their private files.)

Teachers cannot expect writing to be a controlled and well-ordered activity, either on paper or in the room. They also cannot expect it to be quiet.[6] Beginning writers—like more mature members of the club—frequently need to be noisy, to try out spellings, to hear what they have just written or are trying to remember to write, to express the excitement of writing or the frustration of not being able to write. They may need noise for company, to break the silence, just as they may need to walk around. Writing does not have to be a sedentary occupation. But in addition to the possibility of making noise, learners also need opportunity for quiet withdrawal (though unfortunately they rarely all need this at the same time). They need time for reflection as well as for research; the incubation of a text may take days of reading, talking, or simply daydreaming. Few professional writers would claim that all thinking about writing was done while actually writing, or even during deliberate thinking about writing.

For that matter, professional writers would perhaps be unable to write at all in the constrained and inhibiting circumstances in which students are often expected to write. There are, however, ways in which teachers can ameliorate some of the more forbidding aspects of institutionalized writing. One is by ensuring that there is as often as possible an *interested* reader for anything that students write, whether it is the teacher personally, other adults, or other students. School is perhaps the only place where people write (or talk, for that matter) not to interest or entertain other people but to tell them things they already know. Students use language, spoken or written, to demonstrate learning rather than to learn. When so much of what students are expected and permitted to say is regarded as an implicit test, it is all the more important that their efforts at writing find an interested and sympathetic audience. A reader can constitute a purpose, provide a focus, and can be the source of benign and useful feedback and general reassurance. A reader can partake in the writer's pleasure at the very existence of a piece of text, the wonder of the act of creation.

By acknowledging the role of a reader, however, I am not saying that the purpose of writing must be "to transmit information"—that its primary function is to convey messages. Two common uses of written language—to tell stories and to explore ideas—must be distorted if they are to be crammed into the straitjacket explanation of "conveying information." Writing is the construction and exploration of possible worlds, the pursuit of experience, understanding and explanation, and the primary audience is always the writer, whether or not a particular readership is also held in view. In the act of writing, the writer is the first person to interact with the text, which may then be made available to others. We all enjoy sharing the products of our creativeness, but as an experience, not as information. Texts are more than data, they are events—to be lived, not decoded. It is true that writing can be trivialized, regarded as nothing more than a laborious alternative to a telephone call, but I do not see how such a view will enlighten students or keep them participating in the possibilities of writing.

It is also dangerous, I think, to isolate writing as a "subject." Writing should not be perceived as something different, an end in itself. The whole point of the writing act is what it does, the experience and understanding it makes possible. A student who believes that the main purpose of writing is to get a grade and an evaluative comment from a teacher is clearly not likely to develop into an interested or particularly competent writer.

On Testing and Evaluation

Though topics of widespread concern among teachers of writing, testing and evaluation are not discussed in detail in this book. Partly this is because many volumes exist entirely devoted to the topic of evaluation, from many points of view; it is a highly specialized topic. And very often teachers have no choice about what they do because testing is imposed upon them just as much as it is imposed on their students. But I also refrain from discussing this vast topic in detail because I have never seen a testing or evaluation instrument that would help students learn to write or teachers to teach writing; tests are purely bureaucratic tools, and the role of writing teachers is to protect students from them, not to find new and improved ways of administering them.

In this respect, I differ from many dedicated teachers who feel that they have to participate in the design of evaluation instruments because they believe it will limit the damage that is done to their students. Unfortunately, in contributing to tests they help to validate them. And in any case, they have no control over how the tests will be used. The same arguments apply to endeavors to spell out "standards" for writing instruction, in which leaders of influential teaching organizations participate. The "problems" of literacy education are not that teachers lack standards. Endeavors to specify exactly what students should learn, and when they should learn it (which are inevitably discriminatory), always carry the implication that teachers and students who do not meet the standards are inadequate in some way, or not trying hard enough. Also inevitably, national standards are accompanied by national tests, which control and discriminate against schools, teachers, and students even more.

I do not see any point in allocating letter grades or counting misplaced commas as part of writing instruction. (When students say they prefer grades, this only means that they have learned what counts as the currency of many classrooms—and that they normally expect to get high grades. Students who will not willingly write unless given a grade have learned a distorted—though probably accurate in the circumstances—concept of what writing is for.) Grades normally only satisfy students who get "good marks," and then they can be delusory. For students who normally get "poor marks," grading can only be a continual source of embarrassment and discouragement, and an inadequate incentive for "doing better."

Nothing of what I have just written is intended to imply that teachers should not be aware of what their students are learning about writing, or be unable to pass that understanding on to parents or administrators in comprehensible form. But numbers and grades are not comprehensible, or only misleadingly so. Teachers monitor and demonstrate their students' progress by attending to what the students are *doing*.

Focusing on a product—on a single piece of writing a student has done, voluntarily or under test conditions—will not indicate how much a student has learned. Perhaps the student could have done as well a year ago. And perhaps the test item is the only thing the student can do so well (or so poorly). Looking at what students are doing tells a different kind of story. Students who willingly write, who are prepared to enter into a writing task, and show interest in it, and who also read, must be learning about writing—at any stage of their writing development.

The points to look for are easily summed up: Is the student interested in writing? Does the student engage in writing willingly? Does the student read extensively? In short—is the student a member of the club of writers?

This is not to say that the product—what students write—is not important. It is of course a guide to teachers about what a student has been learning; it can indicate the kinds of reading experience and collaborative activity that would help the student. Used comparatively against earlier writing, it can show the "progress" a student is making. For these reasons, *portfolios* are popularly used to reassure parents or administrators that students are learning—although teachers may have to educate parents and administrators about the significance of what the portfolios contain. But portfolios can be threatening instruments if students have no control of them. No writers want writing that is potentially embarrassing to be preserved and possibly used in evidence against them. Students should have the choice of what goes into—and what must be removed from—their portfolios, which should be a compendium of everything the student is proud of, like a professional journalist's cuttings book, and just as personal and private. When writing is literally taken out of a student's hands for administrative purposes, it tells the student only one thing—that the writer does not own the writing.

THE TEACHER'S HANDICAPS

At times when I discuss with teachers my conclusions about how beginners of any age learn to write and read, I am told that I am idealistic and impractical. Schools could never be changed sufficiently to enable teachers to teach in the ways I imply would be most appropriate. (This objection may be true, but my primary concern has been to understand the learning, not to provide prescriptions for instruction. Neither the brains of students nor the nature of writing will change for the convenience of schools.) At times I am told that my conclusions must be wrong. How could they be right, when by my analysis so much is done in schools that can only interfere with the development of literacy? And indeed, if I thought that everything that is done in schools reflects the way learning takes place, then I would certainly have to reconsider my views. But the discrepancies between my conclusions about learning and the practices of schools are easily explained; schools are not primarily concerned with learning. The fact that schools may say and believe that learning is their first concern is beside the point. There are other factors that determine how schools are run; other considerations that underlie many of the classroom practices and constraints that handicap teachers and students alike.

Despite the enormous emphasis on literacy in contemporary education and pressures on schools to promote literacy, schools are not good places in which to learn to write and to read. Before I offer arguments and examples to show *how* this is the case I shall state briefly *why* it is so. (And to avoid premature irritation or despair I should perhaps indicate now that I also intend to make some positive remarks about how teachers can and do overcome the handicaps.)

The reason that schools (and universities, hospitals, prisons, and many other of society's venerable institutions) are not particularly effective in the task to which they are popularly supposed to be devoted is very simple. The principal concern of any institution is the perpetuation and smooth daily operation of the institution itself. Institutions tend by their nature to be resistant to change, intolerant of anything that interferes with their good order and routine, and gripped by a stultifying *inertia*. Their main concern is getting through the day. Ask many teachers about their most pressing concern in the classroom and they will say something like "Keeping the lid on; keeping students quiet so that I can get on with the work." Students have a habit of getting in the way in school, just like patients in hospitals and patrons in many restaurants. That is why schools have rigid routines, not to help the students learn but to keep them under control.

There is a mania for measurement in education, dominating what goes on in classrooms and upsetting almost everyone associated with them, especially teachers and students. Tests are imposed for a variety of reasons—statistical (record keeping, collecting population data), administrative (placement, logistic decisions), political (making comparisons, holding schools and staff "accountable"), and occasionally (and often unnecessarily) diagnostic. Tests are almost inevitably based on very poor theories of what writing and reading involve; they are usually constructed by people whose expertise is in test construction, not in writing and reading. Sometimes it is claimed that tests are atheoretical, which means that no one even gave a thought to what writing and reading involve. The educational world is polarized between those who argue that poor tests are better than no tests (because they see no alternative to tests) and those who argue that no tests are better than poor tests (because they see the damage that tests can do). Between the extremes is a mass of confused and anxious teachers and students.

There is inertia. Teachers do things in classrooms because regulations require them to, curriculum guidelines direct them to, and principals, parents, and the teacher in the next room expect them to; because they were trained to and the program leads them to; because there is a day to be got through; and because the whole business is weighed down with habit and dogma. It is hard to change one classroom, one teacher, or even one school. Entire systems have to be shifted on their foundations, together with the perceptions of students, teachers, administrators, parents, and politicians. Change in schools requires time, effort, will, understanding—and political maneuvering as well.

Schools are odd places. Great pains are taken to group students of the same age and ability level, so it is almost impossible for them to help or learn from each other. Students are expected to learn, and to be interested in, particular things at particular times under the direction of adults who may display little interest in the particular activity themselves. They are required to talk only at the instigation of a supervising authority, in a manner laid down by that authority, to demonstrate what they have learned rather than to learn. The primary purpose of learning (on the part of learner and teacher alike) becomes the allocation of a number or letter grade. Schools are supposed to teach literacy, but only literate students do well at school. Students who have problems with writing or reading create problems for schools, which then tend to blame the students or their home conditions. Reading and writing are trivialized. Failing to become interesting in their own right, they are termed "life (or work) skills" and reduced to matters of reading tax forms and writing job applications. Rather than the pleasures of literacy, the "mechanics" are discussed.

Students are expected to learn to read and write at school. But when researchers took stopwatches into classrooms they found that the actual amount of reading done by individual children in primary grades was four minutes a day,[7] about one percent of the total time. (This was an *average*; good readers did a bit more; poor readers, who might be thought to need more practice, did less.) Researchers found high school students doing less than half a page of writing *of all kinds* in the course of a day, most of it copying or producing incomplete sentences on answer sheets.[8] One percent of the student writing was personal and one percent was imaginative. High school teachers talked 80 percent of the time in class, students 20 percent.[9] Make a charitable estimate of an average of 20 students in a class, and that means each student gets to talk for one percent of the time; 99 percent is listening (or tuning out). And the proportion of writing and talking gets smaller as students move up through the grades. Students in universities who cannot write have probably never done any writing of the kind universities demand, never written a paper, certainly not a critical, analytical one. Even the examinations are multiple choice; writing may be dying from misuse.

Teachers do not believe the figures I have just given. They know they are busy all the time. They think the research must refer to other kinds of school from their own. (Actually, most of the research was done in what would be regarded as liberal, enlightened, middle-class schools.) Teachers do not believe the findings even when the research is conducted in their own classrooms, and they cannot believe the situation has not changed when they are shown a month later that exactly the same thing is still going on. Language habits die hard.

Teachers believe learning must be going on all the time because they believe they are teaching all the time, and it is widely assumed that learning and teaching go together. Occasionally it is noticed that students fail to learn despite the teaching that is done, and even that students might have learned something without the benefit of teaching, but in general it is assumed that schools are places where learning is the predominant concern. Schools are what they are for good reasons—but the good reasons are not generally connected with learning. Teachers and students alike are victims of the handicaps of school.[10]

The Positive Side

I said I would end positively. Schools may not be good places for learning or for teaching, but students often succeed in learning and teachers succeed as well. During only a small part of the day, perhaps during a few minutes of writing, reading, talking, or reflection, somehow the magic occurs, the contact is made, and learning takes place. Despite the handicaps and the complexity of the task, many students learn to write, and to their teachers should go much of the credit. The pity is that the importance of the productive moment is usually not recognized. The credit is given to the day as a whole, to the program, to the drills; even the tests are put in a good light. Teachers become unable to distinguish gold from dross.

And there I think lies the key to the teacher's overcoming the handicaps of school. Obviously there should be every effort to minimize the unproductive aspects of classroom routine, to make the day as fruitful as possible, but to suggest that such a dramatic change could be accomplished easily or quickly would be entirely unrealistic. Unproductive aspects can, however, be *recognized*; they can be distinguished from the parts of the day that are important. And teachers can protect students and themselves.

My own recommendation for how writing and reading should be taught is perhaps radical; they should not be taught at all. Not in any formal sense, as *subjects*. All the busywork, the meaningless drills and exercises, the rote memorization, the irrelevant tests, and the distracting grades should go (to the extent that the teacher can get rid of them). And in their place teachers and students together should use writing (and reading, spoken language, art, and drama) in the course of broader activities. Writing should be used to tell stories and to produce artifacts—books to be published, poems to be recited, songs to be sung, plays to be acted, letters to be delivered, programs to be consulted, newspapers to be distributed, advertisements to be displayed, complaints to be aired, ideas to be shared, worlds to be constructed and explored, for part of the day at least. Students should learn to write in the same manner that they once learned to talk, and continue to do so, without being aware that they are doing so, as they do other things. Teaching writing should be an incidental matter also—teachers showing students what writing can do and helping them to do it themselves.

Implementing my recommendation (which is by no means original) would not require changing the world. It does not demand a one-on-one teacher-student relationship throughout the day. It does not involve great technical skill. But it does need an understanding of how learning takes place, something many teachers know implicitly and respect instinctively.

I mistrust the growing dependence upon programs in education, upon formal and systematic instruction, programming teachers and programming students. The problem is that programs so often seem to work—for their limited aims. They teach trivial aspects of literacy and they teach that literacy is trivial. I do not share the frequent concern that too many students leave school with minimal competence in writing and reading. My concern is that so many students graduate, good and poor writers and readers alike, without the slightest intention of pursuing writing and reading outside school. Poor writers and readers who are interested in literate activities still have a chance. But students who decide that writing and reading should be left behind in the classroom—that they are *work*, that they are *boring*—have no chance at all. They have learned from the wrong demonstrations.

Irrelevant aspects of school need not interfere with learning to write, provided that students are not persuaded that writing is part of the irrelevancy. For part of the day they can be involved in productive activities that are interesting and satisfying. And at such times, when language is used for a purpose, students have their best chance to experience what writing can do and to learn to do it themselves.

SPECIFIC SUGGESTIONS FOR TEACHERS OF WRITING (WITH STUDENTS OF ANY AGE)

- Ensure that a wide choice of reading material is available relevant to your students' interests and to what you would like them to write.
- Encourage your students to *read.*
- Demonstrate reading, especially the kind you would like your students to do.
- Help your students to read (by ensuring they have time, space, opportunity to move about, and any specific assistance they need).
- Make everything as comfortable and interesting as possible to enable your students to *write.*
- Provide all the equipment they might need.
- Encourage your students to write.
- Demonstrate writing, especially the kind you would like your students to do.
- Help your students to write (by ensuring they have time, space, equipment, and any specific assistance they need).
- Bring interesting people into classrooms, especially those who can talk about and demonstrate their own writing and writing habits.
- Encourage *talk* in your classroom.
- Demonstrate discussions and conversation, about interesting events, reading, and writing.
- Practice and encourage civility (on the part of everyone who comes into your classroom).
- Respect your students; do not allow their efforts to write to be used to discriminate against them or to embarrass or humiliate them.
- Respect writing; do not permit written language to be mangled for "instructional purposes" (filling in blanks, combining sentence fragments) and do not permit authentic texts (poems, letters, news reports, stories) to be used for drills, busy work, or tests.
- To assure yourself and others that your students are learning, don't look at what they have done, look at what they are doing; students will always move ahead from where they are if they are writing, reading, and interested.

Some important addenda:

- The above is not a checklist; the items are not to be done one at a time, or once and never again; they are essential elements of a writing environment.
- The elements are not always easy; the way most educational institutions are designed and run does little to facilitate environments of this kind.
- Don't expect to do everything all of the time—be satisfied sometimes if your students see you *trying* to set up this kind of environment.
- Be honest with students (of any age); discuss with them what you are trying to do, and why it may be difficult for you and them to bring it about.
- Protect students; your privilege and responsibility is to help them learn, not to be the agent of their frustrations and failures.
- Don't try to do all this by yourself; innovative teachers need all the support they can get from students, colleagues, parents, and administrators; share your experiences, successes, and difficulties with people who understand your situation.

(Notes for Chapter 14 begin on page 263.)

Retrospect

This book began as an exploration. But the meandering course of the writing and rewriting covered the tracks of where I have been. So perhaps it might be of some interest if I briefly recount where the book led me; what I thought at the end that I did not think or had not even begun to think about when the writing started.

A major landmark in the writing of this book was my growing realization of the role of shared conventions as the point of contact between writers and readers. I began with a rough idea of the importance of writers' intentions and with a rather more substantial feeling for the expectations of readers, but I had no clear notion of how the two might be interlocked. In fact, I used to argue that writers and readers had nothing directly to do with each other, so solid and impenetrable was the text that stood between them. The now-central concept of the pervasiveness of convention in language did not come to me until the first draft of Chapter 7 (although I found I had casually used the term before) and led to a considerable amount of backtracking and rewriting. It also led to a number of other elaborations of my thinking, particularly with respect to learning. The intricate subtlety of everything we learn about language, especially as exemplified through writing, caused me to reconsider how much we come to understand and accomplish without direct instruction, and to revise some of my views on learning and education. The thoughts about demonstrations, engagement, and sensitivity with which I concluded the book did not come to me until near the end, as a possible solution to problems the text itself presented, and went through several reworkings, both in the writing and in my discussions with colleagues and friends.

The focus upon conventions led me to develop fresh ideas about language in general, particularly with respect to what I came to regard as its essentially arbitrary and accidental nature. I also had to think more about thought itself, about the general functions of convention, and about the fact that consistency is so important for many of the brain's concerns. Also new (to me) was the value of unconventionality as a means of establishing new understandings.

The utility of writing in engendering new ideas rather than simply reflecting existing thought was something else I did not have clearly in mind when I began, though I had long believed it to be a distortion and oversimplification to characterize writing (and other aspects of language) as "communication" and "information transmission." The *productiveness* of writing was something that I felt, certainly for myself, but had not put into words. I did not begin with a clear notion of the interaction between "writing and the writer" (the final title did not come until near the end of the first draft).

All these threads led me to think more about storytelling, about fantasy being the parent of reality, and caused me to elaborate some of my earlier writing on learning and on reading. In particular, I was left with a need to explore further the idea of changing writer *specifications* for a text, an analogy that clarified for me the manner in which vague and fragmentary intentions can be translated into specific and appropriate actions so that a coherent text can be produced without ever existing in its entirety in the author's mind. At the end, I was struck by how little of the finished book I could recollect without actually looking back; my specification was still quite sketchy, but a book seemed to have created itself.

Where did all the ideas come from? Many were derived from existing *theory*, the insights and speculations of linguists, philosophers, psychologists, and authors whose writings I had read or reread, sometimes specifically for this book but often for other reasons in the past, perhaps just general interest. A second source was the voluminous mass of *data* collected by experimental psychologists and educational researchers of various persuasions—including myself occasionally—not always for the purpose of shedding light on writing. But then, I have never thought that writing could be particularly different from anything else the brain does.

The third source has always been my own *reflections*, trying to integrate and make sense of the theories and data I have referred to above, the observations of many writers, teachers, and students of all ages with whom I have worked and talked, and my own observations of myself. My fourth source has been *argument*, perhaps the most vital and stimulating form of learning, when two (or occasionally a few more) friends engage in a common pursuit, flushing ideas from their cover and pursuing them wherever they lead, in an exciting collaboration of cooperative opposition. And my fifth source, the solitary but not lonely one, was in my own *writing*, in the confrontation with the words that shaped themselves for me on paper.

And many words there were. The complexity that I found in trying to describe the writing-writer relationship was not anticipated. I must have written five times as many words as eventually remained in the final draft, thousands of them on index cards (my own ideas and other people's), thousands more in scraps of drafts, in rough notes and false starts (the "disposable writing" that I think is so important), and thousands again in the margins and between the lines of the three complete and quite different typescripts that were produced for the book as a whole. I knew I was done (for the time being at least) when there were no notes left. Every jotting that I had ever made about the book had been disposed of, either by inclusion in the text or by elimination from consideration. My desk top was clear, the file folders empty and abandoned, and the wastepaper basket overflowing for the umpteenth and last time. All I had left was a manuscript.

SECOND THOUGHTS
(POSTSCRIPT TO THE SECOND EDITION)

When I committed myself to a second edition of *Writing and the Writer*, I planned to retrace the journey of the first edition, pausing occasionally on the way to make any changes that the subsequent progress of the world, and of my own ideas, suggested to me. But the first I found impossible and the second was difficult.

It is futile, I soon discovered, to dissect a book to examine how it was written. I should have learned that from the first edition, but somehow I thought the situation would be different for a book I had written myself. But authorship makes no difference. A book presents an impenetrable face to a reader, even to its author. Whatever deconstructionists might say, a book cannot be taken apart to uncover anything behind its own structure, or beneath the relationships of the book *as it is*, not as it was or could have been, to the author and to the rest of the world and its history. If I had reviewed all the notes and drafts I used in writing the first edition, and if I had kept a journal of the enterprise, I might have been able to recover something of the journey I made. But that would have been a fragment of biography of the author, not of the book. Books are as solid as houses; they can be taken apart (at the risk of demolishing them), but only to reveal their actual structure, not the scaffolding, false starts, and changes of direction that went into the building. After a dozen years, it was almost as if I was looking at something written by someone else. It was not *my* book I was revising—it was *a* book, and every word had to be carefully read to see what was in it.

Making changes for the second edition was also difficult—but that was a technical problem. I found myself caught in a conflict of technologies, between the "tools of the trade" I used in writing the first edition and those I used in the second. The remainder of this postscript will be in two sections—the first examining this technical problem of revision, and the second a brief outline of the major changes that I found it necessary to make.

Technicalities of Revision

Writing and the Writer was particularly obdurate in revision because it did not exist in "computer-readable" form. I wrote the first edition as a committed typewriter person, necessarily aided by efficient typists for "final drafts." But during the intervening years I have moved easily to word processing, and now I can hardly write without a word processor (although I still prefer to *read* from paper). I like to move around in a text, to do things rapidly, and not to worry prematurely about niceties of transcription. Except for the shortest of notes and brief personal letters, composing and writing final drafts without a computer has become intolerably arduous for me—although I am no longer reliant on typists.

For various technical and economic reasons, my publishers declined to have the entire first edition scanned electronically, which would have produced a somewhat degraded word processor version that I could work with. Nor would they have the entire text retyped on a word processor before I started (although someone would eventually have to prepare it for publication). Short of retyping the entire text myself—which I briefly considered—I was forced to work with a hybrid that existed partly on paper, in photocopied form, and partly on my computer's hard disk. For a while this meant that I had the worst of both worlds. I could not "cut and paste" because the new text existed only in the computer and the old text only on closely printed pages (no double-spaced manuscript here). Word processor designers also talk of "cutting and pasting," but that is metaphorical, an electronic transaction that I now find much more convenient, but incompatible with text on paper.

The hardest part was bringing text from the two sources together, both mentally and physically. I had to print new or revised text that I had typed into my word processor, and try to connect it appropriately with what was left of the photocopied text, by now covered with felt-tipped editorial marks and comments. Eventually I had to do large amounts of retyping on the computer, to be printed and interleaved with photocopied pages. The result was not something I was happy about sending for review and copyediting, and I hope the splices have been sanded down in the published text. At times I sympathized with early brush or quill scribes who found they had to go back to hammer and chisel. In future, I hope, my writing will be supported in the manner to which it has become accustomed—wedded to a word processor.

As I noted earlier, I felt strangely detached from the actual text that I was working on, as though it had been written by someone else. But with a few rather substantial exceptions I didn't find a great deal that I disagreed with, or even that I felt I should rephrase (both of which would have been the case if the book *had* been written by someone else). In other words—the first edition and I still shared a close affinity, even though we had gone our separate ways for a dozen years. As I noted in the first postscript, the differences that the first edition made to me when I wrote it were considerable, and they are clearly still part of me. It is perhaps a little like identical twins meeting after a long separation, and finding how little either has changed.

The conclusion I draw from this is that the changes that writing can bring about in an author may be lasting; one is not the same person after thinking one's way through a book. This possibly explains why it is difficult for writers, especially inexperienced ones, to see how what they have written could be clarified or improved in any way. It is not that they are blind to the text, but that the act of writing—like any other shared and difficult journey—may bring the two participants (in this case the author and the text) irreversibly closer together.

Changes in the Second Edition

I did not make many detailed (focal) changes to the body of the first edition because, I discovered, the cohesive constraints of a professionally edited text are very tight indeed. It was almost impossible to insert or change a word in a sentence, a sentence in a paragraph, or a paragraph in a section, without having to make substantial changes to the whole, even to rewrite. Changes or additions that I had to make tended to be much more global—entire paragraphs if not sections.

I introduced one new chapter, Chapter 11 (The Tools of the Trade), primarily because of things I thought should be said about computers and word processors, scarcely mentioned in the first edition. To round this chapter out, I picked up material on other writing tools, from pencils to wastepaper baskets, from the old Chapter 9. Some references are provided in the Notes.

The remaining chapters (formerly 11, 12, and 13; now 12, 13, and 14) remain on the topics on learning and teaching, but with modification throughout to change a first edition emphasis on learning and writing by "children" to what was always the intention—learning and writing by beginners or inexperienced practitioners of all ages. In the final chapter, I also attempt to be a little more explicit about the critical role teachers have in helping students of any age to become writers. I still steer clear of being prescriptive, and emphasize that decisions about actual things that writing teachers should do must always be made with particular individual learners in mind, but I have tried to focus a little more on what teachers should strive to accomplish rather than on what they should avoid. There are minor changes in wording and emphasis throughout, and about half of the references are updated.

Chapter 3 now includes a brief section on collaboration among writers. A new section on genre is included in Chapter 5 and its Notes, and a notable controversy over the teaching of genre is mentioned in the Notes to Chapter 14. The origins of writing are discussed in a new section of Chapter 6 and its Notes, and some interesting new insights on interest are added to Chapter 7.

Words make a difference, as I found in Chapter 8. In the first edition I reluctantly employed the terms "prewriting" and "rewriting"; these have now been changed to "groundwork" and "review" in an attempt to avoid the slightest encouragement for any view that writing can be divided into stages. In Chapter 9 I have added a distinction between review and editing, both often conflated under the label of "rewriting." Chapter 9 also includes a new section on the writing preferences of writers.

There is and always has been a copious flood of research and publications on spelling. I have not found it necessary to make any fundamental changes to what I wrote on the topic in Chapter 10, although I have thought it useful to add a section on "neurotic attitudes to spelling." Research on spelling and spelling instruction also gets a modest reference in the Notes to Chapter 14. The title of Chapter 12 (formerly Chapter 11) is changed to "Learning to be a Writer" (from "The Learning Brain") to support an additional emphasis on the importance of learners' assuming the *identity* of being a writer. Not unrelatedly, the same chapter also includes a new section on story telling and "the stories of writers." As further clarification, the title of Chapter 13 (formerly Chapter 12) is changed to "Learning the Technicalities" from "Learning about Writing." I do not regard handwriting as a critical matter, but it has significant aspects and as a result the section is rather long; the topic has therefore been moved from the beginning to the end of Chapter 13. In its place is a new and important section on "learning about writing from reading." Another important new section is added at the end of Chapter 13 on "high school and college writers."

The title of Chapter 14 (formerly Chapter 13) has been changed from "On Teaching Writing" to "The Writing Teacher"—a deliberate ambiguity that I hope is noticed, especially in the light of some additional reference that is made to the importance of writing by teachers. A section on testing and evaluation has been added, not as lengthy perhaps as the prominence of these topics warrants but as much as I think they deserve. The chapter has been slightly reorganized to give more prominence to positive things that writing teachers might do, although I still refrain from giving detailed recommendations, which I consider inappropriate from anyone in the absence of direct knowledge of the students involved. I have, however, tentatively added some "specific suggestions for teachers of writing" at the end of the chapter.

The notes have been updated and a number of new sections briefly added: on deconstructionism (Notes to Chapter 2); on "flow" (4); on the vicissitudes of transformational and other technical grammars (5); on the relationships between writing and thought (6); on discourse analysis (7); on implicit learning (12); and on a variety of topics related to writing in schools, including theory based on "cognitive science" (14).

Writing and the Writer remains a *personal* book; it is not a "review of the field" or summary of important points of view. Once again, I haven't attempted to include or even to reflect everything that everyone else has said or done on the topic of writing in recent years. My overriding concern has been to keep the book coherent.

I owe a multitude of debts—to many authors I have read, speakers I have heard, students and teachers I have visited, and friends I have talked with. They are far too numerous for me to mention in any comprehensive way, but I certainly could not claim that I had written this book "by myself." And as with so much else that I have written, *Writing and the Writer* would not be what it is without the patience, guidance, and scrupulous editorial acumen of Mary-Theresa Smith.

Notes

Notes to Chapter 1

1. Louise Rosenblatt (1978, 1980) distinguishes two kinds of reading: *efferent*, where the object is to acquire information as quickly as possible, and *aesthetic*, where the whole point is the experience of the reading itself. For efferent purposes, such as consulting a telephone directory or encyclopedia, we are just as happy for someone else to give us the information we seek, but aesthetic reading is spoiled if someone tells us how the book ends. Rosenblatt properly objects that schools often make efferent reading out of what should be aesthetic—the "communication" orientation. A similar distinction might be made in writing, contrasting the merely efferent, when the sole purpose is to transmit information, with writing whose main purpose is to provide (for writer, reader, or perhaps both) a personal, aesthetic, dramatic, emotional, intellectual, and coincidentally, informative experience.

Popper (1973) argues for the independent existence of books which I assert at the beginning of this chapter. He places books, tools, and all other human artifacts in a "third world" of ideas, as real as but distinct from the first world of physical objects and the second world of mental states. The easiest introductions to Popper's ideas are a brief biography by Magee (1973) and Popper's autobiography (Popper, 1976), which also contains many aphorisms on language that apply particularly to writing. For example (these are paraphrases): We never completely know what we are talking about (because it is impossible to predict all the consequences or to understand all the implications of any statement); it is impossible to say anything that cannot be misunderstood; and increased precision can usually only be achieved in statements at the cost of loss of clarity.

2. Hofstadter (1979) is a remarkable book, half science, half fantasy, on the paradoxes of brains trying to understand themselves.

Notes to Chapter 2

1. Olson and Bruner (1974) argue that learning from experience, from pictures (or film), and from language results in different kinds of learning; that language and other

media are not interchangeable. Their discussion is part of a volume that examines the effects of different forms of expression and communication in education (Olson, 1974). A rather more impassioned argument specifically for the value of writing, primarily in an educational context, is made by Farrell (1977).

2. The contents of this section, including the subheading and the table that follows, are derived from an article published elsewhere (Smith, 1977).

3. Since I shall be arguing in due course that language works so well because it is so conventional, I should perhaps also mention the universal use of language *as* convention, not so much for what it means as for what it does. Such "performative" statements as "I name you captain" or "I fine you $20" are not statements about acts, they are themselves acts; by them the person is named captain or is fined (Austin, 1962; Wittgenstein, 1953). There are many other purely ritualistic uses of language, such as reciting creeds or saying "How are you?", which constitute acts quite independently of their literal meaning. These acts can be performed in nonlanguage ways—for example, by crossing oneself or by raising one's hat; see also Searle (1969).

4. The list is not wholly original. The first seven categories and the phrases used to illustrate them are taken from Halliday (1973). Halliday (1975) provides an excellent description of how children develop various uses for language, initially producing utterances for just one purpose alone but gradually coming to perform several functions simultaneously. In general, Halliday (1970) discusses language functions rather than uses, and he collapses these functions to three major ones (macrofunctions): *ideational*, for the communication of ideas; *interpersonal*, for the expression of feelings; and *textual*, for relationships within series of statements.

Britton (1970a, 1971) has an alternative formulation for the functions of language, extensively used by himself and his former colleagues at the University of London Institute of Education in their studies of children's writing (e.g., Martin, D'Arcy, Newton, & Parker, 1976; Britton, Burgess, Martin, McLeod, & Rosen, 1975). Britton distinguishes three function categories: *transactional*, or language to get things done (related to a wide range of my "uses"); *expressive*, revealing of the speaker or writer; and *poetic*, covering all creative and "artistic" constructions of language. Britton also usefully distinguishes some additional rather specialized functions of language, such as play, practice, and the unique kinds of writing often demanded in school contexts.

5. Language is not restricted to its spoken and written forms, nor does it necessarily lose power by being employed in other modes. After extensive research, Klima and Bellugi (1979) concluded that the sign language of the deaf is just as capable as speech of expressing a full range of human intentions. Sacks (1989) documents the same point even more powerfully and poignantly. It is the brain, not the vocal cords or the pen, that makes language possible and determines the limits to its use, a fact that also seems to be becoming apparent in the recent efforts to introduce chimpanzees to language. Interestingly, we tend to use the word *language* for nonlanguage events if we claim to find meaning in them, even if the meaning is provided unintentionally—hence the languages of music and the arts, of clouds, footprints, tea leaves, and of body postures and gestures.

Some theorists argue that there *is* something special about writing, that it has introduced new modes of thought. Olson (1977), for example, asserts that we could not think in the abstract way we do about the implications of statements if language were not written. (My view is the opposite, not that writing makes a particular kind of thought possible, but that the potential of thought makes writing possible, although there is no doubt that writing can facilitate thought.) In conversation, Olson has also made the interesting argument that people must be writers in order to be able to dispute with writers, that students should learn to write so that they can criticize what they read, not only because they would become familiar with certain tricks of the trade of writing, but also because "only co-equals can criticize." Goody (1977) has also argued that literacy has made possible new modes of thought—indeed, that it radically changes cultures.

6. Language, and especially written language, literally constructs worlds; writing creates the possibility of experiences just as real, powerful, stimulating, and emotionally moving as more concrete aspects of the world around us. A story can create events that might otherwise never occur, possibilities that we can accept or reject, and thus provide opportunities for experience, tests, and arguments that might never otherwise be available. Frye (1963) writes that literature "neither reflects nor escapes from ordinary life; what it does reflect is the world as human imagination conceives it, in mythical, romantic, heroic, and ironic as well as realistic and fantastic terms." Fiction is not the opposite of reality; it is an extension of it. Freire (1972) asserts that to speak a true word is to transform the world, and again Popper (in Popper & Eccles, 1977) claims that "if all language is seen as merely expression and communication, then one neglects all that is characteristic of human language in contradistinction to animal language; its ability to make true and false statements and to produce valid and invalid arguments." Barthes (1968) believes writing to be so potent that it actually delineates and sustains the world in which we live. Literature, especially that of North America and England, he argues, "perpetuates bourgeois myths"; to purify itself (which seems to me improbable in Barthes's terms) writing would have to become completely neutral, formless, and colorless, the "Writing Degree Zero" which is the title of his book. I think there can be no doubt that writing does far more than reflect the world or express ideas; writing creates new worlds that we can construct, modify, and demolish at will.

A continental viewpoint that aroused general interest in some literary circles is *deconstructionism* (or post-structuralism), which holds that historical, cultural, and social forces (and other books) rather than authors create books and their meaning, in fact that books create their own authors. For an original flavor of some of the arguments, see Derrida (1978, 1992); for helpful commentaries, see Culler (1982), Lodge (1990), or Norris (1991), and for a lively critique of the entire approach, see Eagleton (1983).

For the complementary point of view that there is more to creativity than language, Ferguson (1977) argues that nonverbal imagination is responsible for "the outline and details" of our material surroundings; "pyramids, cathedrals, rockets exist because they were first a picture in the minds of those who built them." He quotes Einstein's assertion that he never thought in words at all but in visual and muscular images. Nevertheless, of course, Einstein succeeded in translating this thought into language, or at least in finding language to talk about it.

Notes to Chapter 3

1. There are arguments that the slowness of writing is an advantage because it forces writers to reduce speed and to think about what is being written (Emig, 1978). This view could possibly confuse a disadvantage of writing, that its rate is inevitably slower than speech even when we want to go faster, with the advantage that we can go slower if we wish because writing provides a record of what we have done and we need not fear we shall forget what we have already produced. The danger with the slowness of writing is that we may forget what we wanted to write. I do not see how forcing anyone to think slower can be an advantage, though allowing them more time to think certainly is. In a carefully designed research study, Gould and Boies (1978) showed that two-thirds of the time that experimental subjects spent "writing" a letter (or

dictating the letter in some experimental conditions) was actually spent in "planning," when no writing (or dictating) was being done. Butler (1972) says that writing is like "slow motion thinking with the possibility of replays."

Elsewhere in Emig's (1978) article she argues that for some writers at least the act of physically creating a beautiful artifact is important and motivating. I agree. Even when they cannot help scribbling an untidy mess, most people would prefer not to scribble an untidy mess. A tidy product probably induces as well as reflects a tidy thought—provided the thought is tidily organized in the first place, which sometimes means that it is unlikely to be fresh. Shaughnessy (1977) also argues that poor handwriting interferes with thought—not just because it may be inefficient, but because there is a relationship between the quality of the handwriting and of the ideas it can express. Childish handwriting and childish thought go together, she asserts, without explaining how the relationship comes about.

2. The problem is the limited capacity and persistence of *short-term memory*, the working memory where we hold whatever we happen to be consciously attending to at any particular time. We cannot remember a telephone number and conduct a conversation at the same time (unless the number has previously been committed to long-term memory, in which case it will demand no attention at all). Fairly detailed discussions of my perceptions of short-term memory and attention—I do not distinguish the two—are contained in Smith (1975, 1985). For a comprehensive and technical analysis of attention, including interference among tasks, memory bottlenecks, and competition for effort, see Kahneman (1973). For more extensive discussions of short- and long-term memory, see Ashcraft (1989), Gregg (1986) or Cohen, Eysenck, and LeVoi (1986). For "everyday" memory, see Morris (1988) and for memory for text, Kintsch (1982).

3. Posner and Keele (1973) summarize research related to the manner in which transcription aspects of writing can be performed without conscious attention. Dennett (1991) proposes a pseudo-neurological "parallel pandemonium" model in which different functions of the brain simultaneously perform different functions, such as identifying letters, identifying words, or determining meaning. All systems "shout loudly," Dennett proposes, but only the one that shouts loudest can make itself heard at one time.

For a general discussion of distinctions between transcription and composition aspects of writing, and the relative importance attached to them in school, see Moffett (1979).

Notes to Chapter 4

1. Miller and Johnson-Laird (1975) observe that "The relation of our psychological results to the electrical and biochemical events that we can observe in the brain is so obscure that many philosophers suspect a fundamental conceptual error in the way most psychologists and neurophysiologists think about the brain." An eminent philosopher and an eminent neurophysiologist (Popper & Eccles, 1977) jointly believe they have the problem solved, and other philosophers and psychologists (Ryle, 1949; Dennett, 1991) believe there is no problem in the first place. I shall make no attempt to cite or summarize the extensive literature on language and thought, even where it is profound and influential, such as the contributions of Piaget, Noam Chomsky, or Vygotsky, unless a reference is particularly relevant to my exposition. Jaynes (1976) has a radical way of treating the not uncommon notion that language is the origin of consciousness (see also Note 10, Chapter 5).

2. Observations such as these have been separately made in many different contexts

before, for example, that present knowledge and beliefs are the basis of memory (Bartlett, 1932), of learning (Smith, 1975), of perception and understanding (Hochberg, 1978; Piaget, 1978), and of expectation (Neisser, 1977). Sartre (1962) argues that fantasy is the basis of reality. The entire view is phenomenological (e.g., Merleau-Ponty, 1974) and hermeneutic (see Palmer, 1969). Kelly (1955) developed an important psychological theory of personality around the notion that all our interactions with the world are based on theories of the world that we have ourselves constructed. For a book-length analysis of thinking, see Smith (1990).

3. Tulving and Watkins (1975).

4. We are extremely sensitive to language relating to feelings. With a few words a writer can make us smile, swallow a lump in the throat, or fidget with fear or excitement. Perhaps the reason we respond emotionally to a description in language almost as readily as we would respond to the event the language describes is that to the brain they are relatively undifferentiatcd. Objectively, a spoken or written word is very different from its referent, but to the brain they are both patterns of neural impulscs, to be *interpreted*. There is no exclusive and passionless "word interpreting center" in the brain. The brain responds to the world in its own terms, and it is perhaps not difficult for it to overlook the little intellectual tag "This is not true" or "This is not actually occurring" when there is a powerful emotional component in the interpretation of a "verbal" experience.

5. For example, Heidegger, Husserl, Bergson, Sartre, and Merleau-Ponty. The psychologist who perhaps thought most about the relationship of time and language was the German widely credited with being the first experimental (or "scientific") psychologist, Wilhelm Wundt. In Wundt (1911, 1912) he devoted two volumes to fundamental problems of language, including that of transforming simultaneous events or ideas into sequential language expressions. Some more recent analyses are included in a very dense and technical analysis of the relationship of narrative and time; Ricoeur (1984) notes: "I see in the plots we invent the privileged means by which we reconfigure our confused, unformed, and at the limit mute temporal experience" (p. xi).

Csikszentmihalyi (1990) examines the feeling of "optimal experience" and deep satisfaction that arises from total involvement in what we are doing, which he calls a state of *flow*. In flow, we forget ourselves and also ignore the passage of time. Csikszentmihalyi says that flow is achieved by following a "channel" between boredom (by confronting challenge) and anxiety (by exercising skill) (p. 74), and notes that "mental activities" frequently create states of flow, particularly reading (pp. 49, 50), but also writing (p. 131) and "the use of words" (p. 128). He considers learning as a state of flow (p. 141), but neglects to mention that any state of flow inevitably results in learning.

6. Britton (1971) beautifully sums up the relationship of awareness (which he here calls consciousness) to experience as follows: "...consciousness, in fact, is like the little dog with the brass band: it is forever running ahead, or dropping back, or trotting alongside, while the procession of actual events moves steadily on." He might have added that the little dog often disappears altogether for long periods.

Notes to Chapter 5

1. Most linguists who accept a distinction between surface structure and deep structure would argue that there is more than one level of each. The theory of generative transformational grammar has been through many vicissitudes since first formulated

by Chomsky (1957), including substantial revisions by Chomsky himself (Chomsky, 1965, 1980, 1986, 1988). It is now an ideology accessible only to a small inner circle of linguists initiated into its esoteric mysteries. Nevertheless, the original theory, in a simplified if not misunderstood form, was of great historical importance, helping the new disciplines of cognitive psychology and psycholinguistics to flourish and liberating psychology from behaviorism—as exemplified in George Miller's (1965) revolutionary cry that "mind is more than a four-letter word." Chomsky was the spiritual godfather of what were to become whole language and process writing in educational theory. Today, cognitive psychology has become cognitive science, which is busily reintroducing reductionist mechanistic processes into psychology and education (see Chapter 14, Note 5), and the name of Chomsky is little more than a nostalgic battlecry among veteran psychologists and educators (although well-known to other generations of political dissidents). Chomsky's more recent conceptualizations perceive surface structure as an abstract (i.e., unobservable) level of language that still has to be "interpreted" into sound, whereas deep structure is regarded as a "semantic" representation that still has to be interpreted into meaning. In my simplification I literally go to extremes, treating surface structure as the most observable part of language and deep structure as the most profound.

2. There is a troublesome exception when characterizing surface structure as that part of language which is always observable and has some physical presence in the world—namely, the language that we hear (or imagine we hear) when we talk to ourselves. I argue that *subvocal speech* is not thought (or deep structure) but a product of thought and thus as much a surface structure of language as speech that is uttered aloud. Inner speech—at least that of which we are aware—is different from speech uttered aloud only because it is rehearsed privately in the mind. Nevertheless, it has all the other characteristics of the surface structure of speech: the same vocabulary, the same grammatical structures (although they may sometimes be collapsed into rather telegraphic form), the same existence in time. Subvocal speech obviously does not have a physical existence in the world outside the speaker's head, but it could have—if it were uttered aloud. Thought (or meaning), on the other hand, could not be uttered aloud without first being transformed into surface structure. Vygotsky (1962) argues that subvocal speech derives from social speech that gradually becomes internalized (so that children can control their own behavior in the way it is controlled by the language of others). He then asserts that this inner speech becomes thought when the subvocalization is eliminated entirely, which is a rather different way of saying that thought lies beyond language and perhaps, I think, emphasizes a little too much the role of language in bringing forth thought. But I would not disagree with Vygotsky's general theme that language and thought develop in power and complexity together. Dennett (1991, p. 197) sees talking to oneself as the *historical* origin of thought, providing a coupling (from mouth to ear) where "hard-wiring" within the brain does not exist. Elbow (1987) discusses how talking to oneself may help writing.

3. The role of case grammars in a theory of generative semantics was originally explored by Fillmore (1968) and McCawley (1968). Various categorizations of case relationships were proposed, and simplified listings provided in various introductory texts such as Lindsay and Norman (1977) and Clark and Clark (1977); see also Roger Brown (1973). For a discussion of the history and later status of case grammar, see Cook (1983). A difficulty is that the catalog of possible case relationships in language keeps growing—not surprisingly, perhaps, when one considers the complexity of all the different kinds of relationships we can perceive in the world. For an idea of the enormity of the task of trying to specify even limited domains of relationships (e.g., those related to possession or to relative motion) in language and in our perception

of the world (and to a large extent there is no difference), see Miller and Johnson-Laird (1976).

Like transformational grammar, case grammar and generative semantics have also suffered a decline in popular interest and influence, although once again basic insights have survived in simplified and even distorted form, independently of original theory. I don't think the question of which, if any, of these linguistic theories is "correct" is of crucial importance to the study of writing; writers and educators need not hold their breath. They are simply highly technical and speculative ways of talking about language and thought. Indeed, I doubt if any linguistic theory will ever be proved correct, in the sense of accurately representing the way in which the brain translates meaningful but nonverbal thoughts into the lumpish collocations of words that we pass between ourselves. Such a theory would have to be neurological rather than linguistic. What is important to reflective writers and to teachers of writing is the underlying situation that these theories strive to account for, the fact that meaning is not directly represented in words.

4. There are many texts on "developmental psycholinguistics" that discuss the transformational grammars assumed to underlie infant language. For a classic summary account by one of the modern innovators of child language study see Roger Brown (1973). Gleason (1989) is an excellent nontechnical survey of language learning by a number of prominent researchers, and Aitchison (1989) is lively and informed on both Chomsky and children's language development. Fletcher and Garman (1979, 1986) are compendious collections of authoritative chapters on early language development, and Teale and Sulzby (1986) is an interesting collection of papers on "emergent literacy"—the beginning of reading and writing.

5. As I go on to say, conventions permeate all human behavior and social interaction. For an excellent collection of papers about conventions in general, including but not limited to language, see Douglas (1968). This volume demonstrates not only how cultures depend upon conventions but also the arbitrary or accidental nature of the conventions themselves. An edited volume by Eschholz, Rosa, and Clark (1974) contains many articles concerning oddities and idiosyncrasies in language, showing that what becomes conventional, for whatever reason, overrides all rules and even "logic" provided it serves a purpose. See also the discussion of *register* in language in Chapter 6, beginning on page 77. For a very technical, influential discussion of relationships among intentions and language conventions see Grice (1975).

6. The argument that every aspect of language is based on convention, which is essentially arbitrary, might seem to be contradicted by theories concerning the existence of *language universals* (Greenberg, 1963) common to all the 3,000 or more "natural languages" of the world. Such universals include a separation of deep and surface structures and systems of distinctive sounds from a limited range of alternatives. One might expect many such similarities among different languages, either because they all tend to be concerned with some common events that have a logic of their own or because of physiological limitations; it would be difficult or unnatural for the human organism to produce language otherwise. However, relatively few universals seem attributable to human physiology, and when they are the constraint tends to define a limited range of alternatives rather than a unique possibility. For example, all natural languages have a phonology—a system of distinctive sounds—falling within a range of from 15 to 80 alternatives. (English is a middle-of-the-road language, using between 35 and 45 distinct sounds, depending upon dialect.) Presumably it would be inefficient for a natural language to function with as few as two distinct sounds (like the Morse code) and a system of many hundreds of sounds might be beyond the capacity of the

average tongue to produce or the average ear to discriminate (few linguists can manage more than 100). Yet within that range of alternative sounds from which all languages must select are many thousands of different sounds employed by one language or another. There is no way of predicting how many and what exactly the sounds of any language will be; there is no logical reason why English and Chinese should sound the particular ways they do. As far as their sound is concerned, languages have about as much in common as human anatomy itself. Most human beings are born with one head, two arms, and two legs connected at particular points to a trunk, but within that universal range all manner of variations is possible. One apparent language universal is that in the declarative sentence forms of every natural language the subject precedes the object. It may seem particularly logical to mention who is doing something before whoever or whatever that something is being done to, but this perhaps reflects the way the brain constructs events rather than any logic in the events themselves (whatever that "logic" might be). A complication is that while who is doing and who or what they do it to appear in a predictable sequence in almost every language, what is done does not. The verb may come at the beginning, middle, or end of sentences in different languages; before, between, or after the subject and object which seem so inexorably ordered, with no evident reason for the particular position.

7. For discussions of the variety and significance of nonverbal conventions of language, see Hall (1959, 1966) and also Weitz (1979). Important texts on genre generally (in both speech and writing) are Bakhtin (1981, 1986), but they are detailed and technical; he emphasizes that genre differences in content, structure, and style are culturally determined. There are interesting discussions of genre and related topics in educational settings in Cazden (1992). Feldman (1991) discusses the many different genres of spoken language, particularly in cultures without written language. Bruner and Weisser (1991) have commented that even talking to oneself doesn't come naturally— it requires knowledge of genres and conventions.

8. The problem of defining or explaining "meaning" has notorious pitfalls, partly because the word can itself be used with a variety of meanings in different contexts. In everyday language there is usually no difficulty with the word. We may dispute what somebody means by saying something, but not the meaning of the word "means" in the dispute. Problems arise only when the meaning of meaning in the abstract is debated, rather than the meaning of a particular utterance on a particular occasion. A fundamental distinction can be made between the intrinsic and extrinsic meanings of sentences. The intrinsic meaning of a statement is usually taken to be the proposition it expresses: "Someone is talking in here" means someone is talking in here. Grice (1969, 1975) and Austin (1962) would refer to such meaning as the *locutionary* force of the statement, which is appropriately evaluated with respect to its truth or correspondence to the "facts."

Linguists and other theorists usually focus upon the intrinsic meaning of statements, although in everyday use of language this is often not the main concern. Intrinsic meaning must be distinguished from the reason a statement is produced on a particular occasion; for example, a teacher may say, "Someone is talking in here" (or even the pseudo-question "Can I hear someone talking in here?") when what is actually intended is the command "Be quiet." The purpose for which the statement is made, its *illocutionary* force, may be quite different from its propositional content, and appropriately evaluated in terms of its effectiveness rather than its truth. Everything depends upon whether the intent of the speaker is to make a statement or to produce an effect.

"Speaker's meaning" must also be distinguished from anything a listener might interpret; for example, a child could rightly decide that the statement about talking meant that the teacher was in a sour mood today. The notion of meaning in its intrinsic sense should in any case probably be employed only with reference to words or sentences, and then only when their function is to express propositions. It is stretching the use of the term to talk about the meaning of a paragraph (which may be why schools tend to convolute the matter even further by talking in terms of a "main idea" of a paragraph, when if anything what is referred to is a theme). Certainly books as a whole cannot be said to have meaning in any intrinsic sense (although one would hope any book would be meaningful). If the word *meaning* is appropriately applied to an entire book, then it is clearly related to the general intention of the author: "The meaning of this book is that war is hell" does not refer to the same kind of thing as the meaning of a sentence, and is open to challenge and alternative interpretation by any reader. It is common to talk of authors, as it is of painters, in terms of whether they have anything interesting to say. For painters such a statement is obviously metaphorical, and it should perhaps be recognized that for writers it is metaphorical also. The only thing an author *literally* has to say is what in fact the author writes, no more and no less.

9. There is a large literature on psychological aspects of metaphor; see especially Ortony (1979a, 1979b). Lakoff (1987) argues that language and our perception of the world are constructed out of metaphors related to our bodies and bodily concerns. Samples (1976) makes a strong plea for educational recognition of the mind as a metaphor-making device, emphasizing the importance of writing in providing actual and metaphorical alternatives to "reality." Jaynes (1976), in an interesting and controversial book, argues that consciousness *is* metaphor; that what I have been calling awareness is primarily the interpretation of temporal events in terms of spatial metaphors. This conjecture is interesting in regard to the brain's problem in imposing a structure of "events" upon an unbroken flow of occurrences in time, and in the light of evidence from psychological studies of how the brain comes to terms with time (see Note 11 below).

10. The basis of both verbal and nonverbal communication that is *intentional* (as opposed to "body language" produced without awareness or deliberate intention) appears to be (for the producer) behaving in the way we would anticipate the recipient to expect us to communicate the particular message and (for the recipient) anticipating what the producer is likely to anticipate the recipient to expect.

11. The fundamental answer to the question of how language (and possibly also thought in general) manages to cope with the continuous and unsegmented nature of time is by metaphor, especially spatial metaphor. Specifically, the "before" and "after" of events in time is understood and expressed in terms of the "in front of" and "behind" of objects in space (which often have the advantage of being clearly separated and at least momentarily static). Not only are almost all terms relating to the passage of time spatial in origin (such as *before, after, long, short, near, far,* and *next*) but the appearance of temporal terms and of underlying concepts of time in children's language development seems always to wait upon mastery of spatial terms and concepts of equivalent complexity (Clark, 1973; also Clark & Clark, 1977). It is perhaps also relevant that spatial rather than temporal metaphors are frequently employed to express abstractions—high and low on the totem pole, heights of ignorance, depths of despair, middle management, inner cabinet, upper income, base feelings, shallow thinking, pointed remarks, and peaks of excellence. See Mac Cormac (1985) on metaphor specifically, and Kessen, Ortony, and Craik (1991) on metaphor, memory, and thinking.

12. The classic works on the interaction of thought and language are Vygotsky (1962, 1978); see Note 2 above. There is also a huge psychological literature in this area, both

general and specific—for example, Anderson (1976), Cromer (1974), Fodor, Bever, and Garrett (1974), and Luria and Yudovich (1959). A most interesting work—and also I think the most realistic about the complexity and essential mystery of the issue—is Miller and Johnson-Laird (1976).

Chafe (1992) asserts that many important aspects of language are dependent on and shaped by human consciousness, declaring boldly that introspection is "an indispensable guide" in the study of language. He describes how consciousness can be displaced to experiences remote in space or time, to the past and the future, to the possible and the impossible, with a profound effect on human thought. Chafe also notes that writers of fiction can manipulate modes of consciousness quite different from those encountered in ordinary speech, being free to displace themselves into characters, to take on fictional identities, or to have no identity at all.

Notes to Chapter 6

1. Text, say Halliday and Hasan (1976), is not just a string of sentences. Sentences are interwoven by the various devices of *cohesion* "which give texture to text" and provide the basis of context dependence. Such devices include pronouns (which can refer back, forward, and even outside the text), ellipsis, conjunctions, and various linking markers such as *however, although, and, then,* and *but.* Cohesion devices tend to be the commonest part of any language, children seem able to learn them without effort (or realization) in their mother tongue; yet their use causes the greatest difficulty in foreign-language learning, probably once again because they are essentially arbitrary and conventional.

2. Both spoken and written stories tend to have a similar set of conventions, or *story grammar*, within a particular culture, and spoken and written *discourse* (sequences of context-dependent sentences) tend to have similar structures. There is further reference to story grammars and discourse structures in Chapter 7.

3. Olson (1977) argues that writing improves thought because it must be more explicit than speech in the absence of an immediate recipient. But as noted in the chapter and below, some forms of speech (such as a lecture) can be highly elaborated and explicit, and some forms of writing (such as a personal note) can be most succinct. And the assertion that texts have to be *autonomous*—that they must explain themselves to readers in the absence of the author—has been challenged, in the present book and elsewhere. Nystrand and Wiemelt (1991), for example, argue that there is no such thing as an autonomous text, independent of a reader's interpretation. "Explicitness" is not something an author puts into a text but is part of the relationship between the author and potential readers. Meanings are not fixed, they are "negotiated" (in my view, the way a river or a mountain pass is negotiated, not a contract). See also Nystrand (1986) for a comprehensive examination of "reciprocity" in writer and reader expectations. There is more discussion of these topics in Chapter 7.

Bereiter and Scardamalia (1980) also argue that writing can benefit thought—by providing opportunities for the critical examination of one's own ideas and for their revision. Bereiter and Scardamalia see a dialectic process arising from a "conflict" between the "requirements of the text and the requirements of belief"—and doubt whether the productive resolution is achieved automatically; it must be learned.

Whether there is a *direct* connection between writing and thought—whether people think more efficiently if they are literate—is a tenuous proposition, but there can be little doubt that the printing press, the media, and now computers have made great differences to *societies*, and thus to the people who live in them. People who live in literate societies are forced to think differently about a number of things, and about the way they interact with each other, whether or not they are literate themselves—a point made by Cole and Keyssar (1985) in a more general discussion of the effects of film and other media as well as print.

4. The many ways in which spoken and written language differ, from intimate conversations to formal lectures in speech and from personal correspondence to professional articles in writing, are examined by Chafe and Danielwicz (1987). They note that spoken language uttered on some occasions can be very much like written language, while writing in some circumstances can be very similar to some aspects of speech, and they attribute differences to the formality of the situation, the amount of time available, and the degree of memory support required. At the "written" end of the range (for both spoken and written language) they found more varied vocabulary, fewer "hedges" (like "sort of" and "kind of"), few inexplicit third person references, fewer contractions (like "I'm," "don't"), longer and more complex clauses, more prepositional phrases, and more nominalizations and other devices which appear less frequently in casual conversation. None of these ways of talking appear to Chafe and Danielwicz to be particularly difficult to accomplish; we just do them more often in written language, making maximum use of the elaborating resources of language (and taking more words to say the same thing). Though there has been a great deal of speculation, it has not (to my knowledge) been demonstrated that such elaborations in written language make texts easier to read; they are once again *conventions*—this is the way writing is *expected* to be done.

The relative frequency of nominalizations—the use of nouns like "representation" and "performance" rather than verbs like "represents" or "performs"—in writing is curious. In an analysis of thinking (Smith, 1990), I suggest that a major problem in educational theorizing is that words which are perfectly understandable as verbs—when, for example, we say someone is thinking, learning, or understanding—become a source of confusion and contention when treated as nouns, when we ask such portentous and possibly unnecessary questions as "What is thinking (or learning, comprehension, or meaning)?" By nominalizing, we take a piece of behavior and make it into an abstraction, an entity rather than an action, which we sometimes locate in a person's brain rather than in the person's behavior. Is such a habit, which strangers to Western ways of thought might regard as perverse if not bizarre, largely a consequence of the elaborated way we think it is appropriate to write (and to talk academically)?

Olson and Torrance (1991) is an edited volume containing a number of useful historical and theoretical chapters on relations and differences between spoken and written language, focusing particularly on the way in which written language takes over some of the functions that speech retains in cultures without literacy. Several contributors, including the editors, argue that literacy makes a difference to an individual's knowledge of language, in particular by allowing language to be regarded from a detached point of view, as an object, to be discussed in a specialized metalanguage. Such knowledge is certainly important in contemporary education, particularly in literacy instruction, where much of the teaching may involve talking *about* reading and writing—see especially Scholes and Willis (1991). An earlier edited volume by Olson, Torrance, and Hildyard (1985) examines the possibility of "speaking a written language" and the effect of writing on speech and thought.

5. Register, technically, is determined by the *field, mode,* and *tenor* of a language event (Gregory & Carroll, 1978), *field* referring to the topic that the language is about (all

technical languages are fields), *mode* to its nature (including spoken or written, monologue or dialogue, spontaneous or rehearsed), and *tenor* to the relationship of the producer to the recipient (including aspects of the producer's purpose, whether to persuade, excite, teach, and so forth). For all these aspects of register there are rules (or conventions) that vary with dialect, a complex issue of considerations to which we all usually respond without the slightest conception of their existence or importance.

6. "Plain language" is also a register, and so is "natural speech" as represented in the scripts of plays and films. "Everyday speech" sounds most unnatural when it is translated more or less word for word into a dramatic setting (for example, in the plays of Pinter), while dramatic language usually sounds most out of place in offstage situations. There are conventions for everything, even for representing other conventions. On the conventions involved in "sounding natural" in writing Philip Roth has said, "creating the illusion of intimacy and spontaneity is not just a matter of letting your hair down and being yourself but of inventing a whole new idea of what 'being yourself' sounds and looks like; 'naturalness' happens not to grow on trees" (Roth, 1975, p. 197).

7. Senner (1989) offers a number of accessible essays on the origin of various writing systems, showing that writing was not the invention of one particular group of people, and that it appears to have had its antecedents in drawing rather than in spoken language. Since the development of the alphabetic system, writing has often been modified to correspond more closely with spoken language, but at the same time, spoken language has always been influenced by the structure and use of written language. Written language tends to change less rapidly than speech, and therefore has tended to put a brake on spoken language change (or to drift further apart from it). Even today, many people seem to feel that written language is the ideal form of language, a model for what spoken language should be like. The other origin of written language, pointed out by several of the contributors to Senner's volume, is not so much conventional speech as mathematics—from keeping track of the calendar and of astronomical (and astrological) phenomena to bureaucratic and commercial record keeping. Vygotsky (1978) hypothesizes that both writing and drawing originated in gestures.

For a brief overview of how writing systems differ, for example in terms of the demands they make on writers and readers, focusing particularly on English and Chinese, see Coulmas (1992). Coulmas points out that no purely logographic writing system exists. Chinese, for example, is morpho-syllabic—each character represents a morpheme (meaning) and a syllable. But the logographic (originally pictorial) form is primary in Chinese, with the syllabic connection superimposed, for example using a pictorial symbol for the sun to represent the word *sun* and also the syllable /sun/. Chinese writing has thousands of characters, many rarely used, and it is impossible to say how many are currently utilized, probably at least 5,000. Chinese writing is no more difficult to read than English—perhaps easier. For readers of classical Chinese (before the "reforms" of the cultural revolution) it was certainly easier to read a Chinese text that was hundreds of years old than an alphabetic one because alphabetic writing systems are tied to pronunciation, which changes.

Notes to Chapter 7

1. Tierney and LaZansky (1980) published an article referring to the "rights and responsibilities" of readers and writers as "a contractual agreement." It is common practice to refer to a "reader-writer relationship"(or to *the* relationship between

spoken and written language, between language and thought, or between writers and texts); I do the same at several points in this book. But the key word should perhaps be *relationships*—emphasizing the plurality and complexity of the links, which are never single, never simple, and involve every convention of writing. They are interactions rather than interconnections.

Wason (1980) is one of many authors concerned about the tendency of some people to ignore the writer-reader contract and write sentences that are incomprehensible to other people. As examples, Wason selects the popular targets of civil servants and graduate students—noting that they can often *say* what they mean with more clarity than they can write it. The problem, of course, is that what individuals write is transparently clear to them, and they think it must be to others. Often, they will try desperately to *explain* what the written words are supposed to mean, rather than contemplate changing them, convinced the defect is in the reader. The difficult remedial task is less teaching such individuals to write clearly (a hopeless enterprise when they already believe they are doing so) than persuading them to realize that their writing is obscure. "Careful rereading" may not be the solution, if it only confirms the belief that what has been written is perfectly clear.

2. *Genre schemes* are the structures underlying the organization of different genres of text—one reason that novels, plays, essays, scientific articles, letters, and so forth look different from each other. Many psychological studies have endeavored to demonstrate not only that texts have characteristic underlying structures that enable the "information" in them to be arranged coherently (e.g., Anderson, Spiro, & Anderson, 1978; Rumelhart, 1975) and to be extracted comprehensibly (e.g., Kintsch, 1974, 1977; Kintsch & VanDijk, 1978), but also that such structures in some way represent the way knowledge is organized in long-term memory. Chafe (1977), among others, extends schema theory to all forms of narrative language, spoken and written, as well as to memory, as the basis by which complex events are broken down into smaller units (such as sequences, purposes, and consequences) that can be grasped and expressed in sentences. An analogous notion is that some of our knowledge of the world is represented in the brain in the form of *scenarios* or *scripts* (Schank & Abelson, 1977; Mandler, 1984; Mandler & Goodman, 1982) which describe the appropriate sequences of events for particular contexts, some of which may involve language (turn taking in conversation, the construction of texts) but others of which do not (how to dress, to select a meal in a restaurant, to find one's way around a department store). Just and Carpenter (1977) contains a number of papers on schema approaches to cognition and text construction. For a discussion of how different cultures may have different schemata that result in different understandings of the same text see Steffensen, Joag-Dev, and Anderson (1979).

3. The discipline of *discourse analysis* originally focused on the interaction between speakers and listeners but is now mainly concerned with texts—or at least on *relationships* within texts and between texts, authors, and readers, on "processes" rather than "products." Most discussions of discourse analysis are technical, but an approach could be made through Singer (1990), Coulthard and Montgomery (1981), or Fine and Freedle (1983). There is also a journal entitled *Discourse Processes*. An interesting paradox in all forms of language is that listeners and readers should not be told anything they need not know or can be expected to know already, yet at every level from individual sentence to entire book there must be something that the reader knows to which what is new can be related. For discussions of the "given-new contract" from different points of view see Clark and Haviland (1977) and Halliday (1970). The relative prominence given to different segments of discourse is sometimes referred to as *staging,* discussed by Clements (1977), and Marshall and Glock (1978/79). Grimes

(1975) outlines the view that discourse has three semantic (meaningful) structures: *content* (the propositions it expresses), *cohesion* (binding it into a meaningful whole), and *staging* (the hierarchical organization of content in the text and the psychological process in a reader's mind). Frederiksen (1975a, 1975b) argues again that the content of discourse and of subsequent memory structures after comprehension are identical, a common view which I think puts too narrow and impersonal a meaning to comprehension. See also Horowitz and Samuels (1987) and Flammer and Kintsch (1982).

4. Story grammars are particular kinds of schemata or schemes, conceptualized in terms of predictable settings, characters, plots, episodes (embedded in each other), and resolutions, all of which provide frames for the construction and understanding of stories. In a number of experiments, Bower (1976) showed that "higher-order" (more global) propositions and episodes in stories were easier to identify and to recall, with the more focal ones (in my terms) identified last and forgotten first. The structure is essential, Bower shows. If anticipated constituents are omitted from a story, both comprehension and recall are affected. Stein and Glenn (1979) demonstrate that children who know the grammar of stories (of their own culture) not only use the grammar to understand new stories but will add elements that have been omitted. See also Mandler and Johnson (1977). Todorov (1977) is a highly esoteric and allusive attempt to construct a grammar of plots, examining the codes and conventions that make the meaning of plots possible. Singer (1990), noted above for his discussion of discourse processes, is particularly helpful on story structures.

5. Global aspects of text are easier to identify (Note 4 above) and may blind us to focal detail, a general phenomenon recognized proverbially and demonstrated experimentally by Navon (1977) in a report entitled "Forest before trees: The precedence of global features in visual perception." Norman and Bobrow (1979) discuss what they term *descriptions* in memory which can range from vague to precise, and show that memories can be recalled intentionally at various levels from the global to the focal. We can recall an entire incident or an aspect of that incident. Koestler (1978) has an interesting discussion of hierarchical organizations generally, both in knowledge structures and in the conventions employed to communicate them. Glynn and DiVesta (1979) show that readers expect and utilize all kinds of cues (conventions) in text, typographical as well as semantic and syntactic. Wildman and Kling (1978/1979) argue that semantic, syntactic, and spatial structures but not precise words are anticipated, and Golinkoff (1976) made a similar demonstration with children who were good readers (while those who comprehended poorly tended more to be a "slave to the actual printed word").

6. Popper (1976); see Note 1, Chapter 1.

Notes to Chapter 8

1. An insightful writer on all aspects of writing, especially "prewriting" (which he later termed "rehearsal" and I now refer to as "groundwork"), is Donald Murray (1978, 1980, 1987, 1989). He particularly emphasizes the recursive, interactive nature of prewriting with composition (later termed "drafting") and with rewriting ("revision"). A colleague of Murray's at the University of New Hampshire, Donald Graves, has been a prolific researcher into the place and value of revision for children learning to write (see Chapter 14, Note 4).

2. James Britton (1970b) talks of words shaping themselves at the point of utterance.

Some of Britton's pioneering work on children's language is also cited in Note 4, Chapter 14. For his views on language generally, see Britton (1970a, 1992).

3. William James (1892) wrote eloquently on the limited ways in which we can observe and control our own "stream of consciousness" and in particular on how the decision to extend or terminate a particular focus of attention to some aspect of this consciousness might constitute the mechanism by which our will is imposed on our behavior.

4. Elbow (1973, 1987) argues that the basic problem in writing is in discovering what you want to say, which comes with writing, not in planning or outlining or in putting down ideas already formulated in the mind.

In a speculative chapter entitled "How words do things with us," Dennett (1991, pp. 227–252) says that authors don't have intentions before words (I take it he means focal intentions) but that words come spontaneously and assertively, being selected according to constraints within what he calls "the system" and I would call global intentions. Authors, says Dennett, take credit for intentions they did not have. See Britton's comment in Note 2 above.

5. There is some qualified evidence that exercises in combining short sentences into more complex ones improve writing fluency, one of the few forms of drill that may have some lasting value for a writer (Strong & Marzano, 1976, Strong, 1986). My conjecture is that anything that tends to consolidate focal components of text tends to ease the memory burden for a writer; the more global the peg on which a complex thought hangs, the easier it is to manipulate it. From the reader's point of view the situation may be different; a densely organized text can be at least as difficult for short-term memory as one strung out in a sequence of simple sentences.

Notes to Chapter 9

1. See Note 1, Chapter 8. Murray is also excellent on the making and breaking of writing blocks. He has, moreover, noted an occasional tendency among authors to stop writing when it is flowing, when all is going well, perhaps just to get respite from its control.

2. There is an extensive and diffuse literature on creativity, including a number of volumes looking at the topic from artistic and scientific points of view as well as literary—for example, Perkins (1981), Gardner (1983), and Smith (1990). Getzels and Csikszentmihalyi (1972) found experimentally that creativity seemed to be more a matter of exploration and discovery than any systematic tricks or procedures. Wallach and Kogan (1972) conclude that "divergent thinking" rather than "intelligence" explains creativity in children. Britton (1975) alludes to the importance of "pencil chewing" pauses in the premeditation of writing by children.

3. Perhaps I might provide a personal illustration. From the first draft of the present book I rarely had problems with intentions at a global level. I always knew that I was writing a book about writing within certain circumscribed limits, and tentative chapter headings and general content were never difficult to lay out or to revise. Although ideas about the points a particular chapter should cover may have changed before and during the writing of that chapter, I was never hindered by any general uncertainty of what the chapter I was working on was supposed to be about, or what in general would be in later chapters. I discovered new or different matters to put in subsequent chapters about as often as I decided to make additions or alterations to what I had already drafted in earlier chapters. (I worked on the book as a whole, all the time.) I also had little doubt about what I was supposed to be dealing with in particular sections

of a chapter—the topic of writing blocks, for example, under the present heading. Once again, problems of how chapters should be organized into particular sections tended to be either fairly clear when I began the chapter or easily resolved as the chapter progressed.

Nor had I more than transitory problems at extreme focal levels of composition, with words and sentences. Words were rarely a problem; I was usually inundated by them (when they came at all) although they often came in fragmented sentences, with fractured grammar, incorrect or telegraphic spelling, and marginal legibility. Words sometimes came so fast that I had difficulty organizing them into separate sentences, which in turn tended to become overpacked and diffuse. (I had a greater-than-usual tendency in this book to insert observations in parentheses—or between dashes—an indication that words and ideas were coming faster than I could organize them into simple sentences. I hope to clear up a lot of these parentheses and dashes in the subsequent editing but doubtless enough will remain to provide evidence of their more general intrusiveness.)

The frequent parenthetical observations are part of the problem I had somewhere between my global and focal intentions. This is the problem of organizing ideas at what might be termed the section level. (We do not even have a convenient word in English for this level, lying between the chapter and the paragraph. It might also be referred to as a theme, another word that is very loosely defined and used.) Usually I had a reasonably good idea of the topic I wanted to cover in particular sections and of how the sections might organize themselves within a chapter. And individual paragraphs tended to take care of themselves, in draft form at least, as the sentences were produced. But deciding how to organize (and limit) the content of paragraphs within sections was the critical difficulty. And it was here that I had my most excruciating blocks.

There are perhaps several reasons for my own particular level of difficulty in this book. One is the fact that I was striving to work out ideas as I wrote. I knew that I wanted to say something about writing blocks, for example, but I did not know exactly what I wanted to say, let alone how to organize it, when I came to *explore* the topic in writing. There was also—I excuse myself—the complexity of the subject itself, and the desire to provide *evidence* for assertions, a reasoned argument, so that I was reluctant to leave avenues open or possible questions unanswered. One constant problem concerns overlap and duplication. A statement often leads off in more than one direction, and if I tried to follow both directions at once I was quickly lost. Divergent thinking does not necessarily facilitate the mechanics of writing. On the other hand, I might have wanted to make the same statement, the same general argument, more than once because it was relevant to more than one topic, although stylistically that was often not desirable. (There is more about the writing of the present book in both editions at the conclusion of Chapter 14.)

Notes to Chapter 10

1. "The problem of serial order in behavior" is the title of a classic article by Karl Lashley (1951), who first pointed out that the brain cannot direct "instructions" to the musculature for the production of spoken or written words in the same order in which the sounds or letters of the words are to be produced. There have since been many other research studies and reviews on the subject; see Kelso (1978) and Stelmach (1978). Kelso's volume contains articles specifically concerned with handwriting and with the complex relationship between speed and accuracy. Lashley recognized that

there is always a question of why one particular pattern of movements is initiated rather than another. Why, if we would like the door closed, does the brain initiate the sounds of "Close the door, please," or even "Isn't it cold in here?" rather than "Would you mind passing the jam?" or any other expression? Neither "habit" nor "stimulus-response mechanisms" can explain the relationship of our behavior to our intentions. Lashley, adopting a concept unused in a behavioristically oriented American psychology for nearly half a century, talked of a determining tendency that both initiated and directed the course that integrated patterns of motor behavior take. The term *determining tendency*, like the word *intention* with which it has much in common, may not in itself explain very much, but at least it acknowledges that important aspects of human behavior are not produced blindly or routinely but are related to overriding purposes.

There are some profound problems concerned with how the brain recognizes and reproduces any sequence of events, such as tunes, poems, and either spoken or written spellings. In some respects memory for sequences functions as if they were tapes; we can recognize tunes and poems almost instantaneously from their middles as well as from their beginnings and can reproduce known tunes and poems from almost any part, performing far more efficiently than computers with random-access magnetic tape memories. On the other hand we cannot play those "recordings" backward; it is almost impossible to spell familiar words or to hum familiar tunes in the opposite direction.

There are, of course, no tapes or disks in the brain, nor in fact are continually "reverberating circuits" necessary for long-term retention of ordered sequences. Indeed, the indications are that whatever the brain retains is represented in chemical arrangements, in "states" rather than sequences or even in spatially ordered patterns. Koestler (1978) also discusses the lack of any satisfactory psychological theory of time that can explain how the brain abstracts and recognizes melodies. Jones (1976) and Dennett (1991) endeavor to provide such a theory.

2. The rate at which nerve impulses travel ranges from 20 to 200 feet per second, depending on the diameter of the nerve fiber (the larger the faster), which in turn depends on length (the longer the larger). Thus it can take the brain less time to exchange neural impulses with the hands or feet than with the eyes or mouth.

3. The occurrence of "plateaux" of improvement as a learner progresses from single letters to letter clusters, words, and even phrases was first noted in telegraphists by Bryan and Harter (1899). Little of what should be basic knowledge in understanding language and its use is new.

4. The term *plans* is used for the hierarchically related determining tendencies that direct complex behavior in Miller, Galanter, and Pribram (1960), an original book that retains its relevance and readability.

5. See Note 2, Chapter 3.

6. The "antiphonics" argument of the next few pages will be familiar to anyone acquainted with my writing on reading (see Smith, 1994), where the evidence is set out in even more detail. In the present context, of course, the aim is to provide a basis for looking at spelling from the point of view of writers.

7. Rozin, Poritsky, and Sotsky (1971).

8. Chomsky and Halle (1968) are frequently quoted for their argument that English spelling is close to an optimal system, and not as wayward and unpredictable as it is often taken to be. They also point out that it is a very economical system, which does

not bother to represent anything that readers might already be expected to know (such as the various pronunciations of the plural -*s*). They propose that spelling is related more to meaning than to sound, a claim explored in more detail in a less technical article by Carol Chomsky (1970), and in a highly technical context by Bever (1992).

9. Hanna, Hodges, and Hanna (1971) report studies showing that a computer programmed with 203 rules could spell correctly only 49 percent of 17,000 common words, with nearly 14 percent of the incorrect words having two or more errors. Whether this result is considered impressive or not is a matter of opinion; it is not as good as the average fifth-grader can do. One problem, of course, is that even if the rules do spell a word correctly they cannot guarantee that it is correct. There is still a 50–50 chance that it is one of the words that does not follow the rules.

10. H. D. Brown (1970). For a detailed discussion of the correspondence rules of English spelling (though the author has more faith than I in the efficacy of phonics in reading instruction), see Venezky (1970).

Upward (1992) reports that English undergraduates learning German made fewer spelling errors in German words than in words of their native English. Most of the problems with English involved the schwa (the neutral vowel sound that can be represented by an a, e, i, o, u, or y) or doubled letters, where attention to sound won't resolve doubt. Upward's article, entitled "Is traditionl english spelng mor dificlt than jermn?", is published in a form of "reduct orthography" called Cut Spelling, which removes "redundant letters." He claims this innovation would simplify spelling, but like all efforts at spelling reform, however, his proposal aims at rationalizing a system regarded as defective, rather than one which is essentially a collection of historical conventions.

Notes to Chapter 11

1. Gould and Boies (1978) found that the efficient dictation of relatively brief texts, like letters, could be learned in a few hours, although their experimental subjects still tended to feel that they could not dictate as well as they could write.

2. Problems and possibilities of introducing computers into writing classrooms are discussed by Monroe (1993), Selfe (1989), and Hawisher and Selfe (1988, 1991). LeBlanc (1993) examines how writing teachers can write computer software.

Notes to Chapter 12

1. There may be objections that learning slows down for adults, that the grown-up brain becomes less creative. I must admit the intellectual audacity of adults rarely seems to match that needed and demonstrated by children. But I am not sure of the necessity of the decline. Adults become dogmatic, reluctant to take the risk of testing new ideas (I tentatively suggest). When we discover "what the world is like," when we get a theory of the world that works for most of the time, we become content to stay with it. Many creative artists and scientists remain childlike in their vision, in their sense of wonder, even in what may often be unconventional behavior. The slowing down of learning cannot be a simple matter of hardening of the cerebral arteries or of sloughing off a few million synaptic connections. Some minds retain childlike enthusiasms even while the body wrinkles like an old apple.

2. Popper (1973) proposes that what any individual (or culture) knows is a record of the problems that individual (or culture) had to solve.

3. In a memorable phrase, Chafe (1992) notes that writing is "hospitable to fiction." The author is free to take on a fictional identity—or to have none. Chafe provides a number of illustrations of authors *doing* this, but he does not analyze *how* it can be done—there are no hints for writers. But "finding a voice" is probably not an aspect of writing that can be taught specifically. To learn to do it successfully (or convincingly) needs demonstrations, collaboration, and reading.

4. Halliday (1973). For other arguments and demonstrations that children learn language by understanding its uses, see Gleason (1989), Greenfield and J. H. Smith (1976), Macnamara (1977), Keith Nelson (1983), Katherine Nelson (1974), and Donaldson (1978).

Dickinson, Wolf, and Stotsky (1989) trace the movement of children into literacy, starting with the deep involvement of early exposure to print, including "emotional attachment" to books as well as to the person reading them. They stress the importance for people who respond to children's stories to have the cultural background to understand them. See also Stotsky (1986), and Kroll and Wells (1993). In a detailed study of six families, Taylor (1983) discusses demonstrations of literacy in the home and their consequences for learning at school.

5. Popper (1973) distinguishes a "third world" of human artifacts in which ideas have an existence independent of any actual individual's brain; see Note 1, Chapter 1.

6. Of course you will probably not be able to recollect much of today's newspaper in a month's time because the relationships of particular news items to that particular newspaper will be overlaid by all the other newspapers you will read. You may lose access to the particular newspaper and to the particular items in your memory, but not to the news itself if it has been related to everything else you know. We probably cannot remember now how we learned that Tokyo is the capital of Japan, that the Titanic sank, or that interest is charged on bank loans, but these are all facts that we once learned and have ever since known. Where there is something significant about how or when the fact was learned, then the occasion of learning may itself be retrievable. You would be more likely to recollect the contents of a particular newspaper a month after reading it if that was the last newspaper you read, or different from the newspapers you usually read. We can recollect what is relevant to us, and what we learn is usually far more relevant than the circumstances in which we learned it.

Reber (1989) documents some of the massive amount of implicit learning that takes place without awareness. Bahrick and Hall (1991) note that the longer the period over which something is studied or experienced, the longer it is remembered. (We remember the names of people we know for a few years longer than the names of those we know for only a few weeks.) People who do mathematics in college can remember for half a century what they would soon forget after high school. Foreign language vocabulary fades within three years after one college semester of study, but over 60 per cent was retained 25 years later among students who studied for five college semesters. I don't think these huge differences can be explained in terms of the actual *amount* of study that was done, or of "reinforcement." Rather, the difference must be attributed to the amount of interest displayed, or something related to interest, either at the time of learning or at the time of remembering (or both). As I discussed in Chapter 7, anything that is interesting is more likely to be learned and to be remembered. Anyone who has studied a subject for several years is likely to be more interested in it than someone who lets it go after a few weeks, not because length of study necessarily produces interest, but because interest is likely to be reflected in length of study.

7. For example, Tulving and Thomson (1973), Tulving and Watkins (1975).

Notes to Chapter 13

1. For more about "reading like a writer," see Smith (1988); and for more about the part the author plays, see Meek (1988). Bruner (1986, p. 37) cites approvingly a comment by Roland Barthes that the *great* writer's gift to a reader is to make the reader into a better writer. In a study of the biographies of geniuses (such as Einstein, Pasteur, and Darwin), Simonton (1988) found that "omnivorous reading in childhood and adolescence correlates positively with ultimate adulthood success" (p. 111). He also noted that the geniuses tended to be prolific writers throughout their lives, allowing imagery and even "play" to dominate creative aspects of their thinking. DeFord (1981) reports that children's writing (including their spelling) reflects the kind of reading they do; the richer the reading, the richer their writing. The relationship between reading and writing is not without its dangers. Eckhoff (1983) observed that some "poor writers" in primary school were writing exactly the way their basal readers were written. Cairney (1992) also provides good examples of the same thing. Jacoby and Hollingshead (1990) demonstrate that "reading student spellings can be hazardous to your spelling." Brown, Collins, and Duguid (1989) describe how writing especially is sensitive to the total activities in which it is supposed to be learned; learners do not simply acquire the particular facts and skills that a lesson is supposed to be about; they learn from everything that is going on at the time. Beal, Garrod, and Bonitatibus (1990) showed that experience in detecting unclarities and ambiguities in specially prepared "short stories" helped elementary children to become more competent in revising other people's writing. Scholes and Willis (1991) found that learning to read promotes learning to talk; they also note that the popular notion that there is a "correct" grammar for speech and writing derives from written language.

2. On children's inventiveness in speech and writing, see an article entitled "Let's brighten it up a bit" by Daiute and Dalton (1988). Barbieri, Colavita, and Scheuer (1990) show that children as young as 3 years want to make explanations (for why things are done by themselves or others, or why they happen)—and know how to do so. The explanations are usually more for the enlistment of help in joint activities or to otherwise control events than for communication. See also Donaldson (1986). On children's play, and especially their playful movement into language, see Garvey (1990), Kirshenblatt-Gimblett (1976), Herron and Sutton-Smith (1982), Bruner, Jolly, and Sylva (1976—a compendious early work), and Nelson (1983).

3. Read (1971, 1973, 1975) is frequently cited for his pioneering work on the inventiveness of children's spelling. His research has led a number of educators to believe that competence in spelling necessarily proceeds in *stages*. For example, Henderson (1985) proposes that spelling is a "developmental process," with the kinds of error learners produce changing over time. He does not clarify whether this is part of the development of *children* (a necessary consequence of their physical growth) or simply a reflection of the nature of spelling (just as children learning to swim often swallow a lot of water, not because this is an innate characteristic of children but because it is a normal consequence of trying to swim). The difference is important, because to suggest that the course of the "development" lies in the nature of children implies that all children should go through these stages, that there is something wrong with any child who doesn't, and that "instruction" should follow the same predestined

route—all propositions which I think sense and the evidence fail to justify. Henderson traces the course of "developmental spelling" as follows: pretend spellings, semi-phonetic stage (mainly consonants), phonetic stage (including vowels), spelling patterns (including attempts to represent meaning through spelling), and conventional spelling. It is difficult to imagine that a growing understanding and experience of written language, combined with the pervasive influence of instructional practices, could produce any other result. Nevertheless, Henderson develops his analysis to promote a theory of teaching, starting with most frequent words first, grouped by spelling patterns. The inevitable problem of what should be done with children who fail to learn to spell by such instruction is not addressed.

Hughes and Searle (1991) report on a longitudinal study of two diverse groups of children as they progressed from kindergarten to Grade 5, looking at what they knew about spelling from their correct spellings *and* from their misspellings, and discussing both with children soon after they wrote. They confirmed that there is a progression through what they term a "prephonemic" stage (when children write but ignore or have no knowledge of spelling-sound correspondences), a succession of "phonemic/letter-name" strategies, beginning with how the names of letters are pronounced, a "transitional" stage when the known spellings of words are used as analogies for unknown spellings, and finally "correct spelling." This again suggests that children make maximum use of what they happen to know about written language at any particular time, and the authors confirm that children's reading and writing influenced their spelling strategies.

Like many contemporary researchers, Hughes and Searle stress the importance of "phonemic awareness" (basically—understanding of the way spoken words can be broken down into units of sound corresponding to spelling patterns), but since attempts to spell words phonetically will lead writers of any age and experience to spelling errors more often than not, phonemic awareness is not, by itself, an unalloyed benefit. It may help writers to produce something *closer* to a correct spelling; but whether this will be useful to them depends in part on the tolerance and understanding of whoever reads the approximate spelling. Some new or unfamiliar words will defeat even experienced spellers, and other words are usually quickly learned and spelled correctly even by learners (their names, for example). Hughes and Searle note the importance of children being willing and able to "risk" using their knowledge in actual writing.

A popular exercise in phonemic awareness is technically called "phoneme deletion"—which means answering questions like "What is left if you remove the /k/ sound from cat?" Scholes and Willis (1991) show that this task requires literate knowledge of alphabetical writing and cannot be done by nonreaders. Two cases have been reported from Italy of literate adult victims of strokes that impaired the ability to use vowels in spelling, but not consonants (Cubelli, 1991). One patient left spaces where vowels should be; the other wrote complete words but with a disproportionate number of vowel errors. Neither had any problem if spellings were dictated to them, or with speech comprehension. I mention this as a curiosity only—it is a puzzling condition not easy to explain. The author tentatively proposes that vowels and consonants are stored separately in the brain, or called upon independently, in spelling. But if either were the case, why should consonants be favored over vowels (and fortuitously too, since text without vowels is fairly readable, but text without consonants is not)? An alternative possibility might be that correct spellings are used if they are known, but if they are not, or if they are forgotten, individuals do the best they can, inventing spellings where necessary, and giving priority to consonants that are both easier to learn and less likely to be wrong. This is a strategy children frequently adopt when they begin to write.

Carol Chomsky (1971, 1975) argues that an understanding of spelling helps students make sense of phonics instruction, and that learning to write generally helps them learn to read. Tierney and Shanahan (1991) showed that children who write more are likely to be more enthusiastic and competent readers—and the view is part of Paulo Freire's (1972) "liberation pedagogy" for adults. Bradley and King (1992) found that proofreading correct and incorrect spellings improved the spelling accuracy of both good and poor spellers. However, a few poor spellers were dramatically affected by exposure to incorrect spellings, showing perhaps that if you don't know that a word is wrong, you can learn incorrect spellings as easily as correct ones.

Anxious teachers and even more anxious principals and parents persistently believe there must or ought to be some "systematic" method of teaching spelling that will guarantee success. The usual consequence is an emphasis on words in lists or in artificial contexts, focusing on frequent words, frequent spelling patterns, and words that are frequently misspelled. None of these methods can guarantee that more than a few words will be learned, and then not by all students, despite the pressure of testing that usually accompanies such approaches. They can always claim limited success, and promise substantially more, particularly for students with spelling difficulties. Nevertheless there is no evidence that such treatments ever made anyone a *speller*. They frequently emphasize *pronunciation* (in the name of phonemic awareness), often in conflict with the learner's normal way of pronouncing words, which does not help anyone to spell and frequently causes confusion. See Wilde (1990) and Allred (1993) on all these points.

There is also a prevalent concern that spelling will be overlooked with "whole language" and "process writing" approaches to literacy (see Chapter 14). For many teachers this concern translates into spelling *activities* (Bartch, 1992); see also Wilde (1990). Barone (1992) offers a brief summary of theories of spelling instruction and a review of the role of spelling in "process-centered classrooms," stressing the importance of reading. For other readable review articles on spelling, see Schlagal and Schlagal (1992) and Gill (1992).

4. Calkins (1980) compared a group of third-grade students who received conventional punctuation instruction for a year with third-graders in an adjacent classroom who received no instruction on punctuation at all, but were permitted to write and read freely instead. At the end of the school year the group who received no instruction used twice as much punctuation in their writing and were twice as likely to understand how punctuation was used than the other group, which obviously learned that punctuation was confusing and best avoided. For children's attitudes toward punctuation and editing generally, see Graves (1979).

5. Graves (1979) is a key source on the topic of children and revision in writing. On "disposable writing" see Calkins (1979) in an article entitled "Learning to throw away."

6. Doman (1975).

7. See Clay (1975), an excellent and beautifully illustrated short volume on the progression of young children's writing generally. On handwriting specifically see also Ajuriaguerra and Auzias (1975). Graves (1978b) objects to handwriting being treated in school as an end in itself rather than as a tool, and Markham (1976) demonstrates how handwriting sways teacher evaluation of writing content.

8. It is sometimes suggested that the flood of electronic writing and printing devices is making handwriting lose its importance. It may be a mistake to focus *critical* attention on handwriting, especially at the beginning of learning to write, when so

much is unfamiliar and difficult, but ability to write "by hand" is important to most writers, certainly young ones. Computers or typewriters may take care of legibility problems for readers, but writers must also be taken into account. Beginners especially must be able to make notes, if not finished documents, by hand, and there is nothing more annoying—and I suspect it is not uncommon—than being unable to read one's own writing. The value of *useful* handwriting must be both *speed* and *legibility*, and it can be disastrous for a writer, or a learner (or a teacher) to concentrate on one at the expense of the other. To learn to write unnecessarily slowly is a grievous handicap. And calligraphy should be a separate subject altogether.

Notes to Chapter 14

1. Skemp (1972) distinguishes two forms of mathematics instruction—*instrumental* (teaching the "facts" about how something is done, for example the division of fractions by cross multiplication of numerators and denominators), and *relational* (developing an understanding of why cross multiplication results in division). He argues that instrumental learning has limited applicability but is easier to teach and to drill.

Contentious debate over whether aspects of writing should be taught specifically (as "facts"), rather than engaged in implicitly, is not infrequent. In Chapter 5 and its Notes I briefly outlined the nature of *genre*, referring to the obvious differences between various kinds of text. There has been a considerable controversy, particularly in Australia (Richardson, 1991; Cairney, 1992), over whether genre should be taught as a separate subject. Critics influenced by the work of the linguist Halliday (see Martin, 1985; Kamler, 1993) claimed that as a result of the popularity of whole language and process-writing movements in Australia (e.g., Cambourne, 1988), children were failing to learn genre schemes that they needed to communicate effectively, and were therefore "disempowered." Their solution, which carried considerable political as well as educational overtones, was that both students and teachers should be given direct instruction in the structures and conventions of various genres. Opposition to their point of view was based primarily on the consideration that students (and teachers) do not learn mastery of genre schemes from lectures in linguistics, but by becoming acquainted with them in meaningful contexts, the way they learn other aspects of language. Littlefair (1991), for example, found that British students' knowledge of genre after three or four years of study was directly related to the amount and breadth of their reading.

2. The general argument that children learn from demonstrations, and especially from *models* provided by people around them, is part of everyday wisdom; you learn from the company you keep. Children learn and adopt the language and other behaviors of people they want to be like—first family, then friends, then more distant models. But the general argument has always met with objections. Parents in particular have been quick to point out that every morning they clean their teeth, tidy their rooms, and close the door as they leave. Despite all these demonstrations, the purposes of which are repeatedly stressed, their children seldom seem to learn the same things themselves. The detached objectivity of an anthropologist was required to produce the simple explanation (Mead, 1976). When parents *enjoy* what they regularly do, children quickly learn to do the same things themselves, which is why no doubt they so rapidly learn to do things we would just as soon they would not learn. But when children see parents regularly doing things they do not enjoy doing, children learn what is demonstrated—that doing those particular things is not very enjoyable, and that

parents can be very peculiar people indeed. (How many children see their parents, or even their teachers, writing and enjoying writing?)

3. There is also a pervasive emphasis on *facts*, which it is assumed can be taught, learned, and tested one at a time. I was given two explanations why 7-year-old children in one school were not encouraged or expected to write fantasy. One teacher believed that writing what you know about was surely easier than having to make something up, and another asked how writing could be marked if it did not contain facts that might be right or wrong.

4. Britton (1975, 1992) and Vygotsky (1978) early stressed the social nature of language learning, and a good deal of research has since been done on group structures in writing classrooms. For a summary, see Gere (1987). Graves (Graves and Stuart, 1985; Hansen, Newkirk, and Graves, 1985) claims that beginners learn faster by writing and sharing with their peers than from instruction by teachers; see also Calkins (1986), and Patterson, Santa, Short, and Smith (1993). Dyson (1988, 1989) describes rich spontaneous mutual assistance among learners as collaboration is introduced into writing in an elementary school classroom, changing the thought and attitudes of students and their teacher. Atwell's (1987) influential book *In the Middle* shows how teachers can learn from adolescent students—often regarded as the most difficult age—by engaging them collaboratively in purposeful and satisfying reading and writing. Among many other useful discussions of collaborative classrooms are Bayer (1990), Hudelson and Lindfors (1993), and—in Britain—Styles (1989). Blake (1992) reviews research related to the role of talk in writing classrooms, with particular reference to non-native English speakers. Newman (1991) recounts the experiences of a group of teachers sharing their writing, and in a book entitled *Teacher as Writer*, Dahl (1992) presents reports on the writing experiences of more than 30 teachers and several journal editors, adding advice on how and where teachers can publish.

A journalist, Roy Peter Clark (1987), describes how beginners may be helped to become writers by encouraging them to adopt a "reporter's" role. An actor might encourage children to write and perform plays, or film scripts. The important factor is not the particular content but the *engagement*, by the "teacher" and the learner. Clark has also collaborated on a more specialized book on "coaching writers" (Clark and Fry, 1992) intended for professional editors and reporters but written in a clear and conversational manner that might help many teachers and students.

Torbe (1988) writes of the intimate relationship between language and identity, and of the danger inherent in treating writing in school as a "product." He argues that to call language a "tool" is very imprecise. What kind of tool? And what else is it? Torbe also criticizes exaggerated claims for literacy: Literacy does not necessarily bring social or economic advantage, and such claims do not facilitate learning to read and write—see also Smith (1989). Daiute (1993) attempts to link sociocultural theory, relating learning to social interaction, and development theory, relating learning to personal growth. In a useful review article, she discusses how student writing reflects the student's reading, spoken language, and culture, as well as the kind of help that is available, the specific constraints of a particular task (such as trying to squeeze all the words of a title into one line), and a lively sense of play. Daiute proposes a concept of *youth genres* to underline the distinctiveness of young people's speech and writing, and argues that teachers should have a better understanding of the language of their students (which should not be regarded as an incorrect form of adult language), and be more responsive to it. Adaptation to academic forms of discourse can take many years.

5. Bereiter and Scardamalia (1982) discuss a number of ways in which students fail to

come to grips with rhetorical problems, including "a take-it-or-leave-it attitude," "willingness to put up with recognized weaknesses," and "satisfaction with superficial connections." The authors doubt whether discussions and other school activities have direct effects on such thinking. Instead they prefer external aids that they term "procedural facilitation" which can become part of the "executive procedures" of writers, for example through "problem recognition," the comparison of "mental representations" of an intended text and the actual text, a "diagnostic" phase, and a "monitoring" operator. Behind all the technological jargon seems to be the time-honored assertion that students should be more reflective—and tough—about their own writing. The authors disarmingly conclude that reflection is natural, but nature needs some assistance. One form of assistance they strongly recommend is that writers should talk aloud while they plan and compose; they refer to this as "thinking aloud." "Think aloud protocols" have become an important part of experimental research into writing (see also Flower and Hayes, 1980; Hayes and Flower, 1980). What students and others say while they write or think about writing is supposed to enable them to "monitor their own thoughts" in a productive as well as revealing way; Bereiter and Scardamalia claim it improves student writing. For a later summary of their extensive experimental work into the "control processes" of writing, and its relevance to instruction, see Bereiter and Scardamalia (1987). "Monitoring one's own thought" is also referred to as *metacognition*. In a critical article, Swanson (1990) notes that metacognitive ability is not related to aptitude or the ability to solve problems.

Bereiter and Scardamalia (in Canada) and Hayes and Flower (in the United States) are prominent exponents of the "cognitive science" approach to writing and thinking, remarkable for the variety of ways in which traditional commonplaces of writing instruction are put into the "information processing" language of computer systems. In addition to the examples given in the previous paragraph, cognitive scientists are apt to refer to pieces of writing as "text structures," and to things writers do as "operators" (as in "applying a deletion operator" for "deleting"). Many examples of this arcane way of talking (which is permeating some classrooms) can be found in an edited volume entitled *Cognitive Processes in Writing* (Gregg and Steinberg, 1980). For discussions of the approach from classroom perspectives, with the characteristic titles of "Making thinking visible" and "Writing in real time," respectively, see Flower, Wallace, Norris, and Burnett (1993/1994), and Matsuhashi (1987). Sticht, Chang, and Wood (1986) provide a collection of reports on cognitive science research into writing; the book has a heavy emphasis on military implications, because a substantial amount of the funding for cognitive science research comes from defense sources.

6. A distinction must be made between noise that is relevant and can be ignored, a sign that everything is going well, and noise that is intrusive. The classroom chatter of students absorbed in (and occasionally excited or frustrated by) writing falls into the former category; indiscriminate use of the public address system falls into the latter.

7. Lunzer and Gardner (1979).

8. Fillion (1979).

9. Fillion (1979); Lunzer and Gardner (1979).

10. Detailed analyses of student writing have been made on behalf of the United Kingdom Schools Council by a number of researchers at the Institute of Education at London University. Their publications include Britton, Burgess, Martin, McLeod, and Rosen (1975); Martin, D'Arcy, Newton, and Parker (1976), and Lightfoot and Martin (1988), all emphasizing the ceaseless demand for *transactional* (informational) writing at school. Emig (1971) reports a classic study of writing and teaching in United

States high schools, one of her conclusions being that English teachers who do not themselves write "underconceptualize and oversimplify" writing. Pianko (1979) is similarly critical of college freshmen's writing opportunities. Graves (1978a) offers a detailed and constructive critical report of writing instruction in United States classrooms.

As noted in the Preface, Farnan, Lapp, and Flood (1992) examined over 18,000 articles on writing in the ERIC registry between 1980 and 1989, including reports on over 160 writing projects established in the United States in the decade, but found no documented progress in the amount of writing done in schools or in writing ability. An earlier comprehensive review of over 6,000 research studies on composition, teaching and learning, with 2,000 of them summarized, is available in Hillocks (1986). Among the many findings: The teaching of formal grammar did nothing to improve written composition. "Teacher research" has become a significant movement in writing education; for discussions and examples see Calkins (1985) and Kutz (1992).

In a report entitled *Schools Can Make a Difference*, Brookover, Beady, Flood, Schweitzer, and Wisenbaker (1977) argue that most of the success of schools must be attributed to the "climate" of particular classrooms and most of the failure to a "student sense of academic futility." Bleich (1993) is a more polemical survey of adverse and discriminatory consequence of literacy instruction. The critical risk was perhaps most succinctly expressed more than a century ago: "Of devices for teaching writing, there is no end; and most if not all of them cripple the mind and deform the body. Thank God, the method of teaching children to speak was invented before the schoolmaster appeared!" (Parker, 1890, p. 249).

References

Aitchison, Jean (1989). *The Articulate Mammal: An Introduction to Psycholinguistics* (3rd Ed.). London: Unwin Hyman.

Ajuriaguerra, J. de, and M. Auzias (1975). Preconditions for the development of writing in the child. In Lenneberg, Eric and Elizabeth Lenneberg (Eds.), *Foundations of Language Development* (Vol. 2). New York: Academic Press.

Allred, Ruel A. (1993). Integrating proven spelling content and methods with emerging literacy programs. *Reading Psychology*, 14, 15–31.

Anderson, John R. (1976). *Language, Memory, and Thought*. Hillsdale, NJ: Lawrence Erlbaum Associates.

Anderson, Richard C., Rand C. Spiro, and Mark C. Anderson (1978). Schemata as scaffolding for the representation of information in connected discourse. *American Educational Research Journal*, *15*(3), 433–440.

Ashcraft, Mark H. (1989). *Human Memory and Cognition*. Glenview, IL: Scott Foresman.

Atwell, Nancie (1987). *In the Middle: Writing, Reading and Learning With Adolescents*. Portsmouth, NH: Heinemann Educational Books.

Augst, Gerhard (1992). Aspects of writing development in argumentative texts. In Stein, Dieter (Ed.), *Cooperating with Written Texts: The Pragmatics and Comprehension of Written Texts*. Berlin: Mouton de Gruyter, pp. 67–82.

Austin, J.P. (1962). *How to Do Things with Words*. London: Oxford University Press.

Bahrick, Harry P. and Lynda K. Hall (1991). Lifetime maintenance of high school mathematics content. *Journal of Experimental Psychology*: General, *120*(1), 20–33.

Bakhtin, M.M. (1981). *The Dialogic Imagination*. Austin, TX: University of Texas Press.

Bakhtin, M.M. (1986). *Speech Genres and Other Late Essays*. Austin, TX: University of Texas Press.

Barbieri, Maria Silvia, Federica Colavita, and Nora Scheuer (1990). The beginning of the explaining capacity. In Conti-Ramsden, Gina and Catherine E. Snow (Eds.), *Children's Language, Volume 7*. Hillsdale, NJ: Lawrence Erlbaum Associates.

Barone, Diane (1992). Whatever happened to spelling? The role of spelling instruction in process-centered classrooms. *Reading Psychology, 13*, 117.

Bartch, Judie (1992). An alternative to spelling: An integrated approach. *Language Arts, 69*, 404–408.

Barthes, Roland (1968). *Writing Degree Zero*. New York: Hill and Wang.

Bartlett, Frederick C. (1932). *Remembering*. Cambridge, UK: Cambridge University Press.

Bayer, Ann Shea (1990). *Collaborative Apprenticeship Learning: Language and Thinking Across the Curriculum, K–12*. Mountain View, CA: Mayfield.

Beal, Carole R., Andrew C. Garrod, and Gary J. Bonitatibus (1990). Fostering Children's revision skills through training in comprehension monitoring. *Journal of Educational Research, 82*, 275–280.

Bereiter, Carl (1980). Development in writing. In Gregg, Lee W. and Erwin R. Steinberg (Eds.), *Cognitive Processes in Writing*. Hillsdale, NJ: Lawrence Erlbaum Associates.

Bereiter, Carl and Marlene Scardamalia (1982). From conversation to composition: The role of instruction in a developmental process. In Glaser, Robert (Ed.), *Advances in Instructional Psychology*, (Vol. 2). Hillsdale, NJ: Lawrence Erlbaum Associates.

Bereiter, Carl and Marlene Scardamalia (1987). *The Psychology of Written Composition*. Hillsdale, NJ: Lawrence Erlbaum Associates.

Bever, Thomas G. (1992). The demons and the beast, modular and nodular kinds of knowledge. In Reilly, Ronan G. and Noel E. Sharkey (Eds.), *Connectionist Approaches to Natural Language Processing*. Hove, UK: Lawrence Erlbaum Associates.

Blake, Brett Elizabeth (1992). Talk in non-native and native English speakers' peer writing conferences: What's the difference? *Language Arts, 69*, 604–610.

Bleich, David (1993). *The Double Perspective: Language, Literacy and Social Relations*. Urbana, IL: National Council of Teachers of English.

Bolter, Jay David (1991). *Writing Space: The Computer, Hypertext, and the History of Writing*. Hillsdale, NJ: Lawrence Erlbaum Associates.

Bower, Gordon H. (1976). Experiments on story understanding and recall. *Quarterly Journal of Experimental Psychology, 28*, 511–534.

Bradley, John M. and Priscilla Vacca King (1992). Effects of proofreading on spelling: How reading misspelled and correctly spelled words affects spelling accuracy. *Journal of Reading Behavior, 24*(4), 403–411.

Britton, James N. (1970a). *Language and Learning*. Baltimore: Penguin.

Britton, James N. (1970b). Progress in writing. In Evertts, Eldonna (Ed.), *Explorations in Children's Writing*. Champaign, IL: National Council of Teachers of English.

Britton, James N. (1971). What's the use? A schematic account of language functions. In Wilkinson, Andrew (Ed.), *The Context of Language* (*Educational Review, 23*(3), 205–219).

Britton, James N. (1975). Teaching writing. In Davies, Alan, (Ed.), *Problems of Language and Learning*. London: Heinemann Educational Books.

Britton, James (1992). *Language and Learning* (2d Ed.). London, Penguin.

Britton, James N., Anthony Burgess, Nancy Martin, Alex McLeod, and Harold Rosen (1975). *The Development of Writing Abilities, 11–18*. London: Macmillan.

Brookover, Wilbur B., Charles H. Beady, Patricia K. Flood, John H. Schweitzer, and Joseph M. Wisenbaker (1977). *Schools Can Make a Difference*. East Lansing: College of Urban Development, Michigan State University.

Brown, H.D. (1970). Categories of spelling difficulty in speakers of English as a first and second language. *Journal of Verbal Learning and Verbal Behavior, 9*, 232–236.

Brown, J.S., A. Collins, and P. Duguid (1989). Situated cognition and the culture of learning. *Educational Researcher, 18*(1), 32–42.

Brown, Roger (1973). *A First Language: The Early Stages*. Cambridge, MA: Harvard University Press.

Bruner, Jerome S. (1983). *Child's Talk: Learning to Use Language*. Cambridge, MA: Harvard University Press.

Bruner, Jerome S. (1986). *Actual Minds, Possible Worlds*. Cambridge, MA: Harvard University Press.

Bruner, Jerome S., Alison Jolly, and Kathy Sylva (1976). *Play—Its Role in Development and Evolution*. Harmondsworth: Penguin.

Bruner, Jerome S. and Susan Weisser (1991). The invention of self: Autobiography and its forms. In Olson, David R. and Nancy Torrance (Eds.), *Literacy and Orality*. Cambridge, UK: Cambridge University Press.

Bryan, W.L., and N. Harter (1899). Studies in telegraphic language: Acquisition of a hierarchy of habits. *Psychological Review*, 6(4), 346-376.

Butler, John F. (1972). On teaching composition. *Kansas English, 58*.

Cairney, Trevor (1992). Mountain or mole hill: The genre debate viewed from "down under." *Reading, 36*, 23–29.

Calkins, Lucy McCormick (1979). Learning to throw away. *Language Arts, 56*(7), 747–752.

Calkins, Lucy McCormick (1980). When children want to punctuate: Basic skills belong in context. *Language Arts, 57*(5), 567–577.

Calkins, Lucy McCormick (1983). *Lessons from a Child*. Portsmouth, NH: Heinemann Educational Books.

Calkins, Lucy McCormick (1985). Forming research communities among naturalistic researchers. In McClelland, Ben W. and Timothy R. Donovan (Eds), *Perspectives on Research and Scholarship in Composition*. New York: Modern Language Association of America.

Calkins, Lucy McCormick (1986). *The Art of Teaching Writing*. Portsmouth, NH: Heinemann Educational Books.

Cambourne, Brian (1988). *The Whole Story: Natural Learning and the Acquisition of Literacy in the Classroom*. Sydney: Ashton Scholastic.

Cazden, Courtney B. (1992). *Whole Language Plus: Essays on Literacy in the United States and New Zealand*. New York: Teachers College Press.

Chafe, Wallace L. (1977). Creativity in verbalization and its implications for the nature of stored knowledge. In Freedle, Roy O.(Ed.), *Discourse Processes: Advances in Research and Theory*, Vol. 1. Norwood, NJ: Ablex.

Chafe, Wallace (1992). Immediacy and displacement in consciousness and language. In Stein, Dieter (Ed.), *Cooperating with Written Texts: The Pragmatics and Comprehension of Written Texts*. Berlin: Mouton de Gruyter.

Chafe, Wallace and Jane Danielwicz (1987). Properties of spoken and written language. In Horowitz, Rosalind and S. Jay Samuels (Eds.), *Comprehending Oral and Written Language*. New York: Academic Press.

Chandler, Daniel (1992). The phenomenology of writing by hand. *Intelligent Tutoring Media*, May/August 3(2/3), 65–74.

Chandler, Daniel (1993). Writing strategies and the use of tools. *English Today* 9(2), 32–38.

Chomsky, Carol (1970). Reading, writing and phonology. *Harvard Educational Review*, 40(2), 287–309.

Chomsky, Carol (1971). Write first, read later. *Childhood Education*, 47(6), 296–299.

Chomsky, Carol (1975). After decoding, what? *Elementary English*, 52, 288–296.

Chomsky, Noam (1957). *Syntactic Structures*. The Hague: Mouton.

Chomsky, Noam (1965). *Aspects of the Theory of Syntax*. Cambridge, MA: MIT Press.

Chomsky, Noam (1980). *Rules and Representations*. Oxford: Blackwell.

Chomsky, Noam (1986). *Knowledge of Language: Its Nature, Origin and Use*. New York: Praeger.

Chomsky, Noam (1988). *Language and Problems of Knowledge*. Cambridge, MA: MIT Press.

Chomsky, Noam, and Morris Halle (1968). *Sound Pattern of English*. New York: Harper & Row.

Clark, Herbert H. (1973). Space, time, semantics and the child. In Moore, Timothy E. (Ed.), *Cognitive Development and the Acquisition of Language*. New York: Academic Press.

Clark, Herbert H., and Eve V. Clark (1977). *Psychology and Language*. New York: Harcourt Brace Jovanovich.

Clark, Herbert H., and Susan E. Haviland (1977). Comprehension and the given-new contract. In Freedle, Roy O., (Ed.), *Discourse Processes: Advances in Research and Theory*, Vol. 1. Norwood, NJ: Ablex.

Clark, Roy Peter (1987). *Free to Write: A Journalist Teaches Young Writers*. Portsmouth, NH: Heinemann Educational Books.

Clark, Roy Peter and Don Fry (1992). *Coaching Writers: The Essential Guide for Editors and Reporters*. New York: St. Martin's.

Clay, Marie M. (1975). *What Did I Write?* Auckland, New Zealand: Heinemann Educational Books.

Clements, Paul (1977). The effects of staging on recall from prose. In Freedle, Roy O. (Ed.), *Discourse Processes: Advances in Research and Theory*, Vol. 1. Norwood, NJ: Ablex.

Cohen, Gillian, Michael W. Eysenck, and Martin E. Le Voi (1986). *Memory: A Cognitive Approach*. Milton Keynes: Open University Press.

Cole, Michael and Helen Keyssar (1985). The concept of literacy in print and film. In Olson, David R., Nancy Torrance, and Angela Hildyard (Eds.), *Literacy, Language, and Learning: The Nature and Consequences of Reading and Writing*. Cambridge, UK: Cambridge University Press.

Cook, Walter A. (1983). *Case Grammar Theory*. Washington, DC: Georgetown University Press.

Coulmas, Florian (1992). On the relationship between writing system, written language, and text processing. In Stein, Dieter (Ed.), *Cooperating with Written Texts: The Pragmatics and Comprehension of Written Texts*. Berlin: Mouton de Gruyter.

Coulthard, Malcolm and Martin Montgomery (Eds.) (1981). *Studies in Discourse Analysis*. London: Routledge and Kegan Paul.

Cromer, Richard F. (1974). The development of language and cognition: The cognition hypothesis. In Foss, Brian (Ed.), *New Perspectives in Language Development*. Baltimore: Penguin.

Cross, Toni G. (1977). Mothers' speech adjustments: The contribution of selected child listener variables. In Snow, Catherine E. and Charles A. Ferguson (Eds.), *Talking to Children: Language Input and Acquisition*. Cambridge, UK: Cambridge University Press.

Csikszentmihalyi, Mihalyi (1990). *Flow: The Psychology of Optimal Experience*. New York: Harper & Row.

Cubelli, Roberto (1991). A selective deficity for writing vowels in acquired dysgraphia. *Nature, 353*, 258–260.

Culler, Jonathan (1982). *On Deconstruction: Theory and Criticism After Structuralism*. Ithaca, NY: Cornell University Press.

Dahl, Karin L. (Ed.) (1992). *Teacher as Writer: Entering the Professional Conversation*. Urbana, IL: National Council of Teachers of English.

Daiute, Colette (1993). Youth genres and literacy: Links between sociocultural and developmental theories. *Language Arts, 70*, 402–416.

Daiute, Colette and B. Dalton (1988). "Let's brighten it up a bit"; Collaboration and cognition in writing. In Rafoth, B.A. and D. L. Rubin (Eds.), *The Social Construction of Written Communication*. Norwood, NJ: Ablex.

DeFord, Diane E. (1981). Literacy: Reading, writing and other essentials. *Language Arts, 58*(6) 652–658.

Dennett, Daniel C. (1991). *Consciousness Explained*. Boston: Little, Brown.

Derrida, Jacques (1978). *Writing and Difference*. Chicago: University of Chicago Press.

Derrida, Jacques (1992). *Acts of Literature*. New York: Routledge.

Dickinson, David, Maryanne Wolf, and Sandra Stotsky (1989). Words move: The interwoven development of oral and written language. In Gleason, Jean Berko (Ed.), *The Development of Language* (2d Ed.). Columbus, OH: Merrill.

Doman, Glenn (1975). *How to Teach Your Baby How to Read.* New York: Doubleday.

Donaldson, Margaret (1978). *Children's Minds.* Glasgow: Fontana/Collins.

Donaldson, Margaret (1986). *Children's Explanations.* Cambridge: Cambridge University Press.

Douglas, Mary (Ed.) (1968). *Rules and Meanings: The Anthropology of Everyday Knowledge.* Baltimore: Penguin.

Dowley, Gillian, and Elizabeth Sulzby (undated). *The Social Origin of Narrative Skills.* Unpublished paper, Reading and Language Program, School of Education, Northwestern University.

Dyson, Anne Haas (1988). Unintentional helping in the primary grades: Writing in the children's world. In Rafoth, B.A. and D.L. Rubin (Eds.), *The Social Construction of Written Communication.* Norwood, NJ: Ablex.

Dyson, Anne Haas (1989). *Multiple Worlds of Child Writers: Friends Learning to Write.* New York: Teachers College Press.

Eagleton, Terry (1983). *Literacy Theory: An Introduction.* Minneapolis, University of Minnesota Press.

Eckhoff, Barbara (1983). How reading affects children's writing. *Language Arts, 60*(5), 607–616.

Elbow, Peter (1973). *Writing Without Teachers.* New York: Oxford University Press.

Elbow, Peter (1987). Closing my eyes as I speak: An argument for ignoring audience. *College English,* 1987, *49,* 50–69. Reprinted in Graves, Richard L. (Ed.) Rhetoric and Composition: *A Sourcebook for Teachers and Writers* (3rd Ed.) Portsmouth, NH: Heinemann Educational Books.

Emig, Janet (1971). *The Composing Processes of Twelfth Graders.* Urbana, IL: National Council of Teachers of English.

Emig, Janet (1978). Hand, eye, brain: Some "basics" in the writing process. In Cooper, Charles R., and Lee Odell (Eds.), *Research on Composing: Points of Departure.* Urbana, IL: National Council of Teachers of English.

Emig, Janet A. (1983). *The Web of Meaning: Essays on Writing, Teaching, Learning and Thinking.* (Edited by Dixie Goswami and Maureen Butler.) Montclair, NJ: Boynton/Cook.

Escholz, Paul A., Alfred F. Rosa, and Virginia P. Clark (Eds.) (1974). *Language Awareness.* New York: St. Martin's.

Farnan, Nancy, Diane Lapp, and James Flood (1992). Changing perspectives in writing instruction. *Journal of Reading, 35*(7), 550–556.

Farrell, Thomas J. (1977). Literacy, the basics and all that jazz. *College English, 38*(5), 443–459.

Feldman, Carol Fleischer (1991). Oral metalanguage. In Olson, David R. and Nancy Torrance (Eds.), *Literacy and Orality.* Cambridge, UK: Cambridge University Press.

Ferguson, Eugene S. (1977) The mind's eye: Nonverbal thought in technology. *Science, 197*(4306), 827–836.

Fillion, Bryant (1979). Language across the curriculum: Examining the place of language in our schools. *McGill Journal of Education, 14,* 47–60.

Fillmore, Charles J. (1968). The case for case. In Bach, Emmon and R. T. Harms (Eds.), *Universals of Linguistic Theory.* New York: Holt, Rinehart and Winston.

Fine, Jonathan and Roy O. Freedle (Eds.) (1983). *Developmental Issues in Discourse.* Norwood, NJ: Ablex.

Flammer, August and Walter Kintsch (1982). *Discourse Processing.* Amsterdam: North Holland.

Fletcher, Paul and Michael Garman (Eds.) (1979, 1986). *Language Acquisition: Studies in First Language Development* (1st and 2d Eds.). Cambridge, UK: Cambridge University Press.

Flower, Linda S. (1979). Writer-based prose: A cognitive basis for problems in writing. *College English, 41,* 19–37.

Flower, Linda S. and John R. Hayes (1980). The dynamics of composing: Making plans and juggling constraints. In Gregg, Lee W. and Erwin R. Steinberg (Eds.), *Cognitive Processes in Writing.* Hillsdale, NJ: Lawrence Erlbaum Associates.

Flower, Linda S. and John R. Hayes (1981). A cognitive process theory of writing. *College Composition and Communication, 32,* 365–387.

Flower, Linda S., David L. Wallace, Linda Norris, and Rebecca E. Burnett (Eds.) (1993/1994). *Making Thinking Visible.* Urbana, IL: National Council of Teachers of English.

Fodor, Jerry A. (1983). *The Modularity of Mind.* Cambridge, MA: MIT Press.

Fodor, Jerry A., Thomas G. Bever, and Merrill F. Garrett (1974). *The Psychology of Language.* New York: McGraw-Hill.

Frederiksen, Carl H. (1975a). Effects of context-induced process operations of semantic information acquired from discourse. *Cognitive Psychology, 7,* 139–166.

Frederiksen, Carl H. (1975b). Representing logical and semantic structure of knowledge acquired from discourse. *Cognitive Psychology, 7,* 317–458.

Freire, Paulo (1972). *Pedagogy of the Oppressed.* New York: Herder and Herder.

Frye, Northrop (1963). *The Well-Tempered Critic.* Bloomington: Indiana University Press.

Gardner, Howard (1983). *Art, Mind and Brain.* New York: Basic Books.

Garvey, Catherine (1990). *Play* (2d Ed.). Cambridge, MA: Harvard University Press.

Gelman, Rochel (1979). Preschool thought. *American Psychologist, 34*(10), 900–905.

Gere, A.R. (1987). *Writing Groups: History, Theory and Implications.* Carbondale, IL: Southern Illinois University Press.

Getzels, Jacob W., and Mihaly Csikszentmihalyi (1972). The creative artist as an explorer. In Hunt, Joseph McV. (Ed.), *Human Intelligence.* New Brunswick, NJ: Transaction, Inc.

Gill, J. Thomas (1992). Development of word knowledge as it relates to reading, spelling and instruction. *Language Arts, 69,* 444–453.

Gleason, Jean Berko (Ed.) (1989). *The Development of Language* (2d Ed.). Columbus, OH: Merrill.

Glynn, Shawn M., and Francis J. DiVesta (1979). Control of prose processing via instructional and typographical cues. *Journal of Educational Psychology, 71*(5), 595–603.

Golinkoff, Roberta M. (1976). A comparison of reading comprehension processes in good and poor comprehenders. *Reading Research Quarterly, 11,* 623–659.

Goody, Jack (1977). *The Domestication of the Savage Mind.* Cambridge, UK: Cambridge University Press.

Gould, John D., and Stephen J. Boies (1978). Writing, dictating and speaking letters. *Science, 201,* 1145–1147.

Gould, John D. and Nancy Grischkowsky (1984). Doing the same work with hard copy and with cathode-ray tube (CRT) computer terminals. *Human Factors, 26*(3), 323–337.

Graves, Donald H. (1978a). *Balance the Basics: Let Them Write.* New York: Ford Foundation.

Graves, Donald H. (1978b). Handwriting is for writing. *Language Arts, 55.*

Graves, Donald H. (1979). What children show us about revision. *Language Arts, 56,* 3.

Graves, Donald H. and Virginia Stuart (1985). *Write from the Start: Tapping Your Child's Natural Writing Ability.* New York: Dutton.

Greenberg, Joseph H. (Ed.) (1963). *Universals of Language.* Cambridge, MA: MIT Press.

Greenfield, Patricia M., and J. H. Smith (1976). *The Structure of Communication in Early Language Development.* New York: Academic Press.

Gregg, Lee W. and Erwin R. Steinberg (Eds.) (1980). *Cognitive Processes in Writing.* Hillsdale, NJ: Lawrence Erlbaum Associates.

Gregg, Vernon H. (1986). *Introduction to Human Memory.* London: Routledge and Kegan Paul.

Gregory, Michael, and Susanne Carroll (1978). *Language and Situation.* London: Routledge.
Grice, H.P. (1969). Utterer's meaning and intentions. *Philosophical Review, 78,* 147–177.
Grice, H.P. (1975). Logic and conversation. In Cole, Peter, and Jerry L. Morgan (Eds.), *Syntax and Semantics. Vol. 3: Speech Acts.* New York: Academic Press.
Grimes, Joseph (1975). *The Thread of Discourse.* The Hague: Mouton.

Hall, Edward T. (1959). *The Silent Language.* New York: Doubleday.
Hall, Edward T. (1966). *The Hidden Dimension.* New York: Doubleday.
Halliday, Michael A.K. (1970). Language structure and language functions. In Lyons, John (Ed.), *New Horizons in Linguistics.* Baltimore: Penguin.
Halliday, Michael A.K. (1973). *Explorations in the Functions of Language.* London: Arnold.
Halliday, Michael A.K. (1975). *Learning How to Mean: Explorations in the Development of Language.* London: Arnold.
Halliday, Michael A.K., and Ruqaiya Hasan (1976). *Cohesion in English.* London: Longmans.
Hanna, Paul R., Richard E. Hodges, and Jean S. Hanna (1971). *Spelling: Structure and Strategies.* Boston: Houghton Mifflin.
Hansen, Jane, Thomas Newkirk, and Donald H. Graves (Eds.) (1985). *Breaking Ground: Teachers Relate Reading and Writing in the Elementary School.* Portsmouth, NH: Heinemann Educational Books.
Hawisher, Gail E. (1989). Research and recommendations for computers and compositions. In Hawisher, Gail E. and Cynthia L. Selfe (Eds.), *Critical Perspectives on Computers and Composition Instruction.* New York: Teachers College Press.
Hawisher, Gail E. and Cynthia L. Selfe (Eds.) (1988). *Critical Perspectives on Computers and Composition Instruction.* New York: Teachers College Press.
Hawisher, Gail E. and Cynthia L. Selfe (Eds.) (1991). *Evolving Perspectives on Computers and Composition Studies.* Urbana, IL: National Council of Teachers of English.
Hayes, John R. and Linda S. Flower (1980). Identifying the organization of writing processes. In Gregg, Lee W. and Erwin R. Steinberg (Eds.), *Cognitive Processes in Writing.* Hillsdale, NJ: Lawrence Erlbaum Associates.
Henderson, Edmund H. (1985). *Teaching Spelling.* Boston, MA: Houghton Mifflin.
Herron, R.E. and Brian Sutton-Smith (Eds.) (1982). *Child's Play.* Malabar, FL: Krieger.
Hidi, Suzanne, William Baird, and Angela Hildyard (1982). That's important but is it interesting? Two factors in text processing. In Flammer, August and Walter Kintsch (Eds.), *Discourse Processing.* Amsterdam: North Holland.
Hillocks, George (1986). *Research on Written Composition: New Directions for Teaching.* Urbana, IL: ERIC/National Conference of Research in English.
Hochberg, Julian E. (1978). *Perception* (2d Ed). Englewood Cliffs, NJ: Prentice-Hall.
Hofstadter, Douglas R. (1979). *Godel, Escher, Bach: An Eternal Golden Braid.* New York: Basic Books.
Horowitz, Rosalind and S. Jay Samuels (Eds.) (1987). *Comprehending Oral and Written Language.* New York: Academic Press.
Hudelson, Sarah J. and Judith Wells Lindfors (Eds.) (1993). *Delicate Balances: Collaborative Research in Language Education.* Urbana, IL: National Council of Teachers of English.
Hughes, Margaret and Dennis Searle (1991). A longitudinal study of the growth of spelling abilities within the context of the development of literacy. In Zutell, Jerry and Sarah McCormick (Eds.), *Learner Factors/Teacher Factors: Issues in Literacy Research and Instruction* (Fortieth Yearbook of the National Reading Conference). Rochester, NY: National Reading Conference.

Jacoby, L. and A. Hollingshead (1990). Reading student essays may be hazardous to your spelling: Effects of reading incorrectly and correctly spelled words. *Canadian Journal of Psychology, 44,* 345–358.

James, William (1892). *Psychology: Briefer Course*. New York: Holt.

Jaynes, Julian (1976). *The Origin of Consciousness in the Breakdown of the Bicameral Mind*. Boston: Houghton Mifflin.

Jones, Mari Reiss (1976). Time, our lost dimension. *Psychological Review, 83*(5), 323–355.

Just, Marcel Adam, and Patricia A. Carpenter (Eds.) (1977). *Cognitive Processes in Comprehension*. Hillsdale, NJ: Lawrence Erlbaum Associates.

Kahneman, Daniel (1973). *Attention and Effort*. Englewood Cliffs, NJ: Prentice-Hall.

Kamler, Barbara (1993). Constructing gender in the process writing classroom. *Language Arts, 70*(2), 95–103.

Kelly, George A. (1955). *The Psychology of Personal Constructs* (2 Vols). New York: Norton.

Kelso, J. A. Scott (1978). Joint receptors do not provide a satisfactory basis for motor timing and positioning. *Psychological Review, 85*, 474–481.

Kessen, William, Andrew Ortony, and Fergus Craik (Eds.) (1991). *Memories, Thoughts, and Emotions: Essays in Honor of George Mandler*. Hillsdale, NJ: Lawrence Erlbaum Associates.

Kintsch, Walter (1974). *The Representation of Meaning in Memory*. Hillsdale, NJ: Lawrence Erlbaum Associates.

Kintsch, Walter (1977). On comprehending stories. In Just, Marcel A. and Patricia A. Carpenter (Eds.), *Cognitive Processes in Comprehension*. Hillsdale, NJ: Lawrence Erlbaum Associates.

Kintsch, Walter (1982). Memory for text. In Flammer, August and Walter Kintsch (Eds.), *Discourse Processing*. Amsterdam: North Holland.

Kintsch. Walter, and T.A. VanDijk (1978). Toward a model of text comprehension and production. *Psychological Review, 85*, 363–394.

Kirshenblatt-Gimblett, Barbara (Ed.) (1976). *Speech Play: Research and Resources for Studying Linguistic Creativity*. University of Pennsylvania Press.

Klima, Edward S., and Ursula Bellugi (1979). *The Signs of Language*. Cambridge, MA: Harvard University Press.

Koestler, Arthur (1978). *Janus: A Summing Up*. London: Hutchinson.

Krashen, Stephen D. (1989). We acquire vocabulary and spelling by reading: Additional evidence for the input hypothesis. *The Modern Language Journal, 73*(iv), 440–464.

Krashen, Stephen D. (1991). *Fundamentals of Language Education*. Torrance, CA: Laredo.

Krashen, Stephen D. (1993). *The Power of Reading: Insights from the Research*. Englewood, CO: Libraries Unlimited.

Kroll, Barry M. and Gordon Wells (Eds.) (1993). *Explorations in the Development of Writing*. Chichester, UK: Wiley.

Kutz, Eleanor (1992). Teacher research: Myths and realities. *Language Arts, 69*, 193–197.

Lakoff, George (1987). *Women, Fire, and Dangerous Things: What Categories Reveal About the Mind*. Chicago: University of Chicago Press.

Lashley, Karl S. (1951). The problem of serial order in behavior. In Jeffress, L.A. (Ed.), *Cerebral Mechanisms in Behavior*. New York: Wiley.

LeBlanc, Paul (1993). *Writing Teachers Writing Software*. Urbana, IL: National Council of Teachers of English.

Liberman, Isabelle Y. and Alvin M. Liberman (1992). Whole language versus code emphasis: Underlying assumptions and their implications for reading instruction. In Gough, Philip B., Linnea C. Ehri, and Rebecca Treiman (Eds.), *Reading Acquisition*, Hillsdale, NJ: Lawrence Erlbaum Associates.

Lightfoot, Martin and Nancy Martin (1988). *The Word for Teaching is Learning: Essays for James Britton*. London: Heinemann Educational Books.

Lindsay, Peter H., and Donald A. Norman (1977). *Human Information Processing* (2d Ed.). New York: Academic Press.

Littlefair, Alison B. (1991). *Reading All Types of Writing: The Importance of Genre and Register for Reading Development.* Milton Keynes: Open University.

Lodge, David (1990). *After Bakhtin: Essays on Fiction and Criticism.* London: Routledge.

Long, Shirley A., Peter N. Winograd, and Connie A. Bridge (1989). The effects of reader and text characteristics on imagery reported during and after reading. *Reading Research Quarterly, 24*(3), 353–372.

Lunzer, Eric, and Keith Gardner (Eds.) (1979). *The Effective Use of Reading.* London: Heinemann Educational Books.

Luria, A.R., and F.J. Yudovich (1959). *Speech and the Development of Mental Processes in the Child.* London: Staples.

Mac Cormac, Earl R. (1985). *A Cognitive Theory of Metaphor.* Cambridge, MA: MIT Press.

Macnamara, John (Ed.) (1977). *Language Learning and Thought.* New York: Academic Press.

Magee, Bryan (1973). *Popper.* London: Fontana.

Mandler, Jean Matter (1984). *Stories, Scripts, and Scenes: Aspects of Schema Theory.* Hillsdale, NJ: Lawrence Erlbaum Associates.

Mandler, Jean Matter and Marsha S. Goodman (1982). On the psychological validity of story structure. *Journal of Verbal Learning and Verbal Behavior, 21,* 507–523.

Mandler, Jean M., and N. J. Johnson (1977). Remembrance of things parsed: Story structure and recall. *Cognitive Psychology, 9,* 111–151.

Markham, Lynda R. (1976). Influences of handwriting quality on teacher evaluation of written work. *American Educational Research Journal, 13*(4), 277–283.

Marshall, Nancy, and Marvin D. Glock (1978/79). Comprehension of connected discourse. *Reading Research Quarterly, 14*(1), 10–56.

Martin, James (1985). *Factual Writing.* Geelong: Deakin University Press.

Martin, Nancy, Pat D'Arcy, Bryan Newton, and Robert Parker (1976). *Writing and Learning Across the Curriculum,* 11–16. London: Ward Lock Education.

Matsuhashi, Ann (Ed.) (1987). *Writing in Real Time: Modelling Production Processes.* Norwood, NJ: Ablex.

Mattingly, Ignatius G. and Michael Studdert-Kennedy (Eds.) (1991). *Modularity and the Motor Theory of Speech Perception.* Hillsdale, NJ: Lawrence Erlbaum Associates.

McCawley, James D. (1968). The role of semantics in a grammar. In Bach, Emmon, and R.T. Harms (Eds.), *Universals in Linguistic Theory.* New York: Holt, Rinehart & Winston.

Mead, Margaret (1976). *Growing Up in New Guinea.* New York: Morrow.

Meek, Margaret (1988). How texts teach what readers learn. In Lightfoot, Martin and Nancy Martin (Eds.), *The Word for Teaching is Learning: Essays for James Britton.* London: Heinemann Educational Books.

Merleau-Ponty, Maurice (1974). *Phenomenology, Language and Sociology.* London: Heinemann Educational Books.

Miller, George A. (1965). Some preliminaries to psycholinguistics. *American Psychologist, 20,* 15–20.

Miller, George A., Eugene Galanter, and Karl H. Pribram (1960). *Plans and the Structure of Behavior.* New York: Holt, Rinehart & Winston.

Miller, George A., and Philip N. Johnson-Laird (1976). *Language and Perception.* Cambridge, MA: Belknap Press of Harvard University Press.

Moffett, James (1979). Integrity in the teaching of writing. *Phi Delta Kappan, 61*(4), 276–279.

Monroe, Rick (1993). *Writing and Thinking with Computers.* Urbana, IL: National Council of Teachers of English.

Morris, P.E. (1988). Expertise and everyday memory. In Gruneberg, M.M., P.E. Morris, and R.N. Sykes (Eds.), *Practical Aspects of Memory: Current Research and Issues, Vol. I: Memory in Everyday Life.* Chichester, UK: Wiley.

Murray, Donald M. (1978). Internal revision: A process of discovery. In Cooper, Charles R. and Lee Odell (Eds.), *Research on Composing: Points of Departure*. Urbana, IL: National Council of Teachers of English.

Murray, Donald M. (1980). How writing finds its own meaning. In Donovan, Timothy R., and Ben W. McClelland (Eds.), *Teaching Composition: Theory into Practice*. Urbana, IL: National Council of Teachers of English.

Murray, Donald M. (1987). *Write to Learn*. New York: Holt, Rinehart & Winston.

Murray, Donald M. (1989). *Expecting the Unexpected: Teaching Myself—and Others—to Read and Write*. Portsmouth, NH: Boynton/Cook.

Nagy, William E., Patricia A. Herman, and Richard C. Anderson (1985). Learning words from context. *Reading Research Quarterly, 20*, 2, 233–253.

Navon, David (1977). Forest before trees: The precedence of global features in visual perception. *Cognitive Psychology, 9*, 353–383.

Neisser, Ulric (1977). *Cognition and Reality*. San Francisco: Freeman.

Nelson, Katherine (1974). Concept, word and sentence: Interrelations in acquisition and development. *Psychological Review, 81*(4), 267–285.

Nelson, Keith (Ed.) (1983). *Children's Language*. Hillsdale, NJ: Lawrence Erlbaum Associates.

Newman, Judith R. (1991). *Interwoven Conversations: Learning and Teaching through Critical Reflection*. Portsmouth, NH: Heinemann Educational Books.

Norman, Donald A., and Daniel G. Bobrow (1979). Descriptions: An intermediate stage in memory retrieval. *Cognitive Psychology, 11*, 107–123.

Norris, Christopher (1991). *Deconstruction, theory and practice*. London: Routledge.

Nystrand, Martin (1986). *The Structure of Written Communication. Studies in Reciprocity between Writers and Readers*. Orlando, FL: Academic Press.

Nystrand, Martin and Jeffrey Wiemelt (1991). When is a text explicit? Formalist and dialogical conceptions. *Text, 11*(1), 25–41.

Olson, David R. (Ed.) (1974). *Media and Symbols: The Forms of Expression, Communication and Education* (73rd Yearbook of the National Society for the Study of Education). Chicago: University of Chicago Press.

Olson, David R. (1977). From utterance to text: The bias of language in speech and writing. *Harvard Educational Review, 47*(3), 257–281.

Olson, David R., and Jerome S. Bruner (1974). Learning through experience and learning through media. In Olson, David R. (Ed.), *Media and Symbols: The Forms of Expression, Communication and Education* (73rd Yearbook of the National Society for the Study of Education). Chicago: University of Chicago Press.

Olson, David R. and Nancy Torrance (Eds.) (1991). *Literacy and Orality*. Cambridge, UK: Cambridge University Press.

Olson, David R., Nancy Torrance, and Angela Hildyard (Eds.)(1985). *Literacy, Language, and Learning: The Nature and Consequences of Reading and Writing*. Cambridge, UK: Cambridge University Press.

Ortony, Andrew (1979a). Beyond literal similarity. *Psychological Review, 86*(3), 161–213.

Ortony, Andrew (Ed.) (1979b). *Metaphor and Thought*. Cambridge, England: Cambridge University Press.

Palmer, Richard E. (1969). *Hermeneutics*. Evanston, IL: Northwestern University Press.

Parker, Francis W. (1890). *Talks on Pedagogics: An Outline of the Theory of Concentration*. New York: Barnes.

Patterson, Leslie, Carol Minnick Santa, Kathy G. Short, and Karen Smith (Eds.) (1993). *Teachers Are Researchers: Reflection and Action.* Newark, DE: International Reading Association.

Perkins, David N. (1981). *The Mind's Best Work.* Cambridge, MA: Harvard University Press.

Piaget, Jean (1978). *Success and Understanding.* Cambridge, MA: Harvard University Press.

Pianko, Sharon (1979). A description of the composing processes of college freshman writers. *Research in the Teaching of English, 13*(1), 5–22.

Popper, Karl R. (1973). *Objective Knowledge: An Evolutionary Approach.* Oxford, England: Clarendon Press.

Popper, Karl R. (1976). *Unended Quest: An Intellectual Autobiography.* London: Fontana/ Collins.

Popper, Karl R., and John C. Eccles (1977). *The Self and Its Brain.* New York: Springer International.

Posner, Michael, and Steven W. Keele (1973). Skill learning. In Morris, Robert, and William Travers (Eds.), *Second Handbook of Research on Teaching.* Chicago: Rand-McNally.

Read, Charles R. (1971). Pre-school children's knowledge of English phonology. *Harvard Educational Review, 41,* 1–34.

Read, Charles R. (1973). Children's judgments of phonetic similarities in relation to English spelling. *Language Learning, 23*(1), 17–38.

Read, Charles R. (1975). *Children's Categorization of Speech Sounds in English.* Urbana, IL: National Council of Teachers of English.

Reber, Arthur S. (1989). Implicit learning and tacit knowledge. *Journal of Experimental Psychology: General, 118,* 219–235.

Richardson, Paul (1991). Language as personal resource and as social construct: Competing views of literacy pedagogy in Australia. *Educational Review, 43*(2), 171–190.

Ricoeur, Paul (1984). *Time and Narrative* (Vol. 1.) (Kathleen McLaughlin and David Pellauer, Trans.), Chicago: Chicago University Press.

Rosen, Harold (1988). Stories of stories: Footnotes on sly gossipy practices. In Lightfoot, Martin and Nancy Martin (Eds.), *The Word for Teaching is Learning: Essays for James Britton.* London: Heinemann Educational Books.

Rosenblatt, Louise M. (1978). *The Reader: the Text: the Poem.* Carbondale: Southern Illinois University Press.

Rosenblatt, Louise M. (1980). What facts does this poem teach you? *Language Arts, 57*(4), 386–394.

Roth, Philip (1975). *Reading Myself and Others.* New York: Farrar, Strauss.

Rozin, Paul, Susan Poritsky, and Raina Sotsky (1971). American children with reading problems can easily learn to read English represented by Chinese characters. *Science, 171,* 1264–1267.

Rumelhart, David E. (1975). Notes on a scheme for stories. In Bobrow, Daniel, and A. Collins (Eds.), *Representation and Understanding: Studies in Cognitive Science.* New York: Academic Press.

Ryle, Gilbert (1949). *The Concept of Mind.* London: Hutchinson.

Sacks, Oliver (1989). *Seeing Voices: A Journey Into the World of the Deaf.* Berkeley, CA: University of California Press.

Samples, Bob (1976). *The Metaphoric Mind.* Reading, MA: Addison-Wesley.

Sampson, Geoffrey (1985). *Writing Systems: A Linguistic Introduction.* London: Hutchinson.

Sartre, Jean-Paul (1962). *Imagination: A Psychological Critique.* Ann Arbor: University of Michigan Press.

Schank, Roger C., and Robert P. Abelson (1977). *Scripts, Plans, Goals, and Understanding.* Hillsdale, NJ: Lawrence Erlbaum Associates.

Schlagal, Robert C. and Joy Harris Schlagal (1992. The integral character of spelling: Teaching strategies for multiple purposes. *Language Arts, 69*, 418–424.

Scholes, Robert J. and Brenda J. Willis (1991). Linguists, literacy and the intensionality of Marshall McLuhan's Western man. In Olson, David R. and Nancy Torrance (Eds.), *Literacy and Orality*. Cambridge, UK: Cambridge University Press.

Schwartzman, Helen B. (1978). *Transformations*. New York: Plenum.

Searle, John (1969). *Speech Acts*. Cambridge, UK: Cambridge University Press.

Selfe, Cynthia L. (1989). *Creating a Computer-Supported Writing Facility*. Urbana, IL: National Council of Teachers of English.

Senner, Wayne M. (Ed.) (1989). *The Origins of Writing*. Lincoln: University of Nebraska.

Shaughnessy, Mina P. (1977). *Errors and Expectations*. New York: Oxford University Press.

Simonton, Dean Keith (1988). *Scientific Genius: A Psychology of Science*. Cambridge, UK: Cambridge University Press.

Singer, Murray (1990). *Psychology of Language: An Introduction to Sentence and Discourse Processes*. Hillsdale, NJ: Lawrence Erlbaum Associates.

Skemp, Richard R. (1972). *The Psychology of Learning Mathematics*. Baltimore: Penguin.

Smith, Frank (1975). *Comprehension and Learning*. Katonah, NY: Owen.

Smith, Frank (1977). The uses of language. *Language Arts, 54*(6), 638–644.

Smith, Frank (1985). *Reading*, (2nd Ed.). Cambridge, UK: Cambridge University Press; also published as *Reading Without Nonsense* (2nd Ed.). New York: Teachers College Press.

Smith, Frank (1986). *Insult to Intelligence: The Bureaucratic Invasion of Our Classrooms*. Portsmouth, NH: Heinemann Educational Books.

Smith, Frank (1988). *Joining the Literacy Club*. Portsmouth, NH: Heinemann Educational Books.

Smith, Frank (1989). Overselling literacy. *Phi Delta Kappan. 70*(5), 352–359.

Smith, Frank (1990). *to think*. New York: Teachers College Press.

Smith, Frank (1994). *Understanding Reading* (5th Ed.). Hillsdale, NJ: Lawrence Erlbaum Associates.

Snow, Catherine E. (1977). Mothers' speech research: From input to interaction. In Snow, Catherine E. and Charles A. Ferguson (Eds.), *Talking to Children: Language Input and Acquisition*. Cambridge, UK: Cambridge University Press.

Snow, Catherine E. and Charles A. Ferguson (Eds.) (1977). *Talking to Children: Language Input and Acquisition*. Cambridge, UK: Cambridge University Press.

Steffensen, Margaret S., Chitra Joag-Dev, and Richard C. Anderson (1979). A cross-cultural perspective on reading comprehension. *Reading Research Quarterly, 15*(1), 10–29.

Stein, Nancy L., and Christine G. Glenn (1979). An analysis of story comprehension in elementary school children. In Freedle, Roy O. (Ed.), *New Directions in Discourse Processing* (Vol. 2). Norwood, NJ: Ablex.

Stelmach, George E. (Ed.) (1978). *Information Processing in Motor Control and Learning*. New York: Academic Press.

Sticht, Thomas G., Frederick R. Chang, and Suzanne Wood (Eds.)(1986). *Advances in Reading/Language Research (Vol. 4): Cognitive Science and Human Resources Management*. Greenwich, CT: Jai.

Stotsky, Sandra (1986). On learning to write about ideas. *College Composition and Communication, 37*, 276–293.

Strong, William (1986). *Creative Approaches to Sentence Combining*. Urbana, IL: National Council of Teachers of English.

Strong, William, and Robert J. Marzano (1976). Sentence combining: Pro and con. *English Journal, 65*, 56–64.

Styles, Morag (Ed.) (1989). *Collaboration and Writing*. Milton Keynes: Open University Press.

Sutton-Smith, Brian (1975). The importance of the story-taker: An investigation of the imaginative life. *The Urban Review, 8*(2), 82–95.

Swanson, H. Lee (1990). Influence of metacognitive knowledge and aptitude on problem solving. *Journal of Educational Psychology, 82*(2), 306–314.

Taylor, Denny (1983). *Family Literacy: Young Children Learning to Read and Write*. Portsmouth, NH: Heinemann Educational Books.
Teale, William H. and Elizabeth Sulzby (Eds.) (1986). *Emergent Literacy: Writing and Reading*. Norwood, NJ: Ablex.
Tierney, Robert J., and Jill LaZansky (1980). The rights and responsibilities of readers and writers: A contractual agreement. *Language Arts, 57*(6), 606–613.
Tierney, Robert J. and T. Shanahan (1991). Research on the reading-writing relationships: Interactions, transactions and outcomes. In Barr, Rebecca, M.L. Kamil, Peter Mosenthal, and P. David Pearson (Eds.), *Handbook of Reading Research*. New York: Longman.
Todorov, Tzvetan (1977). *The Poetics of Prose*. (Richard Howard, Trans.) Ithaca, NY: Cornell University Press.
Torbe, Mike (1988). Doing things with language: Skills, functionalism and social context. In Lightfoot, Martin and Nancy Martin (Eds.), *The Word for Teaching is Learning: Essays for James Britton*. London: Heinemann Educational Books.
Tulving, Endel, and Donald M. Thomson (1973). Encoding specificity and retrieval processes in episodic memory. *Psychological Review, 80*, 352–373.
Tulving, Endel, and Michael J. Watkins (1975). Structure of memory traces. *Psychological Review, 82*(4), 261–275.

Upward, Christopher (1992). Is traditionl english spelng mor dificlt than jermn? *Journal of Research in Reading, 15*(2), 82–94.

Venezky, Richard L. (1970). *The Structure of English Orthography*. The Hague: Mouton.
Vygotsky, Lev S. (1962). *Thought and Language*. Cambridge, MA: MIT Press.
Vygotsky, Lev S. (1978). *Mind in Society: The Development of Higher Psychological Processes*. Cambridge, MA: Harvard University Press.

Wallach, Michael A., and Nathan Kogan (1972). Creativity and intelligence in children. In Hunt, Joseph McV. (Ed.), *Human Intelligence*. New Brunswick, NJ: Transaction Inc.
Wason, Peter C. (1980). Specific thoughts on the writing process. In Gregg, Lee W. and Erwin R. Steinberg (Eds.), *Cognitive Processes in Writing*. Hillsdale, NJ: Lawrence Erlbaum Associates, pp. 129–137.
Weitz, Shirley (Ed.) (1979). *Nonverbal Communication* (2d Ed.). New York: Oxford University Press.
Wells, Gordon (1986). *The Meaning Makers*. Portsmouth, NH: Heinemann Educational Books.
Wilde, Sandra (1990). A proposal for a new spelling curriculum. *The Elementary School Journal, 90*(3), 275–289.
Wildman, Daniel M., and Martin Kling (1978/1979). Semantic, syntactic and spatial anticipation in reading. *Reading Research Quarterly, 14*(2), 128–164.
Wittgenstein, Ludwig (1953). *Philosophical Investigations*. New York: Macmillan.
Wundt, Wilhelm (1911, 1912). *Volkerspsychologie, Vols. 1 and 2: Die Sprache*.

NAME INDEX

SUBJECT INDEX